Sri Swami Satchidananda:
Apostle of Peace

Books by Sri Swami Satchidananda
Kailash Journal
Beyond Words
To Know Your Self
Guru and Disciple
The Golden Present
Integral Yoga Hatha
Peace is Within Our Reach
The Mother is the Baby's First Guru
Integral Yoga: The Yoga Sutras of Patanjali
(with full commentary, Sanskrit and index)
Integral Yoga: The Yoga Sutras of Patanjali, Pocket Edition
Integral Yoga Hatha booklet
(with audio cassette instruction)

Other books about Sri Swami Satchidananda
The Master's Touch by Sita Bordow

Library of Congress Cataloging in Publications Data:
Bordow, Joan Wiener
  Sri Swami Satchidananda, apostle of peace

  Includes index.
  1. Satchidananda, Swami 2. Biography. I. Title.
BL1175.S38B66   1986 294.5'5 [B]   86-10533
ISBN 0-932040-31-4

Integral Yoga® Publications
Satchidananda Ashram – Yogaville
Route 1, Box 172, Buckingham, Virginia 23921

Sri Swami Satchidananda:
Apostle of Peace

by Sita Bordow
and others

With a Foreword by Father Thomas Keating

Integral Yoga® Publications
Yogaville, Virginia

The printing of Sri Swami Satchidananda: Apostle of Peace *was made possible by a generous donation from Sri Krishna Yogi.*

We would also like to thank the others whose generous donations helped make the production of this book possible: Savitri DeMeyer, Jean-Pierre and Marie-Therese Colomb, Iain and Isobel Gow, Janaka Grace, and Vimala Laminack.

Blessed is the devotee
of an enlightened Master.
Blessed are they
who can offer themselves
as a flower
in their Master's
puja to the Divine.

This flower is offered in deepest gratitude
for the opportunity to serve.

OM Shanthi Shanthi Shanthi.

Krishna Yogi
Satchidananda Ashram
Australia

Foreword

Many paths lead to the Source. We call this Source the Absolute, God, Brahman, the Great Spirit, Allah and other names depending on our religious frame of reference. The term *Ultimate Mystery* or *Ultimate Reality* might designate best what all these words are trying to signify.

All who seek to participate in the reality of the Ultimate Mystery are united in the same fundamental search. They relate to everything that is of genuine spiritual value in every religion. They resonate to human values wherever they can be found whether in religion, science, art, friendship or the service of others. True unity is expressed in pluralism: unity in the experience of the ultimate values of human life; pluralism in one's unique response to these values in the concrete circumstances of one's life.

Those who truly seek the Ultimate Mystery perceive themselves as citizens of the Earth. Their first loyalty is to the human family as a whole. They transcend the particularities of race, nationality and religion without reacting against them or trying to destroy them. They recognize the profound human values that the world religions enshrine. They work to preserve and enhance them, but not at the cost of dividing the fundamental unity of the human family and resorting to violence. They belong to the emerging global community more than to the nation in which they live. Nationalism is an anachronism in a world of geometrically increasing interaction in ever-expanding areas of human concern.

The world religions have a special obligation in our time to contribute to the cause of world peace. In the past — and even now — their confessional differences have led to violence, injustice and persecution. Each religious tradition has developed teachings and practices designed to foster the full spiritual development of the human person. These common elements need to be recognized, affirmed, and made more available to the world community as powerful means of promoting understanding, compassion and unity among the various races, religions and nations. Spiritual union is the catalyst that would facilitate harmony and cooperation on all levels of global interaction.

The most precious value that the world religions have in common is their accumulated experience of the spiritual journey. Centuries of seekers have discovered and lived its conditions, temptations, development and final integration. This wealth of personal experience of the transcendent bears witness to the historical grounding of the contemporary search. Spiritual seeking is not just a passing fad. Teachers of the spiritual disciplines that have emerged from the world religions should pool their common experiences, resources, and insights for the benefit of the increasing number of seekers in every religious tradition.

The Reverend Sri Swami Satchidananda has devoted himself tirelessly to the promotion of spirituality, transcultural values and understanding among the world religions. His pioneering spirit is now coming to full bloom in the creation of the Light Of Truth Universal Shrine in Buckingham, Virginia. The Shrine is the symbol of his life: a symbol of peace, individual and universal, and of the contribution that the religions of the world can and must make to religious harmony and union among all people.

FATHER THOMAS KEATING
St. Benedict's Monastery
Snowmass, Colorado

Acknowledgements

*In writing this biography of Sri Swami Satchidananda,
we have been given a great deal of help from his many devotees,
friends and acquaintances throughout the world.
Our heartfelt thanks to every one of them.
Among them:*

The Reverend Pierre Benoit, O.P. – Jerusalem
Sri Swami Satchidananda Mataji – Sri Lanka
Sri Kavi Yogi Maharshi Shuddhananda Bharati – India
Sri Swami Venkatesanandaji – Mauritius
Sri Swami Vimalananda Mataji – Sri Lanka
Father A. Boudens – Belgium
Mr. Gene Dadlani – Philippines
Sri Sunil I. Damania – India
Ms. Amma DeBayle – U.S.A.
Mr. Muruga De Neef – Belgium
Mrs. Miriam de Saram – Sri Lanka
Ms. Anna Gervasoni – Italy
Sri Krishnaswamy Gounder – India
Mr. Narada Greene – Netherlands
Ms. Yvonne Gita Hanneman – U.S.A.
Mr. George N. Harilela – Hong Kong
Vijay and Shree Hassin – U.S.A.
Mr. A. R. Hug – Switzerland
Sri P. N. Janakiraman – India
Sri K. Kanagaraja – Sri Lanka
Mme. Janine Lambert – France
Sri A. Maheshwaran – Malaysia
The Reverend Shanthi Mandelkorn – U.S.A.
Mr. Peter Atman Max – U.S.A.
Srimati Sohini Mehta – India
Srimati Sushila Mehta – India
Sri N. Muthiah – Sri Lanka
Srimati Balambikai Nadaraja – Sri Lanka
Mr. G. D. Naidu – India
Mr. Mitra Neuman – U.S.A.
Sri K. Sivagurunatha Pillai – England

Those who worked directly on this book:

Parameswari Adie
Paraman Barsel
Bhaktan Bennetta
Vivekan Flint
Richard Friedel
Uma Knight

Turiya Moran
Ramakrishna Pemmaraju
Swami Premananda Ma
Swami Shantananda Ma
Jayadeva Swanson
Abhaya Thiele
Shuchi Wadhams

Swami Prakashananda Ma, Editor
Swami Sharadananda Ma, Production Supervisor
Anagan Stearns, Contributing Editor

Photos by:

Sri Swami Satchidananda

Cover photo: Amrita McLanahan, M.D.
Maithreyi Andre
Corbit's Studio, Bridgeport, Ct.
Gita Hanneman
George Hausman
Allen Hsieh
Swami Lalitananda Ma
Ganesh MacIsaac
Reverend Shanthi Mandelkorn
Daya Marcus
Amrita McLanahan
Kamala Meredith

Bertil Nadell
Swami Prakashananda Ma
Swami Premananda Ma
Rama Roosevelt
Sita Roosevelt
Chandra Sammons
Swami Shantananda Ma
Swami Sharadananda Ma
Swami Tyagananda
The Vatican
Jerry Wilson
Kalyani Yarusso

and many others whose photographs appear in this book, but whose names do not appear in our files.

Preface

This book is divided into five sections:

RAMASWAMY traces Sri Gurudev's ancestry and early life, up to that time when he decided to detach himself from worldly ties.

SAMBASIVA CHAITANYA describes his spiritual practices and the various teachers with whom he studied before meeting his Guru.

SRI SWAMI SATCHIDANANDA: EAST describes his meeting with his Guru, Sri Swami Sivanandaji Maharaj, and the beginning of his work in Sri Lanka.

SRI SWAMI SATCHIDANANDA: WEST describes his departure from Sri Lanka for a visit to the West and tells of his early work in the United States.

SRI SWAMI SATCHIDANANDA: WORLD TEACHER tells of his service up to the present and how it expanded around the globe.

Interspersed throughout the text are some of the teachings of Sri Gurudev; these direct quotes are in bold type.

May you enjoy and be inspired by the story of this great Yoga Master and servant of humanity. OM Shanthi.

SITA BORDOW

Contents

RAMASWAMY

The story of Kuttiappa; Ramaswamy's birth; devotion in the home; Ramu enters school; the lesson of the matches; young Ramu lectures at a yoga conference; entering high school; the young scientist; Ramu confronts an unjust teacher; lessons from Grandfather; the "Great Bala Vedanti"; Ramu and the untouchables; the hunting trip; helping Father write poetry; Agricultural College; the end of formal studies; Ramu the businessman; Perur: serving as temple manager; breaking the nicotine habit; further business ventures; United Motors; marriage and family life; Ramu goes into seclusion.

SAMBASIVA CHAITANYA

Ramaswamy embarks on a full-time spiritual quest; early spiritual experiences; Palani Hill; study with Sri Sadhu Swamigal; Sri Naga Sai; vision of Bogar; Paper Baba's blessing; two arresting officers learn a lesson; healing powers belong to God; keeping anger in the pocket; in the company of *siddhas;* a profound lesson from Swami Ranga Nath; the wandering mendicant; Sri Aurobindo; Ramakrishna Thapovanam: *pre-sannyas* initiation; a stern teacher — Sri Swami Chidbhavanandaji; the children's hostel; Sambasiva serves in nature cure camps; ministering to the untouchables; Upanishad Vihar; time with Sri Ramana Maharshi; Virupaksha Cave: reaping the fruit of meditation.

SRI SWAMI SATCHIDANANDA: EAST

Rishikesh: at the feet of the Holy Master Sri Swami Sivanandaji Maharaj; pilgrimage in the Himalayas; initiation into the Holy Order of Sannyas; Vasishta Guha: experiencing the highest; All-India Tour; touching hearts and changing lives; a scorpion sting: serving all equally; the wealthy leper: a life is changed on a train; sent by the Master to Ceylon; Guru Poornima is proclaimed All Prophets Day; Kandy: an ashram is built in a garden paradise; healing the wounds of caste and creed divisions; "the revolutionary Monk"; work among prisoners; Buddhists and Moslems ask for advice; a burglar sees an apparition; the Fine Arts Society; courageous pilgrimage to Holy Mount Kailash; Gurudev wins hearts in Hong Kong; Srimati Velammai leaves the body; the *mahasamadhi* of Sri Swami Sivanandaji Maharaj.

Conrad Rooks asks for instruction from Gurudev; sowing spiritual seeds throughout Europe; an audience with H.H. Pope Paul VI; Peter Max meets his guru; two days in New York City; sincere hearts convince their Swami to stay; the Integral Yoga Institute; return to Ceylon; meetings with the Dalai Lama and Lama Govinda; the hippies are transformed; a residence is established for serious students; a landmark visa: the first for a "Minister of Divine Words"; pilgrimage with the Master: the Western disciples take a holy tour around the world; Carnegie Hall: Sold Out!; Ananda Ashram: convocations in the country; the IYI branches out; Gurudev opens the Woodstock Festival; Val Morin: "The True World Order" conference; Yoga Ecumenical Seminary; Annhurst: Yoga Ecumenical Retreat.

The IYI gets a home of its own; India Tour; a visit with the Nameless Swami; the search for a yoga village; dedication of Yogaville East; *presannyas* — some Westerners devote their lives to service; University of Notre Dame: "Doing Prayer"; Aquarius Health Center: Yoga in Harlem; growth of Yogaville; 1974 World Tour; yoga and healing: Integral Health Services is opened; Gurudev initiates the first group of American disciples into the Holy Order of Sannyas; Sri Gurudev becomes a U.S. citizen; doctors and patients take an interest in yoga; more ecumenical programs; Saint Ramalingam; Light Of Truth Universal Shrine (LOTUS); All Faiths Day, 1977; Zinal: European Union of National Yoga Federations; what LOTUS means; searching for the LOTUS site; Music Mountain; building a school for little angels; a new home is found in Virginia; LOTUS groundbreaking; the vision of LOTUS; the Integral Yoga Ministry is founded; LOTUS foundation-pouring; an audience with H.H. Pope John Paul II; ashramites serving in the community; a loving meeting with the Soviet people.

A typical scene in South India.

Introduction: South India

There are not many gods, there is only One.
That One has no name, no form, no place. He is
everywhere — in actuality, neither He, nor She,
nor It. Unfortunately, such abstractions cannot
be grasped by our limited minds. Only when
the mind expands to a greater capacity can we
understand infinite things. That is why, according to our capacity, the Infinite One reduces
Himself to a lower level and appears in all the
different names and forms.

The fragrance of jasmine and tuberose fills the air. The scent of
sandalwood incense and camphor from the thousands of gold-domed
temples blends with other aromas. Lush, emerald green landscapes
bathe in the hot sun. There is a gentleness in the land and in her
people. This is South India.

Here the predominant language is the musical-sounding Tamil — a
language older than Sanskrit. While so many other parts of India have
experienced changes due to foreign invasions, South India retains her
simplicity, her own deep spirituality and the true Dravidian culture.

Everywhere there are temples, shrines and images representing the
Divine, Who manifests in various names and forms. The largest and
oldest shrines contain whole cities within their walls. The simplest un-
covered shrines on street corners and in country villages and fields re-
mind the passerby that God's presence is everywhere.

Hinduism is the main religion, and here is the perfect place to be
reminded of the true meaning of Hinduism. The pure Hindu religion

recognizes God in all names and forms, and in all other religions. The real Hindu will respect a Moslem, a Jew, a Buddhist, a Christian, a Taoist — in fact, he may well feel that he belongs to all these religions as well as to Hinduism. The Hindu even respects the beliefs of an atheist.

The Hindu gods and goddesses do not represent the worship of false idols, as is sometimes thought. The Hindu knows that God is present in everything, but His (or Her or Its) vastness is usually too much for the limited mind to comprehend. Therefore, why not pick a particular attribute of God and focus on that? In Hindu temples one may encounter God represented as the overcomer of obstacles, as the destroyer of selfish attachments; as the Divine Mother, compassionately bestowing wealth on Her children; or as the strict mother who cuts away ignorance. These are but a few of the thousands of manifestations of God. In a Hindu temple one may see God as male, female, or as having no gender at all. There are many paths to the realization of God, but they all end at the same goal.

Ramaswamy

Probably I had all my disappointments in my previous lives. Otherwise, I can't think of any reason why I should have been so contented in this present one. I passed through it all before and must have learned terrible lessons. Somehow I can't recollect anything I was attached to very much, even as a youth. I had the same affection toward everybody and everything.

Ramaswamy

Each individual decides on his or her number of births and the duration of each birth. Every action of ours has its own reaction which we have to face. If we don't have enough time in this life alone to face all these reactions, we are given another body.

Among the shrines and green hills and waters of the South Indian rivers lived a poet-devotee, Kuttiappa. At the age of fifteen, Kuttiappa lost his sight to the extent that he could see shapes and shadows during the day but nothing after the sun went down. To compensate for his loss, he developed his intellect in the study and creation of literature and in the science of mathematics.

With his nephew, he traveled to the temple of Lord Muruga in Marudamalai. Unaware of the presence of the visitors, the temple priest locked the two within the shrine when he left at day's end. Kuttiappa sat motionless in meditation, unaware of the priest's departure. Sometime during the night, he felt very hungry. He called on the Lord to provide food for him. As he finished his prayer, the temple priest entered, instructing Kuttiappa to take the food, which was kept as an offering to the deity, from the temple kitchen. The nephew ran and brought rice and water. After his meal, Kuttiappa went back to his meditation.

When the priest opened the shrine the next morning, and saw the man and his nephew sitting in meditation, he ran over.

"I am so sorry. When I locked up, I didn't know anyone was left inside. You must be starving. Let me give you something to eat."

3

Ramu the Boy Scout, age 10.

Kuttiappa slowly looked up. "You must be teasing me. Last night you yourself instructed me to take the *prasadam* from the kitchen. You even unlocked the kitchen so that we could have these dishes."

The priest examined the dishes in amazement. "I locked these in the kitchen before I left. This is the play of Lord Muruga. He was the one who fed you during the night."

Kuttiappa continued to meditate. He thanked the Lord for this manifestation. Then he concentrated on his condition of blindness, seeking its cause. During the meditation, he was instructed to go to the shrine of Nataraja (the dancing Siva) in Tiru Perur. There he allowed himself to be buried in an underground pit, remaining in the super-conscious state of *samadhi* for forty-eight days. He envisioned himself in a previous birth as a *Brahmin* priest in charge of keeping the lamps of the village temple lit. Instead, he had stolen the butter for these lamps and sent it to a prostitute. The eyes of the temple grew dim; and, in this later incarnation, so had his own.

For the rest of his life as Kuttiappa, the devotee meditated upon and served Lord Muruga.

Six generations later, in the twentieth century, Kuttiappa's descendants — Sri La Sri Ramananda Swamigal and Kandaswami Swamigal, his chief disciple — established their Kaumara Madalayam (a spiritual center and temple for the devotees of Lord Muruga) near Coimbatore, South India. Fifteen miles away in Chettipalayam was the household of their devotees and cousins — Sri Kalyanasundaram Gounder and his wife Srimati Velammai.

Sri Kalyanasundaram was the unofficial chief of the village. He was a landlord who owned three to four hundred acres around the area. Those properties the family couldn't supervise directly were leased to other farmers and worked mostly by untouchables. He had one of the largest homes in the village, and it served as a focal point for local activities. Some days its porch was a court, and those with petty quarrels came before Sri Kalyanasundaram for impartial judgment.

A poet himself, Kalyanasundaram let the house serve as the meeting hall for poets, musicians, philosophers, astrologers. Circuses would set up an arena on the land adjoining the house; acrobats and jugglers, animal trainers and horseback riders performed for the villagers and were treated as guests of the house.

Sadhus and *sannyasis*, wandering ascetics and holy men passing through the area, were directed to Sri Kalyanasundaram's house for free food and lodging. The family served these guests directly, rather than giving the job to the household staff. Srimati Velammai washed

4

the garments of the holy people and cooked their food. Her husband and son brought the food to these honored guests.

In describing this couple, Sri Krishnaswamy Gounder said, "My brother-in-law, Sri Kalyanasundaram, was very advanced spiritually. He was a saintly man, a Tamil scholar, and a widely acclaimed poet. My sister, Srimati Velammai, was quiet and good natured. She was endowed with all of the finest qualities. Only such a woman could bring forth someone of the stature of Swami Satchidananda."

Srimati Velammai was inspired by the holy men and decided that her next child should be this type of person. He should be one with the qualities of wisdom, service to all, detachment and love, as shown by the swamis her family served. She and her husband traveled sixty miles to Palani, the holy hill, to the *ashram* of Sri Sadhu Swamigal. Velammai was given a *mantram* to invoke the Divine Light as manifested in the Sun. She repeated it constantly, developing within a vibration conducive to receiving the type of soul she desired.

Their second son, Ramaswamy, was born on the twenty-second of December, 1914.

The Hindus say that one year in human life is one day in the life of the *devas* (gods). Each month is a portion of their day. Of the months, the most auspicious is *Margali,* the period from the fifteenth of December until the fifteenth of January. To the gods this is *brahmamuhoorta,* the hours just before dawn which are most favorable for meditation. So *Margali* is a very special, holy time; all during that month the *devas* are in meditation. While they were in meditation, Ramaswamy was born — during the "Dawn of the Devas."

Not only does charity begin at home. Everything begins at home, including spirituality.

Ramaswamy ("Ramu" for short) was the landlord's son — served by attendants, heir to those hundreds of acres of farmland. Landlords themselves never worked the land. They acted as supervisors to the untouchable workers. To Ramu, however, their labor appeared to be fun. It was a chance for him to do something different. He walked to the fields and begged the workers to let him use the plow or scatter seeds.

"Sir! What would your parents say? They would be very angry with us if we allowed you to do such things."

Farm work was considered too menial to be handled by the landlord's children.

5

தவத்திரு.கந்தசாமி சுவாமிகள்.

(right) Sri Kandaswami Swamigal
(below) Marudamalai Temple
— where Kuttiappa had the
darshan of Lord Muruga

Ramu's deeply devout parents: Sri Kalyanasundaram and Srimati Velammai (inset).

"Listen," Ramu whispered. "No one is watching. They'll never know if I do it."

In secret, he was permitted to use the farm tools. On some days, he would even sneak off to the untouchables' colony. Such visits were not considered worthy of a landlord's child and had to be made clandestinely.

Meditation is food for the soul. When I was a boy, sometimes I would sleep a little late in the morning and rush in for breakfast. My mother would ask, "Did you meditate?" When I told her that I had not meditated, she would say, "Meditation is more important food than breakfast. If you miss your breakfast, you will eat your lunch well! But never miss your meditation." How fortunate I was to have a mother like that. We learn many great things from our own parents if they themselves have that kind of understanding.

Ramu woke before dawn each morning. In that early stillness, he walked to a farm one and a half miles from the house. An acre of land there was set aside for use as a flower garden. Brightly colored flowers of particular beauty grew here for use in Sri Kalyanasundaram's altar room. Ramu jumped into the irrigation well, washed, and then changed into fresh clothes. Moving amid the heavy scent of flowers, he chose a large selection and carried them back to the house, into the brick temple room with its tiled roof. Next, he sat outside and made sandalwood paste, rubbing the sandalwood against a stone and mixing it with water. After he finished, he quietly entered the cool room to watch his father perform *puja*, the ritual worship of his chosen deity.

The room was fairly large. It had a high ceiling and was covered with various images of gods and goddesses. There was a stone Siva *lingam* (symbol of Siva), and a statue of Ganesh, overcomer of obstacles. Sri Kalyanasundaram's favorite deity was a large, framed relief of Lord Subramanya. The god was flanked by his consorts Valli and Devayani. All were dressed in richly draped cloths and ornamented with real jewels embedded into the relief — both precious stones and artificial ones that formed tiaras, earrings, necklaces and shining bracelets. Even the Lord's spear was dotted with stones. At the end of

8

the ceremony, Ramu's father waved the camphor light. Each facet of the jewels would catch fire, jumping and glittering, then slowly dimming as the camphor vanished.

A bell was rung near the end of the service. The sound drifted outside, and all the household knew the *puja* was almost finished. Srimati Velammai, the children, and all the household staff would gather to join Sri Kalyanasundaram for the closing prayers. Prostrating before the altar, they received holy ash and water from the father and bowed to both the Lord of the Universe and the lord of the house. Just before leaving, the two boys bowed to their parents and received their blessings before starting the day.

The Saraswati *puja* was the greatest and most special of the household ceremonies. It was held during the last three days of the *Navaratri*, Nine Nights Worship.

> **Navaratri is the time to honor the goddess — God as Divine Mother — in her three main manifestations. She is the moving force behind all the aspects of God. The first three nights pay homage to the goddess Kaali or Durga, the destroyer. It sounds frightening, yet what she destroys is everything that stands between the devotee and realization of God. After Kaali has cleared the way, the goddess Lakshmi arrives for the next three nights. She is the goddess of wealth and prosperity. Finally, the goddess Saraswati appears. As the goddess of wisdom, she encompasses all learning including the fine arts; and, of course, she is the ruler of all books.**

On those days of Saraswati *puja*, Sri Kalyanasundaram collected all the books from his library. For this worship, the texts were arranged to form a pyramid, steps leading up and down again. A large picture of the goddess was taken from the wall and positioned so that the book-hill reached her waist. Covering this heap of books were skirts from the temple statues. Ramu's job was the arrangement of all this and her jewels. Carefully, with painstaking concentration, he glued each golden bracelet, each emerald-studded earring and necklace to the head and arms of the goddess.

On the ninth night of the festival, the instruments and tools of the house and field were presented for worship since they are the expressions of the power of the Divine Mother. Then all the family joined in the careful disassembly of the pyramid.

The children of Chettipalayam centered their play around the day-to-day activities of their environment. Instead of "cowboys and Indians," Ramu played "priest and devotee" with his friends. One child served as the grave, omnipotent *guru*; another was the disciple. Their dolls were miniatures of the gods. They constructed temples out of mud and decorated them with leaves and flowers, gathering fruit for a play *puja*. Ramu's dreams and visions focused on the deities as well. He favored Lord Subramanya and the goddess Parvati in particular. On a number of occasions, he accompanied his family on trips to visit the swamis in nearby Kaumara Madalayam and to visit Sadhu Swamigal in Palani.

> **There is only one thing that hurts me. If I feel I have caused anyone else's unhappiness, I won't be happy. Until I see that person's smiling face again, I will feel sorry.**

For several years during Ramaswamy's childhood, the veranda of his house served as the home of the village school. The school day started at dawn, and the schoolmaster had devised a foolproof method for exacting promptness from his students.

The first student to arrive handed the master his cane. The master handed it back to the boy.

"Hold it in your fist," he ordered. Then, he drew it swiftly from the enclosing hand so that the boy could feel the friction and warmth of the cane as it passed from his fist.

The second boy to arrive received, for his promptness, two light raps with the cane. The third, three — a bit harder. Each boy would receive an amount of raps according to his number in line, and each rap would become increasingly harder.

Ramu could stay in bed past dawn. He was still of preschool age; and he could lie in bed on his stomach, under the covers, and listen to the lessons as they wafted to his room on the breeze. He could learn from this comfortable spot, far removed from canes.

The schoolmaster questioned a pupil about the preceding day's lecture. Ramu listened closely. The boy cleared his throat — once, twice. He stumbled over his answer and remained silent. There was a pause.

Revered Sadhu Swamigal, Ramu's family guru.

The household deity: Sri Shanmugar with his two consorts, Valli and Devayani, commissioned by Sri Kalyanasundaram and made by an artist with precious and semi-precious gems.

*Sri Kalyanasundaram with
sons Ramaswamy and
Annachiappa (standing).*

*The family home in
Chettipalayam, where Ramu
was born.*

Ramu stood up on the bed, opened his mouth wide and shouted the correct answer.

"You lazy boy. Can you hear that? Even the little one knows the lesson."

The sound of the cane, hollowly resounding on young knuckles, reached Ramu's ears. Then there was silence, followed by the choking sound of a boy fighting to hold back tears.

Ramu bit his lip and listened. It wasn't the reaction he had expected. He leaped off the bed and ran onto the porch.

"Where did he hit you? Where does it hurt?" He tried to soothe the boy's red hand.

"You little imp. Get away. It was your answer that caused my caning."

Ramu walked back to his room, slowly and uneasily. He had a funny feeling in his stomach. He resolved never to interfere in such a way again.

When he was four Ramu officially entered the veranda school. The entrance of a new child to the school was cause for half a day of ritual. Both new student and teacher were garlanded, and the parents presented the master with a number of offerings, including a new set of clothes.

Sets of palm leaves made up the schoolbooks. The master carved lessons onto the leaves with an iron nail. The imprints were rubbed with turmeric powder to form permanent pages. As each leaf was filled, it was bound with those that had come before.

The students sat upon the stone floor. Each had a pile of sand onto which, with an extended finger, he wrote each new letter and word. Erasures were made by smoothing out the pile.

The parents should not think they have given something of their own to the child. It is the child's own quality that enables him or her to come into a particular family and behave in a particular way.

One of Ramu's household duties was to light all the lamps in the evening. There was no electricity in the village at that time, so Ramu had nearly fifteen kerosene lamps to clean and light each night. The first few times he did this chore, he used one match for each lamp. One evening Srimati Velammai watched him.

While floating in the water, in the lotus pose, Kadappai Sri Paramahamsa Satchidananda Yogeswarar gave satsangs!

"Ramu, you used fifteen matches tonight. At this rate, how many matchboxes will I have to buy for you? You must try to conserve those matches."

"But, Amma, what can I do? By the time I finish with even one lamp the flame is ready to burn my fingers."

His mother gently laughed. "I'll show you how to do it, son." She showed him how to use some cotton and a small stick to make a little torch. With her method, it was very easy to use one match each night. After that, Ramu always remembered his mother's instruction and was very careful not to waste even one match.

One evening the daughter of a poor neighboring family came to the door. They had run out of matches, and in those days one had to travel a long distance even to buy a matchbox. Ramu ran to his mother. "Amma, our neighbor would like to borrow a few matches."

"Of course," Velammai said. "Give her a full matchbox."

"What? A full matchbox! She isn't paying for it."

"Ramu, what did I tell you? Give her a full matchbox."

The boy obeyed but returned to question his mother. "Amma, you don't even want your own son to strike an extra match to light your own lamps. Yet you easily gave away a whole matchbox to that girl. Why, Amma?"

"My dear son. I am so proud of you for your frugality with the matches. It is because you have been so careful that we are able to be generous and serve others."

Ramu understood.

"When Ramu was about ten years old an incident occurred that has always remained fresh in my mind," his uncle Sri Krishnaswamy Gounder remembered. "Often the men of our village would go to a particular fresh water well to bathe. One day a great *siddha* came to our village. His name was Kadappai Sri Paramahamsa Satchidananda Yogeswarar, and at the time he was about fifty-three. He was the author of the famous 900-page book *Jiva Brahma Aikya Vedanta Rahasyam* (The Secret of Vedantic Union of Jiva and Brahma). His specialty was something called *jalasthambanam* — the ability to float on the water in *padmasana*, the lotus pose, while at the same time singing and giving spiritual discourses.

"This kindled everyone's interest; and one day Ramu's father, some other villagers and I went to the well. We all tried to do the same kind of floating and talking but could not. Ramu saw us and wanted to know what we were doing. We told him we were trying out a kind of 'yoga floating.' He laughed and asked why we kept sinking into the water, so we decided to teach him a lesson and challenged him to accomplish this.

"He was eager to try it out. The minute he entered the water, he began to float and recite poetry. This immediately created a big stir, and soon everyone in the village came to watch him floating easefully in the lotus pose and composing Tamil poetry nearly as well as his father!"

A yearly, five-day conference was held in Perur at the Sad Vidhya Sanmarga Sangam of Sandalinga Swamigal Mutt. During that time, a number of well-known lecturers and swamis were invited to address the conference's visitors. Sri Kalyanasundaram was an annual speaker.

In 1921, seven-year-old Ramu asked his father if he could accompany him to the conference, not only to listen but to give a short talk as well. At these spiritual conferences, there was no strict rule about who might or might not speak. If the leaders of the conference agreed, anyone who applied could give a talk.

"Well, it's a big, big gathering. Several thousand people always show up. What will you talk about?" asked the father.

"Ummm. Please suggest a subject for me and give me a few points to discuss."

His father decided on the topic of nonviolence, *ahimsa*, covering the important points. Then he made arrangements to place his son's name on the speakers' roster. Ramu was scheduled to speak on a day when Subbiah Swamigal, a particularly well-known swami, would preside as chairman. Actually, the swami's full name was much longer and quite complicated.

Ramu practiced and practiced — not only his talk, but the correct pronunciation of the monk's name as well.

At Perur, the hour arrived. He felt thoughtful, rather than nervous.

Subbiah Swamigal read from the schedule, "Now, Ramaswamy will deliver a lecture on *ahimsa*."

He smiled at the tiny form of his guest lecturer, who was mounting the platform with such a serious expression. He was the youngest speaker in the history of the conference.

"First of all," a loud, high voice declaimed, "let me offer my humble salutations to the chairman of this session, Sennai Sri Jagathgurupidam Nayachandra Vedanta Bhashkara Srimath Mahamandaleshwara Veerasubbiah Jnana Desikendra Swamigal and to you all."

The perfect recitation of this complex name drew a prolonged round of applause. The swami had never expected such eloquent speech from a child. Embracing Ramu warmly, he lifted the boy onto his lap and instructed him to give the talk from that position.

As long as Ramu lived in that area, he was a guest speaker at the conference.

Ramaswamy joined the Cub Scouts and eventually became a Boy Scout. He entered Sarvajana High School, living in the youth hostel set up for the students in Peelamedu, a neighboring village, and went home about once a month. Then he attended upper high school at the government art college in Coimbatore.

Chemistry and physics fascinated him. His interest was mainly in scientific subjects, rather than history and geography. Scientific subjects could be proved; they didn't deal with theory alone. Things could be put together, manipulated; and there was fun in it also.

Ferreting about the railway station one day, Ramu discovered a gold mine of old batteries which had been thrown away when their current was exhausted. He turned his room at home into a lab and workshop. Its contents spilled into the halls and kitchen, out onto the veranda where the batteries became recharged in the sun. At the time, Chettipalayam's only source of electricity came from Ramu's constructions at home. He also assembled pistons and wheels into a small steam engine.

> **To love your neighbor as your own Self, you must see your neighbor as yourself. Perform your duty as a good neighbor when someone is in distress. Help him. Help her. Do whatever you can.**

At the school, the geography class was held under the supervision of a particularly strict teacher who insisted the students bring a number of textbooks with them to class each day.

One day, the teacher turned his attention to the youngest member of the class.

"Angappa. What is the answer to the question I just asked?"

The boy didn't know.

"You don't know? Well, open your book and read me the information."

That day Angappa had committed the cardinal error of attending class empty-handed. He managed to compose himself, leaned over and borrowed another boy's book. Turning to the proper page, he began to read the required passage in a shaky voice.

"What happened to your own book?" the teacher demanded.

"I-I'm really sorry, sir. I forgot to bring it."

"You forgot!" He raised his eyebrows dramatically. "You forgot! Then why are you coming to class for study?"

Ramu could feel the boy's discomfort within himself. He watched carefully.

The teacher continued, "It's something like a barber going out to give a shave without his razor."

A great silence engulfed the class. Shaving was menial work, below the dignity of boys such as these. They were shocked at the insult.

Angappa began to shake. A barber! He burst into tears. Ramu's sympathy for the boy increased. He was especially fond of Angappa's good nature and innocence. Immediately he stood up.

"Sir," he addressed the teacher. "I have a doubt."

"A doubt? What is it?"

Angappa continued to cry.

"The same doubt as you had."

"What is your doubt?" The teacher was impatient. "Tell me."

"If you go to give a shave, will you forget your razor?" He looked straight at the teacher.

"How can you ask me that?" The teacher's voice rose. "How dare you compare a teacher to a barber!"

"Sir," Ramu answered softly, "I just returned to you the very words you used on this boy. Look how unhappy they made you. When you yourself can't swallow it, how can you expect it of another? And he is just a young boy. Even you, an adult, didn't have the strength to take it. We are here to learn geography, not shaving. You are here to show us the way."

The teacher took a deep breath and nodded his head. He tried to smooth things over.

"Don't worry, Angappa. Forget it. See, someone has even come to take your side."

"No, sir," Ramu corrected. "I am not siding with him as an individual, but I'm siding with his cause. Please excuse me if, in so doing, I have hurt you; but I felt very sad about what I saw."

"All right. Let's forget all these things. Sometimes words will accidently slip out of the mouth," the teacher gently replied.

The events of the day spread to other teachers. For many days, they approached Ramu, shaking his hand or patting him on the back.

"You are really a man of courage."

Ramu (standing in rear on the right) with cousins.

"No. Probably, if the teacher had said that to me, I would have kept quiet. It was Angappa's sorrow that upset me and made me react in that way."

What will make a parent happy? To have beautiful, smart, healthy children who are a little naughty. If they are occasionally mischievous, life will never be boring.

Srimati Velammai's father was a highly respected head man of the village. Sri Ramaswamy Gounder was often called upon to help with difficult judgments since he would always find a wise way to settle a dispute. Once in the Coimbatore court, the District Collector told the people before him, "It's better if you both go to Mr. Ramaswamy Gounder to get this case finalized. If I have to settle it, at least one of you will get hurt. If you go to him, both of you will benefit."

Ramu often visited his grandfather, whom he called "Appa." He had been named after this great man, and they loved each other dearly. Still, Ramu frequently got into mischief when he visited his mother's father.

Sri Ramaswamy Gounder was strictly orthodox and wanted his grandchildren to follow the rules by which he himself lived. For this reason, during Ramu's early school days he had long hair that came almost to his knees. Most of the other boys in school had nice curly crops of short hair, and Ramu wanted very much to follow the fashion. Such a thing could not even be mentioned to his grandfather.

One day a close relative offered to take Ramu on a visit to the sacred Palani Hill. This relative had modern ideas, and he plotted with the young boy to find an excuse for a haircut. Often when someone makes such a holy pilgrimage, he will cut all his hair and offer it to the Lord. This symbolizes offering oneself.

"Aha," reasoned Ramu, "Appa certainly can't complain if I offer my hair to God."

He returned from the pilgrimage and, as was customary, went to get his grandfather's blessings. Sri Ramaswamy Gounder didn't ask one word about Palani; instead: "So, Ramu. I see you have cut your hair. Are you going to keep it like that or be a good boy and grow it back?"

Ramu was a little upset that his grandfather didn't even give his blessings but only cared about his hairstyle. "Well, Appa, it is just growing now. I don't think you should be concerned. As it grows we will see what happens."

His grandfather looked at the boy sharply. No one ever spoke to him this way. "Oh, is that so? I'm going to be watching you to see what happens."

Quietly Ramu stuck to his plan for keeping his hair short, and his grandfather got used to it that way.

There seemed to be many opportunities for mischief with Ramu's beloved Appa. While visiting his grandfather, he often admired the wonderful baths taken by the old man. Because of his orthodoxy, he had a very strict ritual. He would not eat anything until he had his bath and performed his *puja*.

Before drawing the bath water for his employer, Appa's servant would bathe. Then he would take the water from a deep well, boil it in a spotlessly clean vessel and pour it into the tub. Neither the servant nor anyone else could touch the water. It must be totally pure for Sri Ramaswamy Gounder's bath. Young Ramu frequently watched this ritual and admired it. He envied his grandfather the deep vessel filled with hot water, and wished to take such a bath himself.

One day as Appa prepared for his bath, he told Ramu to see if the water was ready. Eagerly Ramu went to check, and as he went an idea came to him.

"Appa," he said upon his return, "the water is ready. It's hot enough now for your bath."

Immediately, Sri Ramaswamy Gounder looked at the boy. "How do you know it is hot enough?"

"Oh, I put my hand in it."

"You dirty fellow! You touched the water? Now how can I take a bath? *You* use the water. Take a bath, then get the servant to clean it and fill it again."

Ramu totally enjoyed his bath.

> **A spirit of detachment doesn't mean that you run away from the world and become no good for it. On the contrary, you are the best person to do something in the world because you have the proper understanding.**

A coatstand stood in Ramaswamy's bedroom. On its flat top was placed a mirror which was particularly prized by Sri Kalyanasundaram.

One day Ramu entered the room and quickly snatched his shawl from the hanger. For a moment, the mirror was suspended in the air. Turning over, it fell to the floor and broke into pieces. Ramu sighed. He recognized his haste but realized there was nothing he could do now to salvage the mirror.

"Muthu," he called to the servant. "Come here. Please collect the broken pieces and throw them in a place where no one will get cut."

As the boy gathered the pieces, Kalyanasundaram reached the room.

"Ramu." His tone was sharp. "That was a very precious thing to me. Did you know how much I loved it?"

"Yes, Ayah," Ramu said quietly. "I know you liked it very much."

"You know that? Well it is obvious you don't care. I don't see any unhappiness in your face about what you have done."

"I really am sad about it, Ayah; and I realize my mistake."

"It doesn't seem so by your expression."

"I just feel there's no need to cry over spilled milk. But if that is what you want, then I'll cry." He turned to the young servant. "Come on, Muthu, stop picking up the pieces. Let us both sit here and cry for a while and see if the pieces will come together again."

Muthu stopped his collecting. Kalyanasundaram became furious.

"You are talking *Vedanta* to me?" He called to his wife. "Hey, come listen to your great *Vedanti*. He broke a precious object and now he talks philosophy over it."

Srimati Velammai entered the room.

"I can tell Ramu genuinely feels sad about it," she commented, "but by your anger, or his tears, you're not going to get it back. When he says he realizes what he has done, you should accept it and finish the matter there."

A long time afterward, Ramu's father was still calling him the "Great *Bala* (young) *Vedanti*."

No person is an untouchable. Differences come, not with the work one does nor the caste into which one is born, but with the state of mind. Essentially we are all one and the same. All are God's children.

Vacation started. Home from school, Ramu walked through one of the farms three miles from his home. On this land which was worked by the untouchables, there was a farmhouse where the family sometimes spent three or four days in order to supervise various projects. When it was cool and dark, the family sat on the stone porch and discussed assignments for the following day with the workers, who sat around red bonfires as bright sparks from the flames shot into the dark night sky.

One day a wind picked up, blowing the clouds into a thick gray curtain. The household staff ran back and forth from the clotheslines, gathering the garments before the oncoming storm broke.

In the fields, the untouchables, dressed only in loincloths, continued their plowing, unmindful of the storm. When they worked they always removed their outer clothes and kept them near the field where they wouldn't get soiled; they dressed again at the end of the day.

Ramu's eyes traveled from the workers, small dots against the cloudy sky, to the buzzing of the household staff.

White flashes of lightning slashed into the ground. The throbbing drum of thunder grew closer as fat drops began to pour, drenching the farm. Still the dots in the fields continued their work, intent only upon completing the task set aside for the day. The mud oozed between their bare toes, and their hair became slick as sheets of water flowed over their heads and ran down their backs.

With the end of the storm came the finish of the day's work. The untouchables shouldered their tools and walked to the huge tamarind tree where they usually kept their clothing. Instead of the piles of soggy material they expected, they found nothing — not a stitch, wet or dry.

Ramu watched them from the veranda, noting their distress. He called one of the workers to the porch.

"Don't worry. All your clothes are safe in the large hole in the tree trunk. I think you'll find them quite dry in there."

The face before Ramu broke into a toothy smile. The worker would have gladly hugged the boy for this news, but instead he stood still and bowed his head to the landlord's son, an action in accordance with the rules of the caste system.

As the untouchable ran off to spread the news, Srimati Velammai approached her son.

"Ramu, how did you know their clothes were in the tree?"

The son recognized her quiet but threatening tone.

"When I saw that the rain was coming, I put them there myself."

"You put them there? You touched *their* clothes? How could you?

The venerable grandfathers: Sri Ramaswamy Gounder (left), father of Srimati Velammai, and Sri R. Nanjappa Gounder (right), father of Sri Kalyanasundaram.

Really, Ramu, you know the way things are." She began to lecture him on the regulations of the caste system.

"Amma, you may lecture all you want, and I am really sorry to hurt your feelings, but how could I let their clothes get drenched when I was able to prevent it? They would have had to spend all the night in damp, cold garments. They might even have gotten sick." Then he placated her. "Come, it's your turn now. I'll perform all the necessary purification processes you desire."

Under her instructions, he removed his clothes and left them outside the house to be washed. Then he took a bath before reentering.

"Well, Amma, it looks as though you'll have to purify the whole farmhouse. Remember I was practically standing inside when you found out about my deed."

"Don't be funny," Velammai said sternly. "You've irritated me enough for one day. Don't make it worse by teasing me."

Ramu was always quick to denounce the injustices of the caste system and could never agree with the long, theoretical explanations of his elders about the differences between one person and another. To him, people were all the same — mixtures of good and bad. While living under his father's roof, however, he respectfully observed the customs since he knew his parents would be terribly unhappy and confused if he didn't. Yet, he never failed to greet the rationalization of these rules with hearty laughter. Later, when he married and had a family of his own, he taught his children, "The workers know all about the land. Don't think they are ignorant. They are wise. You must always treat them as your own family members and respect them."

The same thing can be both good and bad. Whenever you speak of good, bad is also present. The world is a mixture of both. There is not good without bad. They are both sides of the same coin. Both are necessary. We have been given a free will and discriminating capacity to select what is beneficial to us and to avoid what is detrimental to us. Even cobra poison can be used as a medicine.

Though the house of Sri Kalyanasundaram followed a strictly vegetarian diet, there were certain relatives who ate meat. Meat was sometimes served at these homes, though cooked in a separate kitchen with a different set of utensils for preparation and served in a dining room separate from the one in which vegetarian food was served.

The children of these relatives generally played within the thick jungle bordering their home. Many animals lived among the tall shade trees and dripping creepers. Often the boys would hunt and trap in the woods. Once when Ramu came for a visit, he went along on their hunt as an observer.

He followed closely behind the boys, watching them swagger through the bushes, shotguns slung over their shoulders, bragging about the fine kill they were sure to make.

"Shooting doesn't seem to be so very difficult," Ramu thought. "And with all their talk, they rarely ever bring down anything. Shooting seems to be just a matter of concentration. Probably I could shoot every bit as well as they do by simply concentrating."

The boys were busily aiming their guns here and there, not giving their targets much cause for worry.

Ramu stepped forward. "Mind if I try?"

One of the boys squinted at Ramu. "Have you ever used a gun before? I don't remember seeing you shoot before."

"Actually, no, I haven't. But it really doesn't seem to be something impossible for me."

The boy looked at his gun reluctantly. "Well, if *we* haven't gotten anything today, I'm sure you won't. Oh, okay. Here. You might as well try it."

Ramu slowly lifted the gun and raised it to his shoulder. High in a tree perched a pair of birds. Carefully, he pointed the barrel. Aiming well through the sight, he pulled the trigger. Two things happened simultaneously — the gun tore the air with a loud crack, and the larger of the two birds fell from the tree, floating down, turning over and over in midair.

A great rush of accomplishment welled from Ramu's stomach. It was abruptly quelled by a mournful crying sound. The female bird was shrieking through the forest. Down she flew, calling and crying, fluttering nervously over the body of her mate.

Ramu dropped the gun as if it had scorched his hands. Then he too fell to the ground. His blood sounded like the ocean in his ears. His heartbeat speeded to a point where he thought he could no longer breathe and would surely faint. His partners, on the other hand, were leaping and shouting with joy around him.

"Get up, get up." They thought he was joking. "You told us you never shot before. That's impossible. You brought down that bird with one try. How great." They applauded him and danced about.

Their hero remained prone on the jungle floor. Nausea stirred in his stomach. He was filled with disgust over what he had done. He could hear the continued cries of the female bird.

Finally, propping himself up with one hand, he rose from the ground.

"I can't believe I did that."

"Neither can we. You were absolutely fantastic."

"Think what you want. For me, that was the first and last time I'll hurt another creature."

He walked from the woods, followed by his confused relatives.

To the surprise of the boys, Ramu accompanied them another day to the jungle for a shooting trip. Silently, he tracked behind, gunless as usual.

Totally silent, they halted as one. Far away a bird sang briefly. Treading cautiously on her thin, dappled legs, a deer walked toward them, unaware of the boys or their guns.

Two guns were soundlessly raised — painstakingly, slowly. She came closer and seemed to catch the scent. No, she was still approaching, directly in the sights of two shotguns.

An explosion rang out. Ramu, last in line, was shaking with a fit of coughing. As his companions turned quickly to see what had happened, the deer took off and within seconds was far away, leaping through the brush.

The group continued when Ramu's coughing fit subsided. Soon they were gliding soundlessly through the woods again. Not even a branch moved as they passed, not even a leaf. Tension began to set into strained muscles as the hours passed. Then one of the group noticed a small grayish ball snuffling about the roots of a large tree. A rabbit. Even a rabbit was worth the sport after all this time. Before they could raise their barrels, however, Ramu let loose an enormous sneeze. The small animal vanished.

"I knew this would happen if we brought the *ahimsa* lover along," one boy said with annoyance.

"First the deer, now the rabbit. Every animal in the jungle must have run away after that sneeze."

Another said, "The first time I thought your coughing was real. Now your little trick has become quite obvious."

"I'm hungry and there's nothing to cook."

Ramu didn't answer. He began slowly walking, looking down at the ground. "If your problem is really hunger, follow me," he announced. Soon he began gathering wild beans and roots.

Ramu borrowed a pot from a neighbor's house, expertly built a Boy

Scout fire, and cooked the items he had picked.

"It's quite good," a boy said grudgingly.

As they began to fill their stomachs, tempers subsided with their hunger.

"Is this so much worse than eating animal flesh?" Ramu asked.

It is difficult for young boys with full mouths to answer such questions.

We are all playing our parts and in our worldly roles we have various relationships. We have duties toward one another — the child to the parent, the parent to the child, the student to the teacher. We should perform these duties well without becoming attached to them too much.

Ramu was a thoughtful, independent boy. He knew what objectives he wanted and devised his own means for getting them. Although he was against anyone thwarting his plans, he served his parents lovingly, helping them in any way he could. He listened to their advice patiently and respectfully though he didn't always take it. Custom plays a large part in Indian family life, much more so than in the West. He followed the customs to the extent that his parents would be gratified, but he always sought new solutions.

Sri Kalyanasundaram was a poet, widely known throughout Tamil Nadu for his expertise in composing *Chitrabhandanam* — the complex construction of poems into visually attractive designs. There seemed to be no end to the intricate designs Kalyanasundaram would make by playing with words. One poem was done in the form of elaborately intertwined snakes; another was a beautifully drawn Siva *lingam* made by the lines of poetry. There were wheels, complex mandalas, and more. In some compositions every line within the drawing was the same poem. At each point where the lines crossed, the same letter was used. The illustration in this book shows how intricately the words intertwined and how skillful a poet needed to be in order to compose beautiful, clever verses while creating such a complex pattern.

The Tamil Sangam, Tamil Nadu's foremost cultural institution, awarded Sri Kalyanasundaram the title *Chitrakavi* — an honor given to the greatest poets. Later, in the 1950s Sri Swami Sivanandaji gave Kalyanasundaram the title *Kavi Chudamani* (Crest Jewel of Poets).

The kerosene lamps burned into the early morning hours. The

father sat in bed, propped up by pillows, unable to sleep without completing his verses. Ramu would sit by the side of the bed suggesting different words.

"Ayah, why don't you use this one?" The perfect word was offered. The rhythm of the poem could continue unimpaired, and the poem was completed. Sri Kalyanasundaram would pull his son onto the bed, slap him joyfully on the back, shake his hand, and fall asleep.

Ramu entered the Agricultural College in order to round out his schooling. He studied dairy farming, crop rotation and animal husbandry. In the morning and evening he spent some time in prayer and, whenever he had the opportunity, took part in temple services. A month before graduation, he entered the Dean's office.

"Sir, I have just come to say good-bye. I'm leaving school now."

The Dean stood up. "Why? What's wrong?"

"Nothing is wrong. I just feel that I have completed my studies and there are no further courses I'm interested in taking."

"But, Ramu, don't you realize you have only one more month until graduation. Don't you want your diploma? Why not wait until graduation?"

The student looked around the office, scanning the desk and the walls covered with diplomas and certificates, all neatly framed in gold.

"Well, sir, I have no need for a diploma. I've come to this school to take in what it could teach me for my own use. Now that it's finished, I have no reason to stay here just to receive a certificate because I have no intention to use it to get a job. Some people will need their certificate to help them get work, but I wouldn't be using it for that purpose. You have educated me well, and now I'm ready to put all that I've learned here into action."

> **When business people deal with a customer, they should feel they have sold their goods in the proper way, serviced the customer properly, and that the customer will be happy with it. That is fair business. If, on the other hand, they sell the customer trash but still expect the money, it is no longer a business; it's thievery. Business people should be interested in selling the customer products they themselves use.**

Ramu's uncle, Sri Krishnaswamy Gounder, owned a growing

automobile business in Coimbatore and was the first importer of British cars in the Madras State. He also imported motorcycles and metal bodies for building trucks and buses. Ramu was eager to join this type of concern. He was proficient in handling engines and machinery, and his uncle gladly brought him into the business as a partner. These were the days just prior to World War II. The partners foresaw a great scarcity of gasoline and, realizing just how dear it would become, decided to produce engines capable of burning other types of fuel — kerosene or charcoal-burnt gas. They thumbed through the issues of *Popular Science* and *Popular Mechanics* to find the proper instructions and came up with many "finds." From their research, they ordered several of a new kind of bicycle and various shiny gadgets for machinery. Neither of the two had any knowledge of welding, something which was necessary for the production of the needed gas plants for the motor vehicles. Ramu decided to travel to Ceylon (now Sri Lanka) where this training was readily available. He and his uncle began to plan for the trip.

Ramu's relatives in Chettipalayam were shocked. Even trips to North India were rare. In their memory no one in the family had ever traveled to a foreign country.

"Your son is only twenty years old," they reminded Kalyanasundaram and Velammai. "He's still just a boy. How can you allow him to move to a strange country?"

Patiently they explained, "Throughout his life, Ramaswamy has always done exactly what he's wanted. Now that he's a man, you can't expect us to stop him."

Ramu became well acquainted with Ceylon and her culture. He traveled throughout the island, making excursions to various places of religious pilgrimage — the shrines of Kataragama, Munneshwaram and to Adam's Peak. He studied well and returned to South India to serve as the first expert welder in all of Tamil Nadu.

In the worldly, selfish life people live for themselves, using their scientific knowledge for themselves, while in the religious life that same scientific knowledge is utilized for others. Even in the religious field, if people are selfish they are really living a worldly life.

One day, the trustees of the Perur Temple of Lord Nataraja approached Sri Kalyanasundaram with an urgent request.

சிவலிங்க பந்தனம்.

அட்டநாக பந்தனம்.

Two of the many chitrakavi, poems in complex designs, composed by Sri Kalyanasundaram.
Siva Linga Bhandanam and Atanaga Bhandanam.

Agricultural College, Coimbatore, 1933: this small class was chosen from a large number of applicants (Ramu, back row, far right).

"Do you think Ramaswamy would take up the management of our temple? He seems to be the proper person for the job and we are in great need of such a manager. The previous manager has left."

"Well, I really can't answer for him. My son is in Ceylon studying certain technical matters. Probably, when he returns to India, he'll want to go back to his business."

The trustees were persistent. The temple lands were large, consisting of two villages and all their acreage, and had been donated by the kings of India. They waited until Ramu returned and approached him directly.

To Sri Kalyanasundaram's surprise, Ramu agreed. He felt it was an opportunity to serve the Lord.

"I'll do it on a temporary basis," he told them, "until you find someone to your liking who can replace me."

Ramu was familiar with the Perur Temple. Since childhood, he had been very fond of its large statue of the Nataraja — the dancing Siva, arms raised gracefully to the side, one leg balanced in the air between steps.

As the temple's executive officer, Ramu's job was to supervise the temple's finances, organize its festivals, take care of the managing and leasing of temple lands, and oversee the maintenance of the temple.

When all the devotees had left after the final evening prayers, Ramu would decorate the image of Lord Nataraja with all the ornaments in his charge, light the lamps and spend the night in meditation before the flickering flames.

After a number of months the temple trustees found another manager, and Ramu returned to his uncle's business, renewing his acquaintance with both machinery and cigarettes. During his college years, Ramu had picked up more than information about all fields of farming. He had picked up the habit of cigarette smoking.

A third partner had been taken on, Mr. Gabriel, a Frenchman. He introduced Ramu to an extra embellishment, the drinking of great quantities of coffee — not the watered-down variety but a heavily percolated brew of black, syrupy liquid. Ramu mixed his with a few drops of milk and four spoonfuls of white sugar. He had a standing order at a nearby restaurant. Every half-hour an attendant would come in with a steaming, fresh cup and remove the cold dregs of the former one.

When Lady Nicotine comes in, even though you want to divorce her, she won't leave you. Instead, she will dig in deep, to the very mar-

row. Not only that; she will call in her sister, Caffeine. So, take care of your senses. Even if you don't practice *pranayama*, the yogic breathing techniques, don't spoil your regular breathing with the unyogic inhalation of cigarettes.

Ramu leaned over a mass of pistons and oily wheels. He realized his cigarette was cold, hanging dead from his lips. He reached into his pocket for a fresh one and somehow was reminded of a visit to a close relative, a chainsmoker, long before.

He had sat near the relative, playing, as the old man did some work. As the man worked, he smoked, and as he smoked he coughed — retching up sticky mucus. He looked through the phlegm spit into his handkerchief, trying to find something. Calling the boy Ramu to his side, he showed him a small, hard, leathery object.

"Do you know what this is, Ramu?"

"No, sir."

"It is a piece of my lung."

"Your lungs are supposed to be inside your body. How can that be?"

"Because I smoke so many cigarettes my lungs are now flinty, completely ruined. Each time I cough, a little piece like this comes out."

"Icch! Why do you show it to me?"

"To teach you a lesson. Maybe if I show it to you, you won't do the same thing when you are older."

Now, years later, Ramu stood up in his workshop, hand in pocket and realized that he *was* preparing to do the same thing. He withdrew the pack from his pocket and hurled it into the garbage, immediately breaking the habit for life.

As far back as I can remember, I always wanted to be free.

Ramu left the automobile business for the cinematographic field. South India's movie industry was concerned mainly with the production of super-sensational religious myths, glittering with thousands of costumes and extras. He concerned himself with production and distribution. Sometimes, as a representative of the film company, he traveled from village to village. In the smaller areas, he himself did the projection of the movie, handled all advertising and took care of col-

35

lections. As the customers came into the theater, Ramu and the theater's manager would be at the door, dividing the profits right there.

After learning the trade, he returned to machinery and technical matters and started his own welding workshop. He treated his workers more like brothers than subordinates, sitting with them and helping with their jobs.

During World War II, a government ammunitions factory decided to erect a new chemical plant in the Blue Mountains of India. Allied engineers were commissioned to work on the structure, but the project's supervisors needed a master welder. The Labor Commissioner asked for such a man, and various technical engineers gave Ramaswamy's name. A representative of the plant was sent to Ramu's factory and invited him to take the job.

"As you can see," Ramu answered, "I have my own workshop to think about; but temporarily I'll go to your chemical plant and see how the work is proceeding. If I enjoy that work, I'll stick to it and work for you until the plant is completed. Anyway, I'd like to do it as a service for the government."

He closed his workshop and traveled to the plant. Enjoying the work, after a week he decided to wind up all of his workshop's outstanding jobs and close it on a more permanent basis.

Ramu walked through the clanking and grinding din of the plant to the chief engineer's office. As he sat down, he told the engineer about his decisions.

"I think all I'll need is a three-day leave. In that time I can wind up my own business and return here."

The engineer himself was a man with a mission. His answer was one of practiced patience and confidence. "But, Ramaswamy, our work here is of the utmost urgency. If you leave, everyone's work will have to stop until you return."

"Well, sir, it's just for three days."

Slowly, as if explaining a complex theorem to a small child, the engineer stressed, "Ramaswamy, I don't think you fully understand the urgency of our work. No one can work with you gone." Visions of fully paid, loitering workers passed through his mind.

Ramu was equally patient. "Anyway, I must go wind up my own work. I too am still paying my workers all the time I am here. There is also no work for them to do without me."

The engineer grasped the arms of his chair, his practiced patience dissolving.

"Ramaswamy, it is absolutely impossible. There's no way I can grant you leave."

(above) Isn't he businesslike? Ramaswamy the businessman.
(upper right) R. Krishnaswamy Gounder, man of many facets — poet, printer, industrialist, agriculturist, etc.
(middle right) Sri G.D. Naidu, "Automobile King of the East" — South Indian industrialist and inventor.
(lower right) Ramaswamy, 1935.

"If you won't accept my request for leave, please accept my resignation."

The engineer turned away and thought for a long time. Ramu sat patiently, awaiting the outcome of his deliberation.

"According to the law," the engineer smirked, "we can even arrest you and put you in jail for refusing to work on this government project."

"Fine."

"What?"

"Fine," Ramu repeated. "If you want to put me in jail, if that is your chosen course of action, do it. Otherwise, I will leave. My freedom is very important to me and if you don't put me in jail, I'll go."

The engineer offered to double Ramu's salary.

"I didn't come here for money. I came to offer my services to the country. Money isn't my main reason for wanting to be here. Either allow me to go or put me in jail."

The engineer left the confines of his chair and desk. He paced up and down.

"My own son is working here," he said. "At least stay for another few days and train him to take your place."

"I came here to work, not to teach. If you want your son to learn from me, that's fine. I'll take him back to my workshop and give him all the training he needs."

The engineer sat down limply.

"All right. All right," he sighed, beaten, "go back for three days, but as soon as you wind up your business come back here."

Ramu smiled and thanked him. That day he left the factory. If that was the reaction to any infringement of the plant's policy, he wanted no part of it. As soon as he arrived home, he drafted a letter of resignation and sent it to the plant manager.

Soon afterward, a furtive-looking group of men from Central Intelligence entered Ramu's village. They had been sent by the managers of the chemical plant who thought that perhaps this man was a spy. After all, money didn't seem to be the motivating factor in his work so he must have been there for another, more underhanded reason. They checked on Ramaswamy and his family, but left when they couldn't find the desired incriminations.

We go here, there, to this place, to that, always looking for the happiness that is there inside.

United Motors, located in Coimbatore, was founded by Sri G.D.

Naidu, a technical genius and inventor who owned a fleet of buses throughout South India. He was known as the East's "Automobile King." When Ramu was in his early twenties, Naidu decided to open another business (NEW, the National Electric Works) to manufacture electric motors for use in pumping and textile mills. Naidu's factory was unable to handle the copper welding of the rotors to his satisfaction, and he began sending the rotors to Ramu's factory for work. Being a smart businessman as well as a technician, Naidu invited Ramu to join him in the NEW factory, and Ramu agreed — upon certain conditions.

"I will not do it strictly as an employee," Ramu explained. "I must have the liberty of moving around and acquainting myself with the various sections throughout the factory — the electrical shops, the bodywork shops, the casting foundry. I would like to learn about all of the these things."

Naidu agreed. "Do the welding and in your spare time go anywhere in the factory. Learn anything you want. You have full liberty."

Ramu moved into NEW. Very soon he had fully trained a couple of workmen to handle the welding and began to travel about the factory's other sections, learning whatever he could.

The chief engineer called him in for tea and a talk. "Why don't you start supervising the electrical shop?"

Ramu agreed. If he did not actually know anything about a particular section, he would go to the appointed supervisor, watch everything, concentrate and absorb. Within a few days, he had picked up enough information to advise the workers on how to do a better job. He never told them beforehand that he knew nothing of their business. He began to devise ways and means to improve the various sections and to encourage the laborers to turn in more efficient work. He also introduced a system of bonuses as supplements to the salaries.

The engineer sent him from section to section to bring up production. Ramu even worked for a time in the sales department and later took charge of the bus service section at another location.

> **In taking care of your own family, feel that it has been given to you by God to be looked after. Feel that these people have been sent to you. Have your relationships with them, but feel they are the Lord's, not yours. You have not created them, and you are not going to take them with you when you ultimately leave.**

(above) Lord Nataraja and
Sivakami — the presiding
deities in the Golden Hall.

(right) The Golden Hall at
Patteswara Swami Temple,
Perur.

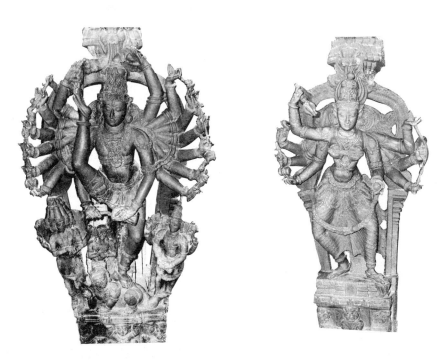

(above) Two of the beautiful statues on the pillars in the Golden Hall — Siva and Kali.

(below) Staff of Patteswara Swami Temple, Perur, 1937, when Ramaswamy was temple manager.

Four great saints whose teachings inspired Ramaswamy during his year in seclusion: (clockwise from upper left) Sri Swami Sivanandaji Maharaj, Sri Ramakrishna Paramahamsa, Saint Ramalinga Swamigal, Sri Swami Vivekanandaji Maharaj.

In India life is divided into four stages. The first is *brahmacharya*, the period of study. During the second stage, *grihastha*, one enters family life. The next stage is *vanaprastha*, and it occurs when the children are old enough to care for themselves. The husband and wife leave the business life, giving up all interest in money and possessions, and turn toward spiritual matters.

At a certain stage, they both take *sannyas* and become renunciates. If one dies before that stage is reached, the survivor traditionally takes *sannyas* vows. *Sannyasa*, the final stage, is entered upon when one gets into the spirit of total renunciation and devotes all his or her time to meditation on the Lord.

Srimati Velammai and her husband were concerned about Ramu's future. He was twenty-three and still a bachelor when most men were married and had children.

"If he doesn't marry now," his mother would fret, "he might be completely absorbed into the *sannyas* life without even tasting a life with a wife and children."

Ramu remained indifferent to their hints and proddings. His workshop filled most of his time, and his interest in a spiritual life had been strengthened by his time at the Perur Temple. Whenever these discussions were brought up, he thought of the various problems of his married friends — economic crises, family illnesses, obligations, attachments.

Eventually, he weighed the pros and cons of the *grihastha* life and decided the lessons to be learned in a family situation were valid and necessary.

During the time Ramu served as the Temple Manager of the Perur Temple, he had become well-acquainted with one of the families which was very active and helpful in the management. In fact, the head of the family had once been a trustee of the Temple. The daughter of this gentleman was very beautiful and very devout. Ramu had watched her regularly visiting the Temple and praying, and now he felt that she was the one he wished to marry. Respectfully he asked for his parents' permission to take this young woman for a wife.

I loved my wife, but at the same time, I wasn't attached to her.

The family was overjoyed with relief, particularly after the birth of first one and then another son. They were confident that Ramu was

43

leading an exemplary family life. It went on smoothly, contentedly and lovingly.

Normally, in Hindu family life, the wife moves into the home of the husband's family. However, Ramu rented a home not far from the factory for the sake of convenience. They lived there quite comfortably with a servant and a caretaker for the two boys. Ramu's monthly bonus was used for luxury items while all their food, vegetables and grains, came directly from the family farm.

Every day he drove to work on his motorcycle. One evening as he drove home through the darkening trees, a picture came strongly into his mind. He seemed to see his wife lying on the bed at home with the neighbors standing by her body and saying that she was dead. Some people might have dismissed this as a busy young husband's anxiety, but the vision persisted. On many evenings, Ramu had the same premonition.

"I left home in the morning, so many hours ago," Ramu would think. "Anything could have happened while I was at work. What if I come home and find my wife dead, and the children crying, and the neighbors all around, just like in the vision? What will I do? How will I react?"

The monologue would continue as he approached the house, leaning into the curves in the dirt road.

"I love her so much, but such things are the Lord's will. If He decides to take her away, who can stop it? I can't worry about these things. When she finishes her duty here, probably she'll just pass on. I can't cry and shout to bring her back to life. If that ever happens, I will have to take it as God's will.

"What will I do with the children if such a thing happens? Again, they are not mine, but the Lord's children. If no one comes forward to bring them up, I'll take care of them."

Five years after his marriage, Ramu was working in the factory when he received a telephone call. His wife had suddenly passed away. He was surprised by his own sense of calm. There was nothing he could do; he had been through the alternatives so many times before. He began to think of the welfare of his children.

Soon afterward he left NEW, though Naidu tried to persuade him to reconsider. It was obvious to his family that Ramu's thoughts had turned to less worldly matters, but they silently hoped this was a temporary result of his wife's death and would, in time, wane.

Ramaswamy became interested in the study and practice of Hatha Yoga, studying three books of yoga postures — two by Tamil writers Mr.

44

Sundaram and Mr. Kumaraswamy, and one by Sri Swami Sivananadaji Maharaj of the Himalayas.

After several months, Srimati Velammai said, "Perhaps it's time for you to consider remarrying, at least for the sake of the children."

Outside the window, in the bright heat, they could see the boys playing.

Ramu looked up. "Are you having trouble taking care of them, Amma?"

She smiled softly. "Of course not. To me they are really a joy."

"Because if you don't want to take care of them any longer, my brother has offered to do so. I can even put them in the *ashram* school of the Ramakrishna Mission. There is no reason for me to remarry just for the sake of the children."

His interest in business and family had come to an end. There was no need for him to learn the same lessons over and over again.

His mother felt this instinctively. "Please, leave them here with us." She felt he would soon be leaving the family for good.

Sambasiva Chaitanya

By renouncing the world, you don't lose anything. Once you give yourself to others, all
others will give themselves to you. In the beginning of this life, people often said to me, "Why
are you renouncing? You have thrown away
your house, your wealth, everything. What are
you going to gain?" I would tell them, "It may
look like I am giving up something, but I know
that I will gain everything."

Sambasiva Chaitanya

Ramu lived in a room in his father's house. He devoted himself entirely to religious study and meditation and became more and more introspective. The mundane noises from outside his room, people talking, floors being swept, doors being opened and closed, began to disturb him. He had become too finely sensitized to remain in the house and requested that his father allow him to live in the flower garden, one and a half miles away.

In this lovely garden to which he had come each morning as a boy, a small patch of land was cleared and an eight-foot square hut was constructed. It was cavelike, with clay walls and a tiled roof. Outside the door, a small stone seat served as a veranda. A fence was constructed at a radius of ten feet, and around the outside of the garden there stood another fence. The two fences were equipped with locks. Ramu had one key; his father, the other.

Ramu would rise and bathe in the large stone well before dawn. Next to the hut, he had planted a small flower garden which he tended into various designs in his spare time. He picked flowers for the morning *puja*. The rest of the day was spent in meditation and the study of books by Saint Pattinathar, a great renunciate; Sri Bhagavan Ramakrishna, Saint Ramalingam, Sri Swami Vivekananda, and Sri Swami Sivananda. To keep his body fit, he practiced Hatha Yoga *asanas*, physical postures designed to bring flexibility to the spine and overall perfect health. His diet was austere, limited to one meal a day at noon consisting of *kitcheree*, a mixture of rice, *dhal* and *ghee*. Srimati Velammai would prepare it in the morning and send it over with a servant. For a while, she tried to induce Ramu to take some food in the evening as well, sending tender coconuts to be left at his door. In the morning, the attendant would find the coconut still outside the door, untouched. After a few days, the practice was discontinued.

This strict regimen continued for almost a year. Ramu shared his small space with a number of snakes and once found a family of scorpions living less than a foot from his bed.

Although he was not aware of it at the time, Ramu already had one very devoted disciple, an untouchable woman. Every day while he meditated, unaware of her presence, she came to the outer garden fence and walked around it once. Bowing deeply, she would say a brief prayer and leave.

Whenever a member of her colony fell ill, she made a special trip to Ramu's hut. After circling the fence and bowing, she took a bit of dust from the ground to carry back to her village. When she came to the home of the sick person, she mixed the dust with water and instructed the patient to swallow it. Many people were cured.

That devoted woman lived to be 104 before she passed away in the late 1970s. Toward the end of her life she was almost completely blind and deaf. Yet Sri Gurudev never failed to visit her when he visited Chettipalayam. He would always greet her warmly, hold her hands and inquire after her welfare, much to the dismay of the class-conscious community.

When a particular *mantram* is repeated, you develop that vibration within you. That vibration attracts a form of the Divine Aspect and, indirectly, the form is created within your mind to suit the quality which you expect. When that quality becomes more and more impressed upon your mind, you begin to perceive it outside as well.

In his flower garden home, during meditation Ramu's first spiritual experiences manifested. As he carefully concentrated on his beloved deity, the goddess Parvati, he felt the small room suddenly glow with light and fill with her unearthly presence. She appeared shining before him. With her was Lord Subramanya. After that Ramu often had such *darshan* (vision) in the small hut.

It was a good situation for introspection and meditation, but Ramu began to feel the need to further explore spiritual life outside those particular confines. As he considered this, he naturally thought of Sri Sadhu Swamigal, one of the main holy men who had frequented the family home during Ramu's boyhood. In fact, Sadhu Swamigal was like the family guru and had given *mantra* initiation to Srimati Velammai. He was a great *upasika* or *tantric* yogi, one who uses geometrical forms or *yantras*, as well as certain *mantras*, *mudras*, and cleansing practices during the course of worship to invoke the presence of a particular deity. Ultimately the *upasika* receives that presence or vision within. Sadhu Swamigal was particularly devoted to Lord Muruga, and it was not surprising that he had an ashram on the side of Palani Hill. That is where Ramu went for the next stage of his spiritual journey.

The holy place called Palani is a hill temple dedicated to Lord Muruga with the name Palani Andavar. For many centuries it has been a place of pilgrimage and meditation for saints and seekers. Many *siddhas* lived and attained *samadhi* in this holy place, and sincere seekers can feel their presence even today. Ramu and his fellow *sadhus* often saw visions of these great *siddha purushas* (personalities of spiritual accomplishment) as they went to and from worship or meditation.

It was still dark when Ramu woke in the early morning. He walked three miles to the river. Unless there was moonlight, only the sense of touch told him when he had reached the water. After bathing, he returned to the hill and walked the two miles around the base before beginning the climb up the one thousand stairs to the top. Ramu always attended the early morning and evening services and often stopped on his way down the hill to meditate at one of the many shrines along the way.

> **If the food you eat is *sattwic* (mild) you will be able to easily harmonize the life force within you. Food that is *rajasic* (hot and spicy) agitates both the mind and that force. *Tamasic* food (food that is old or rotten) produces inertia.**

In addition to Muruga, Sri Sadhu Swamigal was also devoted to Annapoorni, the goddess of nourishment. Due to the manifestation of this "food goddess," thousands of people were fed at the ashram daily — the poor, the sick, as well as pilgrims and visitors who came to Palani.

One evening, the devotees found that there was nothing left with which to feed the people on the following day. Ramu and a few others went to the Master with this information. "Swamiji, there is not even a bushel of rice left. We don't know how we will feed the people. Thousands will be waiting."

Calmly, Sadhu Swamigal said, "Why do you worry? There's a higher authority to worry about that. Just go and sleep. She who has taken care of us all these years will take care of tomorrow also."

At precisely midnight a man from the next village knocked at the door. When the ashramites answered his knock there was a cartload of rice in front of them. In answer to their wondering expressions he explained, "I was sound asleep when a lady in a white dress, like an angel, appeared in a dream. She said, 'Sadhu Swamigal needs rice. Please take it to him right away.' So of course I did what she said."

In the evenings, Ramu and another disciple prepared Sri Swamigal's bed. After putting up the mosquito curtain when the Swami retired for the night, they left the room. Sometimes as they sat and meditated nearby, they heard Sri Swamigal talking to somebody. If they asked about it, they were told, "Keep quiet. You don't need to be spying on me." They finally found out that Sri Sadhu Swamigal often conversed with Lord Muruga and the Goddess.

A kitchen that feeds so many people is hard-pressed to remain always *sattwic*. There were forty to fifty different cooks; and often the meals were laced with curry, chili and spicy condiments. Close devotees prepared food in their homes and brought it to Sadhu Swamigal. Ramu himself had two such devotees — Sri Kalidas, a bachelor, and his elder brother Sadaiappa Chettiar. They sent Ramu lunch each day at noon or took him to their home to dine. There were many evenings when Ramu visited their shop in the center of town. They always kept a cup of milk and two bananas ready for that event.

The holy site of Palani was the perfect place for total purgation, and Ramu's body naturally responded to this. He went through a period when, for no apparent reason, his body purified itself of all toxins. There was a complete burning feeling all over, as if his body were on fire. Ramu would sit in the river for hours in an effort to relieve this sensation. When he emerged from the river, the burning sensation remained. He tried applying sandalwood paste, which is known as a great purifier, but as he covered his entire body with the wet sandalwood, the intense heat from his body immediately dried the paste. This continued for several days and then slowly subsided.

Ramu felt wonderful, not drained and tired as one would after a fever. His body felt amazingly light. It seemed that he could almost fly. In the early mornings when he mounted the one thousands steps to the top of Palani Hill for meditation, he easily cleared several steps at one time. Effortlessly, he bounded to the top of the hill and returned with the same ease. Both body and mind were completely free from any sort of *tamasic* conditions.

(above) The great tantra
yogi, Sri Sadhu Swamigal
at Palani.

(right) Ramaswamy with
Sri Sadaiappa Chettiar
and his younger brother
Sri Kalidas at Palani.

Don't accept gifts. Don't gather too many things. The minute you accept a gift from somebody, directly or indirectly, you are obliged to that person. Then your power of judgment fails. If your mind becomes obligated, it loses the impartial level and becomes one-sided. You start seeing the difference between one thing and another. It is very difficult to live without obligation, but if you care to keep the mind in a serene state, you should follow that practice.

"In Coimbatore, among the Western Ghats, there is a hill called Vellingiri Hill. It has a cave at its top and is far away from the dust and din, amid silent glory and pristine natural purity. There are plenty of caves in these surroundings where, we believe, many saintly people live and meditate.

"I was part of a group of men, headed by Dr. C.S. Ramaswamy Iyer, a leading surgeon and physician. Each year we found time to avail ourselves of a week's leave and went to the hill for our retreat. We camped at a short distance from the cave, and every day we walked to the hilltop to offer our thanks and worship the Lord. It was in the 1940s and, by a strange and grand coincidence, we had the rare privilege of meeting Ramaswamy as a young *sadhu*. His face was always smiling and he had a magnificent personality. He would speak few words, but they were full of similes and metaphors, filled with the Supreme Knowledge. He would always end his speech with 'That is Sat-Chid-Ananda.'

"Not knowing his greatness, we would argue with him from our meager knowledge. Still, his slow, persuasive arguments, couched in simple language, would always drive home his point, and convince us and make us look at his angle, the view of enlightenment. We still remember so many of his words of wisdom."

–A. Sadasivam, Coimbatore, India

At Palani it was the habit of many pilgrims to bring money with them as an offering to the *sadhus* and the poor. One day Ramu was meditating on the veranda of the Samadhi Shrine of the great *siddha* Bogar. A man approached this still figure and held a bag of money for a long time as he watched the motionless *sadhu*. Finally he lifted the bag and turned it over, emptying it over Ramu's body like an *abishekam* of coins. The man quickly prostrated and hurried away down the hill.

Ramu was a bit stunned by the clinking and jangling. It took him a few moments to rouse from his concentration and open his eyes. The pilgrim was no longer in sight, but everywhere was the wink and glimmer of coins, caught in the light of the temple lamps. Money rested on his feet, on the hem of his cloth, dotting the floor around him.

Should he keep it for himself? Should he give it to the ashram? Should he call in the poor and offer it to them?

He looked down and shook his head. "No. The Lord has brought this money here. Let Him distribute it as He wishes."

Ramu stood up, shaking the coins from his lap. First he saluted Lakshmi, the goddess of wealth, then Danadayudapani, who had helped him avoid temptation and the resulting attachment. Then he walked down the hill.

Throughout India's famous places of pilgrimage live many *sadhus* and sincere seekers. Among them there are some imitators. They earn an easy living from the innocent devotees who visit. At the top of Palani Hill, a wealthy young man was confronted by such a *"sadhu"* and his group of disciples. The young man was drawn into a powerful lecture on poverty, during which the *sadhu* pointed to his own lean and indrawn stomach. The pilgrim, greatly affected by these spellbinding words and actions, handed over not only all his money, but the jewelry he wore as well.

As soon as he left the *sadhu*, however, the power of the spell was broken and replaced by a growing feeling of doubt, regret and dissatisfaction about the whole event. He became very depressed about his hasty action.

As he walked down the hill, he met a group of his friends who were asking Ramu questions. When Ramu noticed the man's dejection, he drew from him an account of what had taken place.

Ramu was disturbed by the actions of that *sadhu*. He was well aware of this particular man and his practice of performing *uddhiyana bandha*, a technique of completely contracting the abdomen. Immediately he dispatched one of his devotees to the dwelling of the *"sadhu."* The money and jewelry were soon back to their original owner.

Later Ramu met with the false *sadhu* and advised him to stop playing at renunciation.

"Instead," Ramu advised, "become a true renunciate and serve others rather than preying upon them. Then you will really get everything."

For a while, Ramu regularly visited the Sri Sai Baba Center in Coimbatore. He worked with the center's director Sri A.V.K. Chari and assisted in organizational matters. After an ashram had been built, Ramu continued his involvement, and he was present when a miraculous event occurred there.

It was the 7th of January 1943, Thursday — a day considered especially sacred for worship of one's guru. Many devotees had gathered. A *bhajan* was being chanted. Drums and cymbals played. Lights blazed. Suddenly, a shining cobra appeared in the midst of the worshipers. With open hood, the *naga* (snake) stood very still before the picture of Sri Sai Baba. Normally the sight of a cobra would cause fear in people nearby, but this was not an ordinary cobra. Its manner was worshipful; it seemed to gaze without distraction at the picture of Sri Sai Baba. Several devotees noticed divine markings on the unusually large hood of the serpent. The worship continued. Lights were waved; bells were rung, but the cobra remained undisturbed in its pose before the holy picture. Several hundred people surrounded the visitor; neither the *naga* nor the people were afraid.

Word about the amazing serpent quickly spread throughout the area. Over the next two days thousands of people poured into the Bhajan Mandir to see the *naga*, which remained in the same spot. They felt that it must be a very great and dedicated soul, and worshipers began to shower flowers upon the serpent in a gesture of reverence. Mounds of marigolds, chrysanthemums and other flowers almost buried the *naga*. Even with this rain of offerings, the cobra didn't move.

On the second day, a photographer came to capture the event on film. By this time, however, the *naga* could barely be seen amid the heaps of flowers. No one really wanted to go close enough to clear an area around the serpent. There was only one thing to do. The devotees began to pray.

Suddenly the *naga* jumped out of the flowery mound and literally posed for the camera. The photographer was able to take beautiful pictures of this marvelous creature, and the devotees were even more convinced of the cobra's divine nature.

After forty-eight hours had passed, the devotees reverently prayed to the *naga* to move out of the area so that they could continue their routine worship in the Mandir. The immobile cobra began to move slowly, as one does when waking from a deep meditation. It moved clockwise around Sri Baba's picture and went out into the open. Thousands of people followed the *naga* to a bush where it disappeared. Later, a snake's den appeared there, and that spot is still considered holy ground. Ever since that event, Sri Sai Baba has been worshiped in Coimbatore as Sri Naga Sai.

Your faith and devotion place you in the position of receiving the visions of great beings. Without that faith, you can never get these experiences.

Siddhas are yogis who have supernatural powers, called *siddhis*. One great *siddha* named Bogar had established the Palani Temple and effected its construction. He was a great alchemist and made the Palani deity from a special preparation. Gathering nine poisonous chemicals, he mixed them together in the exact proportion that would make them counteract the poisonous effects. This mixture is called *nava-paashaanam* (nine poisonous chemicals). From it he constructed the deity. During worship there was the traditional pouring of milk, honey, rose water, sandalwood paste and mashed bananas over the deity. Devotees then took a bit of the resulting mixture as *prasadam* (consecrated food or objects). Worship of this deity still continues, and many have claimed that because of the medicinal properties of the deity their hopeless illnesses were cured by taking this *prasadam.*

Often Ramu sat and meditated at Bogar's tomb, "Bogar Samadhi," after his regular worship. One day, repeating his *mantram*, Ramu had a vision. Bogar appeared clearly before him and began to repeat the *mantram* also. He placed his right palm over Ramu's head. The devotee lost all awareness of his body and fell into a "conscious sleep." Peace and bliss surrounded him. The physical world no longer existed.

After one half-hour, he slowly returned to normal consciousness. Bogar's form was no longer before him, but Ramu felt he had received Bogar's blessing and initiation.

With proper understanding, pain and pleasure are the same. Both are lessons. In such a light, pain becomes pain no more. One who understands the world in the proper way will see that pain is there as a great friend and teacher.

South India was full of *siddhas*, many of whom traveled about incognito, never publicly manifesting their abilities. Some appeared to be wanderers, vagabonds, even madmen.

In a small town called Ilanji was a *siddha* known as Paper Baba. He always carried a rolled newspaper under his arm and a stick in his hand.

No one knew his age, but he had been seen around the area for many years. Paper Baba never allowed anyone to live with him as a disciple, but whenever he came across a sincere seeker he would give him advice and send him off with a blessing.

Although he had never seen Paper Baba, Ramu was interested in meeting him and receiving his blessings, feeling it would further his spiritual practices. One day he temporarily placed another man in charge of his duty to feed the people who came to Sadhu Swamigal's ashram and traveled to Ilanji. Once there, he asked where he could find Paper Baba.

"He has just passed this way," came the reply. "Probably if you run you can catch up to him."

Ramu ran to the end of the road but couldn't find the *siddha*.

Another person came along the road, and Ramu asked him, "Do you know where Paper Baba is?"

"There," the man pointed. "Just rounding the corner."

Ramu saw the figure of an old man disappearing around a bend in the road. When he reached the bend, no one was there.

Again he asked, "Have you seen Paper Baba?"

"Over there. Follow that street."

Finally Ramu found the old man. He seemed to be blind, walking along the road cautiously, feeling the way with his stick, a rolled newspaper tucked soundly beneath his armpit.

Ramu crept up quietly behind him. In one quick motion, the old man whirled around.

"Who are you?" he demanded. "Why are you following me?"

Ramu jumped back in surprise but managed to compose himself. "I am a humble seeker, Swamiji. I came for your blessing."

"Who blesses whom? Go! Go away."

Ramu felt a bit puzzled, but still he persisted. "If you are blind, how do you know I am a stranger and that I am following you, Swamiji? Please don't drive me away."

"Oh, you came to spy on me, hmm? Even though I am blind, I can feel if someone is following. Now go. Run away."

"I've traveled a long distance to get your blessings. I can't just run away without them."

"You have seen me. Now you can go."

Ramu stood his ground. "I'm not going."

"I will hit you with my stick." Paper Baba raised his arm threateningly.

"Fine. At least I will have received something from you. If you have decided to bless me in that way I'm ready to accept it."

Paper Baba lowered his stick. "You are a stubborn fellow, aren't you? Very well, come along. Follow me."

Ramu followed him into the richly appointed home of a wealthy disciple. Paper Baba sat in the center of the room and Ramu sat in a corner, watching him.

The great *siddha* called to the wealthy man, "See, here is a dog that was following behind me." He turned to Ramu. *Siddhas* know many things. "You have to feed people. Why are you still following me? Go do your job."

"I came for your blessing."

"All right, come here," Paper Baba sighed. He brought forth a basket of limes which had been presented to him by a devotee. Normally each person present would expect to get only one lime from Paper Baba, but he said to Ramu, "Here, take it. It's all for you. But don't take it all for yourself. Share it with whomever you want."

Ramu accepted this great blessing and immediately started sharing the limes with everyone present.

"That's right," said Paper Baba. "Now take the rest. Don't give away *everything*. Take some for yourself. Now go, and don't keep running after me. Get out!"

As Ramu bowed low before the great yogi, Paper Baba said, "Everything will be all right. Go ahead."

Every evening the ashramites climbed the dusk-covered hill to attend the evening service. Afterward they came down, walked around the hill once and went to the feeding station for dinner.

Ramu sat upon a stone bench, awaiting the dinner bell. He was looking forward to seeing Sadhu Swamigal in the dining hall. As he waited, two policemen approached him. One wore the dress of a sub-inspector, the other was a constable.

"Hey, *sadhu*," the sub-inspector called brusquely, "who are you?"

"You have answered your own question. I am a *sadhu*."

The sub-inspector squinted. "I can see that, but *who* are you?"

"A *sadhu*."

A new tack. "Where are you from?"

"I am from Palani, right here. Before that I lived in Chettipalayam, near Coimbatore."

"Hmm. I see." He filed it carefully in his mind. "What did you do there?"

Ramu remained patient. "I had my own business."

The two policemen looked at each other in surprise and then back to Ramu. "Your own business? Then what are you doing in this type of life?"

"I was tired of all those things and decided to lead a *sadhu's* life."

Doubt crept into the sub-inspector's voice. "Is that the only reason or is there anything else?"

"Yes, brother, that is my only reason. If you can think of a better one, please tell me."

The sub-inspector sneered. "I don't believe you. Nowadays there are all kinds of people disguised as holy men for one reason or another."

These were the days of the Congress Movement for India's independence from Great Britain. Many people had, indeed, taken to dressing as *sadhus* in order to go about their work for India's liberation. The British government was quite worried and was diligently trying to unmask these "spies."

The sub-inspector continued, "You seem to be an educated man. I can't believe you have taken up such a life for the reasons you just stated."

Calmly, Ramu said, "If you doubt my words, there is nothing I can do about it."

"Can you erase my doubts?"

"All I can tell you is: Don't be doubtful."

The sub-inspector had made up his mind. "I think I'd better take you to my superior, the Circle Inspector." He turned to the constable. "Bring him along."

Rather than balking, Ramu stood up agreeably. "Where are you taking me?"

"The station house."

"Fine. Let's go."

The sub-inspector positioned himself ahead of his prisoner, while the constable carefully guarded the rear. As the procession started, the inspector noticed another *sadhu*, half-hidden in the darkness.

"Who are you?" he demanded.

The *sadhu* began to shake violently. "Oh sir, just a *sadhu*...I was born near this area...my parents live here still...I have been here a number of years...you can ask about me from Swami..."

The sub-inspector cut him off, "You seem to be okay." He judged the man's innocence by his apparent ignorance and fear. "Go away."

Instantly, the second *sadhu* disappeared into a side lane.

As the group made its way toward the town, the dinner bell could be heard ringing through the air. They continued toward the station.

"*Sadhu*, are you angry with me? Do you feel sad about this?"

"There's nothing for me to feel sad about. Why should I be angry with you? It is all the Lord's work. Probably He wants to see if I am fit to continue this life, and He's just testing me through you. I am really happy that the Lord is giving me such a test. You are just doing your duty as a policeman. You have been asked to do a certain job, and you are doing it well. I appreciate it."

These words greatly disturbed the equilibrium of the inspector. He motioned for Ramu to stop, called the constable over and spoke with him in a loud whisper.

"I am beginning to doubt that this man is truly a spy. But if we don't bring in our quota of suspects you know what the Circle Inspector will say: 'Can't you do anything? There are hundreds of people roaming around spying, and you don't catch any of them.' But somehow, I don't feel we're doing the right thing in this case."

They started to walk again, discussing the matter back and forth. Ramu caught up to them.

"Sir, you need not worry about me. I know that you have been issued orders to book a number of people and, to all outward appearances at least, you're booking the right sort of man. When you present me to the Circle Inspector, he'll be very happy with you, and your job will be over. Don't worry, I'll explain myself to him when we get there."

The inspector's confidence slipped another ten degrees. "I really don't want to do this. I'm just going to leave you here. Go back to your ashram."

By this time, they were in sight of the lights of the shopping area.

"Now you say I can return to the ashram, but you see, I was waiting to have my dinner. After all this time, dinner is over. You yourself heard the ashram bell as we walked, and that was a while back. Do you want me to return hungry? At least if you take me to the station, probably the Circle Inspector will give me something to eat. Do you want me to miss that meal as well?" It was time to teach these policemen a lesson.

"Sir, I'm terribly sorry," apologized the inspector. "If I had money, I would give you some for food but I have none with me."

"All right," Ramu insisted, "take me to the station. I want to speak with the Circle Inspector."

The policemen were now prisoners of this *sadhu*, unwillingly following him to the station house.

The inspector stopped him. "Just wait here in front of this store. Right around the corner are a number of suspects we picked up before.

I'll go get them and we can all walk to the station together." He motioned to the constable, and they disappeared. After twenty minutes, Ramu also left. He walked over to the temple of Dakshina Moorthi, where he often went to meditate in the evening.

The other *sadhu* who had been so quickly dismissed by the policemen had roused the ashram, telling a number of people about Ramaswamy's arrest. A large group of monks and devotees descended upon the police station to win his release. When they arrived and found him nowhere about, they raced through the station, searching it thoroughly before believing the sub-inspector's story that the *sadhu* had been released somewhere in the center of town.

The party left the station in great haste, proceeding to the store of the Kalidas brothers. Here, too, they found no Ramaswamy so they proceeded through the town, picking up more concerned devotees as the search continued.

Eventually they reached the temple. Entering quietly, they discovered the still figure of their lost brother, deep in meditation.

Ramu felt the presence of a large number of people and opened his eyes. The devotees greeted him with whoops of joy, applause and back-slapping. It was some time before Ramu realized the far-reaching impression that his arrest had made.

As he left the temple in the middle of the crowd, Ramu turned to Sri Kalidas. "Come, let's go to your store where I can have milk and bananas in quiet."

Fifteen days later, the event reached its conclusion. The ashram cooks were a rather fiery-tempered crew, and they decided to take vengeance on the man who had caused their beloved Ramu so much trouble. They lay in wait on the road for the sub-inspector and thrashed him soundly. A few days later, he obtained a transfer to a distant village and moved there immediately.

> **All our continuous ups and downs, coming into this world and going out, birth and death, are due to our *karma*, and to the necessity of accepting the reaction to our actions. We can't escape from it. Once an action is done, either we face the reaction in this life itself or we have to take another body to do it. It is the reaction that binds us, the reaction that uses a body and makes us experience it.**

Sri Kalidas offered Ramu his small hut and its large compound area and went to live with his brother's family. Each day at noon the bachelor sent over a meal of *idli* (little steamed cakes made of rice and *dhal*). This along with *panchamritam*, the temple *prasadam*, comprised Ramu's only meal.

Within this home, Ramu lived in complete seclusion for fifty-one days of rigorous yoga practice and meditation. After a while, not due to any of his conscious actions, many pilgrims coming to the area visited him for instruction. A large number of these pilgrims went to him for healing. For these people Ramu kept a coconut shell container filled with holy ash just outside the hut.

"My child is sick with a stomachache."

"Take a little ash. Go back to your child and put it on his stomach. He will be all right."

One midnight a local man came to the hut. "My wife is giving birth. She has been in labor ten hours already and is in great pain. Please bless her with an easy delivery."

"Take this ash and go back to your home. Mix it with a little water and give it to her to drink."

The delivery was smooth and immediate. Invariably, all of Ramu's cures occurred just as he predicted. He had prayed for this power and received it. Often he would close his eyes and ask, "Lord, please bless me so that I might cure the pains of others."

After a time, though, he began to feel dissatisfaction with his methods. He felt the Lord Himself wasn't pleased. "Do not interfere with the work that is the Lord's," he remembered. "You will only lose all the peace you have gained through your spiritual practices."

He stopped asking the Lord for curative powers, thinking, "Who am I to take another person's *karma* which he must experience himself?"

After that, when people came for cures he would suggest certain changes in diet or special breathing and other practices so that they took an active part in their own healing, and it was not Ramu's effort alone. In this way they could purge their *karma* and not be bound by any reaction.

When you create a particular atmosphere in your life and your family, the soul that has lost its previous body and was waiting for another environment in which to continue its journey, selects your home, goes into the husband's system, into the wife and comes out as a baby. Because you have created a certain type of field and climate, a certain type of seed will come into you.

Hundreds and thousands of devotees were attracted to Palani — all for different personal reasons.

A wealthy widow and her two sons were staying at one of the many *choultries* (housing facilities set up by charitable organizations).

The elder son was married and settled down, but his brother Govindaswamy, at the age of twenty-four, was still a bachelor and the family's major problem. To make up for the absence of a father, the mother had overprotected her son to the point where he had grown up stubborn and totally uncontrollable.

To his mother's great and constant distress, he was a heavy cigarette smoker. Often she reminded him that he was ruining his health. His response was a deep drag on his cigarette and an exhalation directly into her face. The family decided his behavior was the result of adverse astrological influences and had come to Palani to beg intercession from God.

A group of Ramu's devotees suggested that the family visit him to discuss the matter. The mother and elder son left for Ramu's hut while Govindaswamy was out. When he returned to the *choultry* and found out where they had gone he raced after them at full speed and came to a screeching halt inside Ramu's hut.

The *sadhu* was quietly talking with Govindaswamy's family. At the younger son's appearance, the mother and brother became quite distressed and embarrassed. Abruptly, Govindaswamy turned toward Ramu and nodded his head curtly. "*Namaskar.*"

"Come in, son," Ramu replied with a welcoming gesture. "Take a seat. We were just talking about you."

"Aha!" Govindaswamy's eyes glittered. He sat down heavily. "Were they complaining to you about me?"

"No. I merely asked them how many people were in the family and they mentioned your name. Why should you feel that they were complaining about you?"

"They always complain about me," he pouted. "Always find fault with me. Always tell me not to do this, not to do that. I don't like their attitude. They are constantly trying to impose their authority over me."

Ramu examined him closely. "I don't know why they should do that. You don't seem to be that bad. In fact, you seem to be a wonderful boy." Govindaswamy's eyes softened.

Ramu turned to the mother. "What do you find wrong with the boy? He seems to be quite well-behaved. Probably, he is just very straightforward. He wants to know the reason behind things before blindly obeying instructions. When you want him to do something, have a little patience. Explain to him why and how."

The boy interrupted. "Can you hear what this *sadhu* is saying? *You* don't feel that way!"

His mother covered a smile. "Yes, maybe we are a bit hasty with you."

"Well," Ramu advised, "don't be that way. He's a nice boy. He'll be all right if you just try to understand him."

The family prepared to leave. They bowed to Ramu. Govindaswamy performed a stiff semi-bow. As they walked out he said, "I would like to see you again."

"Fine. When you find the time come to see me."

When the family reached the street Govindaswamy said, "You two go on ahead. I want to see this *sadhu* alone. I'll be along later."

Ramu had won over the boy's confidence and after a while told him, "Even though you may be right you should express yourself a bit differently. Others should not harbor bad opinions about you."

"Sir," Govindaswamy admitted, "there is one bad habit I do have. I smoke a lot."

Ramu laughed, "I myself once had the same habit, but when I realized how negative it was I stopped. You seem to have strong will power; it would probably be easy for a man like you to stop. Such a move would make your whole family happy."

Immediately Govindaswamy stood up. "I will show you I do have that will. Nobody has ever presented the solution in such an easy way. I'm going to finish it off now."

He bowed a bit more deeply, left the hut and hurried back to the *choultry*. His family was quite surprised when they saw him hastily removing all the cigarette packs from his baggage.

"You both have always thought I was a weak man. Just watch." He dumped the packs in a heap outside and set fire to them. "No more cigarettes."

His mother was warmed more by this news than by the raging blaze in front of them.

You should never actually become angry. Just keep anger in your pocket. If you need it to clear up an injustice, use it. Then put it away again immediately.

Ramu and Sri Kalidas traveled between Palani and Pondicherry by rail. During the morning the train stopped its laborious squeaking to rest at a station. Kalidas said that he would go purchase some breakfast in the station so that they could eat as they traveled.

Ramu watched as a stream of people flooded into the iron cars. Then he turned toward his friend. "When you go for the food it would be best if you placed a piece of luggage on your seat to make sure no one takes it while you are gone." They still had a long way to go, and only maximum discomfort could be expected if they stood for the journey. Kalidas brought down a piece of luggage and went to buy the food. Ramu looked out the window at the departing figure of his companion.

Many people traversed the aisle searching for empty seats. Seeing the suitcase on Kalidas's seat, they passed it by, but one rather large man leaned his ponderous bulk over Ramu.

"Is that your bag?"

"No. It belongs to my friend. He's just gone to buy some food, but he'll be back any minute."

"In a minute, huh?" The man looked sharply at Ramu. Certain people, even *sadhus*, would cover extra seats so that they would have more room to stretch out during the ride.

Ramu guessed the man's suspicion and tried to ease it. "He'll be back very shortly."

"Well, how about letting me sit there until your friend returns. When he comes back I'll simply get up and go."

"I can allow that only if you promise to get up as soon as my friend returns."

The man smiled tightly. "Of course," he agreed.

Ramu lifted Kalidas's bag; the man sat down, adjusted his body to the seat and made himself comfortable.

After a few minutes, Ramu looked through the window. Sri Kalidas was winding his way slowly through the crowd, balancing the food on his hands.

"Ah," he turned toward the man. "My friend has returned. You can see him for yourself. You'll have to leave now."

The man remained seated, staring straight ahead as if deaf. Kalidas, juggling the food, was rather surprised when he arrived at the seat. Ramu turned toward his neighbor. "Here is my companion. Please do as you promised. Get up and give him back his seat."

The large man glanced up at Kalidas and realized that this type of man wasn't about to fight for a seat. He leaned back, stretching. "Well, I've decided not to leave. After all, why should I have to spend my trip standing up?"

66

"Sir," Ramu persisted, "you made a promise to me. I don't see how you can go back on your word."

The man refused to look him in the eyes. He looked at the floor and said, "I am quite comfortable here. I don't wish to leave."

"You're absolutely not going to leave?"

"No."

"Are you sure?"

"Positive."

Ramu leaned toward him. "Sir, do you want me to throw you out of your seat?"

"You? You could do that?"

"If you really want me to do it."

The man snickered. "I've seen many talk like you. Let's see you do it." He rooted his bulk into the seat.

A terrible, fierce look came over Ramu's face. In a second he took on the appearance of a lion, a jungle beast. He seemed to grow in size. Raising his arm, he turned as if to knock the man out of the seat.

Terrified and shaking, the stranger jumped up and ran from the seat. As soon as the seat was vacant again Kalidas sat down. He and Ramu began calmly dividing the food. Within a few minutes they were eating and chatting as if nothing out of the ordinary had occurred.

The man watched from a corner of the car in amazement. After a while, he approached Ramu meekly.

"Sir?"

Ramu looked up benignly. "Yes, son?"

"I don't understand you at all."

"What don't you understand?"

"Aren't you a *sadhu*, a renunciate?"

"Yes."

"In just a few seconds I saw you turn from a calm renunciate into a wild animal. I thought you were going to kill me, so I ran away. Then, in another few seconds, I saw you turn back into that calm *sadhu*. How could you have done that? Were you really going to hit me?"

Ramu's eyes lit up mischievously. "Would you like to try me again?"

"No, no, certainly not." The man stepped back quickly.

"Don't worry, sir. I won't hurt you."

"How could you get so angry? You're a *sadhu*."

"I never actually became angry," Ramu explained. "I keep anger by my side and if I need it, I just call on it. It's something like having a police dog for a pet. When I no longer have any use for it, once again I keep it by my side."

(upper left) Sri Swami Nityanandaji Kavishwara, famous disciple of Sri Swami Badagara Sivananda.

(upper right) The siddha yogi, Sri Swami Ranga Nath.

(left) "You should be traveling!" Sri Swami Jnanananda Giri, the 160-year-old siddha, predicted that Ramaswamy would travel round and round the world to serve others.

"Thank you." The man picked up his luggage and went into another car. Ramu and Kalidas finished their meal peacefully.

> **Many people are interested in the so-called psychic powers. If you are sincere in your practice and devoted to the attainment of the highest goal, the powers come naturally as a by-product without danger. But the ego can become easily attached to these powers, possessed by the desire for name and fame through them. It is when this selfish attachment takes place that one becomes more and more bound, imprisoned.**

While he was in Palani, Ramu had the opportunity to study with and learn from a number of great *siddhas*. One such being who lived near Palani was Sri Swami Badagara Sivananda. By following a certain strenuous breathing technique, as well as adhering to a strict diet and a heavily disciplined life, he obtained for himself various psychic powers. Many thousands became his disciples. One prominent disciple was the well-known Sri Swami Nityananda of Bombay, who became the guru of the late Sri Swami Muktananda. Often Swami Badagara Sivananda visited Palani to stay for several months; he even attained *mahasamadhi* at that holy spot. Ramu frequently spent time with him. It was Ramu's privilege to attend the *mahasamadhi* day (funeral) of the Swami and to be among the devotees who performed the final rituals.

A friend of Ramu was a devotee of Sri Swami Jnanananda Giri, and he took Ramu with him to have the *darshan* of this reputedly 160-year-old *siddha*. The Swami graciously received him, and they had lunch together. He asked Ramu a variety of questions about himself, all the while referring to things in which Ramu was involved. The Swami seemed to have prior knowledge of his activities although they had never met before. As they spoke, Swami Jnanananda predicted that Ramu would leave India. "This is not the only place for you. You should travel. Many of these people don't appreciate anything. They only want *siddhis*."

Ramu replied, "Swamiji, if you feel that way, let it happen."

The Swami called the photographer and had pictures taken with Ramu. Then he sent one of the devotees to the shrine room for a sandalwood fan with a swan-like handle. He gave the beautiful object to

Ramu, who opened it and began to fan the great *siddha*. One of the devotees whispered, "That fan was such a precious gift. Someone offered it with so much love, and now Swamiji is giving it to you. He must be really happy with you."

Ramu immediately felt that he shouldn't accept the lovely gift. This devotee admired it so much and even seemed a little hurt that it had been given to someone else. When the time came to leave Ramu unobtrusively left the fan behind. He got into the car, the driver started it, and they began to drive away. Suddenly the car stopped dead in its tracks and couldn't be started. At that moment Swami Jnanananda Giri came running out of the ashram with the fan. His advanced age didn't stop him at all.

"You rascal," he reprimanded Ramu, "I gave this to you and you just left it and went away. You shouldn't do that."

"Oh, Swamiji Maharaj, please excuse me. I forgot it. I'm so sorry."

The eyes of the Swami twinkled. "Oh, so you forgot? I know just what you did! Come on, take it." The minute the fan was in Ramu's hand the car started.

These are but a few of the great *siddhas* who lived in and around Palani. Ramu felt blessed to be in their presence and to learn so many lessons.

Ramu learned a profound lesson about *siddhis* from Swami Ranga Nath, a *siddha* and performer of miracles. The Swami's supernatural powers fascinated Ramu, who decided to become his disciple and went to live at his ashram.

Ranga Nath had the ability to materialize things out of thin air. Whenever he ate at the home of a devotee he gave the first handful of food from his plate to the host, as *prasadam*. When the host received the offering he would notice that it was unusually heavy for a small bit of food. Looking inside, he would find a rupee or a sovereign (the denomination differed with the status of the particular host). The devotee would cherish the coin as a sanctified object, believing it would enable him to attain even more money.

Included in Ramu's duties at the ashram of Ranga Nath was keeping the kerosene lamps lit. One day he greeted his guru with the news that the lamps were out of fuel, and he would have to buy some more to replenish them.

"Don't worry," Ranga Nath said airily. "Bring me the empty kerosene tin."

Ramu did as he was told.

"See that empty room? Put the tin in there, close the door and come stand beside me."

As soon as Ramu closed the door on the empty tin, he began to hear the gurgle of liquid filling an empty container. The sound persisted for several minutes. When it ceased, Ranga Nath instructed him to reopen the door and bring him the tin.

It was heavy, and liquid sloshed within. When Ramu peered inside he saw that it was once again filled with fuel.

On another occasion the devotees of Ranga Nath were preparing a hot bath for the Swami when one disciple joked, "How can our guru bathe in ordinary hot water? He should have a more spectacular type of bath."

The students laughed merrily. Ranga Nath looked around at them and bent over the tub. Carefully he dipped his hand into the steaming water and swirled it around and around, forming whirlpools. When he withdrew his dripping hand a heady smell of rosewater emanated from the bath.

On his way out of the ashram to shop for vegetables one day, Ramu realized that the purse he carried was empty. He approached the Swami for some coins.

"Give me the purse," Ranga Nath instructed. He weighed it in his palm for a moment and then returned it. "Open it."

The empty lining was now covered by a ten rupee note.

"Is that enough for you?"

Ramu was disturbed. He had been speculating about these *siddhis* for a long time. "Yes, Swamiji, it is enough." As he reached the threshold, he turned back, "Swamiji, is this real currency?" Always before he had avoided such questions, knowing they would prompt an unpleasant situation.

The *siddha* raised his eyebrows. "Can't you *see* that it's real currency?"

"Well," Ramu said slowly, "if this is real currency, then it belongs to the government. We didn't have it before so it might have been taken from somebody's safe or even from a bank. Now, if you tell me you have created it yourself, then the money is a forgery. If it is real, we have committed theft. In either case we have committed a crime."

Ranga Nath's face grew livid with anger. "How dare you come to such conclusions and make such accusations? Get out of here! I don't want to see you anymore."

"I had already decided to do just as you now wish, sir. Lately, I've not been very happy with matters as they are here. I just wanted to tell you how I felt. Maybe someday you'll come to the same conclusions yourself. Here is your ten rupee note. I'm leaving now. Goodbye." Softly, he closed the door behind him.

Three years later Ramu once again met his former teacher. After Ramu's departure Ranga Nath had gone to a house, locked himself inside and practiced severe austerities. He explained to his distraught devotees that he was staying alive only to see Ramu again. He wouldn't open the house to anyone; but when he heard that Ramu had come, he opened the door. They embraced each other and cried.

"I've been waiting for you," Ranga Nath told him. "I wanted to thank you for opening my eyes to certain things. Recently I have been fasting to purge myself of these faults. Please bless me now to have a better birth next time."

Swami Ranga Nath returned to the small, remote village in which he had been born and lived an austere, ascetic life until his death.

Even with God or the Divine Word, even in serving others, don't be too eager.

The spiritual head of an ashram in Avinaasi passed away and a group of people who knew Ramu and his family suggested to the trustees that he fill the empty position. At this time Ramu's main concern was to lead a simple life, devoted to meditation and study. His only wish was to remain as indrawn as possible at all times, to keep his concentration within rather than outside. At first, he refused the offer. After much prodding, however, he accepted with the condition that he wouldn't have to involve himself with the day-to-day upkeep of the temple and ashram.

The trustees eagerly agreed and with much formal ritual installed Ramu as the new head of the ashram. It was a highly prestigious position.

Shortly after Ramu's investiture the local caretaker, who had been hired to administrate the daily operation of the ashram, disappeared and was never again seen in the temple. Soon the ashramites were coming to Ramu to register their various grievances about housing problems and shortages of food and supplies.

"There is no more rice. Will you please obtain the necessary ration coupons?"

"I don't understand this. Your trustees said they would take care of everything. Why are you coming to me for such things?" Ramu dispatched a delegation of ashramites to the neighboring village where the chairman of the trustees resided.

"When you see the chairman," he instructed, "tell him that unless he comes this very evening to take care of these matters, I'm leaving."

Until late at night Ramu awaited the man's arrival. When it was past midnight he called in one of the ashramites.

"When the chairman finally arrives please give him this bunch of keys and tell him the temple head has gone."

Ramu's career as the head of this ashram had lasted nineteen days.

Really, you don't lose anything by renouncing. Instead, the more you give, the more others will take care of you. Forget yourself completely, and you will find that the entire world is yours.

In 1946 Ramaswamy left Avinaasi and wandered throughout South India as a mendicant. He devised this as a test period. "If there is a God, then He will take care of me." He took two vows: not to keep any money and not to ask anybody for anything, including food.

For four months he wandered wherever his feet took him. During the first three days he had nothing to eat. Eventually he was approached by a man who asked, "Have you eaten? You look hungry." When Ramu replied that he had not eaten in three days the man hurriedly brought him a meal.

When Ramu felt tired he would lie down wherever he was and sleep — sometimes by the side of the road, sometimes on a park bench. He never remained in one area for longer than three days. Often he visited the temples, where he was allowed to sleep on the big verandas and bathe in the ponds. After the morning worship the temple priests distributed food; but Ramu adhered strictly to his vow, never standing in the food line. He would eat only if someone noticed him sitting off to the side and brought him a plate of food.

Sometimes walking, sometimes taking advantage of rides that were offered and sometimes traveling by train, Ramu was able to visit Kalahasti, Madras, Calcutta and Benares.

In those days railroads provided free travel for *sadhus*. A *sadhu* simply went to the railway station and sat on a bench patiently until a railway attendant noticed him and asked his destination. The railway personnel considered it a great blessing to take personal charge of a *sadhu.* The conductor made sure that the holy traveler had a nice place to sit, something to eat and drink, and from time to time he inquired after the *sadhu's* comfort. If there was a change in conductors along the way the first conductor would introduce his replacement to the *sadhu,* and his respectful care would be continued.

Ramaswamy felt something drawing him north toward the Himalayas. In 1947 he decided to leave South India and journey to Rishikesh in the Himalayan foothills. He had heard about the illustrious sage Sri Swami Sivanandaji Maharaj, who had an ashram on the banks of the Ganges. Ramu deeply felt the wish to have *darshan* of this holy being.

At the Calcutta railway station, Ramu sat on the bench waiting patiently for a railway attendant to ask his destination. Half the day passed without a train official noticing him. Other people noticed him, however, and soon many of them gathered around the *sadhu.* They brought food items for him to bless and distribute as *prasad* and sat around him as he gave *satsang.* Finally a conductor came to escort him to a train and be sure he arrived comfortably at his destination.

Unfortunately, an outbreak of political riots plagued the country at that time and caused the blocking of all passages north of Benares. Ramu postponed his Himalayan trip.

Ramu traveled to Pondicherry in order to have *darshan* of the great yogi Sri Aurobindo. Born in the city of Calcutta in 1871, Sri Aurobindo Ghose was a poet, philosopher and educator. He was often viewed as controversially political because he spoke out about Indian independence. Behind the outspokeness was a deeply spiritual vision of India, held by a patriot who believed his country should be ruled by *Sanatana Dharma* (Eternal Law). Sri Aurobindo practiced a rigorous form of *sadhana* for six years in the hope of perfecting himself in order to selflessly serve his country. Following this period he met an accomplished yogi who gave him further spiritual instruction. After just three days of meditation he had numerous spiritual experiences that transformed his life. He left Calcutta and journeyed to Pondicherry, where eager students joined him. Though the Aurobindo Ashram grew up around him, the great yogi spent most of his time in seclusion, practicing yoga *sadhana.* Sri Aurobindo gave *darshan* only four times a year, but through his writings he gave detailed instructions to his students.

Ramu gratefully received the blessings of the great Master and his foremost disciple, the Mother, then continued his journey through South India as a wandering mendicant.

The legendary Himalayan sage, H.H. Sri Swami Sivanandaji Maharaj.

Sambasivam frequently visited Ananda Ashram to spend time at the holy feet of Papa Ramdas and Mother Krishnabai.

Sri Swami Chidbhavanandaji Maharaj of the Ramakrishna Thapovanam at Tiruparaitturai, where Ramaswamy got pre-sannyas initiation and was named Sambasiva Chaitanya.

First the world tempts you more and more
until, one day, you find yourself bound up in it.
Then you say, "No, I don't want it any more."
The world itself gives you this revelation. It
puts up all these temptations so that you can
understand the world first and then turn away
from it with the urge for something more.

Srimati Velammai stood on her porch, looking into the house. She
was crying. She cried many times this way when she thought of her
younger son. Sometimes she said to herself, "We could give him
everything he wants. He lacks nothing here." Yet he called no home
his own. He was a penniless *sadhu*, traveling about. Often she thought,
"Where does he sleep? Who will feed him?"

"Mother." She turned around slowly. Ramu had come for a visit.

"Oh, Ramu," she was still crying. "Is it for this type of life I con-
ceived you and brought you up?"

He gently helped her sit down. "What have I done? What I am now
is your own wish come true."

"My wish? Was it my wish that you should live in poverty?"

With a twinkle in his eye, he started teasing her. "Who else served
all the saints who passed this way? Who prayed for a son just like them?
You could have stopped by just serving them alone, but instead you
molded my character with their words while I was still in your body. If
you had prayed for a worldly son I would have enjoyed myself in the
world!" He raised his arms and dropped them to his sides in mock ex-
asperation. "Mother, you have spoiled my chances for a worldly life!
Could I have become anything other than what I am?"

Put the entire responsibility on God's
shoulders. He is ready to carry everything. In
fact, He is already carrying everything. Let us
realize that and just do as He guides us from
within, free of all burdens and worries. This is
liberation.

Ramu entered the Ramakrishna Mission at Tiruparaitturai, which
was headed by Sri Swami Chidbhavanandaji Maharaj. Chidbhavanandaji was a disciple of Sri Swami Shivananda, one of the twelve apostles
of the famous Sri Bhagavan Ramakrishna.

Sri Ramakrishna was born in Bengal in 1836 and displayed a deep religious fervor even in childhood. The God-intoxicated state that consumed him revealed to his disciples the approachability of the Lord through sincere prayer and supplication. His example of a spiritual life profoundly influenced India and produced many other great yogis such as Sri Swami Vivekananda. Sri Ramakrishna's wife, Srimati Sharada Devi, was a very humble and holy woman; after Sri Ramakrishna passed away in 1886 his disciples asked that she continue as their guiding light. Sri Ramakrishna is still revered as a great God-realized being.

Today the service of the Ramakrishna Thapovanam (Ashram) in Tiruparaitturai is vast. Set on the banks of the Akanda Kaaveri River, it houses a community of monks who are being trained in the spiritual precepts and ideals of Sri Ramakrishna and Swami Vivekananda. Spiritual retreats are conducted by the monks, and spiritual books are printed by the Thapovanam press. There is a residential high school (*gurukulam*) which imparts spiritual training as well as academic learning to its more than five hundred students. Agriculture and dairy farming are among the other activities of the Thapovanam.

When Ramu arrived at the Ramakrishna Mission in Tiruparaitturai, it was much less developed, though it was already under the guidance of the great Master who would make it what it is now. Sri Swami Chidbhavanandaji was born on the 11th of March, 1898, to a traditional agriculturist family. They lived in Senguttaipalayam in the Coimbatore district of Tamil Nadu. He remained unmarried and followed the spiritual path with the guidance of Sri Swami Shivananda. After some time Chidbhavanandaji was put in charge of the Ramakrishna Mission in the hills called Otagamund or Ooti, near Coimbatore. For almost fifteen years he served there, but finally he decided to take a vacation from this busy life and live in seclusion. He traveled to the banks of the holy river Kaaveri. It was an auspicious site for someone living the life of a yogi, for what the River Ganges is to North India, the Akanda Kaaveri is to South India. Chidbhavanandaji managed to live his secluded life in Tiruparaitturai for several years, but his nature was to serve. Slowly devotees started coming to him for guidance; he began to advise them, and a small ashram developed. In its early stages, only four disciples lived at this thapovanam. One of these was Ramu.

It was time for Ramu to plunge even deeper into his spiritual commitment, and he decided to ask for *brahmacharya diksha*. This important initiation is the step into premonastic life, sometimes referred to as *pre-sannyas*. Ramakrishna Order monk Sri Swami Vipulanandaji, originally from Sri Lanka, performed the rites. Perhaps Vipulanandaji's initiation was one reason that years later, after Ramu had become a full-fledged *sannyasi*, the people of Sri Lanka had the privilege of having his service for almost fifteen years.

On the day of the ceremony Ramu and his fellow initiates bathed in the river and received the pure, white garments a renunciate wears until he or she becomes an initiated monk. They were taught the *Gayatri Mantram* and were presented with the sacred thread. This white string, worn diagonally across the body from shoulder to hip, is made up of three strands representing the three subtle nerves of psychic force (the *ida*, the *pingala* and the *shushumna*). From that day until his *sannyas* initiation he was known as Sambasiva Chaitanya.

Chaitanya means absolute consciousness. It is included in the names of all *pre-sannyasins*. *Sambasivam* was the individual part of Ramu's new name. It represents the true harmonizing of the individual soul with the Divine. *Amba* is the name of the goddess Shakti, the cosmic energy. *Siva* is a name of the cosmic consciousness. The goal of spiritual practice is to experience the union of these divine energies.

Included in the initiation's purifying ritual is the shaving of the head and face, leaving only a small tuft of hair on the top of the initiate's scalp. Sambasivam's hair and beard had grown since his days at Chettipalayam. As soon as he shaved, a sudden change struck his system. The hair had served as a shield to neutralize the dense heat of the area. When it was removed, Sambasivam came down with a severe fever which lasted for a number of days. Sri Swami Chidbhavanandaji realized the problem and told the *brahmachari* to grow his hair once again, even though it was not the usual custom.

Sambasivam was placed in charge of the children's hostel attached to Ramakrishna Thapovanam and concerned himself with the welfare of the children in his charge. The hostel contained between thirty and forty children, ranging in age from seven to twelve.

His parents came down from Chettipalayam for the celebration of Sri Ramakrishna Paramahamsa's birthday, and Srimati Velammai asked permission to sleep in the hostel. When she went there with her son at the day's end, they spoke until midnight.

"Amma, I'll be right back. I just have to go and check on the children."

Sambasivam quietly slipped into the dormitory, walking up and down the rows of beds. Gently he lifted chronic bedwetters and carried them to the bathroom. When they had finished he placed them back in their beds, fluffing the pillows and settling the covers over their small forms. He carefully checked each child, replacing kicked-off covers.

Sri Swami Rajeshwaranandaji Maharaj, Upanishad Vihar, Kalahasti.

81

Sri Aurobindo Ghose, Pondicherry.

The great Jnana Yogi, Sri Ramana Maharshi, Arunachala.

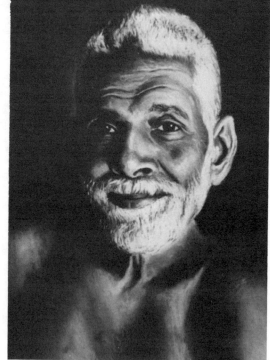

82

Finally, he returned to Velammai. She was in an unhappy mood. Tears dropped from her eyes.

"Amma, what is this? What's wrong?"

"You felt even two children were a burden for you. You left them and came here. Now look what you're doing. You're taking care of forty of them instead. Why don't you come home and take care of your own children?"

"You misunderstood me, Amma. I never said those two children were a burden to me. But if I were home, taking care of those two alone, who would take care of all these? By renouncing, I have not run from anything; instead I have gained even more. *Sannyas* isn't running from the problems of one family. It is taking on the whole world as your family and serving everyone. All older people are now my mothers and fathers, all contemporaries my brothers and sisters, all children are my children. Can you see that?"

"Yes, son." Velammai managed a smile. "But sometimes the illusion, the *maya*, comes before my eyes and blocks my vision. I really know you are doing what is right."

The whole world is the home of the renunciate.

Each day after morning *puja* Sambasiva Chaitanya busied himself with the thorough cleaning of his room. One morning he collected a tablespoon of fine dust, coaxed from cracks in the floor and the far corners of the room. Placing the dust carefully on a sheet of paper, he left the ashram and crossed the grounds until he reached the fence which separated the ashram property from a patch of vacant land. After blowing the dust onto the vacant land, he returned to the building. As he approached his room, he was met by Swami Chidbhavananda.

"Ah, Sambasivam, what were you doing by the fence?"

Sambasivam smiled, eager to tell his teacher of his thorough cleaning. "I cleaned my room of a spoonful of dust. It was that dust I was blowing across the fence."

"Oh, I see. So only this side of the fence belongs to you? The other side is not yours so you feel you can throw dust onto it. Why don't you treat the other side as yours and see that it too is kept clean?"

That was all Chidbhavanandaji said. He didn't give a big lecture to impress his point upon the young *brahmachari*, but those few words were powerful enough for Sambasivam. The lesson became a guiding light in his life.

Sambasivam underwent very strict discipline and training under the watchful and scrutinizing eye of Swami Chidbhavanandaji, who was respected as a very exacting and very great teacher. If a seeker who needed special discipline wished to enter the Ramakrishna Mission, he would be instructed to first enter the Thapovanam under Chidbhavanandaji. If the student was able to persist in this regimented life he would be accepted to live in any of the Mission locations.

While Sambasivam was living at the Thapovanam, Chidbhavanandaji began plans for a large school. Quite a bit of money was needed, money that the ashram didn't have. One day a wealthy man visited the Thapovanam and said, "Don't worry. I can build a beautiful building for your school."

"Fine," replied the Swami, "let's do it right away."

"As soon as I get home, I'll send a check," the man promised.

Not long after that a letter came to Chidbhavanandaji. The gentleman's secretary wrote: "We are sending the entire amount for the building but we have just one request. We would like you to put his photograph in the hall and say he is the one who built it."

Immediately Chidbhavanandaji wrote back, saying, "Sorry, we don't need that money."

Sambasivam and the other disciples were amazed. Their guru had been so eager to build the school, yet he was turning away an offer for all the money that was needed.

When they implored Chidbhavanandaji to explain, he said, "That man is not giving the money for education; he is giving it for the glory of his own name. If I build a college with that money the students who study in it will utilize their education for their own notoriety, rather than for serving people."

This was another great lesson for Sambasivam.

Sambasivam visited Nerur, the samadhi shrine (burial place) of Sadasiva Brahmendra, who was well known in South India as a great siddha and jivanmukta (enlightened person).

During his life, Sadasiva Brahmendra was always in a state of spiritual ecstasy. He was not even aware of his own body. Unless someone physically fed him, he didn't think of eating. One of many stories vividly illustrates this state of mind. One day Sadasiva Brahmendra was walking and came to the palace of a Moslem king. The ecstatic saint, who was wandering naked and totally unaware of his surroundings, walked into the palace and into the women's quarters. Of course, the women were very frightened. Their screams brought the palace guards, and soon Sadasiva Brahmendra was brought before the king. It didn't take long for the king to reach his judgment.

"He deserves severe punishment for his actions. Cut off his hand and send him away." The guards did not hesitate to carry out the wishes of their king. As blood gushed from the place were Sadasiva Brahmendra's hand had just been severed from the arm, the saint quietly turned and walked away as if nothing at all had taken place.

The king was shocked and realized what type of man was walking out of the palace. He immediately had him called back. After the wound was treated, the king asked the yogi to stay in his palace. In fact, he offered him a place of his own within the palace, but Sadasiva Brahmendra was not interested. However, sometimes he would wander in and out of the palace, and the king ordered everyone to treat him with the utmost reverence.

When Sambasivam visited the shrine of the great yogi, he felt a light and a sensation of warmth outside his body as well as within as he received the presence of Brahmendra. The *siddha* was blessing him, and Sambasivam fell into the conscious sleep of *samadhi* for many hours before returning to his normal state.

> ***Tapas* means to symbolically burn your attachments, your mind, your intellect in order to clean them, purify them. Just as you burn dirt to convert it into pure ash, all the impurities are burnt pure in the practice of *tapas*. It is austerity, the acceptance of hardship and pain. The highest form of *tapas* is to serve others while accepting pain for yourself.**

Nature treatment or naturopathy encompasses various methods by which illnesses can be cured without resorting to artificial techniques, medicines, or injections. Toxins are drawn out of the body by the application of wet packs and mud packs. Disease is curtailed through the use of sulphur and other curative baths. Healing is effected by exposure to the sun's rays, by making use of the curative and rejuvenating effects of water and air, by proper baths (spinal bath, hip bath and so on) and various breathing techniques. There are also tonics made from herbs, which are used for rebuilding strength.

Sri Bikshu Swamigal had served as a doctor, specializing in these naturopathic cures before he took the vows of monkhood. After renouncing he set up nature cure camps which he operated out of Saraswati Sangam in Madras. One of these camps was arranged in a small village near Coimbatore, and Sambasivam joined it to learn this healing science. The Swami soon recognized Sambasivam's natural aptitude for this service, and he appointed the *brahmachari* as his assistant. The people soon began to call Sambasivam "*chinna* swami" (junior swami).

Certain areas of India had no doctors within a twenty mile radius. It was to these places that the nature cure camp brought its tents and equipment. When Sri Bikshu Swamigal and his disciples had performed as much service as they could in one area, they broke camp and moved to an equally deserving location, cleaning up the effects of dysentery epidemics, washing patients, nursing entire villages. It was usually the high caste people, the elite of the village, who asked Bikshu Swamigal, Sambasivam and the others to start a camp. Still, the naturopaths would give medication to everyone equally. The untouchables were also given the healing treatments, but there was a restriction. Because of the caste rules, the healers must never touch one of these casteless people.

Everyone had the greatest faith in Sri Bikshu Swamigal and his disciples. If a person came for a little mud pack while one of the doctors was treating someone else, he or she would wait to receive the mud personally from the hands of the healer. Perhaps the doctor would be so busy that he would say, "Go ahead. There is the mud. Take what you need."

The waiting patient would reply, "Oh no, please. I don't want to take it myself. Will you please give it to me? Unless you touch it, it won't work." They had that kind of sincere faith, and it worked.

One day a large cart rolled up to the camp. Many people surrounded the creaking wagon. Lying inside upon a bed of hay, was a huge man. His eyes were rolled up in his head so that he almost appeared to be a corpse. His belly was fully distended, blown up like a giant balloon.

His family members and a group of the *sadhus* removed the man from the cart and, with much difficulty, placed him on the ground. Quickly Sambasivam checked his pulse. It was nearly nonexistent.

"Are there any facts about this man I should know?" he asked the family. They told him the man had not moved his bowels for five days. Immediately an enema was prepared, but the water was blocked and unable to enter the bowels. It splashed down his legs and soaked into the earth.

Sambasivam rolled up his sleeves. Using his hand, he began to withdraw ball after ball of blackened, stonelike fecal matter. After this was repeated perhaps twelve times, a great eruption of foul-smelling liquid and matter gushed from the patient's body and sprayed the entire area, including everyone in the immediate vicinity.

Sambasivam remained by the man's side. Within fifteen minutes the patient's pulse had returned to normal and he opened his mouth. In a weak voice, he requested a glass of water. He received it along with a strength-building tonic. An hour later, the man was again loaded into the cart and driven home by his jubilant relatives. Sambasivam walked quickly to the well for a long-awaited bath.

At another village camp Sambasivam treated a young untouchable girl. One of her eyes was swollen and festering, and he tended the ailment until it was completely cured.

The various caste people of the village heard of this and were incensed. At a hastily organized meeting they decided they could no longer tolerate the presence of a group of *sadhus* who flouted caste rules. They came to the camp as a group and shouted, "You dare to touch those people and then touch us! You dare to treat us as equal to them! Either vacate this camp or we'll set fire to it and drive you out!"

Sambasivam tried to reason with the mob, but they refused to listen. Finally he told them, "You can do anything you want, but we're not going to close the camp."

"All right. You'll see what we do tonight. We'll be back."

After they had left, the other *sadhus* became quite frightened. They approached Sambasivam with the idea of acquiescing to the group's wishes and closing the camp.

He told them, "Don't worry. I'll think of something. Just remain calm." There were many times when he had pondered the inequities of the caste system; many times he had seen its gross imbalance. As a child, his protest had been to ignore caste rules, but now it was time to actively do something about incidents such as these. He walked to the untouchable colony and met with its elders.

"Do you remember when I treated the child for the eye ailment?" he asked.

"Yes, but she's fine now. Did you come to treat her again?"

"No. I came to tell you something. The caste people have said our camp made a mistake in treating the child. They said we shouldn't have done it. Now they want us to close the camp or they'll set fire to it. They have threatened our lives."

"What? You have saved our lives and now there's a danger to your own." They became upset and angered by the injustice.

Sambasivam continued, "The high caste people sit at home, enjoying the fruits of your toil. Day and night, rain or sun, you people go out and bring in the crops for them. Their enjoyment stems from your work. Yet they don't want you to have the simple enjoyments of health and happiness. Such things should not continue. You should put an end to such foolishness."

"Please guide us. Tell us what to do. We are ready to do whatever you suggest."

"Are you ready to stop them from harming the camp tonight?"

"We are ready to give our lives if need be. In half an hour, we'll be at the camp to make sure nothing happens."

Thirty minutes later, a large group of young people from the untouchable community had stationed themselves on the road bordering the camp. They carried large bamboo sticks.

Within fifteen minutes a small group of caste people approached. They bore burning torches which smoked in the night. "You didn't vacate. We are going to burn the camp!" they shouted as they advanced.

The untouchables stepped forward, blocking their way. The high castes were shocked to see this large mass of their own workmen.

"What is this? Why are you here?"

"We have come to protect the camp from danger. If you harm them we'll burn all your homes to the ground. If you don't care for our happiness, if you can't tolerate the treatment of our children, we'll no longer work for your happiness."

The caste people were nervous and confused. They were greatly outnumbered. They called to Sambasivam, "Look at the hatred you have brought between our groups."

"I did not bring this hatred. You are treating these workers as enemies. If you don't wish to help them, hatred will result. This situation is abominable. You shouldn't let it continue. You are all children of God. Why should you let the nature of your births divide you? If not for their labor, you couldn't enjoy life in such a fashion. They are your limbs. You are their brain and their stomach. You should enjoy a give-and-take policy. Think of their welfare and live as a community."

The would-be attackers stamped out their torches. The untouchables lowered their sticks. The camp stayed on for many weeks, serving the needs of all people equally.

Sri Bikshu Swamigal was a good friend to Sri Swami Rajeshwarananda, the great exponent of the *adwaita* (non-dualistic) philosophy, and Dr. T.M.P. Mahadevan, the great philosopher. Sambasivam soon became close to them also and frequently visited the ashram called Upanishad Vihar which Rajeshwaranandaji and Dr.

Mahadevan had built at the holy place called Kalahasti. He loved the beautiful, secluded surroundings and the ancient hill temple to Lord Siva. The banks of the river Ponmugali ("Gold-Filled") were right next to the ashram. He had been working with Sri Bikshu Swamigal for several years, and now Sambasivam decided to stay at Upanishad Vihar for a while. Though Rajeshwaranandaji and Dr. Mahadevan traveled frequently, Sambasivam stayed there and took care of the ashram. With these two great philosophers and their disciples, Sambasivam enjoyed many hours of *satsangs* and discussions about the *advaita* philosophy.

Dr. Mahadevan and Swami Rajeshwaranandaji introduced Sambasivam to Bhagavan Ramana Maharshi, and the *brahmachari* was inspired to spend some time at Ramanashram.

> **By the proper practice of *pratyahara* (withdrawal of the senses) the senses become fully under your control. They become obedient horses, taking you wherever you want. You become a complete master over them.**

The great sage Ramana Maharshi was born in 1879 in South India. At the age of seventeen he had an experience that changed his life. One day he was overcome with a violent fear of death and began to contemplate the source of this fear. Within the same day, this self-inquiry brought him to the experience of Enlightenment. When he got this knowledge directly he was able to experience the Self as different from the body. He never went to any teacher to learn this. He got it directly.

Sambasivam felt blessed to be able to sit at the feet of this *jivanmukta* (living liberated being). To ask the Master a question was to receive a lesson in the thinking of a true *Jnana Yogi*.

"Who is asking this question?" Sri Ramana replied to Sambasivam's inquiry. "Who is having the doubt?"

"Sir, I am having the doubt," the young *brahmachari* answered.

"Who are you?" Sri Ramana persisted. "Find out the answer and come to me then." Suddenly Sambasivam felt the impact of his meaning and vowed that he would find the answer to that question.

During the time that Sambasivam was staying at his ashram, Sri Ramana's body was suffering from cancer, but the sage was obviously not disturbed by the ravages of the disease. It was not so easy for the disciples to transcend that bodily consciousness, however, and they were greatly pained to watch his body's physical deterioration.

When he saw the sad faces around him, Sri Ramana would say, "What kind of yoga is this? Where is your proper understanding? The body is simply undergoing its *karma*. Why do you worry?"

Sambasivam was among those who witnessed the operation that was performed on Sri Ramana's arm. The yoga master was not interested in having the operation, but at the insistence of his close disciples he finally agreed. Still, he refused anesthesia. As the doctor operated, Sri Ramana watched and spoke to his arm as if it belonged to someone else: "Poor arm, is the operation hurting you? Well, just undergo whatever is necessary. I don't know what the *karma* was that makes you have to suffer. I told them not to do this to you, but they insisted on it. The best thing is just to accept it."

At that time Sambasivam found all this too difficult to watch. His heart went out so much to the sage's bodily suffering. As the cancer spread through that body, Sambasivam finally approached Sri Ramana.

"Please, I beg you, Sir, to give me leave to travel on."

"Why? Are you still attached to the body?"

"No. I'm not attached to my body, but maybe I'm attached to your body. I find it hard to face this situation. I don't really feel comfortable in staying and watching the whole thing."

Sri Ramana understood. He raised his hand in blessing, and Sambasivam continued his journey. Fourteen days later, on the day he reached Rishikesh, Sambasivam heard that Bhagavan Ramana Maharshi had left his body. On that day many people saw a beautiful bright star flash across the sky.

The light is always within you but it is up to you to make use of it. Keep the light always in front of you. Follow it always. If you keep that light constantly in front of you to lead your way, you will always be the Master.

There is a cave in Tiruvannamalai known as Virupaksha Cave. In it, Sambasivam meditated. He felt a huge, dark cloud forming within him. Its gray mass expanded until he was completely surrounded in its smoke. Slowly it rose over his head like a mushroom cloud after an atomic explosion. It rose higher and higher until it finally drifted away.

When the density had passed, a feeling of lightness and joy remain-

90

ed within Sambasivam. A brilliant light surrounded him like a globe. He was bathed in its warmth. Gradually it condensed, becoming smaller and more concentrated. It became a tiny spark and entered the crown of his head. He fell into a deep trance which lasted two hours. When body consciousness returned he felt the absence of all unholy, *karmic* vibrations within. A new vibration, filled with light, had taken their place.

Sri Swami Satchidananda — East

Real happiness is within. If you search for it
through worldly or even religious externals,
you will never find it. It is there inside, always
waiting. There is neither the perceiver nor the
perceived. All this is the infinite consciousness.
The goal of our life is realization of spiritual
oneness. Realization of this truth is the birth-
less and deathless state. There is no birthday or
deathday for this consciousness.

Sri Swami Satchidananda — East

In the East, the major forms through which one worships the Lord are divided into six sections. The highest of all is the worship of the guru. It is not the highest because there is a difference between the guru and the other forms of worship but because it is very difficult to worship the guru. There is ample opportunity to lose faith in a living person, while there is nothing to make you lose faith in a picture, a form, or a statue of a god. They are always the same. But a living person is not the same always.

Sambasiva Chaitanya's pilgrimage resumed. In the spring of 1949 he was able to continue on his way north to Rishikesh. As he traveled, he created a particular image of Sri Swami Sivananda in his mind. He imagined that upon arrival at the ashram, an official would give him an appointment with the guru. Eventually his turn would come, and he would be presented to the great teacher. Swami Sivanandaji would be seated in *padmasana* (the full lotus pose), an austere man with his eyes closed. He would be silent. When he finally spoke, his voice would be low, the words mystical and complex. After a few short, blessed moments with the Swami, Sambasivam would be dismissed until his next appointment.

It was the summer season, and Rishikesh was crowded with pilgrims traveling to and from the shrines of Badrinath and Kedarnath, 160 miles further north. For a while before and after their pilgrimage most of them stayed at Ananda Kutir, Swami Sivanandaji's ashram. The ashram housed about eighty permanent ashramites, and three hundred people sat down daily for a free lunch. The entire population of nearby Munikireti took their meals at the ashram. Cows, dogs and hundreds of chattering monkeys were also fed. The area teemed with life in the warm summer light.

Sambasivam arrived at Ananda Kutir at 6 A.M. and was told that the guru was at his private cottage on the bank of the Ganges. To prepare for the auspicious meeting Sambasivam scrubbed his body thoroughly in a nearby part of the river, washed his traveling clothes and changed into a fresh outfit which he had saved especially for this occasion. He bought fruit and flowers to give as offerings and hurriedly went in search of the guru's dwelling.

"Brahmaanandham Parama Sugatam
Kevalam Jnaana Moortim
Dhwandhwaa teetam Gagana Sadhrusam
Tatwamasyaadhi Lakshyam
Ekam Nityam Vimalam Achalam
Sarvadhee Saakshi Bhoodam
Bhaavaa teetam Triguna Rahitam
Satgurum Tam Namaami"

"The greatest bliss, the highest joy,
Embodiment of wisdom absolute,
Non-dual, boundless like the sky
He is the goal of 'Thou art That.'
One, eternal, pure and still,
Witness of the whole universe,
Beyond mind's grasp, of *gunas* free
To that Guru may my worship be."

The one who personifies the qualities listed in this ancient chant is the *Satguru*. I feel very fortunate to have sat at the holy feet of the great *Satguru* Sri Swami Sivanandaji Maharaj. If you see any little bit of truth, knowledge or attainment in me, it is the spark which came from that great Light.

Many steps before he reached the cottage he heard a loud, booming voice and deep, hearty laughter breaking the stillness of the morning. Sambasivam was a bit perplexed. Who would be making so much noise near the Swami's house? He came in view of the cottage. A huge figure was seated comfortably in a cane chair. He was well over six feet tall and weighed a good 250 pounds. The man wore a small cloth *dhoti* which came just below his knees. The rest of his body — legs, chest, and arms — was bare except for a small towel thrown carelessly about his broad shoulders. The man's legs were crossed loosely at the ankles. A few people were seated at his feet, laughing and listening to his jokes. He smiled and clapped his hands frequently. Sambasivam stared. Immediately the shadow-Sivananda disappeared from his imagination. He ran forward and placed his offering at the feet of the guru. Then he prostrated full-length at the feet of his master, staying in that position several minutes without moving. His heart felt full, almost bursting with joy and love. Slowly Master Sivanandaji bent down, holding the hands of the new disciple tenderly.

Finally Sambasivam stood up slowly, gazing at the great swami. In Tamil, Master Sivanandaji asked where he had come from.

"South India."

In rapid succession he inquired when Sambasivam had left his home, how long it had taken him to arrive in Rishikesh, and, "Are you happy?"

"Oh, Swamiji. I am overjoyed to be here."

"Good, good," he clapped his hands. "You have come to the right place. Your troubles are over. Stop wandering and stick to this place. Stay here." He motioned to one of his attendants. "Bring this man some *idli* and coffee."

"Coffee, Swamiji?" Sambasivam's eyes widened — a *sadhu* drinking coffee!

"Coffee," Master Sivanandaji repeated.

"But, Swamiji, in all your books you say coffee is bad and now you are..."

The master smiled at him. "Do you like coffee?"

"Oh, Swamiji, I *love* coffee."

"Do you take hot chutney?" Sambasivam shook his head no. "All right, bring him some *idli* just with *ghee*." Turning back to Sambasivam, the guru asked, "How do you like the rest of the ashram?"

"I was so excited about seeing you, I came directly here without looking at anything else."

"Well then, do you like me? Am I all right?"

Sambasivam had never been asked such a question by a swami. "I really don't have the words to express what I feel. I will say that I'm seeing something completely different from what I expected."

"Ah? What did you expect?"

"Somehow I thought you'd be seated on a big, throne-like seat, meditating. I thought it would be very difficult to see you personally..." Slowly he wove the image before Swami Sivanandaji's eyes.

"Ah, and would you like to see me like that? Only then will you think I'm a big swami, hmm?" the guru joked.

After breakfast he asked one of the *sannyasin* disciples to give Sambasivam a room and told the new *sadhu* to relax. Although the trip had been long and tiring, this order was particularly difficult to follow. All day Sambasivam waited for the evening *satsang* when he could see his master again.

It was Master Sivanandaji's habit to call upon the new ashramites and guests during *satsang*, asking them to sing, play instruments, talk, or in some other way show their talents. That evening he turned his attention toward Sambasivam. "You are a Tamilian. Why don't you give us a lecture in Tamil?"

Sambasivam became suddenly shy. "Oh, no." He looked around in embarrassment. "Swamiji, I'm not prepared to talk."

"Come, come," Master Sivanandaji insisted pleasantly. "Tell us something at least."

Sambasivam came forward, trying to shrink in stature and be less conspicuous. Then he spoke. He spoke of how he had long awaited this opportunity and of his happiness at being in the ashram. "We are so fortunate to be at the feet of a Master who is so simple, so friendly, so loving, and, at the same time, so filled with wisdom." He ended with a short prayer to the *guru*.

"Wonderful! Wonderful!" Swami Sivanandaji applauded loudly. "We have a great Tamil lecturer with us now."

The lesson of my Gurudev's life was service. Always serve, serve and serve.

Sri Swami Sivanandaji Maharaj was a true saint. He lived until 1963, serving all humanity regardless of religion, race, color, caste or creed. He was often called *Jagatguru* (the Great World Guru). Rarely traveling outside India, he managed to send his spiritual vibration to almost every corner of the globe. Thousands of people came to know about the great science of Yoga through his hundreds of books. Many of his disciples are now revered teachers themselves.

Ananda Kutir, "Abode of Bliss," the Sivananda Ashram, Rishikesh, in the valley of the Himalayas.

Sri Swami Sivanandaji Maharaj.

Born in the small South Indian village of Pathamadai near Tin-naveli on the 8th of September, 1887, he apparently possessed an in-born passion for serving others. This manifested at first in his desire to be a physician. After he received his medical degree, Dr. Kuppuswamy (as he was then called) served in Malaysia for several years. During his days of medical practice he never concerned himself about the amounts of fees or the ability of his patients to pay him. Sometimes he went from door to door, serving the poor. His practice was open day and night. "To serve people and to share what I have is my inborn nature," he said.

The aspiration to completely renounce any ties to prestige or position caused him to leave Malaysia at the height of his medical career and return to India to live a monastic life.

In his autobiography, Master Sivanandaji said: "'Is there not a higher mission in life than the daily round of official duties such as eating and drinking? Is there not any higher form of eternal happiness than these transitory and illusory pleasures? The world of names and forms is constantly changing. Time is fleeting!' Such were the thoughts constantly rising in my mind. The doctor's profession gave me ample evidence of the sufferings of this world. True and lasting happiness cannot be found merely in gathering wealth. With the purification of the heart through selfless service, I had a new vision. I was deeply convinced that there must be a place, a sweet home of pristine glory and purity and divine splendor where absolute security, perfect peace and lasting happiness could be had through self-realization."

Dr. Kuppuswamy felt drawn to Rishikesh, and there he was initiated into the Holy Order of Sannyas (the monastic order) on June 1, 1924. The name of Swami Sivananda was bestowed upon him; and, in quest of spiritual vision, he plunged keenly into intense spiritual practices and austerities in the Himalayas. He was blessed by the experience of illumination and received what he felt to be a divine command: "Go thee forth and share thy wisdom with all."

In 1936, with the help of a few devotees, he founded the Divine Life Society in Rishikesh. Master Sivananda chose this title because he didn't want to name the new society for any particular religion or individual. To him divine life meant leading a healthy, happy, peaceful and spiritually prosperous life — something sought by people of all persuasions. Today the Divine Life Society has more than 400 international branches.

Even at the cost of his health, Master Sivanandaji kept serving. He went to the office very regularly and never missed a day. Toward the end of his physical life, in spite of failing health, he was always in his office answering correspondence, checking on the ashram and greeting guests.

In private, Master Sivanandaji's students often referred to him as "Swami Givananda" because of his totally warm and generous nature. Whenever someone came to the ashram Master Sivanandaji would pile the guest up with free books. Sometimes a visitor would protest, "Swamiji, I came by plane and can't carry all these books back in my luggage. The airline company will charge me for them."

"Is that so?" The Master would call to an ashramite, "Come here. Gather all these books, package them in neat bundles, take them to the post office and send them to this man." He never asked so much as the shipping costs in return.

On the ashram grounds, the Divine Life Society ran an *ayurvedic* pharmacy which prepared herbal medicines. At times the devotees were concerned with defraying the high operating cost of the ashram. If a guest visited the pharmacy, they would clandestinely ask him if he wanted to buy some tonic. They knew that once the guest saw their guru, he be given the preparation for free.

Many times the ashram verged on bankruptcy, but the people who supplied the DLS with food, building materials, paper for the presses and so on, freely gave the supplies if funds weren't available. Often a visiting devotee would spontaneously write a check for the exact amount needed to cover the outstanding bills.

Every evening a large group of professional performers showed up at *satsang* to play instruments, sing, dance, act and receive the Master's blessings. Even before such a presentation, he would say, "Bring some hot milk right away. When this man finishes he'll be tired." Or, "Bring this person all the books I have written about music."

One evening the son of a well-known flute player arrived for *satsang*. Master Sivananda was told that the son himself could play the flute a little. Immediately he asked the boy to perform, but the son displayed none of his father's virtuosity. Many listeners covered their ears. As the recital ended, Master Sivanandaji applauded heartily.

"Wonderful, wonderful, Mr. Murugesh. I'm giving you the title of *Sankirtan* Yogi, adept of devotional music."

A devotee whispered, "How can you do that? Such a title will just be meaningless."

The son himself said, "Why are you telling me this, Swamiji? I know I don't play well at all."

"When you are the performer," the guru winked, "you don't always appreciate your music as the audience does."

The following year, the son returned. Those ashramites who had been present the previous year prepared to suffer through this concert as well, but it was as if the father were playing instead of the son. Because of Master Sivanandaji's encouragement, the young man had become an expert at playing the flute.

Life itself is a journey toward Godhead, a pilgrimage.

Beyond a doubt, Sambasivam knew that he had reached his final destination. All the other masters had prepared him for this stage. Master Sivanandaji was unquestionably the one by whose hand he would take the great step of *sannyas* initiation at last.

Traditionally one undertakes a pilgrimage for purification before this initiation, and Sambasivam chose to set off for the holy Himalayan shrines of Kedarnath, Tunganath, and Badrinath — three holy places near Rishikesh. Kedarnath is at the altitude of 11,000 feet; Tunganath about 12,000 feet; and Badrinath is at 10,500 feet. Mother Nature had conveniently provided hot water springs at each of these spots so the pilgrims could take a dip for purification before approaching the sacred shrines. Most of the pilgrimage required walking, and Sambasivam loved his first beautiful first experience of trekking in the Himalayas. He was deeply inspired and often paused to write songs or poems about the journey.

The editors of *Atma Jyothi*, a Ceylonese magazine, heard of his pilgrimage and asked him to write an article for them. Sambasivam was able to incorporate his poems and songs into the magazine piece, which began with the words of a song he had composed:

"Beloved friend, come on. There is so much beauty, so much to see at the silver peaks of the Himalayas. It is a feast for the eyes. Do you know who prepared that big feast? It is all God...Do you see where the Ganges is going? It is running toward the Mother from whom it came, the sea. All these little branches that join the Ganges are all little seekers. The big guru (the Ganges) runs toward the Mother, and all the little seekers join and say, 'We will follow you because we know you are going to take us there.'"

The sight of the peak of Kedarnath inspired a lovely poem in Tamil which translates: "If you take the refuge of the lotus feet of Kedarnathan [Lord Siva] there is no destruction in your life." Glimpsing Tunganath, Sambasivam was inspired to say: "When the mind accommodates the lotus feet of Tunganath [Lord Skanda or Subramanya] it jumps with joy." About Badrinath he said, "If you really cry and shout and call the great Lord of Badri (Lord Narayana or Vishnu) the mind that usually runs hither and thither will stay in one place and get focused."

Being in the midst of these three holy places was almost overwhelming; the energy and power were totally uplifting. On one side was Siva (Kedarnath), on another Shakti (Badrinath, Lord Vishnu), in the middle, Muruga (Tunganath). All three put together are called *Soma Skanda Moorti*, or *Sat Chit Ananda*.

Live for the sake of others. Forget yourself completely. The more you take care of others, the more others will take care of you.

After returning from his pilgrimage, Sambasivam continued his ashram work — conducting Hatha Yoga classes and answering correspondence in the Tamil langauge. Master Sivanandaji would sort the mail, referring certain letters to ashramites who had a particular knowledge of the subject mentioned. Later Sambasivam gave Raja Yoga lectures at the Yoga Vedanta Forest Academy, attached to Ananda Kutir.

There was a financial crisis at the ashram. Since no one was restricted from entering and staying there and hundreds were fed for free each day, a noticeable shortage of money resulted. Sambasivam decided to leave the premises and set an example for the newcomers flooding in.

About three miles from Ananda Kutir was a forest area in which a wealthy man had set up a free shelter for *sadhus*. It consisted of seven small huts, each concealed by the location and the heavy green vegetation of the jungle. At night wild animals roamed the area, treading softly through the bushes. The center of the area was a tiny vegetable garden and a free feeding station managed by a caretaker. Each day at noon he prepared a meal of *rhoti* (a bread) and *dhal* for the seven *sadhus* under his charge. Sambasivam learned that one of the huts was unoccupied and thus available for his use. He was instructed to bring with him a small towel to carry the *rhotis* and a bowl for the *dhal*.

When Sambasivam arrived, the caretaker ushered him to the empty hut and cleaned it thoroughly. It was evening, and within half an hour the caretaker returned to the hut with a portable charcoal stove and a bag of provisions.

"What is this for?" Sambasivam asked.

"I'm going to make you some *rhotis*."

"I thought there was only one meal, served at noon."

"Well, you just came tonight. You must be hungry." The caretaker sat down and went about making the bread. He joined the new *sadhu* for dinner.

The caretaker watched over Sambasivam like a mother hen. He never allowed him to go to the feeding station for food. Each morning and evening the caretaker sent over a cup of milk and, at noon, the usual meal.

"Why do you do this just for me?" Sambasivam was perplexed.

"Somehow I am drawn to you. I feel like doing it. Please let me continue."

Always try to serve others. Don't even call it helping; call it service because you are benefited by that. If a man begs from you and you give him something, you shouldn't think you are helping him. Instead, he is helping you. Hasn't he given you the opportunity to express your generosity? If not for him, you couldn't become a big donor. If no one were there to receive, how could you donate?

Sambasivam returned to the forest for meditation until a special request from his guru brought him back to Ananda Kutir.

A wealthy devotee from Madras had arrived at the ashram with his son and was asking especially for Sambasivam. When he found that the *sadhu* was living in the forest, he prepared to go there at once to stay with him.

"No, no," Master Sivanandaji said. "You can't live in the jungle with him. You won't be comfortable. Instead, let Sambasivam come here and stay with you."

The devotee was quite old and had a rheumatic condition. Quarters were set up for him near the river, and an adjoining room was prepared for Sambasivam. The man remained unsatisfied. He insisted that Sambasivam stay in his room with him, and arrangements were made to accommodate his wishes.

The ultimate quest of the entire world is peace. Only in peace do we have joy; not by acquiring things, not by doing things, not by earning or learning but by dedication. Your entire life must be a sacrifice. Think for the sake of others. Talk for the sake of others. Live for the sake of others. Every action should aim at bringing some benefit to others. To a person with this attitude peace is guaranteed.

It is said that Brahma the creator brought forth four mental sons, the Kumaras, to help him with his work of creation. Because of their absolute nonattachment and spirit of renunciation, the Kumaras refused to be involved in worldly activity. Instead, they chose to lead a life of meditation and were initiated into the highest wisdom by Lord Siva in the form of Dakshinamoorthi (the South-faced one who teaches in silence). These four were the first *sannyasins* (renunciates). Following them on their path of total renunciation of "I, me, mine" — which leads to realization of the true Self — were hundreds, thousands of others such as Vyasa, writer of the *Mahabharata*; Sri Shankara, a religious and philosophical giant; Ramakrishna Paramahansa, Sri Swami Vivekananda and Sri Swami Sivananda of Rishikesh.

The day before initiation, every candidate fasts and spends the hours meditating and repeating the sacred *Gayatri Mantram*. Final offerings are made to all souls, living and departed, in the form of balls of food. Thus the devotee finishes all obligations to humanity. The candidate offers the last ball to him or herself as if to a dead person.

As in *brahmacharya diksha*, the initiate thoroughly shaves his or her head, except for the topmost tuft of hair. This time, Sambasivam didn't worry about becoming ill. The Rishikesh climate was quite a bit cooler than that of South India.

"Are you ready to take *sannyas?*" Master Sivanandaji asked.

"Yes, Gurudev. I'm looking forward to it," Sambasivam answered.

The Master inspected his disciple closely. "You look so beautiful with your long hair and beard. Are you ready to renounce those also?"

In the Tamil language *uyir* is life; *mayr* is hair.

"Gurudev," Sambasivam replied, "in *sannyas* we are supposed to renounce everything. When a disciple isn't even ready to renounce his *mayr*, how can he pledge his *uyir*?"

Master Sivananda called to everyone, laughing, "You see, not only is he ready to give me his life, he's ready to give me his hair also. That's really wonderful!"

July 10, 1949, the day of Sambasivam's *sannyas* initiation was clear and warm. The Ganges sparkled with reflections. With his freshly shaved face and head, Sambasivam presented himself to his guru. The Master looked at him silently.

Sambasivam sat before the orange flames of the sacrificial fire as thousands of *sannyasins* had done before and thousands would do afterward. Into the fire the initiate symbolically offers the body, mind, intellect — in fact, all that could be called one's own. The *sannyasin* feels that all worldly attachment is totally burned at that time, and from that day forward he or she walks forth as a shell, used only as an instrument of the Divine. Even the little tuft of hair is cut by the Master and tossed into the river. In the Holy Ganges river, a *sannyas mantram* is repeated for the first time. The devotee dips into the water three times and walks to the shore where the guru awaits. There the *sannyasin* accepts the *gerua* cloth from the Master. Its color is orange, as if it came directly out of the sacrificial flames. After donning the bright new cloth, the *sannyasin* drops the last remaining article of old clothing into the river. Now the body, the mind, even the dress all belong to the Master.

If this shiny new instrument of the Divine is supposed to serve, the ones in need of service must have some way to call for it. There must be a new name. All are given the title Swami (master of one's own self), and all the names end in *ananda* (supreme bliss) since a *sannyasi* is the most joyous of people. The one who had been called Sambasivam became Swami Satchidananda (Existence-Knowledge-Bliss Absolute). His fellow initiates were named Swami Chidananda (Knowledge-Bliss Absolute), Swami Mounananda (Bliss of Silence) and Swami Brahmananda (Bliss of Brahma).

The following morning business continued as usual. The new Swami Satchidananda waited in his guru's office to receive the daily load of correspondence. Master Sivanandaji entered and studied his new swami curiously.

"Satchidanandaji," he said thoughtfully, "I'm giving you special permission to grow your hair again. You looked so beautiful that way. I want you to look like that again."

He has not cut it since.

One night, while getting out of bed, the devotee with the rheumatic condition fell and broke his hip. For a while he was nursed at the ashram, but soon he insisted that he had to return home. Satchidanandaji traveled 150 miles to Delhi and back, arranging for the devotee's plane flight. The old man told him, "I can't trust my son to take care of me. You'll have to accompany me to Madras and then return here."

Though this would mean a great delay in his return to solitude and study, Satchidanandaji agreed.

After they reached Madras, the man begged the *sannyasi* to remain "just a few more days." Satchidanandaji agreed and arranged his life accordingly. He nursed the devotee twenty-four hours a day. Many nights, just as Satchidanandaji closed his eyes, his patient would whisper, "Are you asleep yet?"

Satchidanandaji's understanding and compassion kept him from becoming annoyed with this task. It was a chance for him to serve, and he recognized the love and faith this man had for him. He remained while the weeks stretched into a month. Finally the cast was removed, and the devotee was able to walk with a cane.

"I've taken so much of your time," he apologized. "Please forgive me. Even though I would love to have you stay here, I know it is time for you to go back to the ashram."

Satchidanandaji bowed to him, thanked him and returned north to Rishikesh.

Ananda Kutir was built on the side of a hill that sloped down to the Ganges. The office, hall, kitchen, hospital, temple and the guru's quarters bordered the river. Located 200 yards above, in the upper section, were the dwellings of most of the ashramites.

For several months Satchidanandaji lived on three cups of milk a day; one each for breakfast, lunch and dinner. In the morning, after bathing in the Ganges, he would drink a cup of milk in the kitchen and take another back to his room for lunch, carrying it carefully up the slope. When Master Sivananda became aware of this practice, he presented his disciple with a thermos bottle so that the milk could be kept fresh and warm until lunch.

The 8th of every month was celebrated as Master Sivanandaji's birthdate. A big feast was prepared. Everyone attended to dine with the Master. When the Master saw Satchidanandaji he would say, "Today you must sit in front of me. Forget about the milk diet for now." He would proceed to ply the devotee with all types of food from his own plate.

Srimati Velammai developed a minor oral infection. A doctor treated it with an extremely potent medicine which caused her mouth to become badly inflamed so that she could barely close it. It became nearly impossible for her to eat or drink. The family grew concerned but they couldn't call in the doctor. After all, he had caused the swelling in the first place. Velammai calmed their fears, "Don't worry. Soon I'll receive something from my son and then everything will be all right."

After two days she received a letter from Rishikesh, 2,000 miles away. Inside the message was a small quantity of holy ash with instructions for her to swallow some and put the rest on her forehead. Minutes after the ash was applied the inflammation disappeared and Velammai could close her mouth normally.

Satchidanandaji received a letter from Sri Kalyanasundaram. It said, "How did you know of her ailment? Now she is fine." It was the first time the *sannyasin* had heard of Velammai's illness.

While living at Ananda Kutir Satchidanandaji often visited Vasishta Guha (Vasishta's Cave) about fourteen miles above the ashram. Living there was Swami Purushottamanandaji Maharaj, a contemporary of Master Sivananda. Originally a member of the Ramakrishna Order, he had become reclusive and in his search for meditative seclusion had settled at Vasishta Guha. This was the perfect spot for meditation, and Satchidanandaji became quite close to this saint during many visits. Purushottamanandaji would sit outside on a small platform talking with the young *sannyasi*, and after some time of inspiring *satsang* Satchidanandaji would ask permission to go inside and meditate.

"My highest experience which was not connected with any particular form was the experience of *Adwaita* or Oneness or Enlightenment. I had that in 1949, a few months after my *sannyas* initiation. It was in midwinter when I visited Vasishta Cave. Vasishta was a great *rishi*, a sage who lived hundreds of years ago. There is a legend that it was in this cave that he performed his austerities.

"I went into the cave, bending down, until after twenty-five feet I reached a large room-like place with a seat. As I sat there and meditated I had the experience of transcending my body and mind, realizing myself as the Omnipresent. I forgot my individuality. It is impossible to explain exactly what this is.

"I must have spent several hours in that state. Then I heard a humming sound, OM chanting, coming from a long distance away. Slowly, slowly, it became louder. As it neared, I became aware of my mind and body. Gently I stood up and went out of the cave.

"For some time, I couldn't see anything in the normal way. All over I saw light, light, light. The whole world appeared to be a mass of light. There was only peace everywhere. The state persisted that whole day.

"Of course, after that I had this experience very often, mostly when I visited a holy place. I had it in Badrinath and almost every day when I went to Mount Kailash. I had it in Amarnath in Kashmir. Even in Sri Lanka, whenever I visited Adam's Peak. I had it in Jerusalem and at St. Peter's in the Vatican."

> The *Bhagavad Gita* tells us "Yoga is neither for the person who eats too much nor for one who starves; neither for the person who sleeps constantly nor for one who doesn't sleep; neither for the person who talks too much nor for one who stops talking completely. The middle path is Yoga."

As usual, the ashramites were gathered for evening *satsang*. It was summer, and the session was held in the cool night air on a terrace adjoining the dining hall.

As the group chanted they could see the impressive form of Gurudev Sivanandaji making his way from his *kutir* along with a number of other swamis, all of whom carried bulging bags. It was the guru's custom to bring a little *prasad* to pass around at the end of the *satsang*; usually it was small pastries or cashew nuts. That evening he also carried a glass container — something special.

He called first to Swami Mounananda, the former editor of Mahatma Gandhi's *Harijan*. "Mounanandaji. Come here. I have something for you. You will love it." He handed the devotee a small green-colored ball. Mounananda placed it in his mouth and smiled. He swallowed it and licked his lips.

"Yogiraj," the Master motioned to Satchidanandaji, "come here. Come on. I'm going to give you something delicious." He smiled at the disciple lovingly. "Shut your eyes and stretch out your hand."

Into the extended palm he placed a small, soft ball. Satchidanandaji assumed it was the same delicacy his brother monk had received before him. Master Sivananda instructed, "Without looking, put it into your mouth. It's a nice surprise."

110

(left) Sri Swami Purushottamanandaji.

(below) 10 July 1949. Immediately following initiation into the Holy Order of Sannyas. The new sannyasi, Sri Swami Satchidananda.

On the banks of the sacred Ganges. Years later, Gurudev referred to this picture of himself with his holy master as "the Jnana Ganga [Master Sivanandaji] and the little creek."

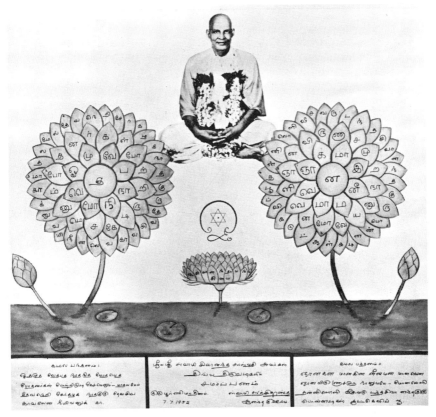

Kamala Bhandanam, *"Song in Lotus,"* composed, sung, drawn and offered to the lotus feet of
Sri Swami Sivanandaji Maharaj by Sri Swami Satchidananda. Guru Poornima Day, 7 July 1952.

TRANSLATION OF SRI SWAMI SATCHIDANANDA'S
LOTUS SONGS

LOTUS SONG # 1 (left): "Beloved Gurudeva, Siva — the Lord of
the Divine Life Society at the Holy Abode called Rishikesh, where the
sound of the recitation of the immortal Vedas by the sages reverberates
constantly — please be a Protector to this humble soul."

LOTUS SONG # 2 (right): "At the golden Feet of Sri Gurudeva
Sivananda — who blessed me with the sun of Superconsciousness to
shed the light of Wisdom in the space of silence, to destroy the
darkness of ignorance of mine and to achieve the liberation — I offer
this flower of song."

A perfect spot for meditation — on the banks of the holy river Ganges.

114

Hatha Yoga class at Ananda Kutir.

115

Satchidanandaji kept his eyes shut and popped the ball into his mouth.

FIRE! His whole body was burning. It was as if a bolt of electricity were coursing his body — seeking out each limb, each cell, each hair follicle. The ball of green chutney had made its way down his esophagus, creating a trail of heat in its wake. The disciple leaped high into the air. Tears began to roll involuntarily from his eyes.

The guru exploded with laughter. He doubled his body and held his stomach. Great tears of mirth rolled from his eyes.

"Look at the Yogiraj," he gasped. "See the yogi. A little chili made him completely upset." He began to shake with laughter again. "Equanimity is yoga. Above dualities is yoga. Above heat and cold, sweet and sour." At last his chuckles quieted and drifted off into the air over the river.

"You should not always take sweet things or live on just milk alone. Occasionally you should take hot things also. Suppose you go into the world to teach and someone feeds you hot curry? If you show such a reaction, how will your host feel? He'll really feel terrible. You should always be able to tolerate anything and everything. Don't stick to one diet always. Learn to digest different things just to see how you'll react."

Satchidanandaji had calmed down. "Thank you, Gurudev. I can assure you this is one lesson I'll never forget."

Treat everyone as the Lord. Feel His presence in everyone. If you see the entire Universe as a divine representation, you will start going out and serving everyone.

A woman named Karina, the wife of a South Indian businessman, came to visit the ashram and practice yoga. She became a devoted disciple of Master Sivanandaji and felt a particular liking for Satchidanandaji. She was concerned that he was not eating a balanced diet and often prepared special meals for him. She treated him like her own son. In fact, she often called him "son." Karina stayed at the ashram for several months before returning to her home in Malabar State. Her homecoming brought with it some sad news. A doctor discovered that she had a tumor; surgery was recommended.

From the hospital in Bangalore, Karina sent a telegram to Satchidanandaji and one to Master Sivananda. "I am going through with this operation and would like to have Swami Satchidanandaji come to be with me during this time. Please, Gurudev, would you send him here?"

Master Sivanandaji knew of Karina's motherly affection and deep respect for Satchidanandaji and recommended that he go to serve Karina during her convalescence. After two weeks in the Bangalore hospital she would travel to Nandi Hills for the rest of her recovery, and Satchidanandaji would accompany her. This gave Master Sivananda an idea. "I want you to take this opportunity to visit some of the places that have been asking for you, some of the other Divine Life centers and other spots where there are devotees. Come back in a leisurely fashion." Gurudev Sivananda had taken a tour of India himself, and he felt it would also be a good thing for his disciple.

Swami Satchidananda left Ananda Kutir on February 8, 1951. His guru watched over him with concern prior to the departure. Mainly, he was thinking about Satchidanandaji's limited diet of milk and fruit.

"Take good care of your health," the Master instructed. "A fruit and milk diet alone will not suit service of an intense nature." At the farewell meal, Gurudev Sivanandaji sat across from Satchidanandaji, making sure his disciple got used to a heavier diet, including hot spices.

"Jai Satchidananda! Go and thrill the hearts of thousands. Inspire all, especially students, to take to the path of yoga and lead the Divine Life."

The devotee prostrated, holding onto his guru's feet, and then left to catch his train.

New Delhi...Madras...Bangalore...down through India to Coimbatore. He lectured at colleges, universities and the homes of devotees. He gave private and public instruction in *asanas* and *pranayama*. New branches of the Divine Life Society were opened at Nandi Hills Station, Mysore and Kumbakonan.

A beautiful Divine Life Society branch opened in Coimbatore and afforded Satchidanandaji's physical family their first opportunity to see him since he had received *sannyas* initiation. The opening of the DLS there was a grand occasion. All the dignitaries came forward to take part in the ceremonies, and many became officers. The mayor became the Coimbatore DLS president.

After a brief stay in Coimbatore, Satchidanandaji was off to other places. In Bombay he lectured and gave *asana* demonstrations all around the area — Shankara Mutt, Asthika Samaj, Sri Ramananda Satchidananda Samaj, Chaitanya Prabha Mandali, Bharatiya Vidya Bhavan, the South India Education Society and High School, and the Naval Accounts Office.

On September 8th he interrupted his tour in Kirkee for a special

Jayanthi celebration in honor of his Gurudev. Then he returned to Bombay for programs at Poddar High School, the Gujarat Hindu Shri Mandali, the All-India Women's Conference at Santa Cruz, and the Sports Club of the Imperial Chemical Industries.

He was consulted about medical problems and prescribed various yogic and naturopathic treatments learned during his time with Sri Bikshu Swamigal.

After eight months, on October 10th, he returned for a brief visit to see Master Sivanandaji before continuing on the tour.

"Satchidanandaji," his guru stated, "you have worked wonders. You have thrilled one and all. I have received letters and reports of admiration from various people. You have created a mighty spiritual stir in the country. You have, by God's grace, rendered an inestimable divine service to the Lord's children."

Swami Satchidananda stayed for a time at Barabanki training college students in *asanas*. Swami Purushottamanandaji was also there visiting his disciples. He and Satchidanandaji enjoyed this chance for a reunion. On the evening of December 31, Satchidanandaji left Barabanki and continued his tour by train. The train passed through the cool night. Lights flickered on in the hills. A man from Lucknow began to speak to the Swami, questioning him about the spirit, the mind and various facets of yoga.

Satchidanandaji left the train at Lucknow, joining his new acquaintance. A number of people were invited to the man's house that New Year's Eve to listen to Satchidanandaji's impromptu lecture on Raja Yoga, the royal path.

On the morning of the New Year his host greeted him. "Swamiji, I wish to take the vow of *brahmacharya*, celibacy. I would also like to give up smoking. Please help me with your strength so that I can stick to these things."

Satchidanandaji blessed his new disciple. He passed on to him a bit of his own Gurudev's energy and waved good-bye to the crowd at the Lucknow Station.

There was a break in his schedule and Satchidanandaji took this opportunity to recharge himself. Leaving the train at Nasik, he wandered free as a mendicant *sadhu*. After several days he went to Bombay to finish the tour.

Bombay was steaming and crowded with people. His visit started with a nine-day celebration at Ramana Samaj, where he lectured on Sri Ramana Maharshi's inquiry, "Who am I?" and led chanting. The organizers of the Ramana Satchidananda Samaj took that opportunity to ask Satchidanandaji to perform the installation of Sri Ramana's statue at the Samaj. This ceremony is called *prana pratishta* and means that the statue is given life through that ceremony. Satchidanandaji felt profoundly privileged to serve in this way.

One year and nine days after its start, Satchidanandaji's All-India Tour ended on February 17, 1952. Later a book was written about the tour. It was a large volume and recounted his activities throughout India.

Real service to humanity is service to the Lord. Don't differentiate from person to person — whether it be God or dog. Treat all the same, as God.

One lovely afternoon, about thirty ashramites and guests were walking with Master Sivanandaji in a wooded area on the upper level of the ashram grounds. It had been a pleasant but long walk, and the sky was almost dark. Among the hikers were a mother and daughter from Ceylon. They strolled as contentedly as all the others.

Suddenly the daughter fell, screaming, to the ground. She had been bitten by a scorpion. Immediately, there was great commotion all around her. Master Sivananda stood apart as if to observe his disciples reacting to a crisis.

There was a terrible dilemma. Aside from the girl, who was writhing in agony on the ground, and the mother, who was anxiously bending over her, all the members of the company were male ashramites. They should never touch a female.

Immediately, a group decided to run back to the main ashram building, get a chair and two poles to make a *dholi* (a carrier), bring it back and have the girl sit in the *dholi*. This way they could carry her to the hospital area close to the bank of the Ganges. While all this planning went on the girl cried in pain.

Satchidanandaji had observed the planning men and the screaming child. Though only a few moments had passed, it was easy to see that it would be a long time before the poor girl had relief from her torture if things proceeded at the present rate.

Even as some of the men started to run back for the supplies to make a *dholi*, Satchidanandaji dashed over, scooped up the girl in his arms and ran to the hospital in time for the effects of the poison to be neutralized. The doctors were able to give her an injection to bring immediate relief, and she rested as her grateful mother sat by her side.

Satchidanandaji walked back to the ashram.

In the meantime, a great furor had grown surrounding this incident. Many of the men were quite upset. "How could a male swami, who is not even supposed to *touch* a woman, grab this girl, *hold* her and carry her?" Satchidanandaji was aware of the gossip, but he simply ignored it.

The gossip reached the ears of Master Sivanandaji. He had, of course, witnessed the whole event but had thus far been silent about it. After several days of this gossip, the Master spoke out. Smiling, he said, "Well, it looks like *you* are the people who are hugging and carrying this girl. Yes, Satchidanandaji picked up her body, took it to the hospital, left it; and there the matter ended for him. He is free. He is not holding anything. But you are all so caught up in that and excited about it; you are still carrying her." The ashram members who had been gossiping realized their folly and felt humbled. They apologized to their brother monk and told him what Master Sivanandaji had said about the matter.

A few months after this incident a dog was found sick and wounded, lying under a tree in the upper level of the ashram. The wounds had festered, and a terrible stench came from the animal. No one would go near it, but of course they wanted to help their fellow child of God. Plans were made to send the dog to the veterinarian in Rishikesh. A horse-drawn tonga was prepared for the trip, but it could not be brought up the long hill to get the dog. Someone would have to bring the animal all the way down to the tonga. None of the monks nearby could bring themselves to touch the malodorous creature.

Satchidanandaji came by and heard of the situation. Quickly he picked up a piece of cloth, gently wrapped the dog in it and carried the animal to the tonga for the trip to the veterinarian.

Afterward, several of the ashramites who had gossiped about him before came forward. "Well, now we know that you really treat everybody equally. We were so disturbed to see you carrying a girl, even though we couldn't help her otherwise. Now we see you carrying a dog that seems to have leprosy as easily as you carried that child. We know now that you are not thinking of them as the bodies. To you it seems that both are great souls, and you are serving them equally."

At the stop in Vilupuram, Satchidanandaji entered the railcar to find one half vacant except for two people. The other half was completely filled with men and women pushed into one another and babies crammed on their mothers' laps.

"Well, there doesn't seem to be any reason for half of the compartment to be so empty," the *sannyasi* thought. "But since it is, I can sit there and stretch out."

"Swami, Swami," a murmur came from the crowded side. "Please come over here."

"Why?"

The people didn't answer. They turned their heads and began to whisper among themselves.

One of the two men on his side of the compartment answered Satchidanandaji. The man seemed to be quite wealthy — expensively dressed and bejeweled. Slowly he said, "I too would like you to sit on the other side, for your own sake; because, you see, I am a leper."

With such an answer Satchidanandaji didn't want to abruptly get up and leave. "It's all right. I can sit here. Nothing will happen to me."

The man smiled and relaxed. Within ten minutes he started talking to the Swami. He spoke of the many years he had suffered from the disease and of the many emotional disturbances his condition had created.

Satchidanandaji patiently explained to him the technical reasons for such a disease, the way in which its progress could be stopped and ultimately cured.

"For one thing," he said, "cigarette smoking will aggravate leprosy."

The man admitted that not only did he smoke heavily, but he took snuff and chewed tobacco as well.

"Why don't you give them up? At least in this stage. The nicotine will only disturb your bloodstream and increase your pain."

The leper inhaled noisily. Slowly he began to show the Swami the waste created by his disease. He pushed up the long sleeves of his shirt. Almost all his fingers were in a state of decay. With one hand he pushed a richly embossed gold snuffbox from his pocket. It was studded with jewels. The sparkling rubies and diamonds contrasted grotesquely with his maimed fingers.

"With your blessings, Swamiji, I'm going to put an end to this. I'll never touch snuff again." He carefully maneuvered the box into his right hand and threw it from the window of the speeding train. It bounced on an embankment and disappeared.

From another pocket he withdrew a matching cigarette box and, while everyone in the car watched in amazement, threw that outside also.

"I'll never smoke, chew tobacco or take snuff again." The leper seemed very content. At the next station his attendant reminded him that it was time to leave the train, but the man had changed his mind. He had decided not to leave just yet.

"I'm going to stay on as long as the Swami does. When he gets off I'll catch a return train and come back."

"Why?" Satchidanandaji asked. "What is the point? I've told you all I know. You needn't continue your journey just to keep me company."

"Well, Swamiji, it's not just by talking to you that I'm receiving benefit, although you've given me some wonderful instructions. Before you sat down near me, I was continually scratching my hands and rubbing them constantly to rid myself of their itching. When you came, the itching gradually went away; and since we've been talking together, I'm completely free of it. For the first time in months I feel comfortable. Please let me keep this comfort until you finish your train ride."

Let the Lord in you be the charioteer. Let Him guide. You just follow.

Srimati Selvanayagi was a young woman from a very wealthy Ceylonese family that owned many acres of land around Trincomalee. When Master Sivanandaji traveled to Ceylon on his All-India/Ceylon Tour, she met him, became very interested in his teachings and eventually went to Ananda Kutir to study under him. *Sannyas* doesn't discriminate between men and women. After a while Srimati Selvanayagi was initiated and given the name Swami Satchidananda. She came from a Tamil community in Ceylon and, because they spoke the same language, the two Satchidanandas often sat and talked.

In 1952, she decided that a branch of the DLS must be started in her home country. She brought the idea to Gurudev Sivananda and asked that the other Swami Satchidananda accompany her to Ceylon to start the organization.

This was the last thing Satchidanandaji desired at the time. He wanted to continue his seclusion and meditation. The other Satchidananda knew of his reluctance, but she had decided upon him because he was an excellent teacher, and spoke Tamil as well.

At Ramana Samaj: Sri Swami Satchidananda is privileged to perform the prana pratishta, *the installation of the statue of Sri Ramana Maharshi.*

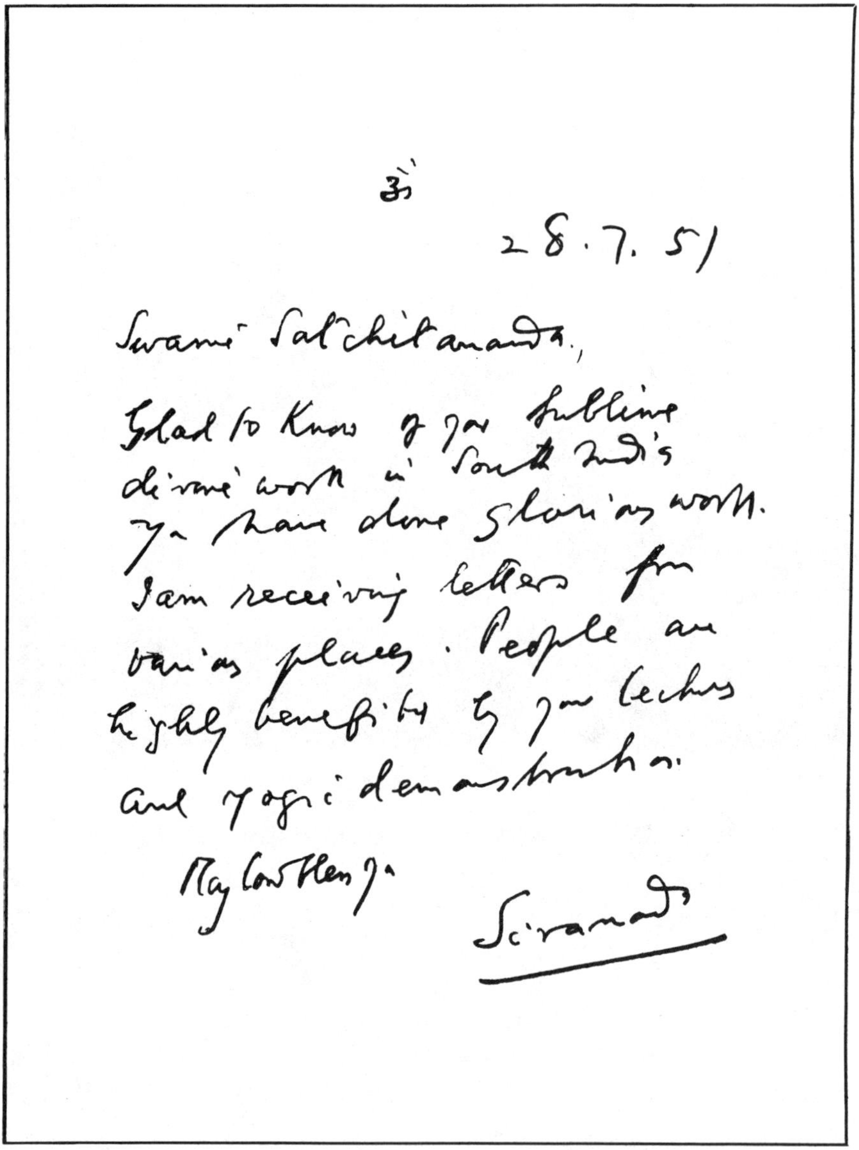

ॐ

28.7.51

Swami Satchitananda.,

Glad to know of your sublime
divine work in South India's
you have done glorious work.
I am receiving letters from
various places. People are
highly benefited by your lectures
and yogic demonstration.

May God bless you

Sivananda

A great blessing — letter from the Holy Master.

A monk, as he tours all over India.

125

Master Sivanandaji approached Satchidanandaji with her request.

"Gurudev," Satchidanandaji replied, "I am not fit to do such work. There may be other devotees who would like to go to Ceylon. I'll be content to stay here and do my work." He thought his refusal would end the matter.

Master Sivanandaji had other plans. "Go ahead. I will work through you. Don't worry."

Satchidanandaji tried another approach. "Gurudev, we are both called Swami Satchidananda. How will people differentiate between us? There will be confusion. What will happen when letters come?"

The Master laughed. "From now on she will be known as Swami Satchidananda Mataji and you can use Yogiraj — the title I gave you. You will be known as Yogiraj Swami Satchidananda." The matter was settled.

At the close of 1952, Satchidanandaji and Mataji left their Master in Rishikesh and traveled down to Bombay. After attending the Jayanthi celebration of Ramana Maharshi, they continued to South India and arrived in Trincomalee on February 1, 1953.

In the spiritual life, all paths lead to the same place.

A new phase of Satchidanandaji's life began at this time. Never again would he find much time for seclusion. He certainly didn't want this recognition, but more and more people began to look up to him as their beloved spiritual teacher, their master, their "Gurudev." From this point onward in this book that is what we will call him.

The two swamis met early in the morning and visited all the fields owned by Mataji's family. Ten acres were selected near Trincomalee. With the help of local devotees, land was cleared and an ashram built. There was a main hall for lectures and classes, a small house for Mataji and another for Gurudev. Construction was completed in September of 1953.

While the ashram was being built Gurudev, lived in a nearby boarding house. He held talks and gave *asana* classes at the Hindu College run by the Ramakrishna Mission.

"You say you are from the Divine Life Society. Why are you giving classes and talking at the Ramakrishna Mission school?"

(top) *Yogiraj Swami Satchidananda and Swami Satchidananda Mataji, the Holy Master's emissaries to Ceylon. (bottom) An auspicious moment. Sri Gurudev places the foundation stone for the Sivananda Thapovanam, Trincomalee.*

"What is the difference?" Gurudev replied to his questioner. "The Ramakrishna Mission is also Divine Life. Every spiritual institution is a Divine Life institution. They have different names but there is no real difference."

"At that time in Sri Lanka there was no free communication between the people and the clergy; those who needed guidance had no one to approach. There was reverence and fear for the clergy, but no love. In short, the swamis and reverends in Sri Lanka then, though noble and compassionate, were kept on a different level from the other people. They kept themselves aloof. They were respected, but they were not teachers to whom anyone in trouble could freely run with love. In the north and east, the orthodox *pandits*, who were Saivites, preached with codes that could not be practiced. Many youths denounced temple worship. They became communists and rebels who scoffed at the idea of God.

"At such a time, Yogiraj Sri Swami Satchidananda Maharaj, professor of Yoga Vedanta Forest Academy of Rishikesh, great disciple of the great Himalayan Saint Sri Swami Sivananda Saraswathi, arrived in Sri Lanka to found a branch of the Divine Life Society. His very first act — most unusual with the existing insular attitude — was to stay at the Ramakrishna Mission. People flocked to see him — some through curiosity, some to criticize, and others hoping to find a monk different from the existing ones. All DLS swamis, like their great master, are simple and humble; and, of course, Gurudev is like that. His attitude bewildered the people of Sri Lanka. He was indeed different from what they were used to. Many *pandits* considered him a threat to the teachings of the Hindu religion, but those who were longing for a preceptor accepted him with gratitude. Yet, generally he was a great puzzle to everyone.

"The rich, the poor, people from all walks of life, of all castes and creeds, of all ages, were treated alike by him. The farmers and the government agents all had to sit together. Only the little children received special treatment. He was a friend to all. This communication between Gurudev and his devotees was something divine. It had to be seen to be believed. The religion he taught was the simple precepts of his great master. 'Serve and love' was taught first, and he practiced what he taught. As friend, companion, counselor, preceptor, his love was overflowing. People approached him with ease for advice. They asked him for guidance about everything from spiritual matters to how to bring up a child, from health problems to designing and building

128

houses and repairing vehicles. Work progressed at a tremendous pace. Retreats were held. Religious classes were conducted. At informal *satsangs*, people opened their hearts to him.

"Priests of all denominations came to the ashram, and Gurudev gave them clarification of their own religions. He did not believe in converting anyone as some other religious leaders did. He did not preach or set any impossible rules to be followed.

"If somebody was stranded without means of conveyance, or the bus was late, he would drive them to their destination. No work was beneath his dignity. What the people did not visibly notice was that they were being transformed slowly and steadily."

–Mrs. Rukmini Rasiah

Guru Poornima Day is held on the full moon in the month of July. It is a day set aside for special worship of the guru and lectures on his or her life. A week before Guru Poornima 1953, the Ceylon Divine Life devotees began collecting pictures of Master Sivanandaji, polishing frames and setting them up around the ashram.

Gurudev thought about this for a while, then told the disciples, "There are people from all different religions coming to me and I have invited them all to this celebration. If they are greeted with these pictures of Gurudev Sivanandaji exclusively, they might feel that their own teachers have been left out. After all, this is supposed to be a day for concentration on the guru, and there are many, many gurus for all the different people."

The devotees set about collecting pictures of masters from all religions. They covered the walls with pictures of Jesus, Buddha, Sri Aurobindo, Ramakrishna Paramahansa, Ramana Maharshi, Siva, Vishnu, Sri Shankaracharya, Saint Ramalingam, and many others.

The day was proclaimed "All Prophets Day" and became an annual event where the various heads of Ceylon's religious factions could come together and discourse on the truths behind the particular religions.

As the chairman, Gurudev summarized with the great universal truth he had believed all his life, the same truth his own Master taught and lived: "Truth is One; paths are many."

Ceylon's Minister of Post and Railways officially opened the new ashram on the 7th of November 1953. Soon afterward construction was started on an orphanage and free medical dispensary. The center also started a cottage industries section where unemployed girls and young women were given jobs doing hand weaving. About forty-five unemployed girls came to the ashram from many different communities. They were Buddhists, Hindus, Moslems and Christians. Gurudev often looked in on their workshop to see how things were progressing.

"Many times when I ask one of you the name of another girl, you say, 'Oh, she is a Buddhist girl' or 'She is a Hindu.' Wouldn't it be nicer if you said, 'She is my sister.'? At least while you are here, feel that you are all living together as one family. Try to feel that oneness."

The young women pulled together as a family. Their work became more efficient. "Why don't you start the day with a prayer? You all believe in God. Probably if you start and finish the day with a prayer, your yarn will not break in the middle. You'll be able to produce even more and earn better wages."

"But our religions are different. Whose prayer should we use?"

"We need not try to find a common prayer. Each day we'll chant prayers from all the religions responsively. That way you will be learning different prayers as well. As each of you repeats the prayers of the others, you'll become even closer to your sisters." That is exactly what happened.

Many people who have felt the misery of the world come to yoga. We don't force yoga onto anybody. Only when people want it do we offer them yoga. "Ask and it shall be given."

Gurudev's devotees loved him so much that they were eager to share his teachings in any way possible. Some of them decided that they would go from house to house, proclaiming the greatness of yoga. Gurudev quickly put a stop to these ideas, saying, "Do not force feed people who are not hungry. They will vomit. Just be patient. If someone asks you about yoga, just tell him a little bit. Then let him think about it. If he wants to know more, he will ask again; and you can tell him more. We are not interested in converting people. Just practice the teachings yourself. Your own health and contentment will be an inspiration to others."

Once a young man — unaware that he was talking to an automobile engineer — boasted to Gurudev about a new gadget he had invented to reduce the consumption of fuel in cars. It was obvious to anyone knowledgeable about car mechanics that this discovery would never work, but Gurudev listened intently and never contradicted his visitor.

When the self-proclaimed inventor had left, Gurudev turned to the ashramites in the room, "Well, he needed love and understanding. He has been very much neglected and needs acceptance. He will come back."

It wasn't long before the young man returned. This time he had come to confess that the gadget was not really a working invention but was a vision of his. Gurudev began explaining automobile mechanics to him.

When Miss R.'s relationship with her boyfriend came to an end she became increasingly depressed and unhappy. At these times she visited Gurudev for advice.

"I don't want to live anymore. I want to commit suicide," she announced.

Gurudev listed her alternatives, advising her on the ways in which she could carry on her life. "You must promise me that any time you feel like killing yourself, you will come to me before doing it. You can only do it after receiving my permission."

She agreed at the time; but a few weeks later her despondency became even deeper, and she bought a bottle of liquid rat poison.

At 10:30 in the morning she closed the door to her room, opened the bottle and prepared to drink the poison. At exactly this time, Gurudev was driving past her house and decided to pay her a surprise visit. He entered the drawing room and asked the servant for Miss R.

The servant walked to the closed bedroom door and tapped on it. "Swamiji is here. He wants to see you."

Miss R. sat very still on her bed. A feeling of fright and extreme embarrassment rose within her. She felt feverish. Quickly she opened her window and threw the bottle into the bushes. "Is he really here? Tell him I'm coming." It took a long time to pull herself together. "What would he think? I gave him my promise."

As the time passed, Gurudev decided to continue on his way. "This was only a casual call," he told the servant. "Tell her I'll see her later."

When Miss R. finally entered the room, her guru was gone. A few hours later she went to the ashram and confessed what had happened. "Gurudev you really saved my life. I'll never try that again."

One day, Gurudev was driving two agricultural officers — a Tamil and a Singhalese — to another town. The wife of the Tamil gentleman was seated in front with Gurudev. After a while, the officers asked, "Swami, do you mind if we smoke?"

"Oh, no. Not at all. Make yourselves comfortable," he answered. The woman in front was a great devotee, and she began trembling with anger at what she considered disrespect toward this great master. Gurudev turned his head and smiled at her.

The men started to light their cigarettes. The woman automatically opened the window to avoid the smoke. The air was very still that day, but suddenly a wind blew in from somewhere. The match was blown out. The matchbox — held by one of the men as he started to light the cigarettes again — was blown out the window.

Simply, naturally, the smoking ended.

The two sides are positive and negative, light and dark. Evil also is God's work. If you say evil is not God's work, then who created evil? There is only one God, and He allows these things to happen — good and the absence of good. Evil is only the absence of good. At the times we call evil, goodness is temporarily hidden just like at night when the sun is temporarily hidden. So the light is always there, but sometimes it gets hidden for a while.

Gurudev sat on the veranda of his cottage, watching a young man approach. The man was running; his face showed strain and anxiety. He reached the guru and prostrated full length, crying and holding Gurudev's feet.

"Swamiji, I am a terrible sinner. I have sinned against you. Please help me. Pardon me."

Gurudev lifted the man from his prone position and had him sit down. "What do you mean?" he asked gently. "How could you have sinned against me? This is the first time I've seen you here. I don't even know your name."

"Well, you may not know why or how, but I'll tell you. My younger brother comes to see you often. He is a very good devotee. But since the very beginning of your arrival here, I hated you — not really as an individual, but I hated your principles. I belonged to a group that doesn't believe in God and particularly not in all those religious rituals. I was its secretary and one of the group's guiding members. We didn't like your staying here in Trincomalee. We thought you converted people and took them into the religious fold. We decided to dispose of you — either by frightening you and driving you away or even by murdering you."

"Well, all this is new to me," Gurudev said. "I never knew anything about it. When did you try these things?"

The man asked him to recollect a few incidents. About three weeks after arriving in Trincomalee, Gurudev had been invited to give a lecture on Maha Sivaratri Day. It was held in February in a temple dedicated to Lord Siva.

"Do you remember a group of young men sitting right in front of you? We were with an elderly man. All during your lecture we made jokes and tried to create a disturbance."

"I do remember, but nothing serious happened. Nobody frightened me."

"The elderly man was the president of our group's branch in another town. We had asked him to come with us in order to ask you confusing questions that would bother you. But somehow he remained sitting quietly throughout the lecture; he didn't say anything. We too failed at creating the desired confusion. After the talk we asked him why he hadn't done his job. He told us, 'I had planned to do it, but I became spellbound listening to the Swami. His thoughts made good sense to me.' That was our first failure.

"Our second try was at a neighboring village where you went to give an address during a temple festival. We sent in a drunkard with a large dog. He reeled through the crowds, scaring people. He was even supposed to set the dog loose on you. Everyone seemed upset by him but you. At one point he asked you a question which you answered quite coolly. That seemed to calm him down. Soon after that, he left the grounds for good."

"The third time was one evening when you were returning from that same village late at night after a lecture. There is a part of the road that passes through dense jungle. We arranged for a group of people to block your car, pull you out and beat you up. Between two trees, they tied a thick rope across the road. We had counted on the fact that there is very little traffic on that road at night. We knew your car and what time you'd be passing. Just when we expected you, another car came down the road. The men had to remove the barricade to let it through. They didn't see that your car was right behind this one. When the first car passed, you followed directly behind and went by safely."

"It's all right," Gurudev assured him. "You shouldn't be so upset.

(top) *Guru Poornima is proclaimed "All Prophets Day," Trincomalee, 1953.*
(bottom) *It set a precedent for hundreds of others throughout the years, in many countries.*

134

The parents were delighted to meet their sannyasi *son at Sivananda Thapovanam, Trincomalee.*

After all, nothing happened to me. Why didn't you continue?"

"I couldn't do it anymore. The whole business began to make me sick. Every night I had horrible dreams. I became frightened of the mysterious power with which you caused our failures. Gradually, some of our close members left and became your devotees. I became certain that something terrible would happen to me. Now I almost feel as if I am going mad. I come to you as a devotee. Please help me. I'll do anything you desire. If you want, I'll set fire to my old office and dispose of it once and for all. I'll get rid of all those people still working against you. I'll..."

Gurudev stopped him. "There's no need to do those things. You were the foremost member of that group. When your mind began to change, you became a good man. The same thing can happen to those people also. Let them see a change for the better in you. Then they'll also be changed. Pray for them. Once you confess, everything is pardoned. Don't bother about the past. Think of the future. Come here often and use your energy to help me with my work."

Let us not think we can learn things only through the intellect. You can read things in a book, but a book can never teach you.

Gurudev was invited to lecture in Colombo, the capital of Ceylon. The editor of *Sunthanthiran*, a weekly Tamil newspaper, prepared to interview him. Mr. Sivanayagam was a hero to thousands of Ceylon's youths because of his intellectual and basically anti-religious viewpoint. He was a well-read, influential man; and, though not truly an atheist, he was against religious ritual of any kind.

At the interview, the editor represented himself simply as a reporter. He devised a number of difficult questions through which he hoped to confound the Swami and show him in a bad light to the readers. To the interviewer's amazement, Gurudev deftly fielded each question, replying with concise and logical answers.

Mr. Sivanayagam became a close devotee. He published Gurudev's answers in his newspaper, alongside the appropriate questions.

"To answer our intricate questions in the proper philosophical way and with common sense, we have a great swami now in Trincomalee — the Swami Satchidananda."

The response of the young readers was overwhelming. They sent

136

hundreds of questions. To answer all of their questions, a regular column, "Way to Peace," was soon featured in the paper.

In Trincomalee a group was formed to open all Hindu temples to the untouchables. Gurudev was a member of that committee, which also included the Chairman of the Urban Council of Trincomalee and a member of Parliament. They organized a large group of untouchables which went from temple to temple, chanting and repeating their demands. From that time on, many temples were open and all people were permitted to enter and worship.

Whenever a chance for further service comes, serve wholeheartedly without losing your equilibrium.

By 1955, Gurudev's travels around the island of Ceylon had greatly increased. People were constantly asking for his services. Trincomalee was located on the northeastern seacoast, a great distance from many other parts of Ceylon. A group of devotees in the hill capital of Kandy decided to start a branch of the Divine Life Society, and they persuaded Gurudev that this was a more centrally located spot than Trincomalee. From Kandy he could easily drive all over Ceylon to answer the requests for his presence. He decided to make the move since Mataji would be in Trincomalee and could easily accommodate the needs of the devotees there.

Beautiful Kandy is surrounded by green hills and lakes. Once its botanical gardens were the largest in the world. Its temperature usually remains in the seventy-degree range. The Temple of the Tooth, the biggest Buddhist temple, is located in Kandy. Its relic is a tooth from the Buddha. Until the reign of Ceylon's last king, paradisiacal Kandy was the capital city. After the foreign invasion, materialism ruled over aesthetics, and the capital was moved to the port city of Colombo.

In September of 1955, Gurudev and the Kandy devotees began to search for a place to house the center. They discovered a lovely coconut garden which contained a huge building — an old *choultry* — and an adjoining temple situated on the banks of the Mahaveli Ganga.

They went to the temple trustees to ask for permission to use this property for a yoga ashram. Immediately the property was handed over, and the devotees set to work repairing buildings and refurbishing the grounds. The new ashram was opened on October 29.

(top) *The Divine Life Society, Kandy Branch, Satchidananda Thapovanam, founded 29 October 1955.* (bottom) *The inaugural procession.*

At first Gurudev lived there alone, but soon devotees came to join him, one by one. Eventually fifteen ashramites lived there by the river, planning discussions, classes and yoga treatments for various physical illnesses.

Kandy was surrounded by tea plantations owned by the British companies. The planters in charge were mostly Britons who ruled like Rajas over the thousands of Indian laborers. The laborers were herded together like cattle into small rooms with pathetic sanitary conditions. Due to hardship, these Indians had gotten into the habit of drinking alcohol. Most of their money went toward this habit, and many of the families were nearly starving. Gurudev beautifully served these laborers. His loving advice and guidance transformed them beyond recognition. To them, he was God Himself. Simultaneously, the transformation in the rulers, many of whom had become devotees to Gurudev, was unbelievable. Soon, the laborers no longer cringed before their bosses, to be booted and whipped as before. Instead they were provided with community centers, reading rooms, places of worship and sanitary facilities. The wives of the planters started visiting the sick and the needy. Into this atmosphere came the riots and massacre of the Tamils in 1958; but the planters protected the laborers.

As the riots took place between the Tamil and Singhalese communities, Gurudev worked for peace and goodwill among the people. People of all nationalities came freely to him for advice and guidance, and he never stopped patiently teaching them about the importance of love for all people regardless of the superficial differences.

A group of college women approached Gurudev and asked what he felt about the dowry system. "Do not encourage it," he replied. "The boys should marry the girls, not their dowries." The young women formed their own associations and vehemently denounced the dowry system. The parents were helpless to protest. The youth of Ceylon felt that, in Gurudev, they had found a loving and understanding father. From the start, his ways had been so radical that by now he was known as the "Revolutionary Monk."

We will never see the world full of enlightened people. If that should happen, the purpose of the world would be at an end because the purpose of the world is to shape people. It is almost like an assembly line in a factory — even as some are coming off the belt as finished pro-

ducts, others are just starting. More and more souls come in, and the world shapes them, reforming their minds. We will always see people in all different stages of development in this factory that is the world.

A branch of the Divine Life Society was inaugurated at Colombo. Then a Jaffna branch was founded. Gurudev made regular visits to the tea plantations to hold discussions and prayer meetings with the workers. His main theme during these talks was an attempt to get the laborers to educate their children and turn them away from chronic drinking of alcohol, and squandering of their limited funds.

He ended each talk in evangelical style. "Is there anyone who disagrees with my point of view that drinking is an evil habit?"

No answer came from the group.

"If you accept that it brings evil effects — sickness, quarrels, wastage of money — how many of you are ready to stop that habit from this day forth? Any person who is that courageous should come forward and take a public vow to stop drinking from today onward. This is the real reward you can give me."

There was a complete hush as each man examined his neighbor's face to see what *he* would do. Cautiously one man came forward. In a low voice he said, "Because of Swamiji's talk I realize the evil effects of drinking. I am really thankful for it. From today onward I promise not to touch a drop of alcohol."

Gurudev lifted the man's arm like a referee with a boxing champion. "Here is a courageous man. Give him a hand." There was thunderous applause. "Let us pray for this man so that he will stick to this vow throughout his entire life." After the silence, he asked, "Is there anyone else?"

One by one men hesitantly stepped forward. There were a few times when more than 150 came up to take the vow.

Once a young man behaved dishonorably toward one of the young women at the ashram. Gurudev was away from Kandy at the time of the incident. When he returned, the boy was so frightened that he took two of Gurudev's devotees with him to help him face the Master. After listening to their explanations, Gurudev suddenly rose with a fierce look and roared, "Do you think my *sannyasin's* robes will prevent me from giving a thrashing to anyone who harms my children?"

140

"*I will never drink again!*" *The tea plantation laborers publicly vowed to stay away from alcoholic beverages. Gurudev gave them his blessings and congratulations.*

Whether he would have done it or not was never known. The boys fled from the room.

In the north of the island, many young people were disillusioned with the way religion had been presented. Communism was spreading among them. This was the most difficult area of Ceylon at that time. Some of the young people were beyond control. Every three months, Gurudev went to this area, conducted long retreats and regular classes in the *Bhagavad Gita*, the *Upanishads*, and the lives of the Hindu saints. These events were attended by people from all areas of Jaffna, and some villagers walked many miles to attend the classes.

Gurudev never spoke against religion. His interpretation of the scriptures and his attitude were such that the young people understood and accepted them. After *bhajan* in places of worship, the last chant of the evening was one for the well-being of all. It ended with the words, "Let the justice of the Saivites prevail." But Gurudev always said, "Let the justice of the Almighty prevail." Those Saivites who had opposed him at the start were very angry about this and tried to disrupt Gurudev's meetings with rude questions. He calmly answered them.

Gurudev had consented to give a public talk in one particular village that was overrun by disruptive communist youths. Some Saivites were arranging to cause trouble at the lecture, and the DLS organizers received calls asking them to cancel the program. The organizers approached Gurudev; they needed advice about whether to cancel or not. Before they even spoke, he said, "Change the title of my talk to 'Hinduism is Communism.' Announce it in all the newspapers, and postpone it by three days."

The meeting was held at an open air theater near a temple and it was filled to capacity for the program. Many boys sat in the trees. The devotees were worried — stones could easily be hurled from those trees. The noise was terrible, and the chief organizer appealed to the boys to listen silently. They could, he said, ask as many questions as they liked after the talk. The rowdy boys became quiet and listened attentively, but some of the others started challenging Gurudev. These people were fanatics and believe that Lord Siva was the only God who could grant salvation. They quoted scriptures with interpretations to suit their beliefs. Gurudev patiently gave the correct explanations and said, "Hinduism is like the ocean. All other religions are like rivers and tributaries flowing into it. This is so because true Hinduism embraces, accepts and accommodates all other religions as valid paths to the same goal. That is why I chose that particular title for this talk. In a way we can say that Hinduism is the real communism because it views all paths as equal."

The *pandits* quietly left the theater, but the students stayed. They had been initially attracted by the unusual title of the talk, but soon Gurudev's words had fired their interest in spiritual matters. They went on asking questions until the early hours of the morning. Untiringly, Gurudev spoke to them, convincing them of the spiritual path.

One student asked, "How can I worship other gods when I worship Siva?"

Gurudev replied, "When you go to visit your parents, will you not pay your respects by greeting the other relatives in the house?" Murmurs of understanding rippled through the crowd.

After this meeting, many sub-branches — called "The Rays of the Sun" — of the DLS were formed. The troublesome youths became Gurudev's ardent devotees and regularly attended the retreats in Kandy.

At Kundasala, near the Kandy ashram, there was a prison camp for inmates who had shown good behavior. This was a minimum security area, where the prisoners farmed the land, harvested the crops, sold the produce and were allowed to divide the profit among themselves. The Divine Life Society members built a temple for these men and regularly conducted prayer meetings. The success of this program was so great that officials soon asked Gurudev and the ashram members to provide the same service at the maximum security facility, Bogambura Prison in Kandy.

At that time only ten or fifteen men were in the capital punishment ward — each one securely locked within his own tiny cell. Only Gurudev and a few others were allowed to go in and talk to the prisoners individually. If they felt that particular men were trustworthy they would suggest to the officials that these prisoners be allowed to come out of the cells for their talks. The inmates were given holy pictures, books and *mantrams* to occupy their thoughts while passing time behind bars. Many of them found comfort and inspiration; quite a few totally reformed and were released from the prison. They attributed this change in their fate to their prayers and the grace of God. One former inmate even turned his farm into an ashram and became a great yogi.

Not all of the prisoners were able to undergo such a change, and one of these men was sentenced to be hanged for murder. Early one morning, Gurudev received a call from the prison warden asking him to come as soon as possible.

"What's wrong?" Gurudev asked.

"This morning we are going to hang that prisoner, and his last request is that you should be here when he is hanged. He wants to be able to die seeing your face. If you feel uncomfortable, Swamiji, we will understand. You are free to refuse. I'm simply telling you his request."

Gurudev gave it some thought. It would be uncomfortable to stand in front of a man as he was hanged. "Who am I to refuse his last wish? Somehow he feels this will help him, and I would want to do anything to bring him comfort at the moment of death. Surely God will give me the strength to face it." He walked out the door of the ashram.

As soon as he spotted Gurudev, the condemned man ran to him and grabbed his hands, crying and begging and praying. "Please, please bless me so that I may get liberated because of this." Gurudev gave his blessings.

The guards led the prisoner to a platform where he stood silently, hands folded in prayer, gazing at Gurudev. His eyes totally focused on the Swami as if he were deeply absorbing that holy vibration. Gurudev stood at his post, three or four feet away, praying for the peace of the man's soul.

Even after the hood was put over his head, the prisoner asked, "Is he still there?"

"Yes, yes, the Swami is still standing here."

The rope was placed around his neck, and the warden silently motioned to Gurudev that he could turn away now. Praying softly for the condemned man, Gurudev turned as the hanging took place.

When you stop running after things, they will all start running after you. When you no longer want things, all the things will want you.

The devotees at the Kandy DLS were concerned about Gurudev's frequent travels. People were constantly asking him to visit their towns or centers, and at least once a month he traveled all over the island. Every time this happened someone would drive to the ashram to get him, drive him to the destination, drive him back again, and then go home. It seemed so inconvenient, for the drivers as well as for Gurudev.

"Swamiji knows how to drive a car," a devotee stated one day. "Why don't we simply collect the money and buy a car for his use?" The others thought this was an excellent idea.

When news of the project reached the wealthy owner of a tea plantation, he came forward to say, "There is no need to go and collect the money rupee by rupee. I will just buy the car for you, Swamiji."

"That is very kind of you, sir," Gurudev replied, "but do you see how happy they all are about this project? Their hearts are in it. If you give the car, it will be *your* car. If they collect the money, they will feel so happy, so proud: 'Ah, we collected the money, contributed the money and bought the car!' There will be a lot of love behind that."

The devotees began collecting, and the contributions came in — one rupee here, five rupees there. One day Gurudev and some others went to Colombo to look at a car. The owner was an Englishman who had brought the car from his home country.

Gurudev first looked around the garage that housed the automobile. It was impeccable. Next he began looking at the car itself. The body looked beautiful. The engine was in perfect shape. Then he looked in the trunk. There were two full bags of sand.

"Why do you have this sand here, sir?"

"Well, Swami, normally I don't use this car much. I have another small car for commuting to work. Once a week or once every two weeks my wife and I go out driving in this car. That's why it has such low mileage. Anyway, we both sit in the front seat, and with the un-equal load the car bounces a bit. So just to have even weight I put the sandbags in the trunk. That way the car doesn't get shaken up."

Gurudev was impressed by this kind of care for a vehicle. "I can see that it is in beautiful condition. I don't even have to drive it. How much do you want?"

"Seven thousand rupees."

"Well, sir," Gurudev said, "this car is worth much more than that, but this is a very good cause. I would like you to sell it to us for sixty-five hundred rupees."

The Englishman looked closely at Gurudev. "I have never seen a man do business this way. You say that the car is actually worth more, but still you want me to sell it for less?"

"That's right. If you sell it for more, you will gain more monetarily. But if you sell it to us for less, because it is a good cause you will reap many more benefits."

"As I said, I have never met anyone like you! You are so frank and honest. Yes, fine. I accept your offer."

The car continued to serve Gurudev as long as he lived in Ceylon. When he left the country the treasurer of the DLS, Mr. Shanmugam, continued to use the vehicle. It served for many, many years without ever breaking down. The love with which it was purchased kept it going.

During a *satsang* at the Trincomalee Divine Life Society, the secretary told Gurudev that one person was not happy about having contributed toward the car. That person had said, "Why should a swami have a car? It's not really necessary for a *sannyasi*. Because you are coming around for contributions I'll give you some money, but I'm not totally happy about it."

When Gurudev heard this, he expressed his displeasure with the idea of taking money from people who didn't believe in the cause to which they contributed. He spoke to those gathered for the *satsang*. "I ask you to be open and frank. Who is it that was unhappy about this contribution? Is there someone among you?"

One gentleman slowly raised his hand.

"Sir, why did you do that? If you weren't happy about it you shouldn't have given the money. Knowing that you don't feel right about it makes me concerned. I would like the treasurer to return that money to you."

"Oh no, Swamiji, it's all right. I gave the money. Now it is being used. It doesn't matter."

"No," Gurudev insisted. "When you buy a car you pay for each part of it. Perhaps your ten rupees purchased a bolt on a wheel. Since you gave it with an uneasy feeling, that bolt might be sitting uneasily. Suppose I am driving over a very rough road, and that uneasy bolt gets shaken off the wheel. What will happen? The car will go into a ditch. Because of one bad nut the whole car will be ruined, and I may be injured also. Please accept your money."

The man humbly fell at Gurudev's feet and started crying. "Please forgive me. I was a fool to think that way. I realize that the car is not for *you*. We are giving it to you so that you may serve us all better. If not for that car you wouldn't have been able to come here today. Now I am giving the money with gratitude and understanding. Please pardon me."

"Don't worry," Gurudev gently told him. "If you truly want to give it now, that is fine. I'm not asking for it, but I will accept it. In the future just know that when you give something it should be with your whole heart. If it can't be that way, don't give it. Never give something with a grudging feeling."

After an interval of one year, Gurudev returned to a particular tea plantation. As he ended his talk, a well-dressed man came to the platform carrying a large multicolored garland. He turned to Gurudev. "I garland the Swami and would also like to offer him this ring from my finger." He slipped off a shiny gold band. "Because of Gurudev's last visit I took a vow never to drink again. From then on I found it very easy to save money. I bought all the jewelry my wife now wears, her silk sari and all my clothing. My child is being educated in a good way. If you all follow my lead, you can have these things too."

Gurudev smiled broadly and returned the ring. "Although I am very grateful, swamis don't usually wear rings. Take it back and save it for your son. God bless you. Stick to your new life and set examples for many more."

A large segment of Ceylon's poor worked on these plantations. Their one- or two-room huts stood in long, straight rows of tin sheet. The women ambled in and out of the huts, cooking, doing laundry, and tending to the crowds of young children who played in the dirt.

Whenever Gurudev stayed overnight he visited the workers in their dwellings before leaving the following morning.

Once he entered the main room of a small hut. Its walls were a collage of color. Framed pictures hung on nails everywhere, covering every wall. The images of Lord Ganesh, Lord Subramanya, Mahatma Gandhi and Pandit Nehru were interspersed with full-length color portraits of various movie stars.

Gurudev pointed to the elephant-headed features of Lord Ganesh. He turned to his host who stood next to his young wife. "Do you worship this picture with incense and camphor?"

The man blushed with pride. "Yes, Swamiji, I do that."

"And to this?" Gurudev indicated Lord Subramanya.

"Yes, Swamiji."

"Do you offer that same kind of worship to this one also?" Casually he gestured to one of the glamorous female movie stars.

The man looked at his feet. "No, Swamiji," he whispered.

"Who is this?" the guru teased. "Parashakti?"

The man could barely be heard. "No, Swamiji, it's just a photo."

"Ah yes. I see. But who is it?"

The wife answered, "Swamiji, it is just a picture of a cinema star."

Smiling, Gurudev looked from the man to his wife. "When you have such a beautiful wife, who is really a goddess, why should you have to look at imitations like this?"

The laborer followed Gurudev's gaze from picture to wife. "Yes," he agreed. "I can see that." He took down the movie stars' photographs and replaced them with pictures of aspects of God.

(top) Board members of the Divine Life Society, Kandy.
(bottom) The final day of the yoga retreat, Kandy Thapovanam.

The Right Hand of Bahaullah, Dr. Samandhari — at right of Gurudev — and the representative of the local Bahai group. At left of Gurudev — Dr. Samandhari's son.

The Bahai faith, founded in Persia in 1863 by Bahaullah, emphasizes the spiritual unity of all humanity. It wasn't surprising that Gurudev felt a natural accord with the followers of such a path; and they were naturally drawn to him. Wherever he traveled, he visited Bahai temples.

Dr. Samandhari was known as the Right Hand of Bahaullah and was deeply revered by the followers of the Bahai faith. He and his son stayed at the Kandy Thapovanam for several days in order to visit with Gurudev and the devotees. The doctor also gave several lectures, which had been organized by Gurudev.

There were many discussions about the essential unity which underlies the wide diversity in the creation. Gurudev and Dr. Samandhari each enjoyed the company of the other. They shared the knowledge that in the Spirit all people are one.

149

My guru was a saint. He never denied anybody anything.

During Gurudev's All-India Tour a young graduate in Bombay had become very attached to him. The man, Mr. Sreenivasan, decided to leave his job and follow the Swami back to Rishikesh. At that time he was employed by a military concern, and Gurudev knew that the man would have a great deal of difficulty if he left this job without giving notice. He suggested that Mr. Sreenivasan come to the Himalayas only after finishing his work.

By the time Mr. Sreenivasan arrived at Ananda Kutir, Gurudev had already left for Ceylon. He wrote to Gurudev for instructions and was told to stay on at Ananda Kutir and eventually, if he wished, take *sannyas diksha* from Master Sivanandaji.

After some time, Gurudev Sivananda noted that Mr. Sreenivasan indeed did have potential as a *sannyasin*. He asked the man if he wished to take initiation.

"Swamiji, I would love to, but I would like to get it from Swami Satchidananda."

Instead of answering, "If Satchidananda is your guru then I am your grandguru and well ready to give you *sannyas*," the Master asked him, "What are you going to do then? Would you like to wait until he visits here or would you rather get his permission to take *sannyas* from me on his behalf?"

"Yes, Swamiji. I will write to Swami Satchidanandaji and get his permission." Mr. Sreenivasan wrote to Ceylon.

Immediately, Satchidanandaji wrote to his disciple: "Don't wait for me. Take advantage of the opportunity to receive initiation from the great Master Swami Sivanandaji Maharaj."

Mr. Sreenivasan accepted his advice but told Master Sivanandaji at the time of initiation, "I am seeing Swami Satchidanandaji in you — not Swami Sivanandaji — please give me this *sannyas* as Swami Satchidananda."

Master Sivanandaji just smiled and complied.

Meat has more toxins than vegetables. It contains purine, and purine gives rise to cholesterol; but that is merely physical. Food has an affect on the mind also. To see the difference between meat eaters and vegetarians, go to any

zoo. See the animals who live on meat. Most of the carnivores must be caged, and even in the cage they become restless; they pace constantly. Look at the herbivorous animals — cows, goats, horses, elephants. With what innocence they look at you. They are so passive. It is not that they are weak; they are strong, but their strength is a passive strength. The tiger can kill the elephant, it has a killing strength, but it can't pull the great weights that the elephant can. We want that pulling strength, that *sattwic* strength.

The University of Ceylon in Perudania is located near Kandy. Shortly after Gurudev's arrival in Ceylon he accepted an invitation to hold a discussion with the students there. As he entered the hall a great buzz began. Ceylon has mostly Buddhist *bhikkus* who are bald and clean-shaven; the swamis in that area have the same appearance. Many of the students had never seen a man like this before — orange gown, shoulder-length hair, a long beard. He was introduced by the presiding education officer, Mr. Somasegaram, and proceeded to give a half-hour introductory speech, pointing out the importance of a vegetarian diet. Afterward, he invited questions.

Immediately, a very dapper-looking student (European clothes, short, slicked-back hair and pointed shoes) stood up and raised his hand. In an eloquent tone he began, "May I ask you a question?"

"Certainly. Go ahead."

"I hope you won't be upset by it."

"There is no need for me to get upset. Please ask your question."

The young man cleared his throat loudly. "Swamiji, you know the cow eats grass." He paused for effect.

"I know, and so does everyone else."

"Then I eat the flesh of the cow. Logically, why can't I say that I too am eating grass?"

The hall shook with applause. The student had apparently rebutted the argument for vegetarianism and successfully defended the eating of meat.

"Logically, you are right," Gurudev responded. "If the cow eats grass and you eat her, then you are eating grass." The students looked approvingly at their fellow debater, who smugly received their glances. Gurudev continued, "Now, do you know what the grass eats?"

(top) The well-known Buddhist bhikku Sri Ananda Maithreya *(far right) often brought his student* bhikkus *to visit Gurudev and seek advice on Patanjali's Raja Yoga Sutras. The bhikku on the far left later became the head of the London Buddhist monastery.*

(bottom) One of many monthly ecumenical gatherings — Hindus, Buddhists, Catholics and Muslims — Father Pillai is on Gurudev's left.

(left) "He teaches people the way to happiness and peace of the heart," said Father Boudens of Gurudev.

(below) At Jaffna Teachers College after a month-long Hatha Yoga course organized by the Education Department.

153

The student was thrown off balance. "The grass?"

"The grass eats mud, and not only that but various kinds of fecal matter also. That is how the grass lives, by eating such a diet. So when the grass eats this, the cow eats the grass, and you eat the cow, logically we can say you are eating fecal matter."

Another uproar ensued. The students hooted with laughter and stamped their feet.

In future talks only respectful questions dealing with the methods and practices of yoga, were leveled at the Swami.

A Buddhist *bhikku* was interested in learning Patanjali's *Yoga Sutras*. He came to Gurudev in order to clear up some doubts. In the course of conversation, the topic of diet came up.

"Swamiji, what food is most beneficial to a person interested in meditation?"

"The simpler the diet, the better. Plain vegetarian food is best."

"In that case I have a problem. As a *bhikku*, I beg for my food from householders. I must eat what they give me, and very often they give me meat."

"Why don't you simply refuse the meat and accept only vegetarian food?"

"Oh, Swamiji, my custom is to not refuse anything the householder offers. I accept it, bow and walk away."

"You need not refuse it," Gurudev advised. "Take it and then offer it in turn to some hungry dogs. When the people come to know that you are not eating the meat, they won't offer it. It is only because they know you eat it that they give it. They would just give you vegetables if that is what you ate."

The *bhikku* shook his head. "No. Our custom is to accept anything that is given."

"That is only the mind's excuse for you to eat meat. Will you eat whatever is offered?"

"We have to."

"Suppose a person gives you a ball of cow dung. Will you eat it?"

When the shock of such a question wore off, the *bhikku* answered, "Yes, yes. I would accept it."

"But would you eat it?"

"Ummm...I wouldn't actually *eat* it but I would use it to wash the room in my hut." (In India and Sri Lanka the floors of village houses are often made of plain, hardened clay. A solution of cow dung is mixed with a liberal amount of water and used to coat the surface of the clay floors, giving them a pleasant green color as it disinfects.)

154

"In the same way, don't actually eat the offered meat. Accept it and let some poor dogs eat it. They will make good use of it."

"Swamiji, I understand. I can see it is a trick of the mind to bring in all kinds of excuses. If I really wanted to live on a vegetarian diet, I could find the means to do it."

Your first duty is to make the body healthy. Without health nothing can be achieved. Not only the higher goal, but even worldly success is based on your health, your physical and mental condition. Whatever you want to do — spiritual, social, national — you have to do with your body. Your thoughts are manifested through your body. You serve through your body.

Sri Tirunavukarasu, a devotee of Gurudev, worked in a bank not far from the ashram. He was asthmatic, and from time to time he was seized by a serious, choking attack. Whenever he felt an attack coming on, he hurried to the ashram, entered Gurudev's office and, without a word, sat by his side. Sometimes he would stay for half an hour, sometimes longer. As soon as the attack passed he would quietly stand up, bow and, again without a word, go back to his job.

"In Tennekumbura, a little outside of Kandy, lives one of the most well-known *sannyasis*, Swami Satchidananda, a beautiful apostle-head who could have come directly from the Passion Play of Oberammergau.

"There he lives very simply, very humbly. No luxury. Nothing to get attached to. In a spacious room that occupies the largest part of his house, there are only the most necessary pieces of furniture: a small writing desk, a seat and a small table with a couple of chairs to receive people who don't sit on the floor in the Eastern way. In the middle, everything is free. There on a mat he does his yoga postures and sits in meditation.

"Against the wall one sees a few Hindu statues, a Buddha and also a Crucifix. Also, a few sayings are hanging there; they give explanations about this strange mixture: 'Truth is nobody's monopoly,' and also 'Truth is One, but the ways that lead to it are many.' The Swami is a Hindu, but he has a reverence for all other religions. He studies the

Holy Scriptures of Buddhism. He reads the Bible. 'One can learn from the founders of all religions,' he says, 'because they are all prophets. They speak in the name of God and manifest in their lives some of His qualities.'

"He teaches people the way to happiness and the peace of the heart. He stressed very much that people who stay in the middle of life should have the courage to retire every day for a few minutes from the hurry of existence and come to rest with God.

"Swami Satchidananda speaks slowly, calmly, simply. When one asks him questions, he does not interrupt but allows the person to speak out quietly. Before he answers he reflects a little while in silence. One feels that he has an immense respect for the people he talks with, that they can teach him something by their questions. When he gives explanations, he speaks with examples and parables — just as Christ must have done.

"I asked him what he finds most difficult in his life as a *sannyasi*. The answer was deep and very sincere, 'It is not easy to be detached from detachment.'"

–from a Dutch article by
Father R. Boudens, a Belgian monk

Selfless people are the most peaceful. They express their state of peace and remain in it by performing every action just for the sake of the action — not by expecting even one thing in return, not even appreciation. If something should come their way, they allow that, set it aside and keep it, maybe pass it on later. But they don't *wait* for results.

Master Sivanandaji was very pleased with the work of his disciple in Ceylon. From Rishikesh, he wrote: "Through dynamic selfless service you have won the hearts of the people of Ceylon. Your radiant personality and spiritual aura attract people to you; and your genuine humility and eagerness to serve all earns their admiration and affection. The newspaper reports reveal that your inspiring discourses command great respect and lead the men and women of Ceylon along the path of selflessness, unity and dynamic service to the goal of peace and prosperity. I pray to the Lord to confer upon you continued radiant health and long life! May God bless you."

A young Moslem man owned a shop in Dambulla, between Kandy and Trincomalee. Though he was of the Islamic faith, he liked Gurudev's teachings so much that he often came to the ashram to practice the various aspects of yoga. He incorporated these practices into his daily routine along with the prayers of his faith. Gurudev always stopped to visit this Moslem when traveling through that area, and he became well-acquainted with the entire family.

On one of these visits the man introduced a young woman to Gurudev. "Swamiji, this is my sister's daughter. For years she has been suffering from severe asthma. I have talked to her about the yoga practices but she doesn't want to learn them from me. Would you mind doing something to relieve her of the problem?"

"Well, I can tell her some things to do, but how will I know if she is doing them properly?"

"Swamiji, I was hoping that she could come and stay at the ashram for a while."

Gurudev was surprised. Normally Moslems don't let people of another faith into the inner section of their house where the women can be seen. Yet here was a devout man sending a woman of his family to an ashram.

"Yes. I am happy for her to come, but I know the rules of your faith. Will your family members agree to that?" Gurudev asked.

"They have all come to know and love you so much. They completely trust you; there is no hesitation at all. We feel she is like your own daughter. She has great respect for you and is willing to go there. Will you accept her?"

"If you have that kind of confidence in me, and if it won't disturb anyone in your family, I will be glad to do it."

The young woman stayed at the ashram for three weeks. By that time, the asthmatic condition had vastly improved. In a state of renewed health, she returned to her delighted family.

Satchidananda Thapovanam, as the ashram was called by Gurudev's devotees, became a meeting place for government officials. People from many different political parties held offices as trustees in the ashram. At one meeting, five different party leaders, Tamils as well as Singhalese, sat down together to discuss the welfare of the center.

Various clergy members came to the ashram as well. They organized an All-Religions Group that met once a month, sometimes at the ashram, sometimes at a seminary, sometimes at the home of a Buddhist or at an Islamic mosque.

Mr. Osmund De Silva, Inspector General of the Ceylon police, became a devotee, and Gurudev began to conduct Hatha Yoga classes for the men in the Police Training School. Many followed Mr. De Silva's lead and became students of yoga. Even though Mr. De Silva was a Buddhist he always visited Gurudev on his birthday in order to receive special blessings.

"Head in solitude and hands in society is a great ideal placed before us by the sages of India. All problems in life will get themselves automatically solved if this ideal is put into practice. The Satchidananda Thapovanam is successfully giving it a practical shape. To be in the calm atmosphere of this *thapovanam* is more than being in solitude. Swami Satchidanandaji goes into society all over the island and goads men and women of right type into religious activities. As such, action and inaction of the *Gita* model is splendidly demonstrated here. I wish this *thapovanam* all success in all of its endeavors."

Sri Swami Chidbhavanandaji Maharaj
Tirupparaithurai

Gurudev was visited in the *thapovanam* by India's philosopher Sri C.P. Ramaswamy Iyer. The Indian High Commissioner, Mr. Guntavia, was also a frequent guest. Gurudev conducted Hatha Yoga classes at the home of Mr. Jean Beloir, French Consul to Ceylon. Mr. Cecil Lyon, the American Ambassador, and his wife became interested in yoga, and they asked Gurudev to conduct monthly classes in Hatha Yoga and meditation at their home for themselves, their friends and the embassy people.

The Kandy municipality organized a civic reception for Sri Rajendra Prasad, President of India at the time. It was to be a big and extravagant affair, but a major problem arose. Who would officially receive the President? Kandy's population consisted mainly of Singhalese and Indian Tamils. If a member of one group were chosen, the other group was sure to feel slighted. Finally the authorities unanimously decided to ask Sri Swami Satchidananda to garland and receive the President on behalf of both groups. Sri Rajendra Prasad was known to be a great devotee of Master Sivanandaji and had visited Ananda Kutir many times. Gurudev could, therefore, represent his guru as well as the city of Kandy.

(top) Sri Swami Chidbhavanandaji is received at the Colombo Airport by Sri Gurudev and Sri Swami Prematmanandaji *(right)*, head of the Colombo Ramakrishna Mission.

(bottom) Gala Jayanthi celebration in Kandy.

159

Visitors to the *thapovanam* left feeling renewed and inspired. The ashram's files were rapidly filling with letters of glowing tributes.

"I had the opportunity to visit the Satchidananda Thapovanam and to receive the inspiring memories of Swami Sivanandaji Maharaj whose ideals and dedicated life of service and *tapas* this hermitage on the banks of a great river seeks to cherish and commemorate. I wish it all fulfillment."

Sri C. P. Ramaswamy Iyer
Nilgiries, India

"My stay at this ashram has been as welcome as an oasis in the desert of life to a weary traveler. The freedom, peace and beauty afforded at this 'Heaven of Rest' gives lasting benefit and solace to a tired soul. I take with me lasting memories of this precious experience and leave the heartfelt gratitude of a Western seeker."

Mr. Peter Bright, England

"It was with great pleasure that I spent three days with my children at Satchidananda Thapovanam, where they had lessons in yoga *asanas*. The radiant personality of Swami Satchidanandaji brings renewed faith and hope to every heart. Spiritual equality for men and women of all religions is one of the greatest gifts of this peaceful ashram. My children and I offer our sincere and heartfelt thanks to all those who are here to help us in one way or other as a labor of love; indeed for them it is a source of spiritual joy."

T. K. Wattegama

Every three months the Jaffna Divine Life Society, which Gurudev had inaugurated, invited him to come for fifteen days and give programs, classes on the *Bhagavad Gita* and discussions of Patanjali's *Yoga Sutras*. The secretary of the Jaffna DLS, Mrs. Rukmini Rasiah, organized a very full schedule indeed. Almost every day Gurudev taught a six o'clock morning Hatha Yoga class. After breakfast he traveled to a local school to give *satsang* for the students. After lunch there was a short time for rest. Then he was off again to another school for the afternoon. Evening brought a regularly scheduled public lecture.

During these visits Gurudev always found time to visit the great *siddha* Yogar Swamigal; he belonged to a long line of *siddhas* who performed miracles, apparently without even meaning to do so.

The guru of Yogar Swamigal was Chellappa Swami, a yogi who kept strict watch over his senses and even played tricks on them. Occasionally he collected provisions for a feast and prepared a special delicious meal. After serving it into his bowl he would address his senses, "Ah, yes. Already you are salivating. What a wonderful meal you are going to have! Are you really so hungry?"

Suddenly Chellappa Swami would kick the bowl so that every tasty morsel of food spilled into the dirt. "Okay, now go and eat it if you are so hungry, you unruly tongue." In this way he trained the senses.

As with many great *siddhas*, Yogar Swamigal did not allow many people to be with him. There were usually one or two disciples looking after his needs, but otherwise he strongly discouraged anyone who wanted to visit him: "What do you want? You don't need me. Just go! Get out!"

It was not unusual for him to be sitting quietly then suddenly turn to a disciple and say, "Ah! Are you aware of that man headed this way? He's coming to ask me which horse will win in the races. Kick him out!" When the obedient disciple went to check, he would see someone just approaching the gate.

Yogar Swamigal was always pleased, however, to see Gurudev. He never spoke much but simply invited his visitor to sit with him. Occasionally the *siddha* simply asked, "How is everything?. . .It's all fine. Everything was already planned long ago. Don't worry; all will be well." Many of the Divine Life Society members were welcomed by him.

One day Yogar Swamigal fell and broke his hip bone. Confined to the hospital room, he refused all visitors and shouted at the well-meaning people who came, "Get out! Get out!" However, when anyone from the Divine Life Society visited, he would say, "Okay. Come in. Sit and chant." He always asked them about Gurudev.

In day-to-day life try to detach yourself from things. This attitude is not one of running away; only a detached person can perform his or her duties well. In fact, a detached person takes care of duties much better than the one with attachment.

By now, Gurudev was very firm with the devotees. Perfection in action, punctuality, performing work as worship — these were some of his strict teachings. Meditation could never be an excuse for neglect of duty. "A true Karma Yogi has the head in solitude and the hands in multitude," Gurudev proclaimed. The devotees ardently strived to follow and uphold all his teachings.

"Few others in the world have the unique combination that we find in His Holiness Sri Yogiraj Satchidanandaji. Direct inner spiritual experience, profound theoretical knowledge of yoga and philosophy, intense dynamism, wonderful organizing ability, child-like simplicity, the capacity to adapt himself to all circumstances and a sparkling sense of humor. It is difficult to find all these in a single person. Hence, it would be well to say that our Swamiji is himself a complete Mission.

"Second to none in selfless service, when he lends his shoulders to the wheel of action, no one can discover in his service and cheerful countenance a ray of superior condescension! He is one with the worker. In the company of yogis and saints he is perfectly at home and holds his own. He is all this, and yet he subtly transcends them all. It is a joy to watch him. As we watch, we learn. We learn to admire him and to be devoted to him.

"In Hatha Yoga he is an adept. But he does not stop there and spend all his time on his head or bellows breathing. He practices and preaches the Integral Yoga, the yoga that enables us to attain integral perfection. Nor does he ignore the day to day activities and problems of man. I have watched him sympathizing with people in their personal problems, consoling them as their mother, counseling them as their father, teaching them as their guru. Life cannot be split into two halves — sacred and secular. It is one, and it has got to be divinized. To Swamiji, therefore, a *sadak's* difficulty in the control of his mind is as urgent as his problem child's wayward ways. To him a yoga student's desire to enter into *samadhi* is as important as a young man's desire to get a job. He helps them both. Thus he has won the hearts of all. They who have lost their hearts to him have gained the passport to the Supreme.

"May our Swamiji be with us on this physical plane for a very, very long time to come. May his blessings be upon us all. May more and more people of the East and West come under his protecting wings, learn yoga and enrich their lives."

Sri Swami Venkatesanandaji Maharaj
Durban, 1962

Gurudev became famous throughout Ceylon. Everyone knew him, even the local thieves.

On one pitch-black night, a burglar broke into a home near the ashram. As he crept toward his car, which was parked in the road near

Gurudev's cottage, the thief decided to see if the guru was away. The house was empty. He thought, "So many people come to this man; he must have a great deal of money and valuables."

The burglar scrambled through a window and searched the rooms. To his disappointment, he could find nothing of real interest except a few odd things and two small purses. Gathering them with disgust, he quickly began to leave the premises.

As he reached the exit door, he stopped dead still. Before him stood a giant figure, taller than the door itself. It was luminous white, shining eerily from head to foot. The apparition seemed to block his way. A ghost! Shutting his eyes, he dropped everything but one purse and fled to his car, trembling violently.

When the ashramites realized that the cottage had been broken into, they hurriedly called the local police. Returning to the cottage, Gurudev found several groups of men hurrying about. Some were examining tire tracks, others dusted the walls for fingerprints, while another group simply stood around authoritatively.

When he checked inside, he found that the only thing missing was a purse containing a rupee and twenty-five cents. All the other items lay on the floor near the doorway.

The burglar was eventually tracked down through fingerprints found on the dropped articles. Still shaken several days after the event, his eyes opened wide and a shiver ran through his body when he repeated his story to the police.

"Swamiji," the police said, "we have caught the thief. He says he is not the man, that his fingerprints were on the items because he used to come and cook for you."

Gurudev checked the ex-convict's photo. "No, he never cooked for me."

"Well, what shall we do with him?"

"If he is so interested in cooking, let him come and do my cooking."

They would have sentenced the thief to such service, but the owners of the neighboring house, also burgled, were not so generous and demanded he be imprisoned at once.

Each temple is a replica of the entire universe.

There are many beautiful temples in Kandy. The main one is Maligawa, the Temple of the Golden Tooth. There, rests a sacred relic

— a tooth from the body of Lord Buddha. Surrounding this famous Buddhist shrine are temples dedicated to various Hindu deities. Ages ago, some of the Buddhist kings in Kandy married Hindu princesses; they had these temples erected so their brides could worship as they wished. Eventually there were no more kings and queens; but the temples remained, and the Buddhists continued worship in the Hindu temples. A curtain was hung in front of each altar, and, after some time, no one but the Buddhist priests remembered what was behind it. Worship services were performed in front of the curtain. At a certain point, the priest would disappear behind the veil and wave the camphor light in front of the deity. But the Buddhist priests didn't really know what to do with a Hindu deity. They honored the deities, but they didn't dare to touch them.

Mr. Paranagama, a Singhalese lawyer, was a Buddhist who felt very close to Gurudev. One day he came to seek Gurudev's blessings; he planned to run for the office of trustee of Pathina Devalaya, a temple dedicated to the goddess Pathini Devi. In spite of the fact that he was a Buddhist, Mr. Paranagama was also devoted to the goddess. Not long after his visit to Gurudev, he was elected to the office.

As a new trustee of Pathini Devalaya, Mr. Paranagama wanted to be sure everything was in order. When he went into the inner sanctum behind the curtain, he was taken aback by the state of things. The whole area was covered with camphor soot; the ancient, beautiful statue of the goddess was black with it.

Mr. Paranagama was a good devotee of Pathini Devi, and he asked Gurudev to visit the temple and tell him what should be done. When he saw the statue, Gurudev felt quite sad. The beautiful goddess was covered with dirt and cobwebs. "This should be cleaned immediately," Gurudev told him.

This direction made Mr. Paranagama and the temple priest very nervous. There is a belief that if one offends the goddess, he or she will be destroyed. "Oh, but, Swamiji, how could we do that? We are afraid to even touch the statue."

"Don't worry," Gurudev assured them. "I will take the responsibility. We are doing it in all purity and love. There is no bad motive here whatsoever. With that kind of attitude in our minds, surely the Goddess won't care even if we, in our innocence, do something wrong."

Methodically, with complete concentration, Gurudev first cleaned the entire area behind the curtain. Cockroaches ran from their disturbed territory. Finally he began cleaning the statue. From under the black coating emerged a beautiful, shining goddess, decorated with precious

gems. After Pathini Devi was installed in her full splendor on a sparkling clean altar, Gurudev had the priest and Mr. Paranagama come to
the ashram. There, he instructed them in the proper way to perform
puja, taught them some special prayers to use and initiated them with
the sacred Devi *mantram.*

**When art is done as an offering to God, it is not
common entertainment. It is divine.**

The enchanting and beautiful dance form of Bharata Natyam was
presented at the Kandy Thapovanam by the great dancer Miss Thiru
Cumaraswamy, who was also Mrs. Rasiah's sister. Everyone was thrilled
by this uplifting performance, and the idea developed to start a Fine
Arts Society in Kandy as a limb of the ashram activities. Gurudev was
glad to encourage this kind of program; he was immediately asked to be
one of the trustees.

Since Miss Thiru Cumaraswamy couldn't travel from Jaffna regularly the Society arranged for a teacher from Colombo to come and conduct Bharata Natyam classes. Interest grew steadily. Soon there were
music and voice classes.

When thirty or forty young students participate in dance dramas,
maintaining order is no easy matter. The frustrated teachers approached Gurudev for advice about keeping the children in line. "First, *you*
should be orderly. Do not get agitated. Then the children will be fine."

Children of all nationalities, creeds and religions studied together in
an atmosphere of love. Hundreds of people benefited from this artistic
and spiritual organization, and the *thapovanam* was very proud of it.
Many who started as small children grew to become well-known performers themselves.

Some people were puzzled. How did fine arts fit in with a spiritual
organization?

To such skeptics Gurudev answered: "Essentially all arts are divine.
When the spiritual aspect is forgotten, it is no longer real art. Then, it
is just dry, with no real life in it. All the great artists were devotees.
Knowingly or unknowingly, they were receiving that talent and inspiration from a higher source. In many temples or churches or other

spiritual places music, dance, theater, art and sculpture are used to express love and devotion for God.

"In Bharata Natyam, all the compositions are devotional songs. Instead of children going off to learn some popular social dance, they can have fun learning Bharata Natyam and learn more about spiritual life at the same time. With the proper attitude all the arts are a joyful expression of God."

Coming from the Hindu tradition, Bharata Natyam is based on Hindu stories and teachings. But the subtle influence of Gurudev manifested in the Fine Arts Society as songs and stories from *all* different religions were brought in. Soon people of all traditions were studying at the Fine Arts Society. Classes were even requested by a local Catholic school; the sisters and priests wanted to study! In the true ecumenical spirit, art was bringing people together in tribute to the unending variety of expressions of the Divine.

BIRTHDAY GREETINGS TO
SRI SWAMI SATCHIDANANDAJI MAHARAJ
on his 45th Jayanthi

Amidst Mother Nature's charming bowers
The Mahavali is rushing;
Her sun-lit waters like golden covers
Her flowing waves go gushing.

Today is our Swami's 45th Jayanthi
Our hearts we link like a chain;
To entwine at his feet in unity
Our homage will not be in vain.

Greetings! To Swami Satchidananda
A prince among men art thou;
Oh! Dazzling spiritual Pole Star
Accept my humble bow.

Thou modern Saint and Seer
Who lives not in cave;
But moves with all who are dear
To help mankind thou crave.

In maya's dark night
  When with miseries we dream;
It's thy knowledge of Light
  Passeth into a happy morn to gleam.

The teachings of asana and yoga
  Are like a Jnana Ganga;
Flowing between banks of Bhakti and Yoga
  Embracing the breeze of Ananda.

Bhaktas and friends cheer him aloud
  To have him among us we are so proud;
Happy are we to be in this crowd
  Our sorrows have fled like passing cloud.

Yonder! the sun is sinking low
  Shadows are falling fast;
But Satchidananda's fame and lore
  Will for yugas ever last.

Outside the moonlight romancing
  With dark shadows of the night;
Our hearts with joy dancing
  In the glow of the temple light.

In a spirit of Universal Love
  You have tied us closely bound
In etheric waves of peace and love
  Your mission goes world round.

Long live thee Himalayan sage
  God grant thee health and long life;
Thy fame to rise in every age
  Giving us eternal life.

Mrs. Padma Bharatharaja
Kandy

A beautiful biography had been written about Gurudev in the Tamil language. After Master Sivanandaji had read it, he wrote:

"You have really made an awakening in Ceylon in the spiritual field.

"I am conducting prayer and *kirtan* for thy health and long life, peace and illumination. Repeat Hari! Never worry. Be merry! Excel in Service! Expand in love! Attune in knowledge.

"Start the day with God. Fill the day with God. Live the day with God.

"With regards, Prem and OM,

Thy own self,
Sivananda"

Sri Swami Sivanandaji Maharaj
Rishikesh, 1962

When you are not aware of the Lord inside, you won't find Him outside either. He must be seen inside first. Then you will see Him everywhere.

High in the Himalayan range is the majestic, glacier-capped peak of holy Mount Kailash, legendary home of Lord Siva. Along the way to the peak are the homes of Tibetan peasants and monks. The farmers live in their tents, high in the rocky hills. Yaks graze lazily on the mountain grasses, tended by black-haired, laughing children. Monasteries cling tenaciously to the bare hills. The more extravagant lamaseries climb over the landscape, level after level reaching up to the sky. The landscape is vast — as awesomely, incredibly vast as heaven.

Prayer wheels and prayer flags spin and wave in the wind — each swoop of the wind whips thousands of flags, vibrating thousands of *mantrams*. Shrines protrude like rocks from the glacier peaks.

In 1958, Gurudev made a pilgrimage to this holy mountain, along with Sri Swami Premanandaji of Poona, Sri Swami Bagawathanandaji of the Himalayas, Sri Praveen Nanawathi of Bombay and Sri Ramdas of Punjab.

The pilgrimage — which is fully and beautifully recounted in Gurudev's book *Kailash Journal* — took two months. They climbed on foot through 800 miles of rocky ups and downs, to a height of 19,000 feet. The group took no oxygen masks, nor were their clothes particularly heavy. Gurudev lectured and visited villages, schools and monasteries along the way.

When a person makes a pilgrimage to holy Mount Kailash, no one asks, "When will you return?" It is enough that one is going to see the

Lord's shrine, circle His peak and receive His *darshan*, His blessing.

Twice on the pilgrimage, Gurudev faced death.

It was late afternoon when the group went through the Undathura Pass, 18,500 feet up. In the morning, the snow in Undathura Pass had been hard — one could walk across it — but, by the afternoon, the snow had become soft. Walking was difficult, especially for the mules with the heavy loads they carried. Recalling this in his *Kailash Journal*, Gurudev said, "It was heart-rending to see the mules struggling to pull their legs out of the snow with each step. At times all four legs would get stuck; we would then have to shove some heavy sticks under their bellies and lift them out of their entrapment. At a number of spots the mules toppled over, scattering the baggage. It did not take long for the provisions to get soaked. Each time we would have to collect the wet baggage and secure it on their backs again. At other places, the deep granular snow was covered by a layer of soft, fresh powder. The feet of the mules were often cut by the sharp icy edges of crevasses lying hidden below.

"Our legs also broke through the frozen snow at times. If one foot sank, the other had to be firmly braced while the leg was extricated and moved ahead. If the pilgrim got excited or alarmed and did not act swiftly and surely, the leg would sink deeper and deeper. If he hastily put the free leg forward, both feet would sink, and he would need assistance to get out. Fellow pilgrims would come quickly, knowing that those feet might soon be frozen in place. Furthermore, both men and mules faced the danger of slipping on the steep path and tumbling down the slope non-stop until they found themselves in the middle of one of the bitter-cold streams of melted snow.

"We were all exhausted when we reached the peak of Undathura Pass at five in the evening. Although we longed to set up camp and rest, we found the Pass to be unbearable. This was a very high spot, and the wind gleefully joined the cold in its chilling task of discomfiting the pilgrims. We had no choice but to climb down the slope. It was a treacherous descent; and the slipperiness of the snow, melting in the afternoon sun, added to the already existing dangers. We took every step with great caution and the firm support of our staffs. Not doing so would have meant either rising from frequent falls or falling never to rise again. The grace of God brought us safely to the bottom of the slope."

When they reached the bottom of the slope, the pilgrims looked back and found that the mules and their keepers had not been following. What had been difficult for the men had been impossible for the pack animals. It was 8:00 at night. The pilgrims stood in the piercing cold without food, tents or bedding. The supplies were all with the mules.

As they entered the Gangapaani Valley, they were amazed to see a tent in the distance. They hurried toward it. What they found was quite a surprise. A man named Pratap Singh and his son Gushall Singh had set this tent up as a tea kiosk only the night before. The tent was small — eight feet by eight feet at the base — and Pratap Singh moved out into the snow so that the freezing pilgrims could huddle inside the tent. They gratefully drank hot, salted tea as they sat by the little fire. Pratap Singh's provisions and the fire took up more than one quarter of the small tent; but to the weary pilgrims, it seemed like a palace. There were no flaps to cover the open end of the tent, and the icy wind chilled them; some suffered from headaches because of lack of oxygen. Squeezed together in the tent, they slept any way they could, leaning against baggage or sitting upright, as if in meditation.

Two of the mule drivers attempted to bring the animals and baggage down the slope. One mule stumbled and rolled down into the valley. A bold rescue team set out to find the mule, but they failed in their efforts. Eventually, the driver found that his poor animal had met its death. The next morning, the other mules were able to descend, but only by leaving the baggage behind. In the afternoon, a few mule drivers went back up and slid part of the baggage down the hill. The pilgrims prepared for another night at the camp in the Gangapaani Valley.

The temperature was often as high as eighty-three degrees Fahrenheit during the day, but after sunset it quickly dropped to around forty-eight degrees. By morning, it was usually thirty-eight degrees.

The icy wind swept across the glaciers as Gurudev got into his sleeping bag that night. As he lay down to sleep, he heard the snow below him begin to melt from the heat of his body. The water soaked through the canvas tarpaulin under his sleeping bag. Near midnight, the cold had seeped through his body to such an extent that he began to shiver violently. He was practically frozen. He felt his heartbeat slow down, his breath stop.

"Oh, Lord, what is this?" Gurudev asked. "I have come all the way here just to worship in Your holy abode. Am I not fit to do so?"

His body broke out in a cold sweat. He sat up and placed his head upon his knees, fighting for breath. Then, gradually, a new warmth swept through his entire system. Life began to seep back in. Gurudev didn't sleep for the rest of that night. Instead he prayed and wept, thanking the Lord for His mercy.

After five weeks of climbing, the pilgrims reached their goal. There, at the height of 19,000 feet, they performed their *pradakshina* — circumambulation of the peak. This formal worship took them thirty-two miles around the peak, up and down the slope at heights ranging from 17,000 to 19,000 feet.

"The *Puranas* describe Mount Kailash as a 'Peak of Silver,'" Gurudev wrote. "Those who have seen Kailash in the rays of the morning sun know what this means. The mountain itself is a radiant temple of grace and beauty. What has man built throughout all of his history that can rival the works of the Divine Architect? The most impressive temples in all the world are but imperfect imitations of the perfection one sees in the *gopurams*, halls, streets and *sanctum sanctorum* of this natural temple where the Lord's presence is seen and felt so strongly."

After receiving the Lord's blessings on Mount Kailash, the group began their descent, still immersed in the feeling of divine bliss. The worship ended with a bath in the frozen waters of the holy Gowri Kundam, dedicated to the goddess Gowri, consort of Lord Siva. Traditionally, pilgrims who have the courage take a dip in this lake before continuing their circumambulation. Many, who felt themselves very weak, would simply touch the water and sprinkle it over their heads.

Gurudev and the other pilgrims stood in awe of the frozen lake. Gowri Kundam spread before them like a sheet of glass, surrounded by icy peaks. Only during the hottest hours of the day, when the sun is at its zenith, could one dare to consider bathing in the waters of Gowri Kundam. They broke the ice and cleared an area so that they could jump into the frigid water. Some in the group performed the bath mentally. One man walked into the water and immediately lost consciousness. He was pulled out, dried with a towel and rubbed with a woolen blanket. Soon his body was warm, and he regained consciousness. Even a single dip in Gowri Kundam is considered a great accomplishment, and a few others managed this heroic feat. Swami Premanandaji, a very hardy person, took many dips. Gurudev took one dip in worship of the Lord, a second dip on behalf of all devotees, and a third for the welfare of the world.

Afterward, as the guide rubbed his body with the woolen blankets, Gurudev wondered if the plunge into the icy pool was really necessary. After some thought, he concluded that it was a good "acid test." It was

171

a test to find out whether one was supposed to go on living, whether a person was really doing what God wanted him or her to do. It was as if the pilgrim were saying to God "Lord, if You still think that I am worthy of staying here and serving people, bring me back from the water. Otherwise, please take me to Your feet." Certainly many people on other pilgrimages had died during or after their dip in Gowri Kundam. He concluded that those who were supposed to stay and continue their service were made to survive.

All the pilgrims felt the blessings of the Divine Mother. They sang in praise of Her and prostrated many times in worship.

One day, exhausted from the rugged hike, Gurudev decided to ride one of the mules for a short distance. The mule wore neither saddle nor bridle. A heavy rain began, and Gurudev took out his umbrella, opened it and guided his mount under a tree. The branches were low, and he was forced to quickly close the umbrella. The sudden snap of the catch frightened the mule, who bolted and threw Gurudev onto a boulder at the side of the path. He fell on his chest, the breath knocked out of his body. "Hari OM," he murmured. His breathing stopped.

"Breathe in! Hard!" The voice came from somewhere within him. It was the unseen force guiding the instrument to finish his work. "Breathe!"

He collected his strength for one deep inhalation. Slowly, his breath returned, and his companions were able to lift him onto the back of a mule. Although every step the mule took on the rocky slope brought increased pain to Gurudev's chest, he knew that he had once again been saved from death.

After he returned, Gurudev was asked, "What did you gain by that pilgrimage?"

He answered: "A great lesson. The lesson is that by such a pilgrimage you realize that nothing you have owned, nothing you call yours will help you to experience God within and without. There are many situations where we depend on money or position or bodily strength. But on the pilgrimage, nothing is going to help you. You might have a strong body; but when there is no oxygen, what are you going to do? You may have millions of dollars, but there is nothing to buy. You may have an important position; you may be a powerful person. But on the pilgrimage, you are more or less a slave to your own mule drivers because they are the people who give you directions. So everything becomes nothing. In a way you are made to learn the worthlessness of

172

everything that you have depended upon. It is at that point you say, 'It's only God's grace that helps me.'

"All these experiences and facing death that many times, they all helped us to realize that without God's grace we couldn't have made it. If anybody can experience this right in his or her own home, there's no need for such a pilgrimage. Unfortunately, it almost never happens that way. Only by making a hard pilgrimage like this does one realize that; then you don't depend on any of those things even though they are around you. You know that without God's help all these things are worthless, meaningless. That's the great lesson we learn from a pilgrimage.

"Sometimes people think of a pilgrimage in a different way. They decide to go to Benares, or Bethlehem, or Mecca. They have a travel agency arrange everything, book a nice hotel, have a nice comfortable car to drive to the door of the holy place. Even in the car, they will have a thermos flask filled with hot drinks. Then they get out of the car, go to the shrine and say, 'Lord, how are you? I just came to see You.' Then they go home and call it a pilgrimage. But it isn't really a pilgrimage.

"On a pilgrimage you go to realize that you are nothing and without God's help you cannot do anything. That is the very reason why, in those days, pilgrimages were made to such difficult areas. Because, truly, God is everywhere. Pilgrimages aren't made with the belief that God can be seen only in that spot. It's that God can be recognized more easily there because you paid such a big price. But the Lord is everywhere; no pilgrimage alone can give you self-realization."

Reluctantly, Gurudev bid farewell to Sri Swami Premanandaji, Sri Praveen Nanawathi, Ramdasji and Sri Swami Bagawathanandaji. Together they had walked a distance of 800 miles. They had ascended to an altitude of 19,000 feet. But the pilgrims didn't feel they had done this themselves. They felt that God's grace, and the prayers of their loving devotees, had led and guided their footsteps.

Gurudev felt drawn to visit the holy place of Amarnath in Kashmir. Just as he had been happy to share a tent with others on the journey to Mount Kailash, Gurudev was now happy to have a little solitude. "Here in Kashmir, the Lord Amarnath has taken abode in a cave at an elevation of 14,000 feet," Gurudev wrote. Within the cave He can been seen in the holy form of a dazzling *Siva Lingam* of pure white snow. This form only appears for a few days each year during the time of the full moon in the Tamil month of Aavani. The full moon day

Two courageous pilgrims about to set out for Mount Kailash.
Sri Swami Premanandaji and Sri Gurudev.

(above) The Holy Mount of Kailash, where Lord Siva dwells. "Who can reach Kailash without His Grace?"

(below) The pilgrim en route to Kailash: the path to God is not a smooth one — often chilling and slippery.

itself is the day especially set aside to worship at His feet. I started out on the 25th of August — four days ahead of this important date — in order to make the pilgrimage at this most auspicious time."

Early on the morning of the 29th, Gurudev left the camp at Panchatharani for Amarnath Cave. It was cold, dark and icy. The cave lies at a height of 14,000 feet. It is fifty-five feet across, fifty feet long and forty-five feet high. Gurudev bathed near the cave in the melted snow of the Amarawathi spring. Then: "With an offering of flowers in my hands and an offering of love in my heart, I entered the cave. My entire body tingled with the thrill. My heart was exuberant with joy. Here I beheld the holy person of the Lord of Amarnath. I clasped my hands and prayed. I fell at His feet in worship. I arose and stood reverently in His presence, wondering at the grace he bestows on His devotees by appearing before them as the *lingam*. It is His gift of grace to allow them this experience of seeing His holy person. The form soon melts away, but the realization of His presence remains with the devotee for all time."

After this pilgrimage, Gurudev returned to Rishikesh. He arrived on the morning of the 8th of September — in time to join the celebration to honor the *jayanthi* of Master Sivanandaji. Gurudev was privileged to narrate, in the presence of his holy master, the experiences of the pilgrimage to Mount Kailash. He mentally offered all of the benefits of that journey at the feet of Sri Swami Sivanandaji Maharaj.

If we always think of others and their benefit, if we travel to aid others when we are called, all calamities, wars, fights and quarrels will cease.

In 1959, Gurudev accepted an invitation from Sri Vasudeva Daryanani, the secretary of the DLS, to give a series of lectures and demonstrations in Hong Kong. He spent two months there and in Malaysia, giving training in *asanas, pranayama,* concentration and meditation.

Hong Kong is an island of about thirty-two square miles. Because of its free trade, it acts as a showcase for world consumer goods, both Eastern and Western. Although the population is mainly Chinese, there are hundreds of other cultures, languages and modes of dress as well. The bustling atmosphere of one of the world's principal ports breeds tension in many residents of Hong Kong. Gurudev made something new popular on the island: yoga, health, peace.

"Swami Satchidananda came to Hong Kong. With his long beard, his appearance was awe-inspiring, but his manners were gentle and his voice was slow and sweet. He stirred the inner thought of our members. Swamiji spoke softly, leading all members to relax from toes to head. To relax our internal organs, he taught a special kind of breathing. Then, absolute relaxation. After a few minutes of the relaxation, upon awakening, members found that they were so fresh — as if they had come out from eight hours' sound sleep. Besides teaching Hatha Yoga classes, he also conducted a tutorial class on Sunday mornings. After the tutorial class he lectured on yoga principles, stressing *yama* and *niyama* (the ethical teachings). He was quite busy by that time. His sincerity and his gentleness have always remained in our hearts."

–Au Yeung Hao Man
Hong Kong DLS

"Yoga and Relaxation" was the topic Gurudev had been asked to address at the Rotary Club luncheon meeting. After the talk, he invited questions from the audience.

"Swamiji, you've been talking about relaxation. I am a film producer. For at least three years, sleep has been a stranger to me. I never sleep. I'm always tense. I don't know how to relax. Can you help me in any way? Can you *prove* that your approach will really bring relaxation to somebody?"

"Dear sir, do you really want to experience that?"

"Oh, yes!"

"All right. When do you want to do it? We are just going to have lunch. Do you prefer after lunch, during lunch or before lunch?"

"Well, I don't know. I can't expect everybody to wait for me for lunch, but I don't mind missing the meal if you give me some way of relaxing." He thought for a moment. "Okay. I'll do the relaxing first."

"All right then. Don't blame me if you become totally calm and don't get any food." Gurudev had a nice blanket spread out right in the middle of the hall. He asked the producer to lie down, and then began the deep relaxation. At first the man resisted. "If you really want to have this experience, you should not resist," Gurudev gently chided him. "You should not be doing this just to disprove my words.

Be sincere. If you really want to experience ease, simply cooperate with me."

"Okay, Swami. I'll give up and listen to you."

Within half an hour, the producer was relaxing; not much later he began snoring. Gurudev left him there and joined the other Rotarians for a sumptuous lunch.

After lunch was finished, they gently woke the very relaxed man. "Swami, I'm your first disciple here! If you could make *me* do this, certainly your technique could help anybody and everybody." He became a dedicated yoga student.

Soon the Hatha Yoga classes were swamped with many more students. Classes were offered at various locations: the South China Athletic Association, the European YMCA and YWCA, the Chung Sing Benevolent Society, the Hong Kong University Alumni Association and the Hindu Mandir. Each class attracted from fifty to sixty students. Before long, the students were asking for meditation classes, and Gurudev added three of these to his weekly schedule. Enthusiasm grew for all aspects of yoga.

Mr. Yen was an eighty-year-old Zen Buddhist and an officer of the Divine Life Society. He listened closely to what Gurudev was saying about the need to develop a desireless or wantless state. "It's the desire that creates all the problems, anxieties, and worries," Gurudev explained. "If we can only learn to be desireless, we can be more peaceful."

Mr. Yen rose slowly from his seat in the audience. "May I ask you a question, Swamiji?"

"Yes, please."

"Ah, well, don't you think that wanting to be desireless is itself a desire?"

"That's a beautiful question. Yes, it's very true. You have to have a desire in order to get rid of desire. Once you achieve *that* desire, what happens? You become desireless; because that was your desire. But at first, you have to have some kind of desire; the mind can't simply stop desiring all of a sudden. So, instead of wanting something selfish, you can have this want to not have any wants. Once that is fulfilled, it will be the *last* desire for you. It acts as a catalytic agent. In the same way, you apply soap — the last piece of dirt — to get rid of the other dirt. When all the other dirt goes, the soap also goes away from the cloth, leaving you completely free."

178

(top) Sri Gurudev was received at the Hong Kong airport by many Indian and Chinese devotees.

(bottom) Office bearers of the Hong Kong Divine Life Society, 1959.

179

(above) At the Lantau retreat.

Facing page: (top) With His Holiness Fat Hall at Po Lin Chi (Thousand Buddhists Monastery), Hong Kong.

Hong Kong DLS activities: (middle) Class at City Hall, Hong Kong; (bottom) Lantau retreat.

Often the Hong Kong devotees would gather for large dinner parties or receptions in honor of their respected teacher. (below) South China Athletic Association class.

"Ah, that's terrific. Wonderful." Mr. Yen became a close friend of Gurudev.

About thirty-five Hong Kong devotees traveled with Gurudev to Lantau, an island twenty-five miles from Hong Kong. There they embarked upon a three-day yoga retreat in an old Buddhist monastery. No roads led to the site. There was no electricity. It was a fantastic success.

In any life you choose, even the worldly one, yoga can benefit you. Through yoga, you will relax more. Through a more tranquil mind, you will be healthier. If you are healthier, you will be happier, more able to accomplish all that you set out to do.

A young Chinese couple came to Gurudev for advice. The wife complained about her husband's nature. He irritated her, she said, and she wanted a divorce.

Gurudev looked at the man. He appeared to be extremely nervous and weak. "Before pressing your divorce suit," Gurudev advised, "wait a few weeks. During that time, begin practicing Hatha Yoga. Then come back to me."

Toward the end of the month, the couple returned. They were holding hands. "We have decided to stay together and not get a divorce," they announced, beaming at each other.

"Oh? Why not?"

The wife explained, "He seems to be more relaxed. He takes things easier. I no longer get upset so quickly. We both seem to have changed for the better. The only reason we can think of is the Hatha Yoga. As we continue it, we find that we are both able to relax. He can control his nerves; he is stronger. I don't seem to be so high-strung, and I don't get irritated so easily."

After that, in his lectures Gurudev announced one more benefit of yoga: "Yoga can help you save your marriage."

Mr. Lee, a man about fifty-five years old, had lost most of his hair due to an illness. Gurudev suggested that he start practicing Hatha Yoga, with emphasis on the headstand. Within four months, Mr. Lee's hair started growing again. Yet another benefit of yoga: Yoga can even help you save your hair!

In Hong Kong, Gurudev became acquainted with a family of people who quickly became devotees and dear friends. These were the Harilelas — a wealthy and successful family who were deeply devoted to God. In the Harilela mansion, each day began with an early morning worship service. The six Harilela brothers always started their work for the day by bowing down on the threshold of their places of business. Gurudev often cited them as an example of devout people. "How often do we see people who worship the threshold of their business place?" Gurudev asked a group of disciples. "The Harilelas do that because they know it is not *their* business; it is God's business. They sincerely feel that they are only caretakers. From the home to the office — everywhere — you see this devotion in their hearts. I think that is the secret of their success in life — total trust in God. They are the living proof that if you have absolute devotion to God, you won't have to worry about anything."

During a television interview, Gurudev was asked to demonstrate some of the *asanas*. One *asana* he performed was *simhasana*, the lion pose — in a kneeling position, he placed his hands on his knees, stretched his tongue toward his chin and focused both eyes on a spot between the eyebrows. The next morning, the television station was surprised to receive calls from several concerned parents. "Who was that man? You should have warned us so the children wouldn't see him. He really became a lion. It was frightening."

Soon Gurudev was known all over Hong Kong.

One day, he was driving through the city. Just as he approached the pedestrian crosswalk, he saw someone step into the road. Gurudev slowed the car and prepared to stop, but the pedestrian stepped back onto the sidewalk and waited. Gurudev continued driving. Within a few yards a policeman stopped him. "Are you the yogi who was on the television?"

"Yes, sir. Did you stop me just to ask this question?"

"Oh, no. You know, you should have stopped back there for the pedestrian."

"Well, I was about to stop when I saw him step back and wait, so I kept going."

"The law is that you should stop and ask him to go first, then continue. But now that I see who you are, I know that you are new to our laws, and you weren't aware of this." Politely, he waved Gurudev on. Yoga even helped with traffic problems.

Sir Turner was the chief executive of the Hong Kong-Shanghai Bank. He and his wife, Wendy, had heard favorable reports about Gurudev and his work. They invited the Swami to tea and spent several hours with him discussing yoga.

The following day, the Turners' six-year-old son, Michael, developed a painful ear infection. They were preparing to leave for a large party, but the cries and discomfort of their child made them hesitate. Lady Turner called her friend Thelma Shanthi Heitmeyer and described the situation. Thelma asked her to call Gurudev.

"Michael is having ear trouble, Swamiji. We don't know what to do. Can you help us in any way?"

"Put a small bit of glycerine on a cotton swab. As you apply it to Michael's ear, repeat a prayer to God. After a while he will sleep, and you can go to the party. In the morning he'll be better."

Soon after his mother applied the glycerine, Michael fell asleep. Late that evening, when the Turners came home, he was still sleeping soundly. During the night, the boil within his ear burst and drained of pus, easing the inflammation. In the morning, the boy was fine.

The day before Gurudev's departure from Hong Kong, about five hundred devotees organized a grand send-off party. It was held in a large restaurant, which the devotees had decorated and prepared in the most loving way. Lectures and speeches of gratitude were given. *Asanas* were demonstrated. The whole event was televised.

Afterward, the group sat down to dine. On the formal white table-cloths sat sparkling silverware, crystal goblets, cut glass bowls of appetizers; and for each person there was a rather large plate holding a whole fish — head, eyes, tail, everything.

Students of yoga are supposed to be vegetarians — especially for their guru's going away party. Gurudev looked at the plate before him. "What is this fish doing here?"

"Oh, Swamiji," the devotees said, "we are so pleased with the service you have given us. We wanted to treat you to our favorite delicacy. We love it so much. Just for our sake, please taste a little of it."

Gurudev couldn't fully believe they were offering him flesh to eat. He thought there must be a motive, perhaps a trick, behind it. He loved them and had faith in them. "Fine. If you really think I'll make you happy by eating this fish, I'll do it." He picked up his knife and started cutting the fish into sections.

The Harilelas: a family filled with faith and devotion.

Students of the Yoga Society, Kobe and Yanaga, Japan, 1961.

All around the room, the devotees were crowded together, peeking over one another's shoulders, watching him cut the food.

"Swamiji," someone laughed, "you must know our trick or else you wouldn't be about to eat that fish."

"It's not a real fish," another said. "It's tofu, soybean curd, colored and flavored and shaped like a fish."

Everyone applauded Gurudev as he raised his fork to his lips and calmly bit into the tail.

Early in April 1961, Gurudev was invited to make a second, more extensive, Far Eastern tour. This time he would cover Japan and the Philippines, as well as Hong Kong and Malaysia. During this trip, a very young but very competent woman came forward to serve as Gurudev's secretary. Eva Ho — who later married and became Eva Kwan — was a high school student, but she arranged vacation time so that she could accompany and serve Gurudev.

His schedule was quite full. Each day Gurudev taught a Hatha Yoga class at 6:00 A.M. Another class began at 8:00. In the late morning, he gave a public talk. In the late afternoon there were more classes; in the evening, another public talk. Often, Mr. Lo Chau, one of Gurudev's star pupils demonstrated the yoga *asanas* while Gurudev explained the benefits of the poses. Interest in yoga was blooming more than ever, and soon Gurudev added a yoga teacher training course to his already extremely busy schedule.

Eva sat near Gurudev at all these programs, translating and recording his words. When the last program ended each evening, at around 10:30 P.M., Eva would transcribe all the day's talks, type them, and have them ready to give the students at the next day's sessions.

The Hay Ling Chau Leprosarium — "The Isle of Happy Healing" — offers treatment to many people suffering from leprosy. In 1961, Gurudev visited the island and spent time with the 200 patients — children and adults. He was very pleased with the way the residents kept busy — supporting themselves by working in the fields, raising rabbits and making a variety of handicrafts. Even though the Hong Kong public helped with the financial support of the facility, most of the patients relied on their own efforts to maintain a livelihood.

Sri Swami Premanandaji, one of Gurudev's companions on the Mount Kailash pilgrimage, visited Hong Kong during this time. The two great yogis enjoyed the opportunity for a reunion. Gurudev and Premanandaji were both busy conducting programs, but they managed to make time in their schedules for an outing together — one much simpler than a pilgrimage to Mount Kailash — to the New Territories and the Castle Peak Monastery.

The Hong Kong devotees often gave dinner parties or picnics in Gurudev's honor. It was not only the delicious vegetarian food that made these gatherings different from typical parties. For these devotees, so-called social events were really opportunities to learn even more from their spiritual teacher.

"On the 24th of May, 1961, Swami Satchidanandaji was invited to a party given by the yoga students of the Hong Kong University Alumni Association. Swamiji addressed the gathering on the importance of *pranayama* in the practice of yoga. . .On the 10th of June, 1961, the Kent Road Yoga Class gave a party in honor of Sri Swami Satchidanandaji. On this occasion Swamiji gave some salient points on yoga. He said that the path of yoga is a scientific one. It is a need of the modern world. When everything is in chaos, we approach yoga to find the solution in us and outside us, to seek the real peace in us and in the world. . .The YMCA yoga students gave a party in honor of Sri Swami Satchidanandaji at the Shamrock Hotel, Kowloon, on the 16th of June 1961. On this occasion, Swamiji explained that through yoga we try to attain perfection in every aspect of our lives. As yoga purifies the body and mind, we will see only the good in everything and never the evil. Our ambition in life is to achieve perfection and to live in eternal peace. In this effort, we approach the path of perfection through the body and mind. . .Now and then, Sri Swami Satchidanandaji was invited to picnics and outings to Sunshine Island, Stanley Beach, Sheko Beach, Big-Wave Beach and to Deep Water Bay, where he would talk about yoga and have wonderful dips in the water. . .On the 17th of June, the traditional Chinese Dragon Boat Festival was held. On that auspicious occasion, Swamiji was invited to watch the colorful race at the Chung Sing Bathing Pavilion. . ."

from the journal kept by Eva Ho

As the time for Gurudev's departure from Hong Kong drew near, he gave two *satsangs* at the Chinese General Chamber of Commerce: "Yoga and Modern Life" and "Man and Mind." He reminded the audience about the essence of the teachings he had given during his stay, and told them about the importance of yoga in all places and situations. "Don't think that yoga can only be practiced in certain situations. Practice yoga right here and right now, in this busy city. In a beautiful, secluded jungle, certain parts of the mind can remain dormant; they stay all bundled up, without the slightest opportunity to reveal themselves. But in a bustling city, evil qualities as well as virtues are revealed. When these problem areas are revealed, we have a chance to improve ourselves. The city is like a mirror in which we see our reflections and correct the blemishes and dirt we see in that reflection."

The members of the Hong Kong Divine Life Society gave a farewell dinner party in Gurudev's honor. Mr. K. S. Fung, President of the DLS, and Mr. Camath, the Indian Commissioner, gave speeches. Then Gurudev expressed his appreciation for the interest that the people of Hong Kong had taken in the great science of yoga. "Every house needs yoga," he said, "and everybody wants to be a yogi, whether they know that term or not. By that, I mean: Everybody wants to be truly happy and peaceful. I am happy that you are using yoga in your lives and, through your own practice, helping others. Remember that you don't need to worry about convincing other people of yoga's greatness. Just let them see the way it is working for you."

In Manila, Gurudev was happy to once again meet Mr. Jean Belloir, who was now the French Consul for the Phillipines. Mr. Belloir had invited Gurudev to stay with him, and he was happy to be the gracious host for his good friend, the Swami.

In the midst of Gurudev's lecture schedule, Mr. Belloir arranged to take his guest to the Manila Yacht Club. Gurudev had never handled a sailboat before, and Mr. Belloir was surprised and impressed at the way the Swami navigated the little boat. That evening, at a small reception, Mr. Belloir highly praised his guest's skill as a sailor. The chairman of the Yacht Club presented Gurudev with a medal of honor and made him an honorary member of the club.

It was not the only honorary membership Gurudev was given in Manila. The local Theosophical Society invited him for a talk and, afterward, made him an honorary member of their organization.

Mr. Belloir invited Gurudev to address the Breakfast Club, a very distinguished group which had as its president the President of the Philippines. Many members turned out for the talk, and many stayed to greet Gurudev afterward.

Two Catholic priests approached him. "Swami, do you know that you have really converted us?"

Gurudev smiled. "Thank you for saying that, Father. But I cannot accept your statement. I'm not here to convert anybody. Probably you could say I have absorbed you. I don't come to convert, but I come to absorb."

The priests warmly embraced Gurudev. "Oh, you really have your own way of playing with words, Swami. Yes, you are very correct. That's what you did to us, absorbed us. It's so beautiful. Thank you."

> **When you take a trip somewhere, you may have to change vehicles during the journey. Sometimes the automobile breaks down and you have to get another one. The body is a vehicle like that automobile. When things go wrong we get it repaired. Today, we can even put spare parts in — new eyes, new limbs, new hearts. But there are still limitations. When nothing can be repaired any longer, when the model becomes outdated, it must be cast aside.**

Just before leaving for the tour of Hong Kong, Japan and the Philippines, Gurudev received news that Srimati Velammai was ill and in the hospital. He decided to visit her before proceeding to Hong Kong.

He went directly to the hospital in Coimbatore and found her lying in bed, small and weak. All around her were friends and relatives with sad faces. Gurudev met with her doctor in the hall.

"She can't survive much longer," the physician said.

Gurudev sat down beside Velammai. He held her hand gently and talked with her about the purpose of the physical form. "Don't expect to remain in this body too much longer." Velammai nodded her head. "Amma, you know how weak your body is now. Do you still want to spend time in this old, dilapidated frame?"

"Son, I know it's not fit to live in much longer. I feel I'm just marking time."

Her attitude was one of complete acceptance, and Gurudev was very glad to see this. "Your attitude is the correct one, Amma. If, by some chance, your body becomes fit once again, let it happen and you can live in it. But you shouldn't demand that. Make yourself ready. Prepare to say good-bye to this world when the time comes. Don't worry any longer about your family, your relations or all the worldly ties you have. They will take care of themselves. Take this opportunity to think of God. Meditate on Him and wait for His call."

191

He spoke to her as a guru to a disciple. He loved her very much, yet felt no attachment. His only interest was in her welfare and comfort.

Srimati Velammai squeezed his hand and smiled, saying she would follow these instructions and begin her meditation that very day.

"Amma, I will pray for your peace."

The friends and relatives, eavesdropping from the next room, had heard this conversation, and they were quite unsettled. As soon as Gurudev came out of his mother's room, they cornered him.

"What is this?"

"How could you tell her things like that?"

"You should not have said that!"

"Instead of encouraging her, you discouraged her."

"How could you tell her she doesn't have long to live?"

Gurudev remained calm. "You all know what I said is true. Even the doctor has told you that. I certainly don't want Amma to die, but I don't want her to live in a body that's not strong enough to support life. When the time comes she should be ready to leave it. Now is the time for her to prepare for that journey. There's no point in my lying to her, telling her she'll live for many years." He turned and walked back to his mother's side. "Amma, I'm going to Hong Kong. I don't know when I'll be coming back. Will you feel bad if I'm not by your side when you leave your body?"

Velammai waved her hand. "No, no. Not at all. All you could do for me you have already done. If, by chance, I go into a coma, I might not recognize you even if you're right next to me." She patted his hand lightly. "Don't worry about my welfare," she consoled him. "Even if this *is* our last meeting, that's fine. We can say good-bye now."

Gurudev embraced her. She kissed his hair and touched his hands for the last time. Then he left her side.

At the end of September, he returned from his tour and went straight to Ceylon.

As he sat in his cottage, a month later, he suddenly felt that Velammai's situation had become critical. Closing his eyes, he envisioned her leaving her body. He went directly to his shrine room to pray for her welfare. When he came out, he walked to his picture of the goddess Saraswati, which hung in the sitting room. He took it from its peg and turned the picture so that it faced the wall.

The following morning, the ashramites arrived for morning *satsang*. They noticed the peculiar position of Saraswati's portrait and asked whether they should reverse it once again.

"No. Let it be."

In the afternoon, two devotees arrived for their appointment. They brought their daughter and newborn grandchild. It was around 3:00 P.M. As he spoke to the devotees, Gurudev held the baby on his lap, bouncing the little one from time to time. After half an hour, one of the ashramites entered with a telegram from India.

Gurudev excused himself and opened the message. It brought the news that his mother had passed away. After a moment of silence, he put the telegram face down and turned his attention back to the guest and the baby. After another hour, the visitors prepared to leave. Gurudev blessed the baby and returned him to his mother.

When the visiting devotees had departed, a number of ashramites crowded into the kutir. A telegram from India signified urgent matters; they asked about its contents.

Gurudev passed the message around. Each ashramite, in turn, became depressed and sorrowful. Many burst into tears.

"Swamiji, how can you just sit there quietly? How could you even play with the baby after receiving such news? You should immediately go to India."

"You appear to be acting very hardhearted, Swamiji. Your mother is no more, but you don't seem eager to get ready to go to India."

The guru's reply was quiet. "Well, what can I do? I can't bring her back to life again. I had expected this. I was prepared for it."

"Is that why you turned the picture around?" In Ceylon, it was the custom to turn all pictures to face the wall when someone died.

"Maybe so."

They looked at their guru in surprise. He had turned the picture around at the approximate time when his mother died.

"Let us all sit quietly and pray for her well-being," Gurudev said.

The group sat in silence, but with the end of their prayers came a renewal of their concern. Their voices rose again, insisting that Gurudev go to India.

"If you really feel I should leave, perhaps you'd better leave the ashram. Every day I hear you repeating, 'I am unborn. I never die.' What's the good of such repetition if you don't really believe it? What good is all your chanting and praying if you can be so depressed about this? Who has died? Has the mother died or was it just her body? When the body is old, it goes. That is natural."

The disciples became silent, somewhat pacified. Later that day, however, Gurudev decided to make the trip to India anyway. He had two reasons for this: to fully satisfy the ashramites, who still brooded silently over the matter, and to make his father happy. Sri Kalyana-sunderam was of a sentimental nature. He was sure to feel hurt if his son didn't attend the funeral.

Indian plane connections were few and far between. Arrangements for flights needed to be made well in advance of departure, and a large amount of red tape was put in the way of processes as simple as changing money. Gurudev was able to get a flight to India. The rest of the trip to Chettipalayam had to be made by train. He arrived the following evening — three days after his mother's death.

When he reached the village, the funeral was in progress. His elder brother had made all the necessary arrangements. Immediately, weeping, disconsolate relatives surrounded Gurudev. He asked them to just sit quietly and pray for Srimati Velammai's peace.

On the following day he met privately with his father.

"I am really surprised to see you," Sri Kalyanasunderam said. "Of course, it makes me very happy, but why did you come? Mother told me you said your good-byes at the hospital on your last visit. Before she died, I asked if I should send you a telegram when she passed. She told me, 'Don't disturb him. He has his own work to do. Probably he is just back from an exhausting tour. Don't bother him with such matters.' When she died, I sent the telegram anyway, just to let you know."

"I didn't come for Amma's sake," Gurudev said gently. "She is no longer in the body. Mainly, I came to console you. If I hadn't come, someday you might have thought, 'If he didn't come to the funeral of his own mother, whom he was so close to and who was so attached to him, will he come for my funeral?' You might worry about that and feel bad. I'm just here to tell you I *will* take care of that. If you want, I'll even be at your deathbed when the time comes."

Sri Kalyanasunderam couldn't answer. His son was exactly right. He felt very reassured by these words.

Shortly after Srimati Velammai's death, her husband took the vows of *sannyas*. He visited a number of places of holy pilgrimage and then settled once again in Chettipalayam to meditate and study.

Later, in 1967, Gurudev had journeyed down through India to Bombay after a meeting with the Dalai Lama. While waiting at the Madras Airport for his plane to Coimbatore to visit his father, he received a letter. He opened it on the plane. Sri Kalyanasunderam was very ill and near death. Gurudev reached Chettipalayam in time to fulfill his father's wish.

Gurudev conducted a retreat in Jaffna in early July of 1963. On the evening of the 14th of July, he was at the home of Dr. Chelathurai, a devotee. A prayer meeting was being held, and all the devotees were seated around Gurudev as he led the chanting. After a while, someone took his place and he continued to watch the *bhajan* from a place near the back of the room. What happened next is best told in his own words:

"About 7:00, a strange feeling spread throughout my body — a burning sensation from head to foot. I felt like fainting. I couldn't understand what the problem was and decided not to disturb anyone else. Slowly, I got up from my place and walked into the front yard. The two daughters of my host noticed this and followed me outside. When they asked what they could do for me, I requested that they bring me an easy chair so I could sit down. Immediately, they went to fetch it. Seeing this, the doctor came outside as well and found me seated in the chair. The girls began to fan me with palm leaves to relieve the heat I felt.

"For half an hour, I was not myself. I felt myself fall into a sort of trance. After a time, I came back to consciousness. The burning had disappeared, but I was left with a feeling of great exhaustion. Almost immediately, a great charge of energy swept through me and the tiredness left. It made me feel completely alert and alive. I told the doctor and his children, 'All right, let's go back in.' I felt that something mysterious had occurred, but what, I didn't exactly know. I knew Gurudev Sivanandaji was ailing at the time, but I could not imagine his passing away. After finishing the *bhajan* and saying good-bye to the devotees, a meal was served by my host. I just had something to drink and returned to my sleeping quarters.

"All night I remained in a deep, meditative state, unable to sleep. Early in the morning, the radio news proclaimed the death of Sri Swami Sivanandaji Maharaj in Rishikesh. It had occurred the previous evening.

"At the moment, my feelings were mixed. I was very sad about my Gurudev's passing, that he was in his body no more. At the same time, though, I was overjoyed with the feeling that my Master had entered into my own system.

"Immediately, I left for Kandy, collected the necessary travel documents and drove to Colombo for a flight. This time there was no problem. My devotees easily got me the proper exchange permit, and within an hour had secured a direct flight to Rishikesh.

"During the final ceremonies, a *Siva Lingam* was erected on our Gurudev's tomb. I had the privilege of holding the *Siva Lingam* in position while Sri Swami Chidananda fixed it onto the tomb with special adhesive. This was during the *pradhista* ceremony.

"After a few days at Ananda Kutir, I made a pilgrimage to Badrinath and stayed there for a week. Then I returned to Rishikesh for three weeks. During that time, Sri Swami Chidanandaji was elected president of the Divine Life Society. I went back to Ceylon."

A true spiritual teacher doesn't need advertisements. Have you ever seen a flower sending out a circular to all the bees saying, "I have honey, come to me!"? No. When the flower is in bloom, all it has to do is be and the bees will come. When the tree is laden with fruits, it doesn't need to send invitations to the birds.

A young American woman filmmaker, Yvonne Hanneman, went to the East on a Fulbright Scholarship to research and document folk art.

"When I flew from Bombay to Ceylon, I met a Ceylonese gentleman on the plane. We spoke about a variety of things. Just as we were leaving the airplane, he asked, 'What are you studying?' 'I'm here to document folk art,' I said. My first step on Ceylon soil was accompanied by his reply: 'Why, there's no folk art here!'

"For the first few months, I'd go to the Ceylonese bazaars and — instead of finding beautiful clay bowls, pottery and pieces of folk art — I'd see plastic this and rubber that. It was so depressing. I found the only pieces of folk art that were fresh and alive were those things the people made themselves to give to the Lord. They brought to the religious festivals things they had made. The Hindus always had fantastic garlands of real flowers to decorate the images with. So religious festivals turned out to be the source of my work. And, when I got into the festivals, in order to do a complete job, I had to learn their significance. Since I'd always been interested in the philosophical side of things anyway, this was a sort of easy slide for me to make. I had read about reincarnation before; and, when you're in the East, somehow the gentleness and the atmosphere make you aware that something else is definitely happening underneath.

"I was referred to several Hindu monks, swamis, to find out the information I needed. None of these swamis, with their matted hair, appealed to me. I had heard they were supposed to be very special people, but to me they didn't seem to be.

"My friend Parvati suggested I meet Swami Satchidananda. She said that he could tell me all I needed to know. When she took me to meet him, he was sitting in a chair on a devotee's front porch. Parvati went and prostrated in front of him. The other people with us followed

196

suit. I thought, 'I'll never be able to do that! How can they lay down in front of him like that?' It was too. . .well, I just couldn't imagine myself doing it. The most I finally managed was a pretty good bow. I noticed he was sitting in the only chair, so I sat on the ground. One thing I did not know was that you never sit equal to a swami or a Buddhist monk. You sit beneath them. And they usually sat on a white piece of cloth, never directly on a chair.

"I was a little nervous at first, but every question I asked, he answered in a wonderfully plain, simple way. Finally, I ran out of questions, but I found him so wonderful to be with that I just started inventing questions. Just his physical presence alone was special. And he could really speak English beautifully. Plus he seemed highly intelligent, with the ability to communicate in succinct, meaningful sentences. I thought that was really amazing. Most of the people I had met in Ceylon never did that. They were too busy finding out how many sisters and brothers I had, how long I was there for, who sent me, etc. But the Swami never asked me any personal questions. I kept thinking, 'He's really together.'

"Pretty soon, I ran out of invented questions, too. He had answered them so smoothly and quickly that I couldn't think of any more. I realized that I was getting a little foolish-sounding, so I said good-bye.

"The next time I came, I had a few more questions, but mostly I just wanted to meet him again. There were little things I noticed about him. He looked, well, solid. I began to think, 'Now, *this* is a swami.'

"I did meet people in Ceylon who were quite jealous of him. They told me things like, 'Oh, he's not a traditional swami. He drives a car. He wears a wristwatch.' But it was obvious to me that he drove a car to get places quickly and serve more people, that he wore a watch so he would be on time.

"All my life up until then, I had always been interested in greatness — working for great people, doing great things. I was really interested in quality. I had worked for Charles Eames and Corbusier, and had always wanted to do something great myself. But on subsequent meetings with Swami Satchidananda, I began to feel, 'This is a great person right here and nobody even knows about him.' It was a new dimension for me — that greatness didn't have to be publicized, and that one could just be oneself.

"Every answer the Swami gave me was logical and complete. He would always throw in little extras. For example, at some of the festivals, people would pierce their skin, gouge hooks into the skin and pull carts with ropes threaded through the hooks. Some would walk on nails, walk on fire, hot coals. I asked Swamiji, 'Is this good or bad?' He said, 'I can't really say if it's good or bad, because what's good for one person isn't good for another. Some people like milk and love to drink it. Others don't like it at all; it makes them almost sick. It depends on your disposition. Basically, you have to be sincere. If you walk around with hooks in your back, showing your mind over matter and devotion to God that way, and the next day you turn around and stab somebody because you got into a fight, it's totally meaningless.'

"At one point, I gave him a couple rolls of color film. I didn't know what else I could give him for answering all those questions. I knew film was rare in Ceylon, and he had asked me some questions about photography.

"One day, I was at a great, grand festival — the *Perahera*. The streets were completely cleared. All the people were lined up on either side, behind barricades. I had been given special permission to walk in the street in order to take pictures. I was walking backward down the street, photographing the elephants approaching. I just kept stepping backward. The next thing I knew, I had bumped into somebody. I turned around and there was Swami Satchidananda — completely laden down with cameras, light meters, movie film. With a big smile, he said, 'I'm using your film!' I thought, 'How wonderful. This is a real swami who can make the jump between East and West, not held down by all the Eastern customs and patterns. He's so practical.'"

Yvonne Gita Hanneman, U.S.A.

"One morning at the Kandy ashram, I went to see Gurudev and found him in a pensive mood. 'Swamiji, are you contemplating how to catch your innocent ashramites tonight?' I asked playfully.

"'I am seeing a vision,' he replied. 'I am seated in a large glass globe, and globes with glowing shrines of all religions are rotating around that central globe.'

"I said, 'But, Swamiji, already the mobile shrines of all religions are revolving around your inspiration.'

"'Yes, but I want the whole world to come together, to love one another in spite of superficial differences and pray to the universal Light, according to their individual beliefs.'

"I always referred to Gurudev as the Star of Bethlehem, because his light showed the location of the Truth, and I said, 'The risen Star has come more than halfway around the world and has only a little more distance to cover.' This was in 1966."

Mrs. Rukmini Rasiah, Sri Lanka

Holy pilgrimage to Badrinath.

Sri Swami Satchidananda — West

The hour before dawn is the blackest time of night. A great change has already begun. We are living now amid violence and confusion, but we are on the brink of a great age of spirituality. Whenever we take a young plant from its nursery and replant it elsewhere, the plant withers. Many of the leaves fall off, but that doesn't mean it is dying. Until it gets rooted, the plant shakes a bit and trembles, but it must face that shaking and overcome it because it can't come to full growth in the nursery itself.

Young people today are being transplanted into another area altogether and so we see this shaking. We see it all over the globe. But I see a very bright future. All the shaking will cease. Slowly, slowly, we are getting rerooted in the right place, with the right ideas. Consciousness is expanding everywhere, and America is going to lead the way. It is time for the West to show the East. There is great peace here and love. We can spread this peace everywhere, all over the world. The West has realized the superficiality of the material life. The West is crying for true knowledge and is getting it.

I have a great hope. There is great awakening. The whole world is going to enjoy the peace through you people. Day by day I see it progressing. All these calamities, all these wars will come to an end. We will all soon be enjoying the bliss of that peaceful sunshine, no doubt.

Sri Swami Satchidananda — West

There is a Divine Plan behind everything. If we allow ourselves to be used as good instruments by that Unseen Force many things can happen in a mysterious, miraculous way. If we interfere with that Plan by introducing our own plan, the egocentric plan, tension will be created. In any event, ultimately, the Divine Plan will win out.

Sri Lanka — known as Ceylon when Sri Gurudev lived there — was a true paradise. With its lovely climate and beautiful scenery it held a great attraction for tourists. Many of the Western tourists visiting Ceylon were directed to Satchidananda Thapovanam, Gurudev's ashram. The entire country knew of the young yoga master and his work. Letters addressed to "Swami Satchidananda, Ceylon" were immediately routed to Kandy.

When these Westerners met him they invariably said, "Swamiji, you must come to the West."

"Fine, fine. If God wants that, certainly I will do it."

Then the tourists would go back to their countries with their souvenirs and color photographs, and the matter would end there.

One evening in 1965, Gurudev was holding *satsang* with the ashramites when the ring of the telephone interrupted. It was Fred De Silva, Kandy's Deputy Mayor and a devotee of Gurudev.

"Swamiji, there is a young American man staying at my guest house. He seems to be interested in yoga and would like to come see you. When can you see him?"

"Well, we are having *satsang* now. He can come right away."

"He doesn't want to meet with you in front of others. He wants to see you all by himself, quietly. Can he come later? Every day he sleeps until twelve or one o'clock in the afternoon. He starts working at five in the evening and doesn't go to bed until three. Ten o'clock tonight will be convenient for him. Can he come then?"

"If he is really interested, let me see him then. It's all right."

At ten, Conrad Rooks arrived at the ashram. He was blond, tan, all-American looking, dressed in a well-pressed lightweight suit.

The floor of the main room in the cottage was covered with a woven carpet upon which the devotees sat cross-legged. There was a chair for the guru and an extra chair for elderly guests or foreigners who were not used to sitting on the floor. Gurudev ushered Rooks to the extra chair.

"Swamiji, I can sit on the floor. I'm used to it." He lowered himself to the floor, legs crossed at the ankles, knees reaching almost to his chin. He was quite proud of his accomplishment.

"Very good. Are you comfortable?" Gurudev asked.

"Oh yes. I am used to sitting and meditating for a long time. Swami, I don't want to take up much of your time. I just wanted to ask you one or two questions about *pranayama, kundalini* and *japa*." (These are not subjects for novices.)

"Fine. You seem to know quite a bit. What are your doubts?"

Gurudev answered the guest's questions one by one. Finally he said, "These few practices are not yoga; they are only aids. A person should practice yoga throughout his life, twenty-four hours each day. A person can't be a yogi for half an hour and a non-yogi at all other times."

As the time passed tension drained from the tanned face of the guest. His hands and even his legs appeared to relax. They continued their discussion. Suddenly Conrad checked his watch.

"Swami, it's 12:30!"

"That's all right. Are you in a hurry to go?"

"No, no. I'm in no hurry, but I had originally expected to return to my house within about twenty minutes. I have left my taxi driver waiting outside all this time."

He ran to the road and found the driver slumped loosely over the wheel — sound asleep. Conrad stayed with Gurudev until two in the morning.

"May I come again tomorrow?"

"Yes. What time will you come?"

"Any time you want. I would like to bathe in the river with you, meditate, learn some more, even take initiation from you."

"In that case, you can come for the bath in the river at 6:30 A.M. Can you make it then?"

"Yes, yes I can."

At exactly the appointed hour Conrad returned to the cottage for the bath. He was fully dressed in his well-pressed suit, cowboy boots and hat.

"Swami, are you ready?"

"Sure, let's go. Do you have anything to change into — a bathing suit?"

"No, but I don't mind. I can just take everything off and bathe."

"You mean you will come for a bath naked?"

"Yes, I'm used to it."

"Well, you may be used to it but this country isn't used to it. Here, take a towel."

Conrad wrapped the towel around his waist and followed Gurudev to the river. The guru walked into waist-deep water and repeated a prayer. Conrad watched quietly and did the same.

During the course of the day Gurudev introduced his new devotee to the techniques of *pranayama* and *japa*. By that time Conrad's cameraman had arrived at the Thapovanam and begun shooting film.

"That's a big camera," Gurudev commented.

"It's a 35mm professional camera."

Mr. De Silva had remarked on the wealth of the young American and Gurudev simply assumed that he had a hobby of making 35mm home movies. Later this footage was incorporated into the professional filmmaker's autobiographical film *Chappaqua*.

After two weeks Conrad decided to stay at least three months. He continued to visit the ashram for daily instruction and discussion with his spiritual teacher. After only ten days, however, he received a cable from his office in Paris. He was asked to return for some urgent business matters.

"Swamiji, I don't know what to do. I'll do whatever you want. Shall I just reply that I'm not coming?"

"No," Gurudev counseled. "That is not fair. If you have some business to take care of, you'd better go back. Settle everything and then come back here."

Conrad left. A month later Gurudev still hadn't heard from him.

After another few weeks Gurudev received a call from BOAC in Colombo. "Swami Satchidananda? We have a ticket waiting for you, round-trip, Colombo-Paris-Colombo. What date will you be flying?"

"I didn't buy any ticket. There must be some mistake."

"The ticket came from Paris."

"Who sent it?"

"A Mr. Conrad Rooks."

(right) Filmmaker Conrad Rooks.
(below) Conrad's first meeting with
Sri Gurudev.

206

"Well, I can't give you a date now. I have no such plans. I will call you after I hear from Mr. Rooks myself."

When BOAC informed Conrad of his guru's decision he immediately sent off a cable: "I have already sent a ticket. I am unable to come to Ceylon so you must come and visit me here for at least two months. Take a holiday and see the West. At least see Europe. Please come."

Within fifteen days Gurudev completed arrangements for the running of the ashram in his absence. He told his disciples he would return to Kandy in a month. The sister of Satchidananda Mataji, Swami Vimalanandaji, who had been initiated into *sannyas* by Gurudev, was put in charge of the Kandy Thapovanam. Gurudev left Kandy on the 22nd of March 1966.

Vimalanandaji, a deeply dedicated servant of God, once described her introduction to Gurudev:

"Some years before I met Gurudev I was waiting for something, though I didn't know what it was. One day I dreamed of a tall person robed in *gerua* cloth. He was holding up his right hand, but I couldn't clearly see his face, and he said, 'Wait for fifteen. . .' I couldn't hear his final words, and I woke up. Because I was waiting for something, in my anxiety I thought 'fifteen days,' but fifteen days passed and still nothing happened. Then I thought, 'fifteen months.' Nothing happened.

"After waiting fifteen years, on February 1, 1953, Gurudev placed his lotus feet in Trincomalee. From the time I saw him I was drawn toward him like a needle to a magnet. I had a strong feeling that no harm could come to me if only I could hold his feet strong and tight. With all my faults and unwanted thoughts, I tried hard to surrender myself completely to him. Oh, what daily struggles I had within me. And Gurudev gave me the strength and courage to win the inner battles."

It is time for the West to lead the way. I can see a bright future for the West. There is a great spiritual reawakening.

It was Easter. On the way to Paris, Gurudev stopped in Cairo, Jerusalem and Rome.

Father Joachim Pillai of the Kandy seminary, a good friend of Gurudev, wrote an introductory letter to Father Benoit, a Dominican monk in Jerusalem who headed the research group of a Bible school. Father Benoit wrote back that he would arrange Gurudev's accommodations there.

In Paris, during filming of Chappaqua.

On his arrival, the Father went across the street from his mission to check on the hotel room for the Eastern monk. As Gurudev waited for Father Benoit's return, the Abbot who headed the school entered.

When Father Benoit returned, the Abbot said, "Why should you let such a man stay in a hotel. I think he should stay with us. Let's offer him a room and invite him to stay here as long as he wants."

Gurudev thanked his hosts and was led to an upstairs room that opened onto a view of the pink roofs of the entire city — its churches, synagogues, mosques and bazaars.

During his stay he attended Mass and held discussions and lectures for the Mission fathers.

"My encounter with Swami Satchidananda was very short but impressive. We had some good conversations about yoga and spiritual life. I asked him for advice about Hatha Yoga *asanas* that I had tried to practice myself, and he asked me to take him to the Holy Sepulchre of Christ.

"I asked him if he would like to see other places like the dome of the rock and so on. 'No,' he replied, 'only the Church of the Cross and the Resurrection.'

"We went there and I was very impressed by the way he knelt before the place of the Cross and prayed with deep concentration. When we went out into the streets people were astonished by the sight of his colorful dress. Some said, 'He is a rabbi!' Others said, 'Oh! Look at Jesus Christ.'

"He smiled quietly and told me, 'Do not pay attention. I am used to that.'

"These days were short but we grew to be good friends."
–*Pierre Benoit, O.P.*

Mr. Duraiswamy, Ambassador from Ceylon to Rome, knew Gurudev well. He met Satchidanandaji at the plane and brought him to his home as a guest. As they sat comfortably in a drawing room and talked, the Ambassador asked, "Swamiji, would you like to meet Pope Paul VI?"

Although he hadn't thought of it before, Gurudev agreed it was a fine idea. Ambassador Duraiswamy called the Vatican and spoke to Cardinal Morello. Although private audiences with the Holy Father were possible, they generally took a week to arrange.

"Swami Satchidanandaji is leaving Rome tomorrow. He has a commitment in Paris."

"In that case," the Cardinal said, "let me meet him for a chat first. Then we can decide about his audience with the Holy Father."

"When do you want to see him?"

"Immediately."

Gurudev and Sri Duraiswamy visited the Cardinal in his Vatican office. A twenty-minute meeting stretched to over two hours as Gurudev answered the Cardinal's questions about yoga and the Hindu religion. When the visit ended, Cardinal Morello said, "I haven't met a person like you before. I think you and the Holy Father must meet one another. I'll arrange for your private audience tomorrow."

The following day Gurudev and the Ambassador returned to the Vatican. Gurudev had thought about the proper way to greet a Pope and decided to do it in the traditional Indian fashion.

They walked through the long, high halls, feet softly clicking in the marble corridors. When they reached the Holy Father, Gurudev took out a lime and offered it to him. The Pontiff was rather surprised and asked, "What does this lime signify?"

"When Hindus go to meet a sage, a swami or a saintly person they bring a lime. It symbolizes an offering and, at the same time, has a beneficial medicinal effect on the system. When you sit for a long time in meditation a great deal of heat is produced. Bile secretion develops. The lime juice cools the system and serves as a remedy."

The Pope smiled and accepted the gift. Gurudev praised the Holy Father's efforts to promote understanding among all Christians. "Now, why don't you come forward to bring the entire world together — all people, regardless of religious or racial differences? It is not only the Christians who should come together. All people should unite in the name of religious harmony. Your word could carry a great deal of weight in helping people realize the oneness of the spirit."

Pope Paul VI nodded in agreement. "Certainly that is a noble idea, Swamiji. But for the time being I think I should concentrate on putting my own house in order before going out to help the whole world."

When Gurudev arrived in Paris on the 6th of April 1966, Conrad was not at the airport. In his place was a secretary. "Conrad is in London. He'll be back in about three days, but in the meantime he hopes you will be comfortable in his home." They drove to Montmartre in a black taxicab, passing tourists photographing the sights, speeding through rotary turns and the narrow cobbled streets, past the River and the cafes.

For three days Gurudev walked around the area, frequently visiting the Sacred Heart Church. A small trickle of people, then larger and larger numbers began to call on him for private interviews. He met Mr. and Mrs. Raymond Lambert, Hatha Yoga instructors.

Two great spiritual leaders: a private audience with His Holiness Pope Paul VI.

"We first saw Gurudev at the Ramakrishna Vedanta Center near Paris. He came with a friend of ours. As soon as he appeared my husband had to leave the dining room and go to the chapel, so struck was he by the appearance of this man. We at once recognized Gurudev as the eternal guru of the Indian tradition. Immediately we felt the significance of his presence for the spiritual work to be done in France."

–Janine Lambert, Paris, France

When Gurudev received word that Conrad was delayed with business in America and would not be in Paris for a while, it seemed the perfect opportunity to fulfill the wish of several devotees. Some devotees from Ceylon were now living in London. They had often asked Gurudev to visit them if he was ever in the West.

These Ceylonese were delighted to have Gurudev visit their London homes. Mr. Sivajnanajyothi, president of the Bank of Ceylon in London, invited Gurudev to stay in his home. The devotees hosted him royally, taking him to see all the sights and proudly bringing their friends to meet this great spiritual teacher. Perhaps most of all, however, Gurudev enjoyed playing with his host's two daughters. The seven- and eleven-year-old girls adored him.

One day, when their father was unable to pick them up after school, Gurudev went to meet the girls. As he waited, the final bell rang and children began running out of the school. When they saw Gurudev, they stopped. "Santa Claus! Santa Claus!" Soon forty children were jumping and dancing happily around him. "Santa Claus, did you get my letter?" "Santa, what are you going to give me for Christmas?" The parents were upset. Who was this strange man, dressed in an orange robe? Why were their children all gathered around him? One of the parents ran to alert a nearby policeman.

"Hey!" the policeman called brusquely. "What are you doing there?"

Gurudev answered politely, "Officer, I came here to fetch the children of my host."

"But why are there so many children around you?"

"Probably you should ask them. I don't know them. I didn't ask them to come to me. They simply came and started calling me Santa Claus."

"Stay here. Don't move," the officer commanded Gurudev.

Finally the policeman managed to gather the excited children and send them off to join their parents. He was still skeptical. "Now, where are the children you came to fetch?"

The girls came forward. "Officer, he is our swami and our friend. He is staying in our house, and he just came to get us after school."

"All right. I see that you were telling the truth, sir. I'm sorry for the inconvenience. You may go now."

This was the first of countless times that Western children would see Gurudev and call delightedly, "Santa Claus!"

The stay in London lasted fifteen days. Conrad had returned to Paris, and Gurudev joined him there before traveling to Belgium.

When the headquarters of the Divine Life Society heard I was coming to the West they asked me to visit some of the DLS branches in Europe to explain more about yoga. I wrote to these different centers from Paris. I received a very loving letter from Aalst, Belgium. It was the nicest one of all. From the moment I received it I felt it came from beautiful people. This letter came from the Kiekens brothers. In Dutch, Kiekens means 'chickens.' Normally it is the hen who gives warmth to the chickens, but in this case it was the chickens who gave warmth to the hen. They received me graciously in their homes, and their yogic family began to grow.

"When we heard that Swami Satchidananda would be available to visit us in Aalst, we immediately sent a ticket and booked the town hall for two lectures. Five days later, Swamiji arrived in Brussels. We met him at the train. He stayed for a week and worked hard with us during that time. Swamiji was the first yoga teacher we had met. He visited our classes, gave directions and criticism, told us how to practice relaxation, breathing practices, how to do *kirtan*. He gave mantra initiation to three people of the group. We learned more in these five days, than we had during all the previous years of our yoga practice. Swamiji agreed to be the patron of our branch of the DLS. For us, he is Master Sivanandaji in disguise."

–*Narayana Kiekens, Belgium*

"For us, he is Master Sivanandaji in disguise." Gurudev speaks at a three-day conference in Belgium.

Yogis of Aalst. (standing, from left) Mrs. Hageman, Ravi, Simonetta, Ram, Narayana, Lakshmi. (seated) Gopal, Nirmala, Siva, Shankar.

214

The monks at Mt. Athos, Greece, were strict vegetarians.

Gurudev and his hosts were on a bus returning from a visit to a spot in the beautiful Aalst countryside. On the same bus were children returning from school. They were fascinated with Gurudev, and asked many questions. "Where have you been? Where are you going now? What will you do there?"

The children disregarded the name they heard when this wonderful person was introduced to them; they knew who he *really* was! A stream of excited young students went running home to tell their parents that Saint Nicholas was going to give a talk in their town that very night. Quite a few people came to the *satsang* that evening because their children had brought them to see Saint Nicholas. They stayed because they were moved by the words Gurudev spoke.

Nine weeks had passed since Gurudev left Kandy. One afternoon he spoke with Conrad about different religions. The filmmaker told him about his trip to Mt. Athos, Greece — a peninsula cut off from the convenience of the modern world. It was surrounded by the Aegean Sea and housed a great number of monasteries. All the inhabitants were monks. No woman, not even a female animal, was allowed to set foot on its stony soil.

"There's no point to my going on about it, Swamiji. I can't explain in words how beautiful, how peaceful it is. You must go there and see for yourself."

Conrad's secretary made arrangements for transportation and accommodations. It was necessary to get a special letter from Greece's Cultural Ministry and a permit for the journey from the monks of Mt. Athos. Reservations were made for Gurudev at the Hotel Nirvana in Athens.

"Very good," he told Conrad. "I will be glad to attain Nirvana."

Once on the peninsula he stayed at the oldest and largest of its twenty monasteries. There were many similarities between Hindu custom and the way in which these monks lived. They arose early in the morning for meditation. They never ate meat.

Gurudev asked the priests the reason for the regulation concerning women. None of the monks seemed to know why it was done. They said it was just custom and didn't seem very interested in the matter. Though Gurudev had great respect for these monks and their path, he still questioned the wisdom of a situation which totally avoided even the most reserved contact with their sisters in God's family.

A letter from Conrad awaited Gurudev in Athens. "I have made arrangements for you to stay another two weeks. Please go to Switzerland as my guest. You will really enjoy it."

Before Gurudev left for Geneva, Conrad asked him a favor.

"Swamiji, there is something I would like you to do for me there. Near Geneva there is a place called Saint-Cerque, which has a small private school. I have heard about this school and want to know if it's a suitable place for my son. You suggested that I put him in a nice school where he can be well-educated and learn responsibility. I'd like you to investigate this one; stay as long as you want and see if it's a good place to send the boy." Gurudev visited Rome and then went on to Switzerland.

There were about forty boys, ranging in age from six to twelve, at the school. Gurudev became their special playmate. He would lie on the rolling lawn, and the boys would hold him by the legs and pull him all over. They would jump about him, laughing and prancing. Gurudev had a fantastic time with them. He spent all his days there playing like a child.

In the evenings Mr. Aubrey, the principal, would invite the local adults to listen to Gurudev's lectures on yoga. While he was there he started a small Hatha Yoga class for those interested.

"How is the school?" Conrad asked over the phone.

"Fine. I am enjoying it very much."

"Conrad, fourteen weeks have passed. I said I would return in one. I'd better go back to Kandy now."

"Swamiji, I've been watching you. I've seen so many Westerners benefit from your presence. Instead of going straight back to Ceylon why don't you go around the other way and visit my country also. Then you can fly back via Japan."

"Well, I really wasn't prepared for such a journey, but if you think it's worthwhile I'll do it." Gurudev had seen for many years how the Lord worked through him, how he was an instrument. This time he allowed his destiny to rest in Conrad's well-manicured hands, at least for the time being.

Conrad's secretary returned to the travel agency and exchanged Gurudev's ticket for one around the world.

Two days later Conrad said, "I don't think you'll enjoy America. It's a crazy, crazy country. If you go there you'll probably develop a very poor opinion of Americans, and I don't want you to think so little of us. You'd better go directly back to Ceylon."

They had to wait another three days for the changed reservation to be confirmed. During that time a young New York artist arrived in

Paris to work on some publicity material for the movie *Chappaqua*. For two weeks Peter Max stayed in Paris, working on the material and finding time to visit and speak with Gurudev.

"The business which I came here for isn't as important as the business of meeting you, Swamiji. You should come to New York so that more Americans can meet you."

"I don't care about going anywhere, but if Providence wants me to go, I'll go."

"I think I'll pray for your visit."

"Early one morning I received a call from someone named Conrad Rooks in France. He wanted me to go to Paris. When I asked why, he said, 'I'm making a movie. Ravi Shankar is here and Allen Ginsberg and Man Ray and Swami Satchidananda, and I want you too.' I never knew what a swami was, even though I'd lived in India in Hindu monasteries.

"Three days later I arrived in Paris. It had been a bad flight. I hadn't eaten and was very tense. Conrad met me, and as we were driving down the Champs Elysee he said, 'Man, what's the matter with you? You look really uptight. What you should do is meet the Swami when we get back to the hotel.'

"I asked him, 'What's a swami?' He said, 'Well, it's a yogi.' This was before yoga was very well known in America. I just remembered what yogis were like in cartoons and so forth, but I thought, 'Okay, so I'll meet a swami.'

"Conrad and I were sitting in the hotel dining room having some breakfast. He had invited the Swami to join us. Across the room were two big golden doors which led into the hotel lobby. I was buttering a roll and having some cold water and feeling better. Suddenly the golden doors opened, and there was this tall beautiful figure with black hair and an orange robe. I said to Conrad, 'Who's *that*?' Very softly he said, 'That's the Swami.'

"The Swami leaned over the table and shook my hand, and I was completely relaxed within two minutes. He offered me some hot cocoa that looked just like his beautiful eyes did.

"Later I went with Conrad to look at some footage from the film. He wanted me to meet with the famous Dadaist Man Ray, but I told him I was a little bit tired and really needed to go back. 'By the way,' I asked casually, 'What's the Swami's room number?' He told me. I walked very calmly out of the building where we had been looking at footage from the film. As soon as I was outside and thought no one could see me I started running. I ran all the way to the hotel and dialed

218

Swamiji's room number. When he answered the phone, he said, 'Hello, Peter? Come on, come on up.'

"In his room, I sat on the floor and he sat on the bed. There was incense all over the room. I asked him questions about yoga, and he answered. I felt that this was the holiest of moments that I had ever experienced. I was amazed that there was a real human being like this.

"During the time I was in Paris, I heard many words of great wisdom from Swamiji. Every time he spoke, I had to think about it all day long. I knew that this was the real reason I was in Paris, and I knew that America really needed him."

–Peter Max, New York City

Conrad changed his mind. "Swamiji, I think you'd better go through the States. . .but don't stop in New York. I mean, every other place is okay. You'd better go to California. It's really a beautiful place. If you avoid New York, the States are very nice."

"All right, Conrad. I have told my friends in London I would visit them again if I passed that way. Also my good brother monk in Montreal, Swami Vishnudevanandaji, would like me to visit him. Please arrange the ticket London-Montreal-California, then Japan."

While in London, Gurudev met an old friend—a Buddhist *bhikku*. In Ceylon, this *bhikku* had come to Gurudev in order to learn about Patanjali's Raja Yoga *sutras*. The two friends were happy to meet once again, and Gurudev went with the *bhikku* to visit the Buddhist center in London. Visiting the center at the same time was the monk who headed the Buddhist center in West Berlin. He was immediately impressed by Gurudev. "Swamiji, you must return with me to Berlin. Since you are in this part of the world, I want to take advantage of the opportunity to have you give some talks at our center."

After five days in Berlin, Gurudev returned to London. Conrad called. "Swamiji, when are you leaving for Montreal?"

"The day after tomorrow."

"Uhh, I think you'd better change it and stay for at least two days in New York. I was thinking; if you go back and people ask you where you've visited and you don't say New York, they'll want to know why. If you tell them I told you not to go, what will they think of me? New York is the world's biggest city. At least for the sake of seeing it, go there for two days. I'll call Peter Max and tell him you're coming."

"Fine. If you'd like that, I'll do it."

He cancelled the direct flight to Montreal and had to wait another two days for his TWA flight to New York City. Conrad telephoned

Peter with the new flight information. Gurudev would arrive in New York late at night on July 31, 1966.

The day before the flight TWA went on strike. Gurudev made arrangements to fly with Air Canada, stop over in Montreal for an hour, then go to New York. The airline agreed to cable Gurudev's new flight information to Peter and also to Yvonne Hanneman.

Though we can't always see it at the time, if we look upon events with some perspective we see that things always happen for our best interests. We are being guided in a way better than we know ourselves.

The transatlantic airliner was filled with passengers — excited, talkative adults and restless children. Stewardesses moved quickly and efficiently up and down the aisles, smiling broadly. Occasionally one of Gurudev's fellow passengers would furtively lean over and take a good look at this man with the long hair and gray beard, dressed in an orange robe, sitting comfortably and reading a magazine.

"Is there anybody meeting you at the airport?" his neighbor asked.

"Yes, I'm expecting one or two friends."

It was almost midnight when they arrived at JFK Airport, International Arrivals. As Gurudev went through customs he looked up toward the glass-enclosed observation deck. It was jammed with greeting parties like pickles in a jar, but neither Peter nor Yvonne was there. The promised cables had never arrived.

A co-passenger kindly noted the problem and suggested, "Why don't you take the limousine with me to the West Side Terminal? Maybe your people will be waiting there."

The West Side Terminal's fluorescent lights glared onto vast, empty halls. A newspaper vendor leaned over his magazines, chewing a cigar, while two janitors made a pretense of sweeping the endless dirty floors with their brooms. Peter and Yvonne weren't there. Gurudev decided to explore the New York telephone directory and call them. He walked to a stand and found four huge books with dog-eared pages.

"My goodness, how am I going to find them in here?" he wondered. After a long search through the pages Gurudev found Peter's number, but he didn't know how to use the coin telephone.

It seemed that hundreds of people were in line at the information section. One harassed-looking lady was taking care of their problems. Eventually she met the guru's gaze.

"Yes?" She looked at his orange outfit.

"Can you dial a number for me?"

"Give it to me."

Before turning to the request of this bearded man she filed her nails, skimmed through a pocketbook and worked on innumerable details. Eventually Gurudev heard the voice of Peter's wife, Liz, on the other end of the phone.

"I'm Swami Satchidananda. I'm waiting for Mr. Peter Max."

"Swami! Where are you calling from?"

"West Side Terminal."

"Peter is at the airport looking for you but I'm home. Please take a cab straight over. It's okay. I'd come get you, but I'm going to have a baby soon, and it's hard for me to get around."

Gurudev waited in front of the terminal for a cab. There was no proper line, and whenever a cab pulled in, someone would run to the curb out of turn and jump in. Finally Gurudev walked to the edge of the curb and waited until a bright yellow taxi pulled up in front of him.

"Where we goin'?"

"I'm going to 118 Riverside Drive."

"That 84th?"

"I told you, Riverside Drive, 118."

"Yeah, yeah. But is it 84th?"

"No, not 84. 118 Riverside."

"84th, 85th, 83rd? Don't worry, I'll getcha there."

The cab driver drove his passenger right to the door.

Gurudev stood in front of the New York apartment and rang the bell. The door opened. The woman inside exclaimed and slammed the door in his face!

Once again he rang the bell. The door was opened a cautious inch. "I am Swami Satchidananda. Is this the apartment of Peter Max?"

Now the door opened wide. "Oh, Swami. I'm so sorry. Please come right in."

Liz had never seen a swami before. Her big blue eyes widened as she showed him in. He put his bag down and made himself comfortable in a white cane chair. The whole living room was white — white rugs, walls, ceiling. Where the walls weren't white they were mirrored. Gurudev looked at the reflection of Swami, Swami, Swami stretching infinitely in either direction. He walked to the high windows and looked down fifteen stories out to the West Side Highway and its line of white headlights and red tail lights, like a school diagram of the circulatory system. The wide patch of black further north was the Hudson River. Little lights bobbed up and down at the 79th Street Boat Basin;

bigger ones swept up and down the waterway. The phone rang.

"Liz, has Swamiji called there?"

"Yes, Peter, he's sitting right here in the living room."

"The living room? I'll be right back."

At 1 A.M. Peter threw open his front door with a resounding bang and raced into the living room.

By the following day the apartment was filled with Peter's friends, all asking questions and all interested in this Swami. After a few hours of speaking, Gurudev excused himself and decided to try finding Yvonne Hanneman.

"The Christmas after I left Ceylon I received a Christmas card from Swamiji. I wrote him a small note and didn't hear from him until the following Christmas when I received another Christmas card.

"The next year I received a letter from London telling me that he was coming to New York for two days and asking if I could make accommodations for him. I wrote back, 'Yes, but please stay longer. There are many people here interested in Eastern philosophy who would like to hear you speak.' The letter must have reached him, but I didn't receive a reply due to a mail strike. I knew what day he was expected, but I had no idea of his flight number, what time he was coming or where I could reach him. Then I realized my name wasn't even in the phone book and, because I was living in someone else's apartment, it wasn't even on the door. I wondered if he would ever find me, but I decided to paint the room he would be staying in, just in case.

"The afternoon after he was supposed to arrive, the family who owned this apartment came home unexpectedly early from vacation. I said, 'I've invited Swami Satchidananda to stay here.' But they didn't have any place else to go so we all decided to stay in one room and give Swamiji the other.

"I continued with my painting. Within an hour there was a knock on the door. I opened it. There was Swamiji looking so beautiful in his orange robes and smiling face in the middle of this dingy, grubby tenement on East 21st Street.

"'How did you ever find me?' I asked him.

"'I had an address from your last letter and just took a cab here. When I didn't see your name I asked the superintendent if he knew a certain photographer. He led me right to you.'

"Swamiji literally had to dig me out of a building in the middle of Manhattan.

"We went to the Empire State building with a friend and her

daughter. We thought the most important thing for Swamiji to be doing in New York was seeing all the sights. We had to wait on a long elevator line, but eventually we reached the top. After a while Swamiji said, 'Wait a minute. I'll be right back.' We were busy looking through the telescopes and having a good time when suddenly I realized Swamiji hadn't returned. I figured I'd better look for him so he wouldn't get lost.

"I walked to the inside of the observation deck and saw a huge bank of machines — sandwich machines, soft drink machines, candy machines — and there was Swamiji, standing right in front of the ice cream machine, reading the directions and concentrating very hard. It was probably the first automatic vending machine he had ever seen. I thought, 'I'd better not be seen checking up on him,' and went back inside.

"About a minute later, Swamiji returned. 'Hello. I have a little surprise for you.' He proudly presented each of us with an ice cream sandwich, taking the last for himself. 'I did it from the machine,' he smiled. 'Quite fine machines. It would be wonderful to have them in your house. You wouldn't have to do any cooking.'"

–Yvonne Hanneman, New York

Though these American children didn't seem to know how to behave I could see they were seeking. I wouldn't expect such treatment in India, but this wasn't India. Sometimes I would think, "Is this the way they behave in front of their own clergy?" Then I would accept it, knowing that they were sincere seekers.

The original two-day stopover passed. Ten to fifteen people crowded into Peter's apartment each evening to watch and listen. Gurudev was glad to see the interest of these Americans. He also began to understand Conrad's warnings. The visitors constantly smoked in his face and sat in front of him, stretching their legs practically into his lap. He patiently accepted it and continued answering their questions.

Gurudev was subject to tremendous discomfort, mostly because of the new students' lack of knowledge. Yvonne herself had no compunction about dragging her guru onto the subways, crowded buses, here and there all over the city. Often she took him to Chinese restaurants. Eventually Yvonne learned of his afternoon rest. After lunch they would go back to her apartment and Gurudev would rest on the floor.

Many Peter Max drawings were inspired by Sri Gurudev.

Dearest Swamiji
You are the sunshine
Happy Birthday —
Love, Peter Altman Max
and Family — 1984

At the evening gatherings, the students would ask, "Swami, what is this *prana?*" while blowing smoke about the room. Finally he asked them not to do this, saying that it bothered his throat. They began to crowd into the bathroom to smoke their cigarettes.

Gurudev spoke wherever he was invited. Many times when people came to see him they were "tripping" on LSD or "stoned" on marijuana or hashish.

"The 1960s were a time of turmoil in America. Young people were noticing the hypocrisy and emptiness of the values of modern society. They noticed the inequality in the world, the hate, the lack of compassion, and the endless fighting. The young people of the 1960s rebelled. Some of them actually fought the system they abhorred by using violence against what they called 'the Establishment.' Some used peaceful means of non-violent marching and protesting, some fought physically, others tried to escape totally by using drugs. Yet, they encountered the same problems within themselves, a feeling of emptiness behind all these actions and attempts to escape. Their music screamed and so did their souls. It was into this atmosphere of confusion and searching that teachers like Sri Swami Satchidananda came to speak about yoga. Only someone of divine vision could look upon the 'flower children' of America and see something beautiful there. In rebellion against their families and society they dressed wildly, acted with disrespect, and many never bathed. But their hearts were beautiful. Gurudev was able to see that beauty beneath the dirt, and he began to patiently teach."

–P.M., *Washington, D.C.*

Liz Max was finding it difficult with the house always crowded, a small child to care for and another one on the way. The group that had formed around Gurudev decided to set up for him elsewhere. Victor Zurbel offered his apartment.

"I'll stay at my friend's. You can use this place, Swamiji."

He told Victor, "There's no need for you to move out just for my sake. If you like you can stay here also."

"All right. I'll be at work the whole day. I'll just come here to sleep at night."

"Swamiji arrived the next morning. I was very busy with work and had very little time to be with him during the day so I told him of all the places nearby which he could visit by himself. 'The Museum of Natural History is one block away; the American Historical Society is on the corner, and Central Park is just across the street.' He warmly replied that he had been traveling around the world and would be quite content just to stay inside. I felt he was a little unsure about traveling by himself so I offered to break away at lunch time and escort him to the museums and the park since it was such a beautiful day. He looked into my eyes with warmth and said, 'I will really be quite happy to stay inside. I have many parks and museums within me.'

"What happened then is difficult to put into words. I felt that I too wanted to discover the parks and museums within myself. I didn't know it at the time, but I had just accepted Swami Satchidananda as my guru. Tears of joy streamed down my cheeks as I bid Swamiji a good day and took off for my office. Incidentally, it was one of the most productive days of my career.

"I had a large bedroom with two beds; I offered Swamiji the large bed and took the little one for myself. The first night he stayed there I came home at about three in the morning, quietly took off my shoes, changed into my pajamas, and tip-toed into the bedroom. There, to my wonder, was Swamiji lying on his back with his palms up in the corpse pose. I got into bed and then realized that I had to be up at seven, but the alarm clock was on the table next to Swamiji's bed and the outlet was underneath his bed. Resigning myself to the fact that I was not about to go crawling under his bed at three in the morning, I went to sleep. But I didn't go right to sleep. First I turned this way, then that way. Then I put my arm under my head, then I turned on my stomach. Swamiji's stillness, however, was making me very aware of my own movements, to the point that I felt like some kind of wild animal next to him. So, imitating Swamiji, I just rolled over on my back, put my hands alongside my body and went into the most wonderful dreamless sleep I had ever experienced.

"I woke up fully refreshed, looked at my watch and saw that it was exactly seven o'clock. Swamiji was not in bed. I went into the bathroom to shower and shave, and when I came out Swamiji was holding a coffee mug, offering its contents to me to drink. I drank the delicious beverage and asked him what it was.

"'Hot milk with honey,' he told me. 'Don't you drink it?' I told him, 'I used to when I was sick as a child.' He smiled and said, 'You should drink it when you are well, not when you are sick. I saw you come in so quietly last night so that you wouldn't disturb me. Very nice of you.' 'But, Swamiji,' I said, 'if you saw me come in then I must have disturbed you.'

"'No disturbance,' he reassured me. 'If the mind is restful during the day it does not even need sleep. I just rest the body and put the mind away, sort of like putting it in a drawer. If I need it I take it out and then gently put it back again.'

"The little things that happened in the weeks that followed could fill the pages of a whole book, but I'll just say that I had the extraordinary privilege of having Swamiji's acquaintance as a friend, only slowly discovering the depth and magnitude of his being. Everything I was learning was by the way of gentle example — how to move chairs, close doors, sleep, eat, and so on. Before Swamiji moved in, my apartment was a storehouse for antiques and old junk. When he moved out of my apartment it was spotless, the walls were clear. While I was uncluttering my apartment I noticed that my mind was getting uncluttered at the same time."

–Victor Zurbel, New York

> By the time many people started coming, they found out I wasn't a very capable cook. They would see me sitting and eating some cantalope or a few bananas and nuts. I never cooked any-thing. They asked me, "What is this? You never cook anything." I said, "I'm sorry. I never learned to cook."

At one discussion Gurudev said, "Disciples usually cook for their guru and help in all ways."

Seven of the women decided to split the week's cooking between them. They each picked a day to go to Victor's apartment and prepare Gurudev's meal. This was the barest, gentlest beginning of their teaching on how to respect and treat a guru. Before that nobody knew; nobody had any idea.

Victor brought a load of clothes to the Chinese laundry. Among the sheets, towels, shirts and pillowcases were a number of Gurudev's silk pajama-like outfits. When he went to the laundry to pick up the clean packages, the laundryman winked.

"Beautiful clothes. You must have a beautiful lady staying with you."

"Oh no," Victor said. "It's a swami ."

The laundryman looked at Victor wide-eyed and handed over the bundle.

228

When the student is ready, the teacher appears.

The crowds of visitors who came to listen to Gurudev grew too large for Victor's apartment.

"We will have to move you to another place, Swamiji. We want you to stay a little longer, and we'll find you a bigger apartment."

Gurudev wondered if this interest could be sustained in his absence. He decided to test it. "All right. Go in search of another apartment and I'll stay a few more weeks. Meanwhile, while you look, I'll go to Montreal and visit Swami Vishnudevanandaji. When the apartment is ready call me."

"We'll get your ticket."

"I already have my ticket."

"We'll get it endorsed for you," the students insisted. "You don't have to bother."

The original ticket read Montreal-California. They wanted to make sure he would come back to them. The disciples bought a new ticket to Canada, with a return flight to Manhattan.

Gurudev flew to the Sivananda Yoga Vedanta Camp, Val Morin. "Swami Vishnu's" center was a jewel — luxurious, modern accommodations for guests, rolling soft green hills covered with tall trees, a blue-black lake shimmering in the summer heat.

Within four days the New York disciples began calling on the phone. "Swamiji, the apartment is ready for you. Come back."

He stayed for a few more days as Swami Vishnudevanandaji's guest and then returned to his new quarters at the Oliver Cromwell Hotel on West 72nd Street.

The suite contained a bedroom, a large living room capable of holding large discussion groups and Hatha Yoga classes, a kitchen and a bathroom.

"How long is this reserved for?" Gurudev asked.

"Only three months."

"*Only* three months?" Gurudev briefly envisioned the Kandy ashram in the warmth of late summer.

"Yes, but if you can't stay that long we'll cancel. It doesn't matter."

Yoga expands the mind by a slow process and by your own work, without external influence. Your will is developed gradually. It is like a fruit that takes its own time to ripen and

229

become sweet. It becomes ready, not by any outside chemical force, not by a sudden pick-up, but in its own time.

Located at West 72nd Street between Central Park and Columbus Avenue, the Oliver Cromwell was mainly a residential hotel with quiet singles in business attire and elderly couples walking their dogs. When Gurudev took up residence there, the lobby was transformed into a psychedelic Grand Central Station.

Young men and women with long, loose, shiny hair and flowery bellbottom pants changed into Hatha Yoga clothes in the lobby's public bathrooms. Long, skinny models in electric green tights and mini-skirts lounged in the venerable armchairs, animatedly talking with advertising executives and photographers in transparent cowboy shirts and handlebar moustaches.

The elevators were jammed.

The youth of New York were ripe for yoga. Many of them came to the apartment in the Oliver Cromwell through "The Psychedelic Experience." The "acid" (LSD) boom was on — sitars, incense, patchouli, saris, silver bangles and Eastern philosophy palatably presented by Alan Watts and Timothy Leary. Somehow it all pointed them toward the study of yoga, although they hadn't the vaguest idea of the disciplines involved.

Still they flocked to see this beautiful man, so serene in orange silk. Then there was his hair — that long, lovely hair so beloved by his own Gurudev. Years before, Master Sivanandaji had foreseen what was to come, how these children with their flowing curls would come to his disciple and see a teacher who understood their needs.

Adults came to him as well. New York's philosophical yoga clique, members of the established yoga and Vedanta societies, warned him against associating with these "flower children." Why, it could ruin his reputation as a Master. Didn't he know these people were drug users, pot smokers?

"These things will drop off in time," he chided. "I only know these children are sincere. I won't stop teaching them. I see the good in all of it."

Two students who had met Gurudev during his trip to Canada were quite taken with his broad ecumenical teachings and universal approach. They left the very next day and drove to New York at the same time Gurudev was flying back. After they met him again at the Oliver

230

Cromwell Hotel they immediately started taking an active part in all the activities surrounding this great yogi. They took responsibility for organizing and managing many of the things that no one had taken care of before.

Blythe Gilmour, who soon received the Sanskrit name Shanthi, and Lakshmi Berg were these highly dedicated students. Shanthi totally organized the suite and bought all the things necessary for a lovely altar. Lakshmi purchased a tape recorder and started taping Gurudev's talks. This was the beginning of a practice that has continued to this day: taping Gurudev's *satsangs* and then transcribing them for easy reference.

"I came to see Gurudev a day after Richie and I were married. My friend Kathy had said, 'You *must* see my swami.' I thought, 'What does she mean by swami? Pointy hat? Crystal ball? But I went with her, mainly out of curiosity. When I saw him I just couldn't believe it. He sat calmly in the midst of so many people. He was so composed, serene. It was overwhelming. At the end of the lecture Kathy introduced me to him. I was very shy. She said, 'This is my friend Joanie. She just got married yesterday.' He gave me an incredibly radiant smile and then held my hands. He said, 'Yes. We can't all be *sannyasis*. Some of us have to marry so we can have all these beautiful children.'"

By now the Cromwell was too small for the growing numbers of would-be yogis. The devotees realized they would have to find a new place. Peter called his friend Victor. "Do you want to help me find an apartment for Swamiji?"

They began the search. Seemingly out of the blue, a man came forward and offered them his apartment for free. The only catch was that it was in the worst shape either of them had ever seen any apartment. Victor vetoed it immediately, but Peter convinced him that they should fix it up — that very weekend. Victor, who was about to go away on vacation, cancelled his plans.

There was still a problem. They would need a small army of people to fix up the apartment in such a short time, and so far they had only themselves. Almost everybody they knew was away for the weekend. Besides, how do you get people in New York to fix up an apartment for someone they've never even heard of, for nothing in return? Impossible.

Peter had another friend who said he would come, and he was determined to go ahead. When they got to the apartment on Friday night there were approximately a dozen people waiting, all strangers to each other. It seemed that Peter's friend had brought a friend who brought another friend and so on. Nobody knew more than three or four people there, and nobody was quite sure just why they were there.

For three nights and two days the group toiled and sweated. At the end of the weekend they were all exhausted, but the apartment was spotless. Then the owner, who had been away, walked in.

"You'll only be using this two hours a day, right? Not on weekends?"

"What? We planned to have Swamiji move in here permanently. We thought you were giving it to us."

"Well, look. I didn't know that. I mean, my friends use this place from time to time, and I crash here on weekends."

A sense of gloom began to settle. Just then in walked Gurudev, whom most of these people had never met. He introduced himself. Sensing that something was wrong, he asked what the problem was. They told him, and Gurudev said it would be best to look for another place.

"Oh, no," someone groaned. "You mean all of this work was for nothing?"

Gurudev calmly looked at each of them. "Do you people all belong to a club or group of some sort?"

"No."

"Then do you all attend the same college or university?"

"No."

"Hmm. Do you all live in the same building or share the same house?"

"No."

"What I am wondering is this: how did you people come together to do all this wonderful work? Are you not all friends?"

"We are now, Swami," someone answered, "but when we started we were strangers."

"So you were all strangers and now you are a large group of friends. Who said that all this work was for nothing?"

They looked at each other and felt that the work was certainly worth something.

Gurudev added, "In the East we call such work Karma Yoga, work without expectation of reward. It is a wonderful practice. Now you can simply leave this beautiful offering for this man and his friends to enjoy."

Kim Jordan rode on the back of Ron Merrian's motorcycle, roaring through the city, on and off, answering each promising apartment ad in the *New York Times* and the *Village Voice*. They located a spacious, old nine-room apartment at 500 West End Avenue and 84th Street. A meeting of the group was hastily called, and money was scraped together for the rent and security.

Gurudev asked, "For how long are you taking this apartment?"

"We've signed a three-year lease."

"But soon I'll be returning to Ceylon."

"We're not going to detain you. Please feel free to go whenever you wish."

At the beginning, a lot of people approached me in the street, but I just accepted it. I knew I wasn't dressed as everyone else was, and I enjoyed their interest.

Gurudev was too dynamic, colorful and striking to blend in unnoticed with the gray of New York. People always turned around to look — in buses, in restaurants, whenever he entered or exited from his apartment building.

One day he stood in front of 500 West End Avenue waiting for a cab. It was a sunny fall day. The rays of sun bounced off apartment windows and the chrome of automobiles, reflecting on the long, peach-orange robe he wore.

A car stopped right in front of him, and the woman who was driving leaned over and rolled down the window. "You should be ashamed of yourself!"

Gurudev looked back at her with curiosity.

"How can you do that. . .a grown man?"

"Do what, madam?" he asked politely.

"Walk around outside in your robe. It's cold out. It's not July, you know. You'll catch your death of cold. You'd better go home and change at once."

Gurudev looked down at his long warm robe.

"Better put on something warm!" she warned, then rolled up her window and drove away.

Faith makes everything possible. Faith itself is God.

Bilious green walls, bare floors, peeling wallpaper — this was the new home of the yoga center. After two days a skeleton force of workers began repainting, replastering and rescraping in shifts of several hours each.

George Eager had surpassed his shift many times. He continued plastering, stripping off peeling paper, and painting far into the night. His chronic kidney problem began acting up. As Gurudev passed through the dark hall he noticed George in a doubled-up position.

"Are you feeling sick?"

"Oh, it's nothing, Swamiji. I've had this kidney problem for a long time. It always goes away."

Gurudev walked to the kitchen, got a glass and filled it from the tap. He held it up, closed his eyes and whispered a chant. Giving it to George, he told him to drink the water.

"It will make you urinate quite a bit, but don't worry."

George drank the water, and a few minutes later cleaned his brush and caught a subway for home. As he rode downtown he was struck by an overwhelming urge to urinate. He leaped off the train at the nearest station and dashed into the men's room. The water he passed was thick, profuse and of a green-black color. Until very late in the evening he urinated frequently. The pain left his kidneys and never returned.

Peter Max telephoned Gurudev. He and Liz were very worried. Their son Adam had come down with a high fever; he wasn't eating anything and couldn't sleep. The doctors had tried a number of remedies to bring down the fever, but nothing worked. Gurudev immediately went to their apartment.

Again he chanted softly over a glass of tap water. "Take a few drops of this water on a spoon and give it to Adam."

Carefully they opened their son's mouth and dripped the water in. He swallowed it. Quite soon the boy began to cry. He was hungry and tired. The fever had passed.

It took all of Peter's will power to prevent him from drinking the rest of the water himself.

> Integral Yoga is a combination of specific methods designed to develop every aspect of the individual: physical, emotional, intellectual and spiritual. It is a scientific system which integrates the various branches of yoga in order to bring about a complete and harmonious development of the individual.

(top) The devotees reserved a suite for Gurudev in the Oliver Cromwell Hotel for "only three more months."

(middle and bottom) First home of the IYI, 500 West End Avenue, where many daily classes were conducted.

Hatha Yoga classes were set up on a regular, permanent basis. Friday evenings were set aside for lectures. Gurudev alternated teaching with Lakshmi, whom he had trained in Hatha Yoga instruction. During the day Lakshmi worked as a school teacher; in the evening and on weekends she acted as the secretary and treasurer for the organization which was rapidly forming around Gurudev. Despite her busy schedule, she happily cooked for him and served as his secretary; she knew that his schedule was even more full than hers.

Each month eleven of the original members pooled their money and paid the rent. Shanthi Gilmour began to work on the organization's incorporation, and the group decided that the center needed a name.

"Any name you like is fine," Gurudev said.

A list of proposed names was submitted: Satchidananda Sangha, Satchidananda Center.

"Why don't we call it the Divine Life Society?" Gurudev suggested.

"Swamiji, people in this country are tired of such words — 'divinity,' 'purity.'"

"Well," he said. "Then the name should have yoga somewhere in it."

"Satchidananda Yoga Sangha."

"Our teaching here is an integral one, a synthesis. The word 'integral' was used very often by my master. Integral Yoga should come in somewhere."

The group decided on Integral Yoga Center.

Gurudev suggested, "Why don't we call it Integral Yoga Institute?"

Visions of other institutions — jails, mental hospitals — passed through the minds of the devotees.

"Well, Swamiji, in the East that may all be fine, but here 'institute' has a negative connotation."

Gurudev kept smiling. "No. I think that would be better: IYI."

The new organization was named the Integral Yoga Institute.

Two years later Yvonne was leafing through some notes in Gurudev's Ceylon diary. On one page was a proposal for a new ashram and center. Printed in large letters were the words "Integral Yoga Institute."

"Recently we attended a Friday night discussion during which you were asked about fear and how to deal with it. You replied that fear is really fear of losing something — whether material loss or loss of health or part of one's body or life — and you went on to explain that only through nonattachment can one conquer fear. My wife was particularly drawn to this idea, and it made a very deep impression on her.

Unknown to her at that time, she was to lose a part of her body through major surgery because of a malignant tumor in her breast.

"At the time of her hospitalization she was able, through meditation on your words regarding anxiety and loss, to maintain excellent spirits both before and after surgery and to achieve an attitude of nonattachment that has astounded all who have had contact with her during this time. She also related that, to her astonishment, you seemed to appear to her on the evening following the surgery, and that the feeling of peacefulness and strength which your image evoked was a great and timely gift."

> **You can perform *japa* (repetition of a *mantram* or sacred word) in the midst of your day-to-day work. Then, when it becomes a habit, even when you are working intensely a portion of the mind will keep repeating the *mantram* always. Even in deep sleep your mind will do this work. That means that you have locked one end of your chain to a holy place while the rest of the chain remains still in the outside world.**

The IYI grew through word of mouth. One person would go to a lecture, listen to Gurudev, and bring ten people the following week. Many took up the regular practice of Hatha Yoga and meditation. Eventually, some of these students became interested in an even deeper connection with their guru. To those who sincerely wanted this connection, Gurudev gave *mantra* initiation.

Prospective initiates fasted the day of the initiation and maintained silence. Before the initiation they bathed, dressed simply and neatly, and brought flowers and fruit as an offering. The fruit symbolized the dedication of the fruits of all their actions to the Divine; the flowers represented anything which the initiate especially wanted to offer to the Lord or to humanity. After a *puja* (worship service) each initiate individually entered Gurudev's private meditation room, where he transmitted to them a *mantram*.

"When I walked into the meditation room it was as if the whole room were alive. I could see the air currents moving. The tiny room

237

was rocking and vibrating, and Gurudev sat so still in the middle of it all just like God."

By the second initiation the group of initiates had increased to fifteen; by the third, there were forty.

> **I never asked the students to stop using drugs, I never forced them. I do feel these drugs are dangerous, powerful and hypnotic. They give a brought-in experience, not developed by one's own self. It's not a genuine spiritual experience. It is something like a medicinally-induced sleep. Can you call that type of sleep as good as the normal sleep? They said they wanted to expand their consciousness. But when the drugs failed them they turned to yoga consciousness. As they continued the purifying yoga practice, their use of drugs simply fell away naturally.**

Timothy Leary made an appointment to see Gurudev. He arrived at the IYI with a number of people and began to tell Gurudev about his LSD experiences.

"Have you had any experiences without the drug so that you can compare the two?" Gurudev asked. "It would seem to me that the experience of complete calm and tranquility could not be obtained through any foreign agency."

"That's not so. We do have such experiences."

"I have heard of a number of incidents when people became emotionally upset during LSD 'trips.' Why do such things happen?"

Leary explained, "They don't know how to use it. They don't prepare themselves. They just take it. I don't approve of taking it in that way. I'd like to have an ashram where people could prepare themselves properly and then take the drug."

"In that case, why have you publicly said that the drug is good and everyone should try it? If you hadn't revealed such information it wouldn't have gotten into everybody's hands. You would have been able to give it in a more scientific, controlled way."

"Scientific truths should be expressed to everyone," Leary replied. He admitted he had discussed this matter with his two colleagues. They had desired to keep the findings secret. He had opted for openness.

238

"Timothy, is it not a dangerous thing you have done? Now you have no control over it."

"Perhaps it is, but it's completely out of my hands now. Instead, I tell people if they want to try it they can come and stay with me. I wanted to have your opinion about it also."

"Well, I have no experience with LSD. If you want to try it you can, but personally I feel it's not the right approach. You have called these saint-making pills. To my knowledge, it takes lifetimes to create a saint. When you claim these pills can create saints, which takes so much time normally, why don't you try to create lesser things? For instance, if you could make a pill that would create an instant engineer or an instant doctor, which takes only a few years of study, think how much time and money could be saved. It would really be wonderful. Why don't you show the world you can create engineers and doctors before trying to create so many saints?"

There is a great difference between the ancient yogis and the present day ones. Today you are drawn out 100% in every way, from head to foot, through all your senses. Every cell of your body is being drawn out. There are hundreds of artificial forces at work. With all that, if you are still able to listen to a talk on yoga it is really great. In the old days, apart from working and eating there wasn't anything else in the way of recreation. To choose to practice yoga wasn't as great as it is today.

A public lecture was planned for December 1, 1967, in New York's Community Church. The IYI had asked poet Allen Ginsberg to introduce Gurudev. A number of Gurudev's older devotees and acquaintances heard that Ginsberg was to give the introductory speech, and they strongly objected. Gurudev asked the IYI why they had chosen the poet.

"He has a great appeal for thousands of youngsters. They all love him. His presence at the lecture will attract more young people."

"Fine," Gurudev said. "Let him do it."

When Gurudev heard that Ginsberg had met Master Sivanandaji in Rishikesh he was even more interested in having him give the speech.

For weeks before the lecture the IYI students had covered the city with posters and handbills — a full-face portrait of Gurudev printed in sepia tone. Gurudev stared gently and sweetly from tenement walls, construction fences, telephones poles. It seemed as if every apartment in New York had a stolen Swami Satchidananda poster on the wall.

The church was filled. Even those who had objected came to see what would happen. Many who had voiced opposition apologized to Gurudev. The lecture had attracted hundreds of young people, and attendance at the IYI grew rapidly.

Gurudev attended a devotee's Christmas party. The great musician Ravi Shankar attended, and so did Allen Ginsberg.

"Swamiji," Ginsberg said, settling on the floor next to him, "I'm going to give you a surprise Christmas gift."

"Fine, but I don't see anything in your hands."

"It's not to see, it's to feel."

"Yes?"

"Having met you, I have begun to feel I should give up smoking. My Christmas present is this: a promise to you that I will stop smoking."

Gurudev embraced him. "That's wonderful. Really great!"

Several months later a devotee said, "Allen has started smoking again. He said, 'Tell Swamiji I have fallen from my promise and won't come to see him until I stop again.'"

As Christmas drew closer, Gurudev called the IYI members together. "I have to go back. There are many people in Ceylon who have been waiting patiently. I have to think of them too."

"When will you come back?" they asked.

"You mustn't think that I will just be coming back. There is work I must do, and many people there want me just as you do. There is a need there."

"But we need you too, Swamiji."

"Yes, you feel that way now, but this is a country where things change quickly. After a couple months you may forget me. Perhaps this yoga is only a fancy, something of which you will grow tired."

"No, we'll continue with our work," they promised. "We'll keep giving classes and playing your tapes while you're away. As soon as you reach Ceylon you can finish your work and then return to New York permanently."

"Well, I won't promise anything. It all depends on where the need is greatest. We'll see what happens."

Unless you understand the world and its truths, you can't understand the Higher Truth.

Nobody can just ignore the world, run away from it, escape from it and try to understand the Higher One. It is impossible. Even the so-called renunciates, if they have not understood the world, if the world doesn't drop from them by itself, if they fear the worldly life, if they shun it for selfish reasons, they will certainly get caught by it one day or another because they have not let it go by natural processes.

The world is an examination field. You are being tested here, purified, given experiences. You are being made fit to understand the Higher One. The world is not a fetter but a help. It is going to shape you and make you fit to reach the Goal.

The plane took off on a cold, gray January 4th in 1967, and flew to Chicago. There, Gurudev stayed with Sri Swami Bhashyanandaji at the Ramakrishna-Vivekananda Center.

A convent was nearby, and when the sisters learned of Gurudev's arrival in Chicago they invited him to speak at their cloister.

Entering this convent was like entering a high security prison: through one door to a hall, a peephole swiftly opened and shut, through a second door, closed tight, into a third. Finally there was a small room. Gurudev was to sit on a chair directly in front of a window. On the other side of the window were a number of seats. It was like watching television. He watched as the black-clad sisters filed into the room on the other side of the screen. The sister-in-charge sat directly in front of Gurudev. He spoke about yoga, its aims, its benefits; and at the end he asked a question.

"Sister, why must these nuns always be confined?"

The sister-in-charge hesitated. Nervously she glanced at the nuns behind her. "They are being trained. They spend most of their time in meditation."

"Yes, I know. But why can't they come out and see how the world is? They seem to be kept completely away from the world as if it were a dangerous place for them. That will create the wrong impression about the world outside. Moving about in the world and performing service should strengthen the conviction of a monk or a nun, while hiding from the world will often make for a weak foundation."

Early days of the IYI: the growing family.

Peter Max and Sri Gurudev on the Mike Douglas Show.

The sister-in-charge looked anxiously at nuns behind her and back to Gurudev.

He continued, "I don't think it is a natural growth. It's something like keeping a plant indoors without fresh air or sunlight. That plant will not have a natural growth. It will become pale and lose its color. The world itself is a big university. There is a lot to learn from it. They should be allowed out now and then to see what's happening there and to test their reactions. Then they can return to seclusion and analyze their feelings."

The faces behind glass lit up. The sister-in-charge became a bit shaken and leaned toward the glass, lowering her voice. "Swamiji! You should not tell them all these things. We can talk about it privately. They've already brought such ideas forward, and now you're just stirring them up."

Gurudev's voice retained its previous level. "That's fine, that's good. They should do that. They should bring up such things."

"But, Swamiji, we have to listen to the hierarchy. We can't just do what we want."

"Well, make the hierarchy aware of the situation here. Unless they know there is a problem, they won't do anything about it. 'Ask; it shall be given.' The child must cry so that the mother will know it's hungry and can feed it."

The plane carried him to Arizona, over convoluted desert-scapes, glowing pink in the twilight. He visited the Grand Canyon and Los Angeles, including stops at Marineland and Disneyland, then went on to San Francisco.

When asked to comment about it, Gurudev said: "The moment I went into Disneyland I felt like a young child. I went on the riverboat, the monorail, and on another small boat that takes you to a magic land where dolls are playing and jumping and dancing. At the same time I was fascinated by the human mind behind all these mechanical marvels, how great it was to come up with such ideas. Everyone I saw there, especially the grownups, behaved like children and forgot their worries, troubles and tensions.

"The Grand Canyon showed the great force of nature. By constantly rubbing and rubbing and rubbing, you can cut so very deep. In the Grand Canyon you can learn from nature how perseverance will allow you to gain whatever you wish. How that river cut down and down through the rocks! There is a Tamil saying: 'As the ant crawls, the rock is worn away.' The rock is so much heavier than the tiny ant, but still, if the ant constantly takes the same route over the rock again and again, he will eventually create a furrow. Just by constant trying, you can achieve anything you want."

The plane flew over the Pacific to Hawaii, Japan, Hong Kong and Malaysia.

A huge reception was assembled at Colombo in Gurudev's honor. It was February 22, 1967, almost a year since he had left for one month. Hundreds of friends and devotees greeted him. There were receptions in Kandy, Trincomalee and Jaffna.

A pile of letters from New York awaited him at his cottage. They all said very much the same thing in different words:

"The members of the IYI have asked me to write and urge you to come back as soon as possible."

"There has been a mass spiritual awakening and a coming together of all people who can sense this. Thousands of people gathered in Central Park for a 'Be-In' just to be together. There was meditation, chanting, dancing, kite flying, loving and everybody dressed in colorful clothes with flowers and feathers. The only thing missing was our Swamiji. Come back soon! We all love you very much."

Gurudev met with Cecil Lyon and his wife. The American ambassador asked him to return to the United States. He had visited the Institute and seen the work being done there.

"Your presence is really needed in America, Swamiji. It would be very nice if you went back."

Gurudev meditated on the situation carefully. It really seemed that God was guiding him to return to America. The people of that country were sincerely hungry for spiritual guidance. They asked for help in the way Gurudev had described to the nuns in Chicago: "When the child cries, the mother will recognize the hunger and feed it." The good and sincere devotees of Ceylon were already learned in the yogic teachings, and there were other *sannyasis* to guide them if need be. The decision was made.

The devotees in Ceylon were very unhappy about Gurudev's return to the United States. He told them, "I've been here for the past thirteen years and I've served all of you and the country as much as possible. God seems to be sending me to the West, where the need is greater. Every two years, at least, I'll try to visit you all here."

Not all Tibetans are holy; they are just like anyone else. I have been to that country and seen

them. They are just normal people. There are many monks. The holy people have taken the Chinese invasion easily. They feel it is a test and that it is God's work. Many people, however, really feel the pain. They feel quite bad about it. If you are possessed of that higher sense of wisdom, nothing is bad. All is good. Usually those who believe in God the most are those who are tested most.

Conrad Rooks sent a cable from Paris: "Would you like to join me in a visit to Lama Govinda at Almora?"

Lama Govinda was a scholar and authority on Tibetan religion. Gurudev wrote back to Conrad, explaining that he wished to stay in Ceylon until mid-April to celebrate the Tamil and Singhalese New Year with the devotees. After that he could visit Almora.

Conrad joined him at the ashram, and after the New Year's celebration they traveled to Bombay and New Delhi, where Gurudev met India's Prime Minister Indira Gandhi. Gurudev recalled this visit for his American devotees: "Indira Gandhi was a wonderful surprise. We visited her at her residence, and she was so humble, so simple, so down-to-earth. She walked into the room as if she had just come from an ashram, very loving and gentle. She wore a plain white sari and a *mala* around her neck. When she saw me she bowed down and made me sit in the largest chair in the room, while she took a small one by my side."

Gurudev and Conrad visited Lama Govinda. "In Lama Govinda I saw a great scholar and authority on Tibetan Buddhism. Because of his constant involvement in Tibetan scriptures and practices, he has imbibed all that great peace and serenity." They traveled on to Benares, Katmandu, and down to Darmashala for a meeting with the Dalai Lama.

The Dalai Lama sat in a chair, a slight, delicate, bespectacled young man with intensely glowing eyes.

Conrad felt like a tiny intruder at a meeting between two giants. Gurudev asked the Dalai Lama about the psychedelic interpretations of various Tibetan yoga books. This way of seeing the ancient teachings was popular in the West at the time.

"No drug can give you these experiences," the Tibetan holy man stated. "They can be reached only by going deep into meditation and not by any external agency."

"What about the opening of the third eye? There are books that claim this can be achieved by an operation."

"There is no external action involved. The third eye exists not on the physical plane but on the more subtle, spiritual level. It can be experienced only through deep meditation." He didn't approve of the modern interpretations of the secret Tibetan practices. Perhaps these questions were for Conrad's benefit, since Gurudev obviously knew the answers all along.

Gurudev later remarked, "I could feel a sanctity in the Dalai Lama. Although he appeared a bit young and modern, one could feel a higher spiritual experience pervading him. I felt a great deal of warmth in his presence."

Some of the Kandy ashramites had left the Thapovanam; they didn't wish to remain without Gurudev's physical presence. The temple authorities were requesting the land back for their own use. Vimalanandaji suggested they look for a new piece of property. A coconut grove was found nearby, close to the river. The disciples cleared the acre-and-a-half, and Gurudev laid the foundation stone for the new building.

On May 24, 1967, he returned to New York City.

"Sri Lanka was the starting point of Gurudev's life as a world teacher, and the first Satchidananda Ashram was founded there over thirty years ago. Swami Vimalananda Mataji, Gurudev's first *sannyasin* disciple, has been head of the ashram ever since Gurudev came to the West. She and our beloved brother Mr. P. Shanmugam take care of Gurudev's every need when he visits the island. Seeing how they relate to him, one would imagine he had never left. When I mentioned this to Mataji, she replied, 'Of course, child. He never has. I have never missed him because he has simply never left!'"

–Amma DeBayle

"His plane was due from Paris at four in the afternoon. So around two o'clock people gathered outside the IYI on West End Avenue to begin a caravan to JFK airport. It was a beautiful spring afternoon and Swami's people were happy and smiling and hugging each other.

"They piled into cars and drove to the airport and reassembled in the upper lobby of the International Arrivals Building, where they waited for Swami's plane. They looked great with bells and flaming colors and flowers. And they stood around the top of the escalators waiting and not talking very much and admiring the building.

246

"One of them had a movie camera. He wound it and started to shoot, down on his knees and zooming in. Not much action. Just people waiting.

"But suddenly there was an audience. The camera convinced a hundred other passengers that there was indeed something strange about the people in colors, just standing around. They were making a movie. A hundred people formed a semi-circle around Swami's people, watching them, waiting, careful not to walk through the middle.

"Swami's plane was late so this went on for three hours.

"Finally he arrived and came through customs, beaming and radiant, and his people came to him loving with garlands of flowers and gathered around him to walk slowly a foot off the ground through the terminal, softly singing 'Hari OM,' into a Swami orange sunset behind the limousine outside."

–The Village Voice

> **We can see the same spirit in everybody only when we know we are that spirit, *Atma* or Self. Only a person who has understood his own Self can see that same Self in everybody. Until then, you can never see others in this way. With that spiritual vision you see that you are not different from anybody else. It is with this understanding that Jesus said, "I and my Father are one." Because he himself became the holy spirit, he was able to understand the holy spirit.**

Gurudev's New York students were delighted by his return, but there was one event that soon disturbed their feeling of well-being. While Gurudev was in India he had received a letter from Lakshmi saying that she would like to invite a woman who was visiting from India to stay at the IYI. Gurudev had replied that the guest was welcome. Later he received another letter saying that both Lakshmi and Shanthi had been attracted to this woman's way of teaching, and that they would like to go with her back to India to study with *her* teacher although they wanted to wait to see Gurudev before leaving.

When he returned to New York the two women explained that it was not only the difference in teachings that appealed to them; they were not happy with the students who were coming to the IYI. Once again the hippies were unwittingly discouraging people of more sophisticated tastes who were studying with Gurudev.

"It's really too much for us to handle these hippies," Shanthi and Lakshmi explained. "We never expected that a great person like you would be surrounded by people of this type. We just can't tolerate them. If you really want our services, you shouldn't encourage them. Other people will be driven away too. If you think those hippies should be allowed to come here, then probably we should be leaving. We respect you, but we can't stand these pigs."

Gurudev said softly, "I am sorry to hear you say all this. All I can see is their beautiful, searching hearts. What you call pigs are my kids."

Years later Gurudev described this incident and commented, "I really felt a little pain in my heart when they said that, because I knew these kids were wonderful people. They were very serious and sincere in their seeking. Superficially they looked different, and it would take time to clean them up and make them look better. Probably these ladies didn't want to take that much time."

To their ultimatum, he replied, "I'm not asking you to go; you have decided to go. If you don't have that kind of compassion, you are free to leave if you wish. I cannot and will not decide whom to serve. It's just not possible. God sent me to serve them; and, if it is God's will, the IYI will survive. Whatever you do I will still love you."

Lakshmi and Shanthi continued with their plan to leave for India. They still loved and revered Gurudev and even asked for his help in preparing for the trip. He was happy to serve them in that way too. He took them shopping to help them pick all they would need in India.

"I still have some financial matters here," Lakshmi said. "I should be receiving some money and will need to have it sent to me in India. Swamiji, would you please take care of that for me? Would you deposit the money in my account and see that I get parts of it regularly?"

"Fine. I will certainly do that for you."

When the time came, he even drove them to the airport and saw them off.

Many of the students were totally mystified. "Swamiji, they are literally deserting you. How can you do all these things for them when they are dropping all their work for the IYI? Why aren't you angry with them? You seem to be calmly helping them, taking them to the airport, doing their banking for them. Aren't you at least a little disappointed with them?"

"Why? That's the way they want it. They wanted to come; they came. Now they want to go; they are going. Maybe they want to grow in a different way. If I am thinking of their welfare, I should allow them to do what they want. I can give certain advice, but I will never force anyone or try to hold onto them. If they find that they are not happy in what they've set out to do, they will always know that they are welcome here."

"But, Swamiji. . ."

"It's the same with you people too. If you want to stay with me and learn, fine. If tomorrow you also want to go somewhere else, you are free to do that. I'm not going to stop you. I didn't ask you to come; still you came. As long as you think that my lessons, my teachings, my words are helping you, wonderful. The minute you feel that you would get better help somewhere else and want to go, also wonderful. It's almost like owning a restaurant. If you think the food is better at some other restaurant, why should I stop you from eating there?"

The students understood, and interest in the IYI grew. Gurudev began training more people to teach Hatha Yoga. Those who wished to teach yoga were required to honestly represent those teachings by being strict vegetarians, and non-smokers. They would not use alcohol or drugs, and would be neat, clean and simply-dressed. Many young people became conscious of the need to lead a pure life: caring for body, mind, and the welfare of others. The hippies were becoming yogis.

Conrad arrived in New York.

"This city is hot and dirty in the summer. Swamiji shouldn't have to stay in the city all the time," he told the devotees.

The next day he ordered a car and chauffeur for the IYI's disposal so that they could look for a summer house for Gurudev.

A devotee had leased a country home in Port Jervis, New York — a mountain area bordered by Pennsylvania and New Jersey. The house was surrounded by woods and cliffs, narrow, twig-choked streams and fields of wildflowers and weeds. There were two buildings: the house itself and a small cottage a few hundred yards distant. Devotees could come up, ten at a time. The cottage was repainted for Gurudev's use.

"The 'ashram' was set high on a hill reached by a winding, well-rutted private road which cut through pines and hedges. The end of the summer was very hot. The air was always still. Five of us were visiting the house that weekend with Gurudev. After lunch Gurudev suggested we take a walk in the woods. We walked behind the house into the pine forest. It was warm and heavy. We walked until we reached a meadow. There was a rusty plow with white flowers growing near the driver's seat.

"We sat down on the grass and repeated some OM chanting. We all lay down with our arms over our heads, watching the clouds. I closed my eyes. I was still awake, but I felt as if I were dreaming. I was moving very quickly through the clouds, higher and higher, looking down at myself and everyone else lying on the ground. Within a split second I was back on the ground, sitting bolt upright. All the others were in the same position, sitting bolt upright, as if snapped from a deep sleep all of a sudden.

"Slowly Gurudev sat up and smiled at us. We followed him back to the house. Later when we compared notes, we found that we had all shared the exact same experience."

Marriages motivated only by physical beauty, money or other worldly reasons will be bondage. But if there is a spiritual attraction, the marriage will be made in heaven. A wedding is between two reflections of God, two pairs of eyes that see one vision. They are dedicated to serve each other and all of humanity.

Vijay and Shree Hassin were the first American couple married by Gurudev. A week before their yoga wedding, their parents gave a huge Jewish gala for them at a restaurant in the Bronx. Shree stood about five feet tall in her new white heels and long satin gown; Vijay stood dressed in tails and top hat with his arm about her shoulders. The bridesmaids wore gold-trimmed saris and sandals. All the friends of the couple dressed in wide, embroidered Indian shirts and loose pants. Both a Jewish grandfather and Gurudev blessed the breaking of the *challa* (ceremonial braided bread).

A mammoth piece of meat was ceremoniously rolled to the center of the floor, steam rising from the roast beef in great clouds. The bandleader gave a signal, and his group played "I'm an Old Cowhand from the Rio Grande." He motioned happily for the bride and groom to come up and give the first cut to those pounds of juicy beef. Vijay turned to his guru anxiously, "Gurudev, is it okay? I mean. . ."

"It's just for the ceremony, for your parents. Go ahead."

Vijay and Shree hurried back from their selfless service to join their table for vegetable curry and rice.

By the end of the evening the entire assemblage had joined in a circle, dancing and singing "Hari OM" and "OM Shanthi."

The following weekend, forty guests traveled to Port Jervis for a ceremony performed by Gurudev. Afterward they ate *upma*, the preparation of which had been supervised by Gurudev. Pine branches covered the house. Wildflowers were twined into Shree's hair. She sat in the late afternoon in her white sari. Gurudev carefully constructed twigs into a special configuration for the fire. It rose smokey and odorous into the darkening sky. He scooped ash from the fire, mixed it with *ghee* and passed it to each guest for application to the forehead.

May the indwelling Guru guide you all. May you be loving instruments in the hands of the Master.

The *jayanthi* (birthday) of Sri Swami Sivanandaji Maharaj was celebrated at New York's Village Theater. Two thousand people came to watch Gurudev's devotees give tribute to Master Sivananda. There was a dancer performing traditional Bharata Natyam and one doing modern dance. There was a sitar player and a jazz musician, as well as a Hatha Yoga demonstration and Gurudev's lecture.

Gurudev was invited to Belgium as the main speaker of the First International Yoga Convention. Later he visited Aalst, which had been transformed into a town of yogis. The whole town appeared to be involved directly or indirectly with yoga practice. Gurudev was welcomed by the mayor at a civic reception and was presented with flowers and the town's plaque. He lectured on the realization of Oneness through meditation and met the *bala* yogis of Aalst, a large group of children. Through his stories and parables Gurudev initiated them into Divine Life for children as taught by Master Sivanandaji. His face appeared in newspapers and magazines throughout Europe. Father Bouden had known Gurudev in Ceylon, and he invited the yoga master to visit his monastery in Gijzegem on December 5th and address the students. On the 8th and 9th, Gurudev addressed the Brussels Yoga Convention.

At the Brussels yoga center known as *Dharma*, Gurudev was welcomed with a poem read and written by Usha Devi:

> *Eternal map, sweet and transcendental,*
> *Such a star, come from such a faraway kingdom.*
> *You shine at the door of the sanctuary*
> *And you spread your warm radiance.*

It is you who awakens, in the heart of our souls
A hope always being reborn.
Although our eyes are veiled or distracted by the
   agitation of the world
It is you again who recalls to us the infinite
   compassion which illumines the door
   of the sanctuary
Where we must shine for all eternity.

After lecturing in Ghent, Ostende, Antwerp, Mons and Cherleroi, Gurudev returned to New York for a *jayanthi* celebration in his honor.

Each devotee received a book, and many received an extra gift, a yoga name: Rama, Sita, Krishna, Radha, Narayana, Hari, Siva, Jai, Uma, Arjuna, Aruna, Shankar, Maji, Asoka, Karuna, Valli, Muruga, Vimala, Vidya, Gita, Parvathi, Maheshwara, Subramanya, Atma. The names would serve as a constant reminder of their spiritual goal.

As classes continued to expand, once again more space was needed. Fortunately, this time it wasn't necessary to move. A second large apartment across the hall became available and doubled the size of the IYI. At about the same time, many of the students who had gathered around Gurudev expressed an interest in living at the IYI. They wanted an environment conducive to the yogic practices. In addition, they needed help and guidance in living a yogic life. Gurudev discussed it with them, telling them about traditional ashram life and asking them if they were really prepared for the self-discipline involved. They said they were.

For most, ashram living was a completely new experience. Until recently many had been living undisciplined lives on their own in the city. In the IYI Gurudev laid down rules of conduct based on the yogic scriptures and established a schedule that everyone was expected to follow. In this way the students gradually took over the responsibility for running the IYI, for maintaining a clean and orderly environment, and for teaching many of the classes. For most it was a difficult but rewarding experience.

"When I first moved into the New York IYI, I felt I had been reborn into a large family. For the first time I had many brothers and sisters to talk to, to work with, to study with, to be with. But along with this joyous feeling came the normal problems of daily living. Having to deal personally with so many people tends to point out your own strengths and weaknesses. It's easy to blame another person you can't get along with, but if you're having trouble getting along with half the household, you know you should do some soul-searching. You just can't get away with a lot of the selfishness, aloofness and laziness that you can when you're living alone. That doesn't mean you won't *try* to get away with it, and it doesn't mean that you will be able to get rid of those tendencies all at once. But there will be much less tolerance for those qualities and a greater acceleration of the process of getting rid of them."

The experiment was a success. The students were happy with their new home, but not everyone was happy about it. Some of the parents of the students were very upset, particularly those with strong religious ties. They felt that yoga was taking their children away; not just from them, but from their tradition. Such fears were understandable, and Gurudev would talk to such parents at great length — in person if possible. Often he would simply get an angry telephone call from a parent demanding to know what he was doing and threatening to take legal action. He would always invite them to come to the Institute, to see how their children were living and how happy they were, so that the parents could understand yoga better. Many parents came away from these visits with the understanding that yoga actually helps one to better understand his or her own religion, to be an even better Christian or Jew. It was not unusual for the parent to leave with a sincere interest in studying yoga more.

Sometimes, however, the irate callers didn't listen to anything Gurudev had to say. It was as if they not only did not know about yoga, but they did not *want* to know, only to judge. At such times Gurudev had the good fortune to be able to turn to someone else: a religious teacher from the student's own background, someone who was sympathetic to yoga himself. One such teacher was Rabbi Joseph Gelberman of the Little Synagogue in New York City. Through his intervention, many of the parents were reconciled to the involvement of their children in yoga, and many of the students were spared the ordeal of a direct conflict. From this, the relationship between Gurudev and Rabbi Gelberman continued to grow. Soon they began to give an annual program called "The Swami and the Rabbi" in order to further the goal of ecumenical understanding.

"Dear Swamiji,

"After some thought I felt I wanted to write this letter to let you know how I and the rest of the family who visited last week felt about your whole setup.

"I must admit that at first we all had a lot if misgivings because of what we read in the papers and hear on TV, to the point of being frantic. But after my third visit, all doubts and suspicions have completely vanished.

"We have seen the wonderful work you have done with your young people. Through your great spiritual guidance, compassion, and your love of mankind you have molded these young people to lead a good, clean life, dedicated to the spiritual work of God. They radiate a peacefulness and happiness from within. Their kind consideration, compassion and loving concern for one another and everyone in general is really beautiful and something which one seldom sees today in our society. Also impressive is their discipline which they have learned to master from your spiritual teachings.

"I notice the wonderful change in my daughter and feel very happy now to know that she is a part of your spiritual community. I have no qualms about the wonderful life she is leading.

"You are doing a beautiful job, and the fruition of your work certainly shows. God bless you and keep you in good health for the wonderful work you are doing. Please continue."

–Florence Holt, Connecticut

Gurudev was asked to give lectures outside the IYI. He spoke at the Buck's County Seminar House, Public School 42 in Manhattan, Vassar College, Columbia University, Mt. Saviour Monastery, the Lions Club, Ohio University and Princeton. At the end of January he flew to California and Hawaii for lectures, television appearances and radio interviews. New students came; outside classes formed. The Hatha hall outlived its usefulness as a lecture room, and lectures were moved to the Unitarian Universalist Church.

"In 1967 I was living at the Institute, acting as secretary. Vijay and I were working on a film script for Conrad, and he asked me to come to Los Angeles to do a rewrite. About two days before leaving, I asked Gurudev if I could go, and he gave me his permission. As I was about to leave to meet Conrad and go to the airport I went to say good-bye to Gurudev.

"He was sitting at his desk as I came in, and he said, 'Sita, don't go.'
" 'What?'
" 'No, I don't want you to go.'
"A thousand things rushed into my mind at once: 'What should I do? Conrad will be upset if I don't go. He's counting on me. But if I do go after Gurudev said not to, something terrible is bound to happen.

Maybe the plane will crash. Maybe we'll get into a car wreck on the way.' I decided Gurudev had some inside information and walked over to the phone to call Conrad and cancel.

"'What are you doing?' Gurudev asked.

"'I'm calling Conrad to tell him I'm not going.'

"He took the receiver from my hand and placed it on its cradle. Then he started to laugh.

"'What's so funny?'

"'It's all right, Sita,' he laughed. 'You can go. But now I know you'll come back.' He kept on laughing and laughing. He had just been testing me through this little joke.

"'Don't miss your plane,' he said gently. He gave me a hug and pushed me lightly out the door."

Peace is your own true nature.

On a hot night in early summer hundreds of people arrived at random and slowly filled the large Unitarian Universalist Church. They had come for one of Swami Satchidananda's public talks, which were now given every week. Many came regularly to the talks, but many were coming for the first time. It was like other gatherings in the city where strangers came together for a short time and then dispersed. The atmosphere was one of excitement. There was also a quality of curiosity and its underlying restlessness in the air. One of the things that contributed to this was the war in Vietnam.

In the late 1960s opposition to the war was growing rapidly. Increasingly the opposition was expressing itself in violent terms. People who came to hear Gurudev talk wanted to know how he felt about the war. There was often an edge to their questions, a challenge.

Gurudev, of course, was aware of the war and was also aware that people were in danger of taking on the qualities they opposed. He knew that you cannot end violence with violence; that you cannot treat violence in one place and ignore it in another. He could see that outward violence comes from an inner disturbance, a lack of peace in mind and heart, and that whatever qualities we want in the world we must first find in ourselves. He would ask his listeners to consider the true meaning of peace — not something external, something to be fought over and won, but something that we already have within. If we do not disturb that peace within, he would say, then we will be able to share it with others. It begins with each of us.

(right) A special satsang *was held at the Universalist Church in honor of the Jayanthi of Sri Swami Sivanandaji Maharaj. Sri Gurudev stood at the podium to address the large audience. (below) One of many hundreds of Friday night lectures at the Universalist Church, New York City.*

"I'll give you a small story," Gurudev said. "One day a businessman was in conversation with some of his partners, who were visiting him at home. His son, a very intelligent boy, kept coming into the room and asking questions. In a way, he was interrupting the conversation. To keep the boy away for a while the man looked around, saw an old world map from a magazine, tore it into pieces and then gave it to the boy. 'Son,' the father said, 'I know you are very smart. These are the parts of the world. Try to put them together again.'

"The boy didn't hesitate. 'Okay, Dad, I'll do it.' He went into a corner and started to look at the pieces. He really did not know much about geography. He just saw lines and names entered here and there on the pieces and was a bit puzzled. Then, casually, he turned over a piece of paper and saw a small nose. He turned over another piece and saw a finger. So he started turning everything over and found the different parts of the human body. It was easy for him to put together the human body because he knew where the eyes should be, where the arms should be, and so on. He placed them together, taped them and then turned it over. There was the whole world intact. He rushed to his Father and said, 'Dad, it's okay now.'

"The father never expected the boy to put it together so quickly. 'Son, I really thought you knew nothing of geography. I just wanted to keep you busy for a while. How did you do it?'

"'Dad, it was easy. Just turn it over and see.'

"The father turned it over and saw the human figure. 'What did you do?'

"'Well, I didn't do much. I just set the man right; automatically the world became all right.'"

Gurudev paused a moment. "See what a great truth it is? You set right the person, and the world becomes all right. People always want reformations to happen outside rather than within themselves; but even if it is peaceful outside, if you do not have the eye to see it, then you will not realize it is peaceful. Only a peaceful mind can make a peaceful world. So the best thing is to change the individual. Then we can easily see that change happening in the world."

Through such simple stories Gurudev conveyed some basic truths to his listeners. Not everyone was convinced, but at least he had persuaded them to listen and to consider a deeper dimension to the conflict. When the program was ready to close, he would request that everyone participate in a short meditation.

"Let us sit and calm our minds and then think of all the troubled minds around the world. Let us send our loving, peaceful vibrations to them. Let us share and radiate those peaceful vibrations to all in need.

Do not think that it is useless. There is nothing more powerful. Such vibrations reach everyone and help the whole world. So let us do a short chant for peace and then meditate."

Then he would lead everyone in a chant of "OM Shanthi" (OM Peace). As the chant got softer the lights would dim until everyone was sitting in silence in the dark. For a few minutes there was no sound and no movement among hundreds of people. They were united in a living, peaceful silence so unique in the city. When they left they would not feel quite the same as when they first arrived.

> **The renunciate is not a loser but a gainer. Instead of belonging just to one fenced-in area, he or she belongs to the world. The renunciate belongs to everybody, and everything belongs to the renunciate. In a way he has added to his family. A truly renounced person is the richest one in the world. Who is that person? The one who possesses nothing. To want nothing is to have everything.**

Gurudev was still in America on a temporary visa. The New York IYI, which had begun to grow up around him, was determined to keep him in their country and made every effort to acquire a permanent resident visa. The right kind of visa was one given to religious ministers, rather than to someone sponsored by a group. There were many difficulties, however. One was that the authorities had never given such a visa to a religious teacher from another country. Gurudev was even told, "We have been sending religious ministers to other countries, but we have never given a religious minister a permanent visa to this country. Even though there is a provision for that, so far we have never opened that channel." Because of this, there was a reluctance to set a precedent.

The IYI persisted even though it looked as if there was every chance of being refused. An interview with the Director of the Immigration Department was arranged, and Gurudev attended.

"Why do you want to stay in this country?" the Director asked.

"I have no desire to stay," was Gurudev's reply.

"*What?*" It was the very first time in the history of the Immigration Department that the Director had heard someone who applied for a visa saying such a thing. "Do you really mean that?" he asked.

"Yes, sir. I do mean that."

"Then why did you apply?"

"The people want me here and are asking me to stay. For that reason I have applied."

"Suppose we say no?"

"Fine then. You are not saying no to me; you are saying no to them, to your own people. It's between you and them. I have nothing to gain or lose."

In addition to the interview, petitions and letters poured into the Immigration Office:

"Swami Satchidananda is a holy man. Whether he receives the people that will inevitably seek him out in a church, by a river or in Grand Central Station it will make no difference. Whether he is allowed to remain or should he be banished to Tierra del Fuego, it will make no difference. He will still be a holy man." — J.A.C., Design Associates, New York City. . ."My name is Julius Zupan, a house painter. I have a son, Larry, twenty-seven years old. It is more than a year since Swami became an influence on Larry's thinking, and Larry's activities with him have proven most rewarding — physically, morally and spiritually." — J.Z., New York City. . ."As a Roman Catholic monk engaged in the study of Eastern religion and philosophy, I want to state that I have known the Swami from the time he came to this country, have had the privilege of discussing with him at length his religious and philosophical views and am convinced that his presence here in the United States serves a spiritual need felt by representatives of many different religions." — Brother D., New York. . ."I have appeared on religious and secular platforms with the Swami and have heard his sermons preached throughout the city. Young people, for whom spiritual, physical and inspirational guidance previously appeared meaningless and impractical, 'come to scoff and remain to pray.'" — Rabbi J.G., New York City.

"Anyone having watched Swami Satchidananda addressing many hundreds of youngsters on the greens of Griffith Park in Los Angeles lately on a sunny winter day, could not fail to see the deep religious awakening his address brought to these young people. They were truly drinking in — absorbing — every word offered. It was truly a sermon to the living soul." — E.H., Santa Barbara, California. . ."As an officer of the United States during World War II, I was officer-in-charge of the Ground School Administration of more than 10,000 Naval Aviation cadets and therefore have some idea of how badly young people need the sound advice of Swami Satchidananda of the Integral Yoga In-

259

stitute"...B.A., Greenwood Lake, New York..."I am a seventeen-year-old high school student. For the past six months I have been studying yoga. Prior to this I had been a frequent user of drugs for close to two years. Among the drugs that I have used are marijuana, hashish, codeine, amphetamines, methedrine, barbituates, LSD and STP. I have smoked marijuana on more than 100 occasions and taken LSD more than twenty-five times with dosages to 2,000 micrograms. After studying yoga principles I have completely stopped taking all drugs and have even stopped smoking cigarettes and drinking alcohol." — M.E., New York City.

"I believe that Swami Satchidananda is an asset to this nation because of the fine work he is doing in the teaching of this ancient philosophy of yoga." — J.G., United States Information Agency, Washington, D.C...."As a psychiatrist, I have sent several patients to this man, feeling that they could benefit from his teachings." — L.B., New York City..."The almost two thousand students from Manhattan College and Mt. St. Vincent who attended his lecture here on campus last week did not think they were attending a philosophy lecture or they would not have been there. They were greeting a man who was addressing the spiritual needs of the younger generation. He was saying the same things the Church has been trying to say; but, by saying it to them in a different way and a different context, he is saying it so they will listen." — D.C.H., Assistant Professor, Department of Theology, Manhattan College..."From the moment I first talked to Swami Satchidananda I began to realize that he understood my questions and could help me find the answer within me and that in him I had found someone who could bring that answer to the surface. I had long ago lost faith in my Protestant upbringing and become an agnostic. The beautiful faith I had in God as a child became more and more distant as I got caught up in the confusion of everyday life. Swami Satchidananda has taught me that God does exist and that He is everywhere if we only take the time to stop and look for Him." — F.C., Cambridge, Massachusetts..."I teach here in the graduate school of drama at Yale, and I am a playwright (my play, 'America Hurrah,' is running currently in New York). In both these capacities, as well as personally, I have been greatly enriched by my contact, through his classes, with Swami Satchidananda during the past year. Any true understanding of foreign cultures must come through the authentic work of such inspired and modest men in our midst. On such understanding lies our best hope for a peaceful world." — J.C.I., New Haven, Connecticut.

"Recently the Swami lectured in a seminar at Daytop Village, a therapeutic community for ex-narcotics addicts. The people in the community were moved by Swami's presentation and found it very rewarding and helpful. The influences of Swami on the Daytop community will remain with us and we all feel enriched at having had the benefit of being exposed to him." — L.S., Staten Island, New York. . ."The Swami has been a great inspiration and help, not only to myself but to hundreds more. Such Christ-like figures with genuine words of peace and love have sustained the world from time immemorial. How necessary they are in our own troubled times." — J.W., American Book Company, New York City.

Finally, through hundreds of letters, the dedicated efforts of Yvonne Gita Hanneman, and the services of lawyer Lyle O'Rourke, a decision was reached.

August 2, 1968

Dear Friends,
Perhaps you have by now heard the good news about the approval of Swami Satchidananda's permanent resident's visa, but I want to thank you personally and also thank you on behalf of Swamiji and the many friends and students of the Integral Yoga Institute.
Your support was a great help in winning the case. In the final analysis, it was this kind of interest expressed by the American people that decided the favorable results.

Yours in the service of the Lord,
Yvonne Hanneman, Board of Trustees

The visa was granted. Gurudev's was the first visa ever to be given to "A Minister of Divine Words."

The India tour was a strenuous journey. In most places we stayed at youth clubs. What was most surprising was the reaction of the Indian people to the American students. Even I didn't expect such a thing to happen! At least in front of others, the students behaved very nicely, seriously, well-disciplined. Through them, America was seen in a better light.

It was time for the dedicated young yogis to visit the place of their guru's birth. The tour took off from Kennedy Airport on August 1,

1968. Traveling around the world with Gurudev wasn't merely a glorified vacation. Instead, it took on all the characteristics of *sadhana*. There was hardship, illness, as well as inspiration and education. The group ranged in age from late adolescence to senior citizens and was made up of about twenty members, both men and women. Gurudev, with his flowing hair and orange robes, and his American students with their flowing hair and pastel pajamas were an instant crowd-gatherer.

New York. San Francisco. Los Angeles. Honolulu. Tokyo. Osaka. Hong Kong. Kuala Lumpur. Bangkok. One of the main purposes of the tour was to visit as many holy places as possible, particularly those where people had dedicated their time and energy to seeking enlightenment. They visited the Buddhist shrines of Nara and Osaka in Japan, as well as temples in Thailand. At last they arrived in India.

Traveling to Benares by rail, they reached the sacred Ganges River and decided to take their first bath in its waters. Under Gurudev's direction they proceeded to the river in the morning. Gurudev rowed about the group in a boat, instructing them about how to perform the cleansing of body, mind and heart.

One of the group's members entered the water wearing a wristwatch and carrying his umbrella. As he waded in further and further his arm lifted higher and higher until all that was left above water was a head, an arm, and an umbrella.

Gurudev rowed over to him. "The idea is to renounce everything when you enter the sacred Ganges, to leave your worldly possessions behind. It seems you're still a bit attached."

The devotee laughed, returned to the shore to detach himself from these final possessions, and replunged.

They were obviously the first Americans in quite some time to enter a second-class Calcutta hotel. The proprietors of the hotel's restaurant tried to make them feel at home.

"And what kind of prime meat, roast or steak will you have?"

"We're vegetarians. We'll just have some rice and vegetable curry."

"Cocktails? Whiskey?"

"We don't drink."

A three-piece, Glenn Miller style 1930s jazz band appeared just as the guests started to repeat their meal prayer. Finally the musicians realized that the group wasn't interested in ballroom dancing and quietly disappeared.

In the same city they received an audience with a great holy woman, Ananda Moya Ma. The grace and dignity with which she and Gurudev received one another formed a lasting image for those present. The usual greeting of garlanding became a very sacred, brief ceremony between the two.

India has many temples which non-Hindus may not enter. Puri Jaganath Temple followed this rule, but Gurudev made a special request at the office. "These people are very interested in Hindu philosophy."

The authorities remained rigid. "Only you may go in, Swamiji."

The group sat down cross-legged on the road. Gurudev led them in chanting: "OM *Namo Bhagavate Vasudevaya, OM Namo Bhagavate Vasudevaya.*" The sun set and the sky darkened. Rain began to fall. People darted around them, running to shelter. It poured in sheets, in blankets of water. The group continued to chant and did not move.

The onlookers were incredulous. "See how devoted they are. Even we couldn't stay outside in such a downpour. It would be a terrible thing to stop them from having *darshan* in this temple."

The authorities remained adamant, rain or no rain. Quietly, the temple priests entered the *sanctum sanctorum* and brought out garlands and *prasad.* They garlanded this amazing guru and his equally astonishing disciples and offered them the holy *prasadam.*

The peace was so strong at Buddha Gaya that the group wished to stay longer than planned. It was here Buddha had attained enlightenment.

"Okay," Gurudev agreed. "We won't go to the other place. We'll just sit here awhile."

They sat under the cool darkness of a bodhi tree for *satsang.* Gurudev spoke about the way of the Buddha. After worshipping in the temple, the group repeated a chant they had learned from Gurudev at the IYI. "*Buddha bhagavan, Buddha bhagavan, Buddha bhagavan paahi maam; Bodhi Satva, Bodhi Satva, Bodhi Satva raksha maam.*"

A number of monks stood around the group. They seemed excited. "What was that chant? We want to know that *mantram.*"

Gurudev repeated it for them. Taking out his notebook, he wrote it down on slips of paper. One of the monks wandered away, clutching his paper and carefully repeating the chant over and over.

We hear a lot about ecumenism now. My Master, Swami Sivanandaji, was an embodiment of that spirit. If you have seen his pictures, you might wonder who he is. Sometimes you see him with a nice Muslim cap, sometimes

with a tennis racquet in his hand. You can see him with a beautiful cross adorning his broad chest. He was everything. He was a Buddhist, a Christian, a Muslim, a Hindu, a Jew. This broad outlook went beyond his religious work. He was a doctor; he was a playmate. He was a mixture of everything; he accepted everything, and everyone. That is the secret of why everybody felt at home with him, and by his mysterious and miraculous touch he was able to lift people up.

"We visited Ananda Kutir in Rishikesh. It was during the Jayanthi Celebration for Sri Swami Sivanandaji. Master Sivanandaji's presence was so strong, we kept expecting to see him come walking around a corner. On the night of his birthday they showed movies of him. That's when I understood something about our Gurudev I had never understood before. It showed Sivanandaji near the end of his life — full of vim and vigor, very active, very sharp. It showed him walking here and there, shaking hands with people, greeting guests. And it was just like Gurudev; he has taken on the qualities of action his Master had. The way Gurudev gives someone a piece of *prasad* is the way Master Sivanandaji did. The way he stands is the way Swami Sivanandaji did. The way they spoke, expressing what they knew, was so similar. And it's not an imitation; Gurudev just does it. He doesn't think about it. So many times he says, 'I'm not doing anything. It's not Satchidananda. It's my Master, Sri Swami Sivanandaji, working through me.' And it's true. On the physical plane I saw it."

I had to keep an eye on all these people.

The group traveled by *bogie*, a railway car that could be hooked up to various trains. Gurudev warned them, "Be sure to lock up everything each time you leave the train."

The doors were locked and checked carefully, but the windows remained wide open to catch the infrequent gusts of breeze which stirred the hot, dusty air. One afternoon Subramunya's trousers disappeared from their hook next to the window. He made a general announcement, "Everyone has to keep their windows shut at all times. My pants were stolen right through an open window."

Within a day every member of the group was carefully adhering to the rule. Windows as well as doors were locked and checked thoroughly.

The following evening Gurudev called Subramunya to his compartment. "Keep this safe condition always. Here are your pants back."

"Gurudev watched, even from afar, all our transactions. I always tried to be very careful about handling the group's money — always keeping my money in one pocket, the group's money in another, a separate envelope for receipts. But still I wanted to be at ease and soak in what was happening a lot of the time, especially when we were in places of worship.

"One time we were in Haridwar. There was a great celebration, a beautiful festival where you could buy flowers, leaves and candles. They had stalls where they sold all this paraphernalia for worship. You would light a candle on a leaf, say a blessing over it, and put it into the Ganges, which flowed right through Haridwar at a terrific course. You couldn't even swim; that's how fast it was. There was a big chain rope and steps leading down because as soon as you got in up to your waist, if you let go, you'd be washed downstream. It was really forceful.

"The river was rushing by; and there were thousands of people all over, lighting candles, putting them on leaves and floating them down the river. The Ganges was aglow with light. Bells were ringing and *mantras* were chanted. We were doing this too, the whole group and Gurudev. It was one of those crowd scenes. I had just laid out money for our worship items, and all of a sudden it was time for us to have our group worship and give our offerings to Mother Ganga. Well, I got absorbed in it and really tried to worship the river. Suddenly the money I had been carrying was gone. Just carelessly, for the first and only time on the trip, I had slipped it into the pouch of my airline bag instead of under my *kurta*.

"It was gone and I really got upset. It wasn't so much the money, but I had put it into my receipt envelope with all the other receipts and they were gone too. I thought, 'What am I going to do? Swamiji's really going to be angry with me.' All along he had been cautioning us about pickpockets. He said people would be attracted to us for many reasons.

"After the ceremony Gurudev came up to me and said, 'Did you lose something?' He held up the missing envelope in front of my eyes and waved an admonishing finger at me. He had picked my pocket to teach me a lesson."

265

The holy cave Vasishta Guha. American devotees meditating with their Master.

(left) The great saint of India, Ananda Moya Ma. (below) American devotees on pilgrimage to India.

From India, the group went to Kandy. True to his word, Gurudev returned to Ceylon, this time bringing the eager young American devotees. If the people of the Kandy ashram had met these Americans a year before and then witnessed their transformation to this state, they would have known that it was a great service to let their beloved guru go to guide the youth of this foreign country.

The Americans were struck by the rich beauty of Kandy. With irony, Gurudev commented, "This is what I left to come to New York City."

"Instances of Gurudev's fatherly affection abounded throughout the trip. On one occasion in particular I had the opportunity to see this. While we were staying at the Kandy ashram, we visited the Temple of Kataragama, where I was bitten by a malarious mosquito. This manifested three weeks later in the form of high fever and the disease. I found myself greatly weakened and losing much weight due to constant perspiring. In the beginning, before we knew whether it was malaria or merely a high fever, I decided to take an enema and try to cleanse my system. Gurudev arranged for the necessary apparatus and brought it back to where we were staying. I was so weak that I had trouble standing and walking to the bathroom. Gurudev said a few quick words, telling me to call upon my natural strength. 'Use your will. Come on, apply yourself.' Throughout the night he nursed me, happy to perform the most menial and distasteful jobs."

Krishna contracted dysentery in India. When he reached Ceylon he was treated with a highly powerful medicine which ate through the walls of his stomach and infected his whole system with polyneuritis. He became weaker and weaker. Unable to eat, his weight fell to under 100 pounds. Gurudev took him to the hospital. A group of doctors from the ship Hope came to visit the hospital and decided to take Krishna to the ship the next day for an operation.

During the night Krishna fell into a strange sleep. It was more reality than dream. He was back at the ashram and seemed to be steadily rising above it. All the American ashramites were outside on the ground waving to him, saying good-bye. Up in the air he met Gurudev, who held him and said, "Good-bye. I can take you no further." Krishna said, "I understand." He experienced a great feeling of freedom, elation, ecstasy — of illumination all around. He was entering into a great source of light.

He opened his eyes. He was back in the hospital room, and it was morning. Sun streamed through the windows. The doctors returned to take him to the ship. They hurriedly examined him. His fever had broken, and his body had begun to heal. They left him in the hospital to recover.

In the Hindu calendar, every day of the week belongs to a particular deity. There is a day for creation and one for destruction. Thursday is the day for worship of the guru. At the ashram some of the devotees fasted on this day.

Gurudev knew of this practice. On Thursdays he would greet them at the cottage as usual, but he would have some special *prasad* awaiting them — a box of chocolates, the ultimate temptation. Each of the fasting devotees reacted to Gurudev's offer in his or her own way. Some thought, "Oh no. If I eat one thing I'll never be able to keep up the fast." Others, "I'll just take one and save it for tomorrow." Still others, "A treat from Gurudev. Of course I'll eat it."

Eventually one Thursday they asked him, "Gurudev, what are you doing to us?"

"If you have the right attitude about *prasad*, it is not food. You are taking a blessing. If you take it with that consciousness it won't even affect the digestive system."

"He gave us everything. At one point, he gave us a spiritual experience also. It was one evening at meditation. After an hour, I wasn't meditating very much. My legs hurt. I was thinking, 'Well, it must be close to the end by now.' I was still repeating the *mantram* but without too much devotion or feeling. Suddenly I felt very uplifted, very concentrated again. The pain in my knees disappeared. My *mantram* started repeating itself, while I watched the whole experience. I felt a part of it and away from it at the same time. My *mantram* stopped. The only thing that existed at that moment was sound. The *mantram* was just there. I could somehow look at it and perceive it visually. I was seeing sound. Endless sound. The same sound. It was all there at once. It had no beginning, no end. I was in that presence for who knows how long. As long as it lasted it was eternal time. It was timelessness. I felt no physical existence or consciousness. At the same time, there was me and there was this. But we were existing at the same time.

"After a while the mind came back in, but I was able to witness the mind. The body came back. Time came back, but still I could watch time. Thinking came back; I could watch thinking. Someone started chanting to end the meditation. I watched myself repeating the chants. I heard Gurudev's voice among us. After the chants I bowed, sat up and opened my eyes. I became aware of other people around me, that we were in a meditation room, in an ashram, in Ceylon. It was like waking up to the physical world. I looked around, and, as I did, I saw Gurudev just walking out the door. I hadn't heard him come in.

"He had brought this consciousness to us. Krishna, Kala, Jai, Ishwara, Hari and I all looked at one another. We all knew what had happened. Without saying anything, we could see it in each other. We had shared this consciousness. Gurudev has that consciousness all the time."

The group returned to India. They visited Chettipalayam and Coimbatore, where Gurudev gave lectures at the Divine Life Society.

"Living like this, in such a small group, so close to our guru is bound to cause major changes in all of us. Even though we may not see these changes manifested for a while the seeds are certainly being planted. I am slightly aware of subtle changes working in my own mind. Everything here is calm, curative, purifying, rebuilding."

The American disciples were taken to the tea plantations with their guru. All four thousand workers had been given the day off to see Swami Satchidanandaji. It looked like a postcard of St. Peter's on Easter Sunday. Hundreds stood on ridges, in trees, balanced on each other's shoulders for a better view. Mothers held up their infants to receive Gurudev's *darshan*.

At noon Gurudev sat high on a platform where all could see him and get his blessings. The hot summer sun, low and orange, beat down on the crowd. Sweat ran in profusion. While the blessings were given, not a word was spoken from 4,000 pairs of lips.

To these workers, God had descended from Mt. Kailash and taken a body for that day. They struggled to touch his feet, to prostrate before him. They chanted, thousands of voices echoing to the name of the Lord and Gurudev.

After India, the party visited Europe and the United Kingdom before returning to the United States.

As long as the mind is restless and constantly creating waves on its surface you are not able to get the correct clear reflection of the Self. That's why a tranquil mind is the goal.

"Swami Satchidananda has more than his share of charisma. The Swami is just back from an around-the-world trip that he made with a group of his students. He is giving a lecture at Carnegie Hall on January 31." — *New York* Magazine.

Carnegie Hall was sold out for that lecture.

The beautiful concert hall was alive with the sound of a theatre filled with people eagerly waiting for the program to start. Gurudev sat backstage, calmly playing with the child of a devotee. Eric Javits, cousin of Senator Jacob Javits, mentally rehearsed the words he had prepared to introduce Sri Swami Satchidananda.

Suddenly a reporter appeared backstage and anxiously approached Eric. "Where is the Swami. I want to ask him for a copy of his talk. I don't think I'll be able to follow it all, and I want to quote him correctly in my article."

Eric Javits laughed. "It doesn't appear to me that he has anything written in advance. Normally, he doesn't prepare ahead of time. He simply talks extemporaneously."

The journalist couldn't believe it. Someone was speaking in Carnegie Hall without a prepared talk? Impossible. "Let me just ask him myself. Where is the Swami?"

Eric was still smiling. "He's right there in the corner, playing with the child."

"Swami? Swami, excuse me."

"Yes?"

"This man says that you don't prepare your talks."

"That's correct."

"Swami, do you know that there is a hall full of people — almost 3,000 people — waiting there to listen to your talk? Do you really mean to tell me that you haven't made any preparations? How could that be?"

"Sir, I'm telling you the truth. I haven't prepared anything. Really, I never feel that I am the one giving a talk. Someone Else does the talking. So I'm not worried; I'm just enjoying playing with this little one."

"Then who will talk?"

Gurudev looked up at the journalist. "Well, you just go, have a seat, wait and see who talks."

Much later in the evening, the crowd left Carnegie Hall. The air of the street was humming with their conversation. "That was great!" "What a wonderful talk." "This evening has really changed my life." "Fantastic!"

*

CARNEGIE HALL 77th Season

Friday evening, January 31, 1969, at 8:00

SWAMI SATCHIDANANDA

Yogiraj Sri Swami Satchidananda

IN CONCERT

PROGRAM

Introduction by Eric Javits

Lecture by Swami Satchidananda

Asana Demonstration by Students and Instructors of
The Integral Yoga Institute
Peace Chanting led by Swami Satchidananda

Sponsored by the Integral Yoga Institute, Inc.
Founder-Director: Yogiraj Sri Swami Satchidananda

Carnegie Hall, 31 January 1969: sold out!

TONIGHT'S ARTIST

Yogiraj Sri Swami Satchidananda was born in India into a highly spiritual family. After finishing his schooling, Swamiji entered the field of technology. He tried his hands at many fields. He worked in industries as diversified as the automobile, electrical, mechanical and cinematographic. For a time he worked in church management as well. But none of these endeavors brought him the lasting joy he sought.

At the age of twenty-eight, Swamiji started upon his full-time spiritual quest. For several years, he practiced intense sadhana in seclusion. He made holy pilgrimages and acquainted himself with various spiritual paths. In 1947, he met his Master — His Holiness Sri Swami Sivananda Maharaj, the founder of the Divine Life Society. On July 10, 1949 in Rishikesh, he was initiated into the Holy Order of Sanyasins (monkhood) and given the name Swami Satchidananda (Existence-Knowledge-Bliss Absolute). A year later, his master conferred upon him the title of Yogiraj, for his mastery of the intricate techniques and processes of the Yogic science.

Swamiji is well versed in the Vedantic philosophy as well as being adept at both Raja and Hatha Yoga and has lectured extensively in India and Ceylon.

He has also organized branches of the Divine Life Society and other Yoga centers in India, Malaysia, Singapore, Hong Kong and the Philippines. He is the Founder-President of the Divine Life Society Branch and Thapovanam (Yoga Seminary) at Kandy, Ceylon.

In 1966 Swamiji visited New York

for two days. Here he met many students who wanted to study under his guidance. In August of 1966, the Integral Yoga Institute was founded.

On August 1, 1968, Swamiji, together with twenty-five students began a pilgrimage. They covered the entire Northern Hemisphere stopping in more than fifteen countries and dozens of cities. Spreading the teachings of Integral Yoga, Swamiji also visited centers in Hong Kong, Malaysia, Ceylon, India and Belgium.

Swamiji will accept invitations for lectures and may be reached through the Institute for personal interviews.

Gurudev was often invited to Ananda Ashram as a guest speaker. He became a friend and guide to its members, and they offered him use of the ashram as a weekly retreat, reserving a cottage on the grounds for his personal use.

Members of the IYI arrived on the weekends. The grounds were tilled and reseeded; a partially destroyed building was reconstructed; the hazardous bridge to the island was dismantled. Vegetable gardens were put in. Fresh coats of paint were applied. Gurudev was everywhere — repairing the tractor, working on a stereo set or car, supervising the disciples.

"One day he scolded me for allowing the workshop to be dirty and sloppy. I had been sitting on the floor and had not stood up when he came in. He really lit into me when I was too dull even to stand up.

"'Stand up. You don't even show your guru the respect you would pay to your father or grandfather.'

"I thought he was really angry, and I was terrified. In the middle of his tirade of admonitions, he stopped abruptly and turned to my wife. 'I'm not being too rough on him, am I?' he winked."

Evenness of mind. He taught this balance in many ways. Sometimes he gave the devotees specific instructions, completely reversing them the next day.

There was an old station wagon at the ashram, faithfully serving its purpose as a work horse. Gurudev instructed Maheshwara never to drive this car over twenty-five miles per hour. Soon after receiving this instruction, Maheshwara drove Gurudev back to the ashram from the local garage. He crept along at 25 m.p.h. Gurudev kept checking the speedometer and playing with the gearshift as Maheshwara tried to guide the car.

"What's wrong with the car? Is the engine broken?"

"No, Swamiji."

"Why are we going so slow?"

"The car is fine. You told me to drive it at this speed."

"I said that? Come on. Go faster. We have to get home."

He chuckled and patted Maheshwara on the shoulder as the car picked up speed.

It was about 8 P.M. when Gurudev arrived at the cottage with two disciples. It had started drizzling rain on the way from the city. The temperature was near freezing.

"Is it warm in the house?" they asked.

274

Ananda Ashram — one of many satsangs with Sri Gurudev.

"Oh, yes," Shanthi Norris promised. "As soon as the thermostat is on, it really heats up." She flipped it on. Nothing happened. "It takes a few minutes." The radiators remained stone cold.

Gurudev called from upstairs. "Shanthi, what is happening?"

"The thermostat isn't going on, Swamiji."

Down he came, dressed in orange robe, orange crocheted cap, black rubber boots and an open tan ski parka over his shoulders. He tromped out into the slushy drizzle to the boiler room in back of the cottage. There were sounds of tinkering and grinding, calls for a hammer, a screwdriver. Then could be heard a low, slowly increasing vibration, just like when your car motor turns over after you've almost given up on a cold gray morning.

The ancient boiler had met its match. Gurudev strode back into the kitchen and ordered a hot chocolate.

"I met Swami Satchidananda on a sunny spring morning at Ananda Ashram, after coming all the way from California. The first time I heard about him, I was staying at the Abbey of New Clairvaux, a Trappist monastery north of Sacramento where my cousin Brother Paul was a monk. I was wondering if I could become a monk like him. But at the same time I was reading a lot about yoga, especially the *Yoga Sutras of Patanjali* and the *Gospel of Sri Ramakrishna*. I wanted to have a guru like Sri Ramakrishna, always God-intoxicated, caring nothing for the world. I believed that personal possessions limited my freedom so I had already given away or destroyed almost all my belongings before coming to visit the monastery. My cousin, a real monk, actually had more personal possessions than I. I also believed that a religious aspirant should not work. He should let God take care of him. He should not make any decisions for himself. I believed what I read; that when the disciple is ready, the guru appears. So I was just waiting for him or her to appear, to guide me in the choice of whether I should become a monk or follow some other path to find God.

"Then a letter reached my cousin from another monk in a Trappist monastery in Massachusetts. The letter contained news that an Indian swami recently visited them to talk on yoga, accompanied by some disciples who gave a demonstration. When Brother Paul told me the news I immediately wondered if this swami was the guru I awaited. Right away I urged my cousin to find out more about him. We found out his name was Yogiraj Sri Swami Satchidananda. The 'Yogairaj' reminded me of the Raja Yoga of Patanjali so I was encouraged to sit down and write him a letter — my first one to a swami. I introduced myself, stating my sincere desire to find a guru and asked him what to do. Although I had never seen this swami I somehow felt confidence in him. There was a long wait for his reply, three weeks or more.

"When his letter finally came, with my name neatly typed on it, I felt a tremendous excitement. The letter began, 'Dear Child.' Even this was enough. This simple, direct, loving address produced such a feeling in me that I didn't have to read another word to know it was a master speaking. But would he accept me as one of his disciples? The Swami noted my keen interest in yoga and invited me, if I wished, to come see him in person so he could better come to know me and guide me on my path.

"I prepared to start my pilgrimage to New York by renouncing the very last of my possessions except for what seemed absolutely necessary to the trip. In a way, I wanted to test my faith in God's love for me. If I could reach New York in spite of the obstacles, it would prove that God wanted me to go to the Swami. I emptied my pockets of money. I gave Brother Paul my silver pin souvenir from the Golden Buddha Temple in Bangkok. I even threw away my glasses. Standing on a fallen tree trunk above a creek, I recited, 'The world is a dream. I will never work again,' and tossed the glasses into the water. After all, I didn't need them except to work. I supposed that the Swami would take care of me in his ashram.

"Early, before sunrise the following morning, after the morning prayer, Brother Paul hugged me good-bye at the monastery gate. He made me wear his blue denim jacket over my shirt. But only a few hours later, as I walked down the road and the day warmed up, I took off the jacket and left it hanging over a bridge railing to be found by someone who needed it more than I. I was glad to free myself of one more binding possession. Less than a week later, by the grace of God, I was dropped off in Manhattan. I was cold, wet and hungry but excited to be near the end of my pilgrimage. I called on a former acquaintance, who let me sleep on his floor.

"When I reached the IYI the next morning, Hari Zupan met me and read the Swami's letter. He told me to telephone upstate where the Swami was spending the week.

"Near the waiting room phone was a big framed photograph of an Indian man with very long, dark hair and beard. 'Is that the Swami?' I asked. 'Yes,' I was told. He looked like a real swami, very holy looking. Hari dialed the ashram and handed me the phone. When Gurudev himself answered the phone, I knew it must be him by the sound of his voice, but I hesitated to say 'Is that you?' or something disrespectful. I asked if I could please speak with Swami Satchidananda. The voice asked me who was calling. I told him my name, mentioned the letter, and again requested to speak with the Swami. There was a pause. Then quietly but clearly, in an almost musical way, he said, 'This is he.' I felt an electric sensation. In a rush, I told him how I had come from California to meet him and asked if I could come up to his ashram.

" 'Yes. When?'

" 'Now. Today.'

" 'No, not today. Come tomorrow morning.' Another day to wait. I was learning that the guru doesn't necessarily appear all at once. Sometimes he appears step by step.

"The next morning I had a good shower, changed to clean clothes and took the first bus from Port Authority to Ananda Ashram. Even without my glasses I spotted the wooden arrow on the pole near the bus stop, pointing toward the ashram. When I reached the main house, a man came around a corner and told me to follow him to Gurudev's cottage. As we walked across the grass, under the trees toward the white cottage, I expected to be led to a cool, shady room with incense burning and the Swami seated in meditation.

"But my guide steered me slightly to the side of the cottage, toward a small, yellow tractor standing in the bright sunshine. Suddenly my eyes focused on an orange form of a man with long black hair, crouching beside the machine and working on it like a mechanic. Could this be the Swami? A holy man working on a tractor? I couldn't believe it. The man looked like a swami with his orange clothing and long hair but there was a screwdriver in his hand. He seemed to be scraping mud out of the air filter with it. I just couldn't understand it. Sri Ramakrishna wouldn't even touch money with his hands, but this swami was actually working on a tractor. My guide said something to the man in orange. I heard the word 'Swamiji' so I knew this must be the Swami. Then the young man left. I was completely confused. I didn't know what to do. To my relief, Gurudev didn't seem to notice me much. He just kept working on the tractor. There was a tool kit laid open beside him on the grass. After a while I sat down in a cross-legged position a few feet from him and waited for him to say something. In the silence, I began to adjust to the situation. This was the first swami I had ever seen in my life. If I had been introduced to him in a cool, shady room with incense burning, I probably would have been frightened speechless; but outside in the fresh air and bright sunlight, my awkward feeling melted away although my mind felt numb.

"Gurudev gently asked me a few questions about where I was from and so on. It was relaxing to start off with something easy instead of how to find God. He asked me how I had come to the ashram.

"'I walked,' I answered, meaning that I had walked from the bus stop.

"'From New York?'

"'Well, no,' I had to answer. 'A friend loaned me some money for a bus ticket.'

"He asked me how I could be free if I had to beg for money. What right did I have to beg for money when I had strong hands to work? 'Look,' he said. 'I am repairing this tractor rather than calling a mechanic from town. Be independent and not a burden on anyone.' I was simply amazed. Really this wasn't the kind of swami I had expected at all, one who would tell me to go out and get a job! If I got a job, wouldn't that mean accumulating personal possessions again? I told the Swami about renouncing all my personal possessions.

"'And what,' he said, 'did you do with your glasses? You threw them away I suppose.' How did he know that? He smiled and said, 'Swamis are full of surprises.' As if to prove it again, he called to someone in the cottage to bring him his glasses. His glasses? A swami wears glasses? A young woman brought them and held them out to him. To my ever-increasing surprise, he didn't take them right away. For about thirty seconds the woman silently held them motionless in the air, directly in front of my gaze, as if Gurudev purposely wanted me to notice them. I began to think, 'Who am I to be without glasses when even Swami uses them? Who am I to be without work when even Swami works? I'll go get a job to be independent and not a burden on anyone. If I don't follow his advice, he won't be pleased with me and I can't call him my guru.

"Gurudev must have known I was trying to make such a decision. He said, 'Yes, go and get a job. Be independent. I will help you.'

"'You said you would help me,' I repeated. 'These are the words I wanted to hear.' I felt ready to make any sacrifice to please him, even to go and get a job. I realized that he would not be an easy guru and not at all what I had imagined, but my heart told me to follow him.'"

Everywhere things are happening well. Our people who have taken up the Institute work are showing real interest. I seem to feel there is a great hope that many more centers will come up.

The IYI set off, pioneer-style, for the West Coast. During the summer of 1969 Krishna and Narayana traveled to Los Angeles; Shree and Vijay to San Francisco, Ishwara, Kaniah and Ramana set up an Institute in Connecticut, and another one was started in New Jersey.

In July Gurudev flew to Detroit, addressing a convention of two hundred Catholic nuns. Then he accepted invitations to Hawaii, San Francisco, the Esalen Institute at Big Sur, and Los Angeles. There were lectures, television appearances and interviews, radio programs in San Francisco, and *mantra* initiations.

The interest in Gurudev's teachings and in the Integral Yoga Institute was growing dramatically.

Music is the celestial sound, and it is sound that controls the whole universe, not atomic vibrations. Sound energy, sound power, is much, much greater than any other power in the world.

They didn't know they were creating history as they gathered in Max Yasgur's cow pasture for the Woodstock Festival-Aquarian Exposition — three days of free music, free food, free entertainment. Almost all of the most famous contemporary musicians had volunteered to perform at the Festival — for free. When the fences couldn't hold back the almost half a million young people, the promoters chopped up the ticket booths for firewood. Soon there were miles of tents — green, red, blue, orange — on the hills. There were open kitchens for cereals and vegetables. The sun burned down, and then it poured rain. The ground turned to mire, but good spirit and a loving consciousness never faltered.

The promoters had expected a few thousand people, and as they watched many more than that pouring into the farm for the festivities, they became concerned. Such large numbers gathered in much less than perfect conditions usually made for trouble. One of the people in charge had met Gurudev and felt that his calming vibration could have a soothing effect on the crowd.

The roads were too choked with cars and people for his car to pass so a police escort drove Gurudev toward the site. A boy fell off the back of a speeding car, and Gurudev sat by him until help arrived, rubbing his head gently and soothingly. When the roads became too clogged even for the police, a special helicopter was pressed into service, lifting Gurudev high into the air above the hundreds of cars parked every which way, and the thousands and thousands of people milling like tiny ants below. How he loved it, this smooth soaring above the festival, descending finally into the midst of it. Backstage he sat on a makeshift wooden stepladder, waiting to go on. Out front were 400,000 people.

"My beloved sisters and brothers," Gurudev began, "I am overwhelmed with joy to see the youth of America gathered here in the name of the fine art of music. In fact, through music we can work wonders. . .

"One thing I very much wish you all to remember: with sound we can make or break. On certain battlefields animal sounds are used. Without such sounds — war cries — human beings couldn't become the kind of animals that kill their own brethren.

"So I am very happy to see that we are all gathered to create some 'making' sounds rather than 'breaking' sounds, to find that peace and joy through the celestial music. I am honored for having been given the opportunity of opening this great, great music festival.

"America leads the world in several ways. Very recently, when I was in the East, the grandson of Mahatma Gandhi asked me, 'What's happening in America?' I said, 'America is becoming a whole. America is helping everybody in the material field, but the time has come for America to help the whole world with spirituality also.'

"That's why across its length and breadth we see people, thousands and thousands of people, yoga-minded, spiritual-minded. So let all our actions and all our arts express yoga or unity. Through the sacred art of music let us find peace that will pervade all over the globe. Often people shout, 'We are going to fight for peace!' I still do not understand how they are going to fight and then find peace. Therefore, let us not fight for peace, but let us find peace within ourselves first.

"The future of the whole world is in your hands. You can make it or break it. But you are really here to make the world and not to break it. There is a dynamic manpower here. Hearts are meeting. Here I really wonder whether I am in the East or West. If pictures of this gathering were shown in India, the people there would certainly never believe that they were taken in America; for here the East has come into the West.

"I, with all my heart, wish a great, great success to this music festival. Let it pave the way for many more festivals in other parts of the country. I have met the organizers, and I admire them. They have come forward to do a job, but the entire event is in your hands, not in the hands of just a few people. The entire world is going to watch this.

(above) San Francisco: one of the first IYIs.

(below) At the legendary Woodstock Peace Festival: Gurudev sets the tone for an unprecedented gathering of hundreds of thousands in peace and harmony.

Sivananda Yoga Camp, Val Morin, Quebec, Canada: the True World Order Convention, 1969, brought together many of Master Sivanandaji's illustrious disciples. Front row, from left: Sri Swami Pranavanandaji of Malaysia, Sri Swami Sahajanandaji of South Africa, Sri Swami Sivapremanandaji of New York, Sri Swami Satchidanandaji of New York, Sri Swami Chidanandaji of Rishikesh; Second row, from left, Sri Swami Venkatesanandaji of Mauritius and Sri Swami Vishnudevanandaji, the host.

The entire world is going to know what the American youth can do for humanity. Every one of you should feel responsibility for the outcome of this festival.

"Once again, let me express my sincere wish and prayers for the success and peace of this celebration. Thank you."

Woodstock amazed everyone. Despite adverse conditions, the thousands of people lived together in total harmony for the duration of the Festival. No comparable gathering before or since could make that claim.

> **Normally, in the spiritual way, a *mantram* is selected for you by a guru, an adept, guide or Master. You might think, "Can't we select it ourselves?" You are certainly at liberty to do that. But still, there is an advantage in going to a Master. When the guru selects something for you, it comes with a little momentum duly charged with his or her own vibration.**

Gurudev conducted a three-day seminar at a convent in Quebec, Canada — St. Augustine's. He gave lectures, Hatha Yoga classes, discussions. At one meeting he explained the theory of *mantra japa*. On the following day he was to leave early for Val Morin. A number of sisters came forward. They asked to be initiated. Thirty-five showed up at 6 A.M. for the ceremony. He was very happy with such attendance.

"You really understand the universality of it. *Mantram* doesn't pertain to any particular religion. Rather, it is based on universal sound vibration."

> **Sri Ramakrishna Paramahamsa used to tell this story. Once, a number of people went to a huge fruit garden that was surrounded by a high wall. They were told that delicious fruits and delicacies abounded within. Slowly, a number of people went to the wall and started to climb. With great difficulty, they reached the top. As soon as they looked over, they could see hundreds of ripe mangos, papayas, pomegranates, trees bending low with red apples and cherries,**

bushes bursting with berries. Looking at this lush array, these people lost control and jumped in, one after the other. But a handful, reaching the top, refused to jump. They thought, "If I jump in, what will happen to all the thousands of people outside? How will they know about this place?" These people called to the crowds behind them, "Hey, everybody, everything you could want is within this garden. It is a divine garden. Come. Come on. All of you. This is how I reached the top: first one foot on this stone, another on that." They acted as guides and led the thousands below, helping them climb to the top, step by step. Until everybody climbed into the garden, they themselves wouldn't budge.

Such people are the prophets, the *avatars*. And that is their mission. Until all the others have jumped in, they just watch and guide. They are satisfied to see the joy of those they lead.

"The True World Order and Its Actualization" was held at Swami Vishnudevanandaji's yoga camp August 30th to September 4th, 1969. It was a summit conference of gurus. Swami Vishnu was joined by Gurudev, Sri Swami Chidanandaji of Rishikesh, Sri Swami Venkatesanandaji of Mauritius, Sri Swami Sivapremanandaji of New York, Sri Swami Pranavanandaji of Malaysia, and Sri Swami Sahajananda of South Africa. Six hundred students pitched their tents among the trees and participated in the program of meditation, lectures and *asanas*.

This meeting was a reunion of Divine Life Society branch leaders and initiates of Master Sivanandaji, most of whom had not seen one another since their days at Rishikesh. It was a meeting to exchange ideas about various ways and means of reaching the greatest number of people.

To be in the presence of any one of these great children of Swami Sivanandaji was a great blessing and a moving experience; to be with so many of them at one time had a deeply inspiring effect on all those fortunate enough to attend.

Interest in Gurudev's teachings was growing rapidly in Europe, and not long after this reunion he embarked on a European tour to speak at the many places that had eagerly invited him. His first stop was Copenhagen, Denmark. In Aarhus he gave a talk and answered questions. One query was about the nature of death.

Gurudev replied: "I believe in life after death, but I do not think it is very important to think about. If you take care of today, your tomorrow will be taken care of. Why should you worry about tomorrow or yesterday? Think of the golden present. Lead a good life now. Likewise, forget the past. What is past is already gone. But what you sow today, you reap tomorrow."

He visited France, and after a lecture in Toulon he agreed to visit an ashram on his way to the Marseilles Airport. The ashram was housed in an old multistoried chateau. After lunch Gurudev's hostess showed him to a room where he could rest.

"You know," she said, "in this room they used to kill rabbits."

After lunch Gurudev rejoined the group.

"Did you have a nice rest?" inquired his hostess.

"Yes, I did; but there were rabbits crawling all over me."

From Marseilles he flew to Milano, where one hundred fifty students awaited him, chanting, ringing bells, playing flutes and drums. After that he gave *satsangs* in Verona, Padua, Florence and Rome.

In Switzerland he gave programs sponsored by Mr. and Mme. Hug before going on to England, the last country on the tour.

"I was a pianist with a jazz group in Europe. To say the least, being a jazz musician means there have been many temptations over the years toward smoking. I almost completely resisted, but one time I slid a bit into some too easily accessible hashish. When I heard that Gurudev was coming to give a lecture three months from that time, I thought, 'Good. Three months is enough time to clean myself up for his arrival. Gurudev will never know about the smoking.'

"So I diligently stopped smoking all substances and got more regularly into the *asanas* and meditation. When Gurudev arrived there was a nice little reception for him. I turned up in my neatest 'whites,' my hair and beard neatly trimmed, and of course the most beatific smile I could muster. While I was there, someone asked to see the nice yoga picture I kept in my wallet. After I showed it to him, Gurudev looked right at me and asked if he could have the wallet.

"'Hmm,' I thought. 'He's testing me to see how generous I am.' So

I said, 'Oh yes, take the wallet. There isn't much money in it, but you can take anything you need.' Gurudev started sniffing it and said, 'I don't want your money, but don't you have just a little something else in here? Don't you keep just a little toke or something? Just a bit of grass?' He looked right into my eyes as he said this, one of his famous penetrating looks, you might say. All I can say is that I've never been able to touch or smoke even a twig since that day, nor do I even want to."

Do not judge others. If you see someone who is unrefined, who is doing wrong things, that only means he is taking his first steps. He is falling down. Probably you were like that once, and someday he will be like you. He will pick himself up and learn to walk. Someday he will even run. Today's saint was yesterday's sinner. What was once crude oil is now high octane fuel. All it needs is a little refinement.

The IYI continued to grow. New Institutes opened in Washington, D.C., Detroit and all around the country. During this time Gurudev continued to live in New York, and each Friday evening he gave a public talk at the Unitarian Universalist Church, within walking distance of the Institute. The IYI, in addition to offering a full schedule of classes, also began to conduct many special programs outside the Institute. There were children's classes and adult education classes, classes at the United Nations and classes at the Postgraduate Center for Mental Health. One place classes were given was Horizon House, a center for the treatment of drug addicts. The classes were so well received that Horizon House hired two teachers from the IYI to work full-time, to incorporate yoga into its program for drug rehabilitation.

Gurudev visited Horizon House several times and gave a number of talks there. Wherever there was a sincere interest and an invitation, he would go: churches and colleges, conferences and festivals, radio and television. Sometimes he would even receive an invitation to speak at a prison. This was the case when he gave a talk at the Lorton Complex, a federal prison near Washington, D.C.

"In the late 60s I was arrested in the District of Columbia for selling ten pounds of hashish. I was able to post bail right away, and thus I avoided dealing with the experience of incarceration at the time.

"As the court case slowly moved along, I met a woman who was quite different from my usual flashy numbers. She started taking me to Swami Satchidananda's talks at the Universalist Church in Manhattan. Because of my interest in her, I usually went along except for those times that I wanted a cigarette or when I couldn't handle the semireligious feeling that would come over me. (It wasn't part of my idea of a successful image.) Sometimes I was able to understand that what the Swami said was valid and meaningful. I saw a balance of opposites in him — male and female, laughter and seriousness, speech and silence — an equanimity.

"Back in court we lost motions, and then we lost the trial. As my court scene got worse, my yoga scene got better. There was still that place inside me that resisted it, that was unwilling to accept any help. But still, the new awareness was growing.

"The turning point was my *mantra* initiation at a retreat at the end of the summer. I was profoundly affected by the experience. There was a whole new energy happening. Old habits and thought patterns fell away. Then, in April of the following year, when I no longer felt any connection with my old life, I met my due *karma*. Judge John Sirica sentenced me to two to six years incarceration plus $10,000 in fines.

"I was shipped out to the Lorton Complex in Virginia and placed in the maximum security facility, which was surrounded by a forty-foot wall. I managed to keep my *mala* beads, and I made enough room alongside my bed to do the Hatha Yoga postures. For three grueling weeks I had no contact with the world at all. A nervous rash broke out all over my hands. I took to writing a poem in Sanskrit for my beloved guru. First I wrote the poem in English; then I tracked down each word in a Sanskrit dictionary and copied this new and unfamiliar alphabet. It was three weeks of work. Without those hours of intense concentration, I think I'd have gone crazy.

"There was a fellow who was sleeping near me. He was finishing up a five-year sentence for bank robbery. He watched me do my *asanas* and meditation for a while and began to ask questions. Soon he was doing the postures too. My *sadhana* seemed easier with someone doing it alongside me. (There were also those who threw paper at me while I was doing the poses.)

"At last I was moved into a dormitory with a hundred other men and began working in the office as a clerk. It was wonderful to be able to help them open up to the potentials of yoga. We began to meet twice a week in the chapel, once for Hatha Yoga and once for discussion and *satsang*. There were now about ten of us in the yoga group.

"I was in touch with a beautiful fellow from the Washington IYI. It took some of my old manipulation games, but we finally arranged for him to teach in the prison once a week. Then beloved Gurudev received permission to visit. Through 'channels' we were able to print up posters and pin them up all over the institution. It was even announced over the loudspeaker system. Everyone worked toward the event. Gurudev spoke to almost one hundred of us."

At Lorton Gurudev told them:

"Thank you for inviting me. I am happy to be here. Yes, I am aware that I am in a place where people come to be corrected. It is something like a repair shop where things are restored to their proper shape. That means you are supposed to be in a particular shape, and somehow you have gotten out of that shape. You were once well-formed, somehow you got de-formed, and now you have to be re-formed.

"So don't think that anyone is punishing you. The intention is not punishment; the intention is to help you to return to your original state. And don't think that this is the only reformatory. The entire world itself is a correctional institution. All through life we slip from our original state and are reformed again and again.

"How did we slip from our original state? By our own thinking. Through wrong thoughts our minds become disturbed. We lose our peace. Question your mind: 'Why am I disturbed?' You may try to put the blame on someone else. But that is not the right answer. If we really analyze, ultimately we will come to this one truth: we just wanted something for ourselves. Most crimes are committed for the sake of this selfishness. If only we can get rid of that selfishness and think in terms of the whole world, the mind becomes pure and peaceful.

"Make use of this opportunity. Don't send out undesirable thoughts of hatred or resentment. There is no need for it. Suffering is to be accepted. Accept it and purge out all the sins accumulated by your past deeds, whether yesterday's or yesteryear's or yesterlife's.

"Many have done this. I have visited many correctional institutions, and everywhere I see this. If even one person in an institution gets interested in yoga, through that one more and more will get interested and get benefited. So set an example. Then you can walk out as well reformed, beautiful people — peaceful and useful to the entire community."

"After the talk I gave Gurudev what I could (a tomato from the prison garden and a bean pie) as an offering. He gave me his blessings

Rabbi Joseph Gelberman, Sri Gurudev and Br. David Steindl-Rast, O.S.B. Interfaith gathering at Fordham University.

Do you feel the joy? Annhurst, first of many ecumenical retreats: Br. David, Sri Gurudev, Rabbi Gelberman and Fr. George Maloney.

Another one of many such retreats. They are great treats to many minds, young and old.

and told me to continue the fine work.

"Later I was moved to a minimum security facility. I was granted permission to leave every Friday evening to attend the Raja Yoga classes at the Washington IYI. But as winter set in, things became more difficult. My diet was poor. In addition, there were several setbacks in my court motions to be released. I became more depressed than ever. At the height of my depression, the men and I were again blessed with a visit from Gurudev. His radiance and love energized everyone. When I told him of my darkness, he made a motion with his hand like a rising sun. He told me the darkness would be gone. I do not believe in magic, but I do believe that because of the strong faith which I have in my guru I was able to pull out of the bleakest of times.

"Now, many years later, I am a successful businessman with a beautiful wife and children. Gurudev is dear to the whole family."

–M., New York City

> To see the unity in diversity is Yoga — to see the same consciousness in everyone. Once we realize that oneness, we don't divide people because of color, country, caste, community, creed or language. With that basic understanding which we call Yoga, you feel the oneness. Whoever realizes that Yoga or union will always love the whole universe as part of his or her own Self.

A number of people representing different spiritual groups met in New Hope, Pennsylvania. Gurudev went there with his friend Rabbi Gelberman. At the end of the gathering Gurudev suggested, "We feel so happy about coming together now. Why don't we make this happen more often? We will let people know that although we have superficial differences, if we look deeper we see that all paths have that common Source."

Another participant, a Benedictine monk named Brother David Steindl-Rast, was taken with the idea. At his suggestion, the Center for Spiritual Studies was started, and its board of directors included Gurudev, Brother David, Rabbi Gelberman, and Eido Tai Shimano Roshi. The group met once a month, sometimes at the IYI, sometimes at the Zen Center. Soon the students of the teachers came also, crowding the limited facilities. They began to look for a larger setting.

As a result, it wasn't long before YES, the Yoga Ecumenical

Seminary, was created. YES was a retreat site established in Saugerties, New York. There was a twenty-six room main house; the large grounds included a secluded waterfall surrounded by woods at the foot of a mountain. In the summer, people could come together to share a common experience, whatever their particular beliefs. Here clergy members, laity and students of different faiths participated in a schedule of Hatha Yoga, prayer, meditation, Karma Yoga, and *satsang*. YES became a haven away from the city, a place of physical and spiritual rejuvenation. The response was enthusiastic. On weekends as many as thirty or forty people enjoyed vegetarian meals, swam in the streams, and shared chanting and music and common space.

The high point of these ecumenical programs and the response they generated came at the end of the summer of 1970. It was then that the first Yoga Ecumenical Retreat was held at Annhurst College in Connecticut.

There were wide lawns, peaceful pathways, and brick buildings — none more than five years old. Annhurst was a Catholic college in the rural Connecticut town of South Woodstock. For weeks in advance the retreat was advertised by the New York IYI. The hundreds of people who took classes saw the bright, attractive posters announcing ten days of vegetarian diet, ten days of Hatha Yoga and meditation and talks, and — most striking of all — ten days of silence.

Those who took classes at the IYI came from various life styles. They were artists and actors, housewives and students, dropouts and advertising executives. They all came to the classes carrying the tensions of the city with them, and left relaxed and peaceful; but yoga was still a new thing to them. Most had little idea of the full dimension of yoga, and most knew Gurudev only from the pictures on the walls.

Still, the posters were intriguing. The retreat sounded intense; at the same time, it sounded like fun and a great way to finish off the summer — an experience.

In fact, it was a new kind of experience. Before now, Gurudev had given public talks, and he had given small weekend programs for students who were more involved; but never before had all the practices, the total experience of Integral Yoga, had been available to everyone. Later, in the 1970s, programs of this kind would become common; they would be given by all kinds of spiritual groups, all across America. In 1970, however, it was a new thing. Nobody at the IYI knew how many people would come, and nobody knew how well it would go once it was underway.

On Friday afternoon in New York City chartered buses carried some of the retreatants from the front of the IYI to northeastern Connecticut. Others went by car, some by train; some hitchhiked. That evening 250 retreatants spilled out onto the Annhurst campus. Somehow, in the seeming chaos, they were all assigned rooms and given an evening snack before the orientation. In terms of numbers the retreat was already a success beyond expectations; but the questions remained. What would happen next?

It was not only the staff or the retreatants who didn't know what to expect; the sisters who ran Annhurst College were full of misgivings. First and foremost their doubts had to do with yoga. Wasn't this a religion that was foreign to their own? Wasn't it wrong to allow such a retreat at a college devoted to Christian teachings? It was Brother David who allayed their fears; in fact, it was he who had made the arrangements for the retreat to be held there. He also convinced Father George Maloney, a Jesuit priest from Fordham University, to take part. The sisters were somewhat reassured by this, but they were still uncertain.

Their doubts also had to do with the retreatants. They imagined their campus inundated by droves of undisciplined youngsters, hippies perhaps. All this wild energy: would it be uncontrolled, destructive? When the buses rolled in, they saw that many of the retreatants were young, in casual clothes, some with flowers in their hair; but then, many were older, quite distinguished looking, some with gray in their hair. It was hard to tell what to expect.

"The retreat was a new experience for me. I had taken some Hatha classes, but I didn't know anything else. Then, first thing, I get this schedule. 'It says that morning wake-up is going to be at 5 A.M.! And we're going to meditate for an hour! And we're only going to have one solid meal a day!' Suddenly I didn't know what I'd gotten into. I didn't know whether I could make it.

"Morning came. Or rather, someone came around to wake us up while it was still dark. We went out under the stars to a place where we would sit for an hour to meditate. I don't know how I did it, not moving or making any noise. I doubt if I meditated much, but as the closing chants began the sun began to rise in front of us, over some far woods. Despite the discomfort, somehow I felt good.

"Each day was full of things to do and things to think about. The hardest part was the silence. There were hundreds of people but no talking except for the lectures given by the guest speakers and the retreat staff. All these feelings began to come up in me, old feelings, painful feelings, and there was no one to talk to. I had thought I was quite illumined, but now I could see that I wasn't. I began to feel really disturbed by all the surfacing thoughts in my mind, but everyone else looked so peaceful. I felt I must be the only one who was disturbed. Yet, in the midst of all this, I would have these incredibly peaceful times myself. I would be upset at one time and very content an hour later.

"I started sitting up front during the talks. I wanted to get a clear impression of the different teachers. At first they seemed the same to me. I mean, they were obviously from different backgrounds; but they seemed to be on the same level somehow. Then, as the days went on, I began to sort them out. I began to appreciate each one for what he was. I was especially moved by Gurudev. It wasn't so much a matter of what he said — although that was very meaningful — but who he was.

"After a few days of ups and downs, things began to get better for me. I began to feel more relaxed with the schedule, with my own mind, and with what these different teachers were saying about selflessness and leading a spiritual life. I began to feel a lot lighter, and I noticed that the whole vibration of the retreat seemed to get lighter too. For the first few days the retreat had seemed endless; by the last day, I wanted it to go on forever. I vowed that when I got home I would not lose what I had found here."

On the last morning of the retreat, all the retreatants were crowded into the *satsang* hall for some final words from Gurudev and the other speakers. Afterward, lunch would be served and the buses would take everyone back to the city. Silence was officially over, but the crowded hall was still silent. Most of the retreatants sat cross-legged on the floor in front of the stage. Others sat on chairs along the sides. Among those sitting were many of the nuns who were on the staff of the college. During the ten days they had gradually begun to attend the talks; some had even taken Hatha Yoga classes. Now everyone was waiting.

Gurudev began by introducing a special guest, his good friend Mr. C. V. Narasimhan, who held an important post at the United Nations. Mr. Narasimhan told the retreatants that he wished to sing them a traditional song of India. He said that the important thing was that there was a moment in the song which could be called a "moment of truth," and that they should listen carefully for that. Accompanying himself on a small harmonium, he sang.

Afterward, Gurudev introduced each of his fellow teachers in turn: Brother David, Rabbi Gelberman, and Father Maloney. Each spoke of his own experience of the retreat, revealing for a moment an intimate aspect of himself that hadn't been shown before. Gurudev also invited the Mother Superior to speak, and she confessed her early fears about the retreat. Those fears, she explained, had been dissolved by the retreatants. She complimented them on their beauty and self-discipline and said they would all be welcome again. With arms open wide in a gesture of embrace, she concluded by saying, "OM Shanthi, OM Shanthi, OM Shanthi OM."

Finally, Gurudev addressed the group:

"Beloved friends, in yoga we are supposed to transcend the ego, to transcend all the selfishness. But it seems I still have a little way to go. I say this because I still seem to be a little selfish. When I hear the beautiful words of the Mother Superior, I can't help but feel a little proud and happy. I feel like a proud papa for all of you who have done so beautifully on this retreat; and I am happy to have had the opportunity to serve you. I want only to serve. In a way, this is a selfish desire because such service brings peace and joy. So I want to go on serving, to serve as long as I live. My whole life is only for this. There is no other reason for me to live."

The first Annhurst retreat was an end to something and also a beginning. It was the culmination of Gurudev's first few years in America. At that point, in August of 1970, with the retreat highlighting Gurudev's ecumenical teachings, it seemed that the "flower children" of the sixties had blossomed under his guidance into the flowers of a new decade.

Sri Swami Satchidananda — World Teacher

A renunciate belongs to the whole world. He or she cannot be limited to one place or caste or country or creed. If a person is limited, then what has been renounced? Limitation means that one still has something to renounce. It is this complete renunciation that is an important requirement in understanding God, because God has no limitations. He is unlimited. Even the term "He" is used only for simplicity and convenience; God is neither He nor She nor It. No individual can know God. One knows God only by becoming unlimited.

Sri Swami Satchidananda — World Teacher

One day someone said to me, "I don't even
know what you are doing to make things grow,
but I see the ashrams and IYIs growing more
and more." The reason for that growth is that it
is not my work. We don't proselytize. We just
go about everything humbly and quietly. Many
people who see this for the first time say, "My
gosh! I didn't even know that all this was happening. Why don't you have more publicity?" I
just say, "If God wants it, people will know."
Yes, it is God's work. God is taking care of
everything.

The New York IYI was growing rapidly, and the members began
looking for a second center. In 1970, they found a wonderful six-story
building on West 13th Street. Hari Zupan, one of the administrators of
the IYI, negotiated with the real estate agents. Everything was going
smoothly, but when it was time to sign the agreement, Hari learned
that $1500 more was needed to make the downpayment. The IYI real-
ly didn't have any way to raise that kind of money.

At the same moment Hari was negotiating, Gurudev was at 500
West End Avenue, sitting and talking with Alice Coltrane. The
famous musician was a devotee, and she had come to speak with him.
Their conversation was interrupted by a phone call from Hari letting
Gurudev know that more money was needed for the downpayment.
Gurudev listened to Hari's words, but offered no solution to the prob-
lem. He returned to the room where Alice was waiting.

(left) A new home for the growing IYI
— 227 West 13th Street, New York.
(below) "There's nothing lacking in
him!" The Nameless Swami lovingly
gave his blessings to Gurudev.

(above) Everywhere he travels, Gurudev meets with the Brahma Kumaris. Pictured: At Mount Abu.

(right) Following in the footsteps of the Master. American devotees on tour in the Himalayas.

"You know, Swamiji," Alice said after Gurudev sat down, "I have been coming here and benefiting so much from your teachings. Is there anything I could do to help the center? Is there anything you need?"

He simply said, "Whatever you feel moved to do, you can do."

"Well, do you need anything urgently?"

"In my life there is no urgency."

"Okay, fine, Swamiji. Thank you. I don't want to take up any more of your time; I should go now." She left, but not much later she knocked on the apartment door. "I'm sorry to bother you, Swamiji, but I forgot my purse." As she came in, she said, "You know, I'm really embarrassed about this. I came with the idea of giving some contribution. Then when you said that there was no urgency, I thought I would wait and give something later. But it seems that God wanted me to make a donation immediately. That must be why I forgot my purse and had to come back for it. I'm going to write a check right away."

Without consciously knowing how much was needed, or for what, Alice wrote a check for $1500 — just in time to make it possible for the IYI to purchase the property on West 13th Street. If only a little more time had passed, the IYI would have lost the building to someone else.

Somehow, everything was being taken care of.

A village is a small place from which we evolve to feel that the whole world is a big village. We are all members of the same family.

In late 1970 and early 1971, Gurudev was on a world tour. The three American disciples who traveled with him were deeply moved by the love and dedication they saw in the devotees of India, Sri Lanka, Europe and the Far East. As Americans who often had the opportunity to be in Gurudev's physical presence, they were humbled to see these people from other parts of the world, people whose faith and devotion were unwavering although they rarely were able to be with their guru in physical form. Many told beautiful stories about visions or dreams they had in which Gurudev appeared and gave them some guidance. They always felt his presence strongly, in spite of the fact that he was on the other side of the world.

In South India, Mr. Giri of Coimbatore asked Gurudev to join him for a visit to the Nameless Swami. This holy man lived in a house that belonged to a wealthy landowner, but he lived simply in a sheltered

304

area on the roof of the building. He rarely saw visitors, and this meeting was a great honor. Mr. Giri and the devotees sat quietly on the floor as Gurudev and the Nameless Swami talked. Once in a while, the Nameless Swami would turn his head away from the others and talk very animatedly to — it appeared — thin air. Shanthi Mandelkorn, one of the devotees in the group, felt that he was talking to some being she was unable to see.

The Nameless Swami asked Gurudev to go into his meditation room. Gurudev entered, bowed and sat down. "You stay here," commanded the Nameless Swami. "Don't go back to America. We need you here." He quickly left the meditation room and locked it behind him.

Time passed, more time than was necessary just for a joke. The devotees were perplexed and concerned. It certainly seemed that the Nameless Swami meant what he had said. Did he really intend to keep Gurudev locked in that room so he couldn't return to America? If so, what on earth could they do to remedy the situation? The Nameless Swami was a highly evolved being; it wouldn't be right to question his actions. They sat and worried in silence.

Finally, the Nameless Swami unlocked the door. Gurudev slowly walked out. He was quiet and radiant. It was obvious that he had been meditating during his "imprisonment." The Nameless Swami led him to a chair and sat him down. He stood behind Gurudev and gently stroked his head, saying, "There is nothing lacking in him. There is nothing lacking in him."

The Nameless Swami always had a harmonica with him; he played one for a few moments and then gave it to Gurudev as *prasadam*. Eventually, it was time for Gurudev and the devotees to leave. The Nameless Swami lovingly gave his blessings to the visitors, and Gurudev continued his trip back to America.

When Gurudev returned to America after that world tour, he brought back with him a dream, a vision. It was not a new dream, but he was expressing it for the first time to his American students. It was the dream of a community founded on yogic principles, a community where all who wished to follow a yogic way of life could come and live. Following the ecumenical axiom "Truth is one, paths are many," residents would live and work together in fellowship. It was not to be a community just for the IYI or just for Americans, but a model for the whole world. If one little village could live in harmony, perhaps others would be inspired to do the same — following whatever spiritual teachings they preferred. Eventually, perhaps the entire world could live harmoniously together, in spite of superficial differences. Gurudev described this model town as "a yoga village or a yoga-ville," and the name "Yogaville" stuck.

This vision immediately sparked great enthusiasm among the students, young and old. Committees were formed, bringing together all those who lived in the IYIs with all those who, although they lived outside the IYI, were very much part of the family.

The idea immediately touched the hearts of many devotees, and donations began to come in. One couple, both of them teachers, saved thousands of dollars from their joint income and donated it to Yogaville. At the same time, Sister Agnes Therese — a Catholic nun from Wichita, Kansas, who had attended the Annhurst retreat — contributed one dollar a month from her ten dollar allowance toward the fulfillment of this dream.

Despite the general enthusiasm there were many difficulties. It was important to find a place that was both suitable and affordable. For a while it looked as if Yogaville would be located in Virginia, but that particular prospect faded. More than a year passed, and the right property had not been found. Still Gurudev continued to talk about Yogaville wherever he went — not as something that was important for him, but as something which could serve as an example of love and cooperation for the whole world.

"After many months of concentrated searching for the right property for Yogaville, we all gave a joyous sigh of relief when the 'perfect' land, with the 'perfect' price, on the 'perfect' location finally appeared. Group followed group to see the land and to make plans. Gurudev made a special trip there before the final decision was made. He drove all over the property. He loved it, and the news spread across the country like wildfire. This was the realization of a dream in Gurudev's heart, as well as the hearts of many others. We were all full of expectancy as we neared the day on which the final papers were to be signed.

"A very dear friend of mine came one day to visit Gurudev. The three of us were sitting having tea; and, as we were talking, a phone call came. Gurudev answered it. We heard him saying, 'Yes?. . .Hmm, hmm. . .Wonderful. . . Aha, aha. . .Wonderful. I understand. . .That's fine. . .Yes. Wonderful! Thank you for calling. OM Shanthi.' That was his end of the conversation.

"The little tea party came to an end, and after a pleasant afternoon my friend departed. That evening I was looking over some last minute business with Gurudev when he casually mentioned that we had lost the land. He said that something unexpected had occurred, and the deal had fallen through.

"'Oh my God, Swamiji, that's terrible. How could that happen? When did you hear about it?'

"'This afternoon. The phone call came while we were having tea.'

"'*That* phone call, Swamiji? But you sounded so happy. And I heard you say nothing but "Wonderful, wonderful!"'

"He gave me a look between surprise and amusement, and shrugged his shoulders, saying, 'Sure, Amma. When things come, wonderful! When they go, wonderful!'"

Amma DeBayle

It was the winter of 1972, a year and a half after Gurudev first sparked everyone's interest in Yogaville, when an estate was located in Pomfret Center, in the rural northeastern part of Connecticut. The property had fifty-eight lovely acres, much of it wooded. It also offered the great advantage of providing the necessary facilities for a community: a fifty-room house that had been built around the turn of the century, but which was very solidly constructed, and an adjacent building where classes and lectures could be given. It was only a few miles from Annhurst College, where the IYI had already conducted two retreats.

Before the Connecticut ashram was found, the West Coast devotees had purchased a lovely summer resort in Seigler Springs, California. For a while, everyone spoke of Yogaville East and Yogaville West. However, the enthusiastic and inexperienced Integral Yogis of California had not looked carefully enough at all aspects of the property before making their purchase. In spite of the Yogaville West ashramites' hearty, pioneering spirit, as well as a thriving cottage industry (Integral Yoga Foods) and Sri Gurudev's encouragement, the obstacles were too many to overcome. This first Yogaville West was sold in 1973. As always, experience was a great teacher. The same devotees who had been a little naive about real estate in 1972 were among the best and wisest counselors for later decisions about Satchidananda Ashrams, East and West.

Yogaville is an abode of perfect dedication — an inspiration to express the True Self; an embrace to all nations, cultures and creeds; a community expressing the unity in diversity

through a life of purity and serenity; a model world of health and harmony, peace and prosperity; a spiritual center for study, research and growth. Let us walk together, talk together, live together, love together.

The dedication of Satchidananda Ashram — Yogaville East, on the 14th of April 1973, was the culmination of almost two years of effort. It had absorbed a tremendous amount of time and energy on the part of everyone connected with the IYIs. During this time, though, something else was developing. Some of the disciples who had been with Gurudev for several years had begun to think more seriously about commitment. They began to think in terms of a life dedicated to spiritual service. In response to this interest, Gurudev began to talk more about renunciation. He did so cautiously, knowing that it was a delicate subject, one that would raise many questions and feelings in the minds of his listeners.

At first, people were not ready to understand what I was telling them about the importance of renunciation. However, slowly some people came forward, each dedicating his or her entire life to selfless service. When I saw that they sincerely wanted to do this, I made that fact known publicly by initiating them into *pre-sannyas*. To take *pre-sannyas*, one should feel ready to renounce everything one calls "mine." Mainly, it is selfishness that is renounced. There were some people who wanted to be dedicated in that way but still had some doubts; for them, taking *pre-sannyas* put a sort of fence around them. Publicly letting others know they were living a fully dedicated life made it easier for them to stick to their commitment.

In February of 1973, at Yogaville West, the first group of fourteen devotees was initiated into *pre-sannyas*. The event caused a great deal of excitement and questioning in the IYI. Everyone knew that this ceremony, officially called *brahmacharya diksha*, was the same one that

Gurudev himself had received many years before, when Sri Swami Chidbhavanandaji named him Sambasiva Chaitanya. Clearly, it was a time of testing for those who felt drawn to the renunciate life. The initiation was the first step toward *sannyas* itself.

Some devotees were confused. Not everyone felt attracted to the monastic life. Could it be, they wondered, that only by taking monastic vows they could serve others and show their love for Gurudev? Their guru was quick to put these fears to rest. "From the point of view of spiritual attainment," he said, "it makes no difference. The only difference is that a renunciate is more free to serve. A householder has to think of his or her family obligations first; a renunciate can just go and serve wherever needed. But don't forget that many great saints were also householders. It is not the form, but the dedication that is important."

For the *pre-sannyas* initiation, the candidates cut their hair short. After the ceremony, Gurudev placed an orange scarf around each new *pre-sannyasin's* neck. Now their individual names were preceded by "Brother" or "Sister" and followed by "Chaitanya." They would live their lives as *sannyasins*, and find out if the path of total renunciation was really right for them.

> It does not matter whether you are a householder or a renunciate. For the spiritual purpose, it's all equal. Whether you are a monk or a business person or a doctor or a construction worker, whoever you are does not matter. You can lead a spiritual life by leading a dedicated life.

"Just before I met Gurudev, I had three wishes: to meet someone with understanding who could guide me, to find work which I could dedicate myself to, and to find a partner I could love. When I started as a full-time worker at the IYI, those first two wishes had been fulfilled. The third was forgotten because all my energy was channeled toward Gurudev and the Institute work. At that time I was working closely with Siva. Suddenly — or so it seemed — Siva and I, who had worked together as brother and sister, fell in love. Siva had hoped to become a monk, and he had some hesitations about getting married. Eventually, he made the choice to marry.

"Gurudev performed a beautiful wedding ceremony for us at the IYI.

(top) Ecumenical gathering. Brother David, Rabbi Gelberman, Sri Gurudev, Sri Swami Venkatesanandaji, Father Maloney.

(below) Ashramites pose with two great masters on the back lawn of the new Satchidananda Ashram - Yogaville East, in Pomfret Center, Connecticut, in 1973.

310

A visit from one of Sri Gurudev's beloved brother monks, Sri Swami Venkatesanandaji of Mauritius.

(top) *The Tibetan Buddhist Kailash Sugendo visits the West Coast Integral Yogis, 1973. Those in the photo wearing scarves are the first* pre-sannyasis.
(below) *United Nations: meeting with Secretary General U Thant.*

312

He told us that two partners should be like two wings of the same bird or like two eyes; they should work together. 'Two people who share the same goal and marry can also be good renunciates. You will be a beautiful yogic couple, and you will teach others by your example.'

"Since then, this has been a constant reminder and inspiration to us. Just as Gurudev guided us through our courtship and married us, so he has been at the heart of our marriage. I feel he will always be with us. I remember that after the ceremony he told us, 'Just as you are married to each other, so, in a way, I am married to you both.'"

Please do not feel I am here as a Hindu. If you want to call me a Hindu, then I am a true Hindu, not a sectarian Hindu. A true Hindu is a person who embraces everything.

"Now that we have an ashram, maybe Swamiji will stay mostly in one spot. People can come there to see him, and he won't have to travel so much." Many devotees had this thought, but there was very little chance of its coming true.

Of course, Gurudev never arbitrarily decided to go anywhere. He only traveled in answer to invitations to speak and conduct programs, and those invitations were steadily increasing. More and more people looked to Gurudev for direction in ecumenical understanding and spiritual direction. The interesting thing was that his reputation spread in a very quiet way. With his charismatic personality, his wit, his comfortable way with people, his handsome countenance, he could easily have become quite famous; and many devotees felt he should be. Their intentions were good ones: "Gurudev is so marvelous. Everyone should be aware of his greatness." Some of them began thinking of public relations campaigns. Gurudev, however, didn't want that. "If the Lord wants people to know about me, it will happen naturally." It did happen naturally. He has become very well known all over the world; and he is highly respected by all who know of him.

"One day, Sri Ravi Shankar was going to be interviewed on a radio program I produced. Because of my profession, I was used to meeting celebrities, but I was particularly thrilled to have a chance to meet this great Indian musician. While talking with him before the interview, I shyly asked, 'Mr. Shankar, do you know Swami Satchidananda?'

"His gentle eyes lit up, 'Oh, yes. He's a lovely person.'

"'He's my guru.'

"'Then you are very fortunate,' he said, 'There are some wonderful spiritual teachers, but there are also some charlatans who take advantage of innocent people who don't know any better.' He was almost angry as he thought of these false teachers. Then his voice softened, 'Ah, but Swami Satchidananda. . .he is a great teacher.'

"When the interview was over, he said good-bye to the interviewer and then turned to me. His eyes twinkled as he said, 'The next time you see Swami Satchidananda, give him my love.'"

J.C., Washington, D.C.

Even those who didn't know about him could tell there was something special about Gurudev.

This was a typical scene: He was on his way from one program to another program and had a wait between flights — this time in Boston. The day was particularly hot, and the Boston devotees had arranged for him to wait in one of Logan Airport's V.I.P. lounges. That way, he could have some refreshment and perhaps even a little nap before continuing his journey.

The devotees sat very quietly near their guru as he sipped a cool drink. They were hoping he could rest a bit from his busy schedule.

Suddenly a man walked up to Gurudev. "Excuse me, sir. I don't want to disturb you, but I couldn't help coming to ask you something. I don't know who you are, but I can tell just by looking at you that you're a very wise person."

"Yes? Well, I don't know if I can answer your question; but, certainly, I will be glad to answer if I can. What is your name?"

The man introduced himself; Gurudev introduced himself. Several of the devotees had immediately recognized this man as a celebrity, and they were excited. After he introduced himself to Gurudev, one disciple said, "Swamiji, he's a very famous singer."

The news didn't change Gurudev's demeanor. He continued speaking to the celebrity with the same gracious, loving tones he had used to talk with a derelict who had approached him on the streets of Boston a few months before.

There in the V.I.P. lounge, this man gazed longingly at Gurudev. He was searching for something. After they had spoken for several minutes, he asked his question: "Sir, please tell me: what is love?"

"It is very simple. Love is a one-way street. It is giving and giving, totally, without asking anything in return."

The troubled expression in the celebrity's eyes softened, and he

314

smiled as he said, "Thank you. Somehow I knew you could give me the answer."

Gurudev had been asked to speak during a program at the University of Notre Dame, one of the most important and influential universities in the United States. The five-day workshop was titled "Doing Prayer," and it was being given for 190 Catholic nuns and priests from all over the country. Their job was to teach other members of the clergy. Each of the five days was given over to one person, to give the group practical experience in a particular form of prayer. Gurudev was the only "non-Christian" in the workshop, and he had been asked to speak about the Eastern form of prayer.

On the first day, Gurudev participated in a program about image prayer, given by the Reverend Morton Kelsey. Reverend Kelsey led the group by describing in detail an inspiring scene from the life of Jesus for the group to visualize internally.

In a discussion afterward, Gurudev mentioned that this reminded him of a practice that is often done in India. Many devotees who live too far away from a holy place to visit it in person often sit and make a mental pilgrimage. If done with sincere devotion, they can experience the Lord's presence or *darshan*.

On the second day Gurudev taught an early morning Hatha Yoga class for more than 150 of the nuns and priests. Then he led them in a walking meditation across the campus to the main lecture room. At their request, Gurudev performed a beautiful worship service. As always, he began with some prayers and chanting. As he conducted the *puja*, he simply and softly explained the meaning of each action as he offered flower petals, waved the camphor flame, and so on.

Afterward, he led the way downstairs where lunch was waiting for them. The participants chanted as they entered the dining room. Each one took a candle and lit it from the single flame that Gurudev had brought from the altar. Soon the room was full of glowing lights as everyone followed Gurudev in a prayer of thanksgiving. They had previously asked Gurudev to suggest a menu, and they all enjoyed his choice of a vegetarian meal.

Later, Professor William Storey, the theological leader of the conference, thanked Gurudev for the moving experience of the *puja*. He spent a long time enthusiastically praising Gurudev's words and devotion, but Professor Storey had one doubt.

"I hesitate to bring this up because I feel so positive about Swamiji's presentation," he said, "but I feel obliged to mention this because of the job I have been asked to do. Swamiji made one remark about eating an apple with the attitude that one is eating God's body. I think I understand what he is saying. But for me, there are serious distinctions among the kinds of 'presence' of God. For example: Christ as being present in every person (which is a great theological truth) and Christ as being present in the Eucharist. They are not the same form of presence. The transforming power of God, as I understand it, which can take place because of the yielding character of bread and wine, doesn't take place so easily in man because of the unyielding character of flesh and blood. So it's when you get into these distinctions that I start to feel uneasy. But that's enough of that, because I don't want to put a damper on all the positive things I've said; and I mean those positive things very profoundly." Father Storey asked Gurudev if he would care to comment.

"Well," Gurudev started, "a little on the last point, which our Father Storey was a little hesitant to say. I'd like to ask: Is there anything wrong in seeing the Lord's body in an apple? Do we in any way bring Him down to a lower level or commit any sin in seeing it like that? He may not be present in the same way as in the Eucharist. But where is the harm of seeing Him there? On the contrary, we are elevating the apple to a higher level. It depends upon your feeling. Not all the people who receive communion see the same way, feel the same way. To be more frank, I have taken communion many times and have watched others who come and take communion. To some of them, it is just a piece of bread. But when I receive it, I feel that I am actually receiving Him. So it's the *bhavana*, as we call it, the feeling behind the action. If you have the right feeling, everything is the Lord's body.

"After all, what is Christ? Who is he? Just a body? We say Christ was crucified. What is it that was crucified? Certainly not Christ. Nobody can touch Christ. Nobody can nail Christ. He is the true spirit of God. It is the body that has been nailed, the body in which Christ lived. When you talk about 'Christ being born in you,' you mean the spirit. The spirit is always in you, untainted, unaffected by all these things. So, as such, it is the son of God, or God Himself. Every expression is the son of God. An apple is the son of God. We can treat it that way, if we can see it that way. We see the Mother Earth. Anything that comes from the Mother Earth is mother's milk. It is the essence of Mother. If one doesn't have the faith, then even in the Eucharist — the bread and wine — one may not see anything. Personally, I feel that when I walk on the Earth, I am walking on the breast of my Mother; when I sleep, I feel I am sleeping on Her lap. So there is nothing wrong in seeing everything as Divine. If you treat everything as Divine, it becomes Divine. If you have the faith, you receive the benefit."

After Gurudev concluded his remarks, one of the priests in the workshop stood up to speak. "I'd like to share something that I've realized during the last few days. I sense that I have not become what I am supposed to be. I don't think that the interest many Christians have in the East is an interest in setting aside our Christian faith. Rather, we see in the holy people of the East a certain awareness. Swami Satchidananda has become who he says we all are. If I, as a Christian, were to become who I say I am, I think I too would be able to go beyond the Eucharist to the apple. The real difficulty is that many of us have not really become who we say we are, so we dogmatically think that the apple cannot be God's body. But if we were to become like Saint Francis, for example, what would we see that apple to be? I haven't realized it yet, but I sense that it has to do with what we really are."

The workshop was deeply appreciated by all the participants. They had been inspired by Gurudev's presence, and the program itself evoked a great deal of response. Everyone involved felt renewed.

In Missouri, Gurudev met with Dr. John G. Neihardt, author of *Black Elk Speaks*, an account of the life and teachings of a Native American holy man. As the two sat holding hands, Dr. Neihardt recited some of his poetry, in which he described his early experiences of oneness with Creation. Gurudev and Dr. Neihardt were together a long time, sometimes without speaking. Dr. Neihardt brought out and put on the "Morning Star," a holy relic that Black Elk had given him. At the end of the meeting, Dr. Neihardt said he felt that Black Elk and Gurudev were the same breed, as if both "Indians" were from the same tribe.

> **Let your love be a universal love. Always doing something good to others; that is love. Let everything that is in your presence make use of that love. Love is concern for other people and other things. Love is doing good to everybody, trying to remove pain from the lives of others. Sometimes it means even undergoing the pain yourself. Utilize your love for the benefit of the Creation.**

One of the unusual things about the many talks Gurudev gives all over the world is that he almost never mentions the IYI. He never uses his public talks as a way of promoting the organization that has grown up around his name. Yet the Integral Yoga Institutes continue to grow. In the early 1970s, IYIs opened in Dallas, Texas; Boulder, Colorado; Detroit, Michigan; Garfield, New Jersey; Hartford, Connecticut; Montreal, Canada and Washington, D.C. Many more would follow.

One development that was very gratifying in this way was Gurudev's growing relationship with an organization in Harlem, called the Aquarius Health Center. A few people had criticized Gurudev because the students at the IYI seemed to be mostly white and middle class. Some felt that Gurudev should do something more to bring the teachings of yoga to the black community. The IYIs were open to all people, but Gurudev's way was never to force his teachings onto anyone.

Then, in the mid-1970s, the people who ran Aquarius became acquainted with Gurudev and began to feel close to him and his teachings. There were difficulties, however, because many in the black community felt that they should not be associated with a group outside that community; so the relationship grew slowly. Finally, Gurudev was invited to speak at Aquarius, and of course he accepted.

The atmosphere when Gurudev arrived for his talk was one of keen anticipation and some tension. Gurudev evidently felt that himself, for he began by saying, "Beloved friends, let me calm down a little. Normally I don't get excited, but today somehow it seems to be so. Ever since my arrival in this country in 1966, I have been looking for an opportunity like this. But somehow my nature is not to push myself. I only wait for an opportunity. As the Bible says, 'Ask and it shall be given. Knock and it shall be opened.'"

Gurudev went on to talk about the unity in diversity that is yoga, and about the power of love and nonviolence. By the end of the talk, the listeners had visibly relaxed, and there was a wonderful feeling of harmony in the room. This was reflected in a letter which the staff at Aquarius sent to Gurudev, in which they said, "Quite often, when people speak of the need for love and universal brotherhood, many blacks tune out; they have heard it all before. Yet, your talk was different. Your message of universal love and brotherhood was not just in your words; it was reflected in you. It *was* you."

This talk marked a turning point, and the ties between Gurudev and Aquarius became closer and closer. Eventually Aquarius became an official Integral Yoga Teaching Center.

A clean ego would make you say, "I like to

serve everyone. I'm not here for my sake. My main purpose in living here is to be useful to people." Even to think that way — "I like to serve" — you need an ego. That shows us that ego by itself is not bad. It is the unclean, self-centered ego that causes all the problems. To clean the ego — that is the reason why we don't do anything for our individual selves in the ashram. As ashram members, whatever you do, you do it for the sake of the entire village. That's how you begin, with one village. And then it becomes the entire state, the entire country and the entire world.

In the spring of 1974, after almost a year of continual travel, Gurudev returned to Yogaville East for a while. From the original group of six ashramites, the community had grown to almost thirty, including several married couples.

Cottage industries had begun, and a large organic garden was under cultivation. The IYIs needed a central coordinating office, and that was established at the ashram. Soon an audio/video department was started, as well as publications and program coordination offices.

With Gurudev present at the ashram most of the time, visitors began to come from all over the world. In the spring of 1974, the ashram had the honor of hosting Mr. C.V. Narasimhan of the United Nations; Sri Swami Kriyananda, founder of Ananda Ashram and a disciple of Paramahamsa Yogananda; the Reverend Seung Sahn, a Zen Buddhist master whose own center was in nearby Providence, Rhode Island; and Gurudev's brother monk, Sri Swami Venkatesanandaji, from Mauritius.

The ashram also provided the opportunity for the Americans to meet their fellow devotees from all over the world. People from all parts of the United States and other countries began to spend their vacations at the ashram.

That Light is within and without. It is in you, in everybody, in everything. Wherever we recognize that Light, we express our devotion. It is that Light which we call the guru. We should always remember this. The guru is not the body,

not the form and name. It is the spirit. It is the
Light that is guiding our lives. It is the
awareness itself. It is in you and it is everywhere. I am only an instrument, physically, to
let you see that Light. You came with that Light,
with an open heart. If you had not opened your
heart, you could never see that Light through
this form. Don't make the mistake of thinking
that it is coming just from me. Your own Light
is simply being reflected back to you. Don't
think that in the name of "surrender" you
should surrender to someone else. No. You are
surrendering to that Light which is your own
true nature.

In the fall of 1974, Gurudev undertook a three month tour of India,
Sri Lanka and Hong Kong. Two of the most noteworthy events of this
trip took place in his original homeland of Tamil Nadu in South India.

At Gurudev's birthplace, Chettipalayam, his family members and
other devotees decided that the house of Gurudev's birth and boyhood
should be converted into a hospital in his name. On the 21st of
November, Gurudev inaugurated the hospital in a ceremony that included the Indian doctors who would be devoting their services to it,
and the next day the hospital staff began to see patients.

An Integral Yoga Institute was opened in Coimbatore. This was the
first IYI in India. It would be administered by Sri Sengottuvelan, a
leading advocate and disciple of Gurudev.

One sunny morning in South India, a large group of people came to
Gurudev for his *darshan* and blessing. They bowed before him as they
offered the fruit they had brought. Such prostration is a matter of form
in India, and is virtually automatic for everyone when they come into
the presence of a spiritual master. But one young child refused to bow
before Gurudev. The parents were very embarrassed and tried to make
the boy bow. Gurudev gently intervened. "No. Don't force him. By
doing that you will only create a resentment and distaste in him. That
is what is happening today with all these young people who cast off
their family's religion because it was forced on them. Please don't
make that mistake. Just let him see your example." Then, holding out
a banana, he turned to the child. "Come," he said, "take this." The

child hesitated, then came forward, took the banana and ate it happily by Gurudev's side.

It seemed that Gurudev was inspiring good health care everywhere, and not long after his return from the East, he presided at the opening of another clinic. This one was Integral Health Services — a center based on a natural and holistic approach to healing — in Putnam, Connecticut, the town nearest the ashram. IHS, which grew out of a one-woman medical practice, was headed by devotee Sandra Amrita McLanahan, M.D. Through her efforts it began to grow, and its staff soon included trained nutritionists, chiropractors, psychologists and other practitioners. It brought much-needed help to the surrounding area, but its service didn't stop there. News of this excellent clinic spread. *Prevention* magazine wrote a glowing article about its service and philosophy. People began coming from all over the country, and even overseas.

> **I go wherever I can serve, wherever people want me. It is not wealth or fame that attracts me; it is your sincere hearts. Wherever I feel that sincerity, it is a joy to serve. And the more I serve, the more I wish to serve.**

Between 1970 and 1975, Gurudev made three trips to India and two to Europe. In Europe, he met with his many longtime devotees and friends as well as the growing numbers who had newly become interested in his teachings.

In the spring of 1975, he spent two days in Aalst. On the first evening, he spoke at the Town Hall, where he had spoken on his first visit in 1966. This time, the hall was completely packed. All three hundred chairs were taken, and everywhere — in the middle, on the sides, in the front — people were sitting on the floor. Many were standing behind Gurudev.

On behalf of everyone, Lakshmi Kiekens — wife of Narayana Kiekens — garlanded Gurudev. Narayana, president of the Divine Life Society of Aalst, sat near Gurudev and beautifully translated his talk.

"I put some seeds here nine years ago," Gurudev said, "but the merit goes to the fertile soil and to those who took care of it. So I pass the merit on to Narayanaji, the yogi guru of Aalst."

He placed the flower garland around the neck of his translator, but

Narayana descended from the stage to garland his brother Siva, secretary of the Divine Life Society.

"That is the sign of yoga!" Gurudev proclaimed. "They refuse even the merit. One says, 'It is he,' the other says, 'No, it is he.'" Gurudev was visibly moved by the whole evening, and at the end he said, "Know that I love you all. I have a soft corner in my heart for Aalst. It is in this town that they made a saint of me. During my first visit we took a bus once, and children who were coming from school thought I was Saint Nicholas. So whenever I want to become more saintly, I just think of Aalst."

During the next two weeks, Gurudev traveled to Brussels, to the Hague, to Antwerp, to St. Niklaas, and then to Paris. He met continuously with people, giving talks and *satsangs* throughout each day. From Paris he went on to Nimes, where he spoke to an overflowing group of yoga students, answering their questions late into the night. Even after the questions and answers were over, he found the time to give a private *mantra* initiation. At six the following morning, he began his journey back to the ashram in Connecticut.

"The plane would land in about forty-five minutes, back on American soil. I sat reviewing in my mind the succession of events that had made up the last two weeks as I traveled with Gurudev. He had been at the center of all the events, and yet never did he pass judgment on anyone in word or action. Never did he lose his amazing vitality, kindness and good humor. He seemed ever new with the newness of each moment. Although I had seen all these qualities throughout the years, I had never before experienced them all at once, changing from moment to moment at what seemed the speed of light. The message it gave me was: Elasticity of mind, equanimity, is yoga.

"I began to ponder how necessary this quality is in order to serve to the extent that I saw Gurudev doing. Without it he could not possibly do what he does. I also began to wonder how I could become like that, feeling that I would never be of real use in life until I did.

"Gurudev, perhaps sensing a certain nostalgic feeling I had because the trip with him was coming to an end, signaled me to come and sit next to him. I did, and took advantage of the opportunity to thank him and tell him what was on my mind.

"He was leaning back in his seat. His hands — on his lap, palms up — were open and relaxed. He slowly turned his head toward me, and ever so softly said, 'You see, I have no personality of my own. And when you are nobody, then it is easy to become anybody or everybody, in answer to the need of the moment.'"

Amma DeBayle

Imagine a heaven. How would that heaven be? Everybody would be loving and living happily together. We can make a heaven like that. It's easy to say that we want a peaceful world. But before we can make the whole world a heaven, we have to start somewhere. If we can't make a heaven in this little place, then what is the point of talking about a peaceful, heavenly world all over?

Retreats continued to be among the most popular of the IYI programs. In June of 1975, another ten-day retreat took place at Annhurst College. A huge tent was set up on the campus grounds, and the hundreds of retreatants gathered there each evening for *satsang*. The tent and the crowd of people gave these programs a quality reminiscent of spiritual *satsangs* in India. Like many previous retreats, this one was honored by the presence of Brother David, as well as other spiritual teachers from a variety of faiths. On the final day of the retreat, there were some special guests. Andre Van Lysebeth, president of the Belgian Federation of Yoga and longtime friend of Gurudev, is well known throughout Europe as a yoga teacher and author. He spoke to the retreatants. Sri N. Mahalingam, prominent industrialist, president of the Sri Ramalingar Mission, and supporter of Gurudev's work in India, also addressed the assembly. Later, along with several other visitors from India, Mr. Mahalingam toured the nearby grounds of Yogaville, with Gurudev as his guide. Brother David later recalled:

"The last day of the third Annhurst retreat hovered between spring and early summer. Swamiji's mood seemed to mirror that glorious afternoon. He was surrounded by eight or ten friends, mostly from India. For me it was an unexpected treat to be among them, for I would have had to leave earlier if Swamiji had not generously arranged to have me taken back to my monastery in a private plane the next morning. Now he was proudly giving us a tour of Yogaville.

"We looked with admiration at the great improvements that had been made in the short time since the IYI had acquired these buildings, and we marveled at the dedicated work and perseverance of the ashram community. After Swamiji had shown us all that could be seen, he showed us, as it were, what could not yet be seen. There we stood on a gentle June meadow, and Swamiji conjured up before the eyes of our imagination the lotus blossom design of a temple — celebrating, by its very architecture, the unity in diversity of the great spiritual traditions. Looking at his face, we could almost see the finished structure reflected in his eyes.

"My mind flashed back to my first meeting with Swamiji, almost a decade before. Memories of a first meeting often retain an exciting freshness which even much deeper encounters later on never surpass. I can remember the smell of the elevator and the fragrance of incense at the door of Swamiji's apartment. But what I remember best from that first meeting is the immediate feeling that we belonged together, the spontaneous conviction that we shared a deep dedication, which made it natural for me to trust Swamiji as if we had known one another for ages.

"That trust remained and grew. The next time we met, not long afterward, I was ready to share with him a secret hope I had not shared with many people. I needed only to give him a bare outline of my dream: a community in which different groups of earnest seekers, each following their own spiritual tradition, would work and worship together and so bear witness to their deep unity — not threatened, but enhanced, by diversity.

"No sooner had I finished talking than Swamiji sat back, looked at me with big eyes, and said, 'You thief!' Then he took paper and pencil and drew a quick diagram of his own dream, which I — he jokingly claimed — had simply stolen from him. I treasured that sheet with Swamiji's scribbles for years and later gave it to the IYI when Yogaville was founded. In its very center was the first indication of a concept which now had grown into that lotus blossom design.

"We've shared much in those years since our first meeting. We have faced problems together, and we've had just plain fun at times. There have also been moments of sadness and moments of deep joy. The bond that seemed to unite us from the beginning has stood the test of time. My first intuition of belonging proved valid. The core of the lotus blossom is still the most beautiful symbol of this belonging.

"Every so often, someone to whom I'm being introduced will ask, 'Brother David? Are you Swami Satchidananda's Brother David?' The 'yes' with which I reply means more than an ordinary 'yes.'"

The dedicated ever enjoy supreme peace. Therefore live only to serve.

Guru Poornima, the full moon day in July, is the day when devotees honor their spiritual masters. For almost ten years, Gurudev's American devotees had come together at this time. There was extra excitement, however, as Guru Poornima 1975 approached. Hundreds of disciples, students and friends traveled to Yogaville East from all over the United States and Canada for the week-long festivities. Every Integral Yoga center, from Hawaii to Montreal, was represented; and there were distinguished visitors such as Justice P.S. Kailasam, from as far away as India. All were awaiting a climactic event.

During the week there were programs and seminars. There were wedding ceremonies, *mantra* initiations and *pre-sannyas* initiations. Each evening, Gurudev gave *satsang* in Sivananda Hall, the ashram's large meeting hall.

It was a glorious week, but the event everyone was awaiting with special anticipation was the one that occurred on Guru Poornima Day itself — 23 July.

Very early in the morning, in a solemn and sacred ceremony, twenty-eight of Gurudev's senior disciples — men and women — were initiated by their spiritual master into the Holy Order of Sannyas. Before donning the orange robes symbolic of renunciation, the new monks took vows of poverty, celibacy and obedience, and dedicated their lives to the selfless service of all God's creation. Although Gurudev had initiated other disciples in the East and in Europe, this was the first time that American disciples had taken the final monastic vows. These were disciples who had gone through the testing period of *pre-sannyas*, and who had chosen a life of dedication — of service to God and humanity — in the same spirit Gurudev himself exemplifies.

"On the day when I was blessed with initiation into the Holy Order of Sannyas, I felt quite different than I ever had before. I sat with my fellow candidates chanting and waiting for Sri Gurudev to arrive for the ceremony. We had been up all night preparing for the event, but none of us was tired. I felt elevated, but not elated. It was — dare I think it! — real *sattwa*. I was totally content. When Gurudev arrived. . .well, it's hard to express in words. He always looks so beautiful, but at that moment he was even more beautiful than I had ever seen him, and far more beautiful than anyone or anything I had ever seen.

"Throughout the ceremony, throughout the day, and for many days to follow I was honestly on a level of consciousness much different from what I was used to. Even though my ego eventually managed to come onto the scene again, I knew that I would experience that level of consciousness again and that someday it would never leave.

"The path of *sannyas* has not always been easy for me. But, deep down, it has always been joyous; and I have never wanted to leave it."

S.P.M., *Virginia*

After the ceremony, under a brilliant sun, Gurudev presented his new *sannyasins* to the hundreds of students and guests who were waiting on the back lawn. They appeared radiant, beautiful, and transformed in their new orange robes. The effect of them all together with Gurudev was stunning. It was not just the shaven heads and the orange robes; something very deep had taken place. There was a transfiguration which left many who saw these new monks with a feeling of awe. Gurudev introduced each one by his or her new name. Brother Vivekan had become Swami Asokananda; Sister Amaleshwari had become Swami Gurucharanananda Ma; Brother Arumugam had become Swami Murugananda; Sister Susheela had become Swami Sharadananda Ma, and so on.

Soon enough, everyone would become familiar with the new forms, the new names, and soon enough the *sannyasins'* hair would grow back — just as Gurudev's had twenty-six years before. But on this day, there was an unforgettable impression: a turning point had been reached, both in the lives of those individuals who had become *sannyasins* and in Gurudev's spiritual mission. Everyone now knew that there would be others to carry on Gurudev's work, that a great and ancient order which would survive and grow had been successfully transplanted into Western soil. From this time on, there were many "Swamijis"; and more American disciples began referring to their spiritual master as "Gurudev."

The *pre-sannyas* period is a testing time. Some devotees expressed the desire to lead that kind of life and later, after trying it awhile, changed their minds. *Pre-sannyas* is not a court-of-law decree. If people wanted to change, they could do so. But from *pre-sannyas*, a number of

students took the vows of *sannyas*. Even from that, one or two might want to go back to the householder path, and who can stop them? What is the point of trying to stop them? If anything like that happens, I won't be surprised. I have even seen people in India become monks and later become householders. I would never condemn anyone for it. Most people who have left the *pre-sannyas* or *sannyas* life and become householders remain very close to me.

"I think my life had been leading in the general direction of *sannyas* ever since childhood. But I couldn't relate to the form for an awfully long time. To be frank, I couldn't tell whether it would 'work' for me. Some of the people who had taken the *pre-sannyas* vows couldn't uphold them, and I could see it wasn't working for them, even though they were trying to preach the ideals. Then I became very close to someone who wasn't trying to preach anything. She was simply living her *sannyas*. By her example, I could see it was the individual who has to make the whole process work. She also convinced me, more by example than by her words, that I could do it. With Gurudev's blessing, I was initiated into *pre-sannyas* and eventually I took *sannyas* initiation."

S.N., California

The parents of the American *sannyasins* seem to be accepting it just fine. Of course, before someone takes *sannyas*, their parents get to watch them trying out this life in *pre-sannyas*. If someone has just come into the IYI, the parents might not understand; but after watching their growth, parents are usually satisfied with what their children are doing. I suggest to the people who want to take *sannyas* that they show their parents — through example — that this is right for them, rather than taking initiation against their parents' wishes. Once they take *sannyas*, they no longer see their parents as parents, but as people they love equally with everyone else. Otherwise, what has been re-

**nounced? They don't reject their parents, but
they don't segregate one group from everyone
else and say, 'Only *this* is my family.' The entire
world becomes their family.**

During the month of August, 1975, Yogaville East was the host to
eighteen men and women who were taking part in the ashram's first
yoga teacher training program. All eighteen lived at the ashram,
following its intensive schedule and sharing in the problems created by
a shortage of water. It was hard, but they didn't seem to mind — once
they got used to it — and each Friday evening they had the opportunity of having *satsang* with Gurudev. This was the beginning of what has
grown to be one of the most respected yoga teacher training programs
in the country, now attended by people from all over the world.

Unexpectedly, toward the end of the summer, arrangements were
made for a visit to the ashram by Sri Swami Chidanandaji, president of
the Divine Life Society. This visit was made possible through the efforts of the World Fellowship of Religions, a group seeking unity among
all religions. They were sponsoring a tour by Sri Swami Chidanandaji
and by Sri Muni Sushil Kumarji, one of India's most renowned Jain
monks. An orthodox Jain, he was making a courageous break with the
2,500-year-old Jain tradition by coming to the West.

The ashramites and the teacher trainees were fascinated by the appearance of Sri Sushil Kumarji, who, in keeping with Jain tradition,
wore a mask over his mouth to avoid harming even the most minute
form of life. At *satsang* that evening, he gave a stirring talk. Then
Gurudev introduced Sri Swami Chidanandaji.

At first, he pondered out loud how to introduce this illustrious being
who is so widely known and revered and who is, in Gurudev's words,
"my spiritual twin." Swami Chidanandaji smiled at Gurudev's introduction, and with a twinkle in his eye, said, "Just say to them, 'Your
uncle is here.'"

The majority of those present had never met Swami Chidanandaji
before. They were moved by his presence and the beautiful way he expressed the teachings of his master, Sri Swami Sivanandaji Maharaj.
They felt it was a great blessing to be in the same room with these two
great children of the great spiritual father.

**I don't really belong to any one country or
organization.**

328

The world traveler — one of many visits to France.

(top) Hatha Yoga class at Princeton University.
(below) Yogaville East: Gurudev playing with the children.

(top) *Working in the ashram's auto body shop.*
(below) *Four ashramites from the Pomfret Volunteer Fire Department. Ashram members volunteered their services in the neighboring community in a variety of ways.*

331

The ashram hosts the Venerable Seung Sahn of Providence Zen Center and a group of his students.

(top) The birthplace honors Gurudev. Reception at Coimbatore airport.

(below) "The deity I served for many years and worshiped many nights." Visit to Perur Temple.

333

(right) Sri Gurudev
with "his" Brother
David.
(below) A tender
moment with Rabbi
Gelberman.

Pada Puja, *Guru Poornima at Satchidananada Ashram, Connecticut.*

Sri Gurudev with his "spiritual twin," Sri Swami Chidanandaji, the illustrious President of the Divine Life Society, at Yogaville East.

336

(top) Judge Robert Zampano presides as Sri Swami Satchidananda becomes a United States citizen. (below) A day of greatness: Sri Gurudev initiates the first American disciples into the Holy Order of Sannyas.

337

The year 1976 was America's 200th birthday, and on the 20th of February, at 2:22 P.M., a special event took place. Sri Swami Satchidananda became a United States citizen.

Judge Robert Zampano presided over the event in a Connecticut District Court. Also present was the lawyer whose services were so helpful in this process — Mr. Lyle O'Rourke, the same lawyer who had served Gurudev ten years before in acquiring a permanent resident's visa.

That evening, Gurudev spoke to the family at the ashram about what had happened and expressed his appreciation.

"Thank you very much for making me one of you. But it really was only a matter of legality. Otherwise, I have been an American for the past ten years. Wherever I go, I feel that I am one of that group. The reason is that I don't seem to really belong to any one country.

"In 1966, when I came here, they all called me a hippie because I was in the midst of hippies. And I was happy to be called a hippie, since that is the only way we could establish a proper communication. Even the Supreme God — the nameless, formless God — when He comes down to our level, He also has to take some name and form. Unless you are on the same level, you cannot communicate, you cannot even understand each other.

"When a grown-up person wants to play with the children, he or she has to get down on all fours and crawl and talk their language. This same person may be a famous philosopher, someone with many letters after his name. But if he is going to use all his education with the children, they will get scared. They won't even come near him. So he has to talk in their own language, crawl like them. Only then will there be proper communication.

"So as soon as I walked into this country, I felt that. And if you remember my talks, you remember that very often you heard me saying, 'We Americans,' because when you are in America, you are an American. . .

"To really know God is to renounce all your limitations. This is the reason why you see in almost all the different religions — whatever be the country, caste or community — all the God-men and God-women have renounced their narrowness. No real sage or saint or prophet has ever said, 'I belong only to this country or that group or this community and not the others.'

"It is we who limit them, because we are still limited by our own narrowness. When we are narrow, we say, 'Moses belongs to us.' 'Jesus belongs to us.' 'Buddha belongs to us.' We limit them. But ask Moses and Jesus and Buddha, 'To whom do you belong?' They will certainly answer, 'We belong to everyone.'"

This same year, 1976, marked the tenth anniversary of Gurudev's arrival in America, and his grateful U.S. devotees wanted to celebrate this event on a grand scale. A gala commemorative celebration took place at the Cathedral of St. John the Divine, in New York City. Nearly 2,000 people filled the world's largest cathedral to hear many of Gurudev's students and friends pay tribute to his greatness and his transforming influence on their lives. Amma DeBayle, Arjuna Zurbel and New York attorney Deva Barrett told how Gurudev's teachings had helped change their lives. Mr. Hari Harilela of Hong Kong; Indian Ambassador to the United States, Mr. T.N. Kaul; Proctor Sri S. Kanagarathnam, of Sri Lanka; and Rabbi Joseph Gelberman all joined in praising Gurudev's work. A multi-media presentation saluted his years of service in America. Choirs sang. A commemorative volume called *A Decade of Service* was presented.

Afterward, Gurudev quipped that, with such a wonderful ten-year celebration, he would certainly plan to be present for the twentieth year as well. Everyone was delighted to hear this, knowing that the guru's words — even presented as a jest — are not spoken lightly.

Ten years of Gurudev's service had brought great changes to the lives of the American devotees. Many who had suffered from poor health or drug and alcohol dependency were now vibrantly healthy. Minds were more calm and clear. Lives were more happy, dynamic and serviceful. Some of the devotees had become monks. Many had married and become parents. Where there had once been hippies, there were now doctors, nurses, chiropractors, lawyers, administrators, writers, contractors, housewives, teachers, actors, engineers, physicists, musicians, entrepreneurs — all of them bringing the yogic attitude of Karma Yoga to their professions and interactions with others.

Gurudev told the devotees that there would inevitably be changes after all these years, especially now that some of his disciples had taken the *sannyas* initiation. Speaking not long after the celebration, he said, "It's not possible for me to have a close relationship with thousands of people on the physical plane. Anyway, students should not depend so much on the person; the teaching is what is important. Still, I give public *satsangs*, but I don't see people privately that much. And I have trained a number of people whom I know can handle many of the questions that have been asked of me. After ten years of constant service here, I think it's time to give a little rest to the body. Just because I'm not available for personal interviews, it doesn't mean I don't love people or want to serve them. I am serving now through my trained students, and in planes above the physical."

Somehow I seem to be speaking more and more to medical people about yoga. The time has come. Yoga is genuine. It may take a little longer to show results in treating ailments, but those results will be permanent.

Although Gurudev had indicated that he would not be serving so much on the physical plane in the future, he was still invited to speak all over the world, and, in response, he kept traveling continuously. The year 1977 seemed to be filled with invitations for him to address medical and other health-related groups. After ten years, evidently the time had come for yoga to enter the mainstream of Western health awareness.

During this year, Gurudev was invited to speak at the national convention of the American Medical Students Association in Chicago, the Johns Hopkins University Medical School in Baltimore, the National Institutes of Health (NIH) in Washington, D.C., the Himalayan Institute's Congress on Meditation-Related Therapies, the Baylor College of Medicine in Houston, and numerous other medical and health-related conferences.

For Gurudev's lecture at the National Institutes of Health — an organization of about 6,000 workers within the Department of Health, Education and Welfare — Dr. Amrita McLanahan introduced him to the full auditorium of 600 doctors, nurses, technicians and invited guests. As he always does when he talks about health, Gurudev emphasized prevention, saying that health or ease is our normal state. "Dis-ease," he explained, "is simply a disturbance of that ease. When looked at this way, the important question becomes: What do we do to disturb our ease? When we know this, we know the *cause* of ill health, and it is then relatively simple to prevent it."

The health professionals listened attentively as Gurudev cited four factors as the cause of almost all modern health problems: smoking, drinking, improper diet and stress. The yogic approaches to the first three of these are well known. In dealing with them, Gurudev highlighted the importance of *prana* — not just oxygen, but the cosmic vital energy. It is this which brings light to every cell of our bodies and which burns out all the toxins. It is even more important than what we eat, because it provides the digestive fire, without which any food produces toxins. By proper breathing alone, Gurudev said, we can prevent and cure almost all ailments.

The fourth factor, stress, led Gurudev to talk about the yogic understanding of the mind and the emotions, how it is vital to have control over the mind so that we are not constantly disturbed by anxiety. This is the importance of meditation. But even more important, he said, is leading an unselfish life, because selfishness is the root cause of all disturbance.

With masterly precision, Gurudev summed up the whole yogic approach to life for all these health professionals: "Let us have an easeful body, a peaceful mind, and a useful life. What more do we want?"

Inspired by Gurudev's talk, a successful yoga program was started at NIH for patients and staff. The program combined Hatha Yoga, meditation, and Raja Yoga.

The growth of interest in yoga in the medical field at this time seemed nothing short of astonishing. Around this time, the official newspaper of the American Medical Association published a long, very positive front page article describing Gurudev's presentation at the medical students' convention in Chicago. In the early fall, Gurudev gave an address at the prominent Baylor College of Medicine in Houston, arranged by medical student Dean Ornish.

In this talk, Gurudev emphasized that we are responsible for everything that happens to us. We make ourselves sick or keep ourselves healthy by our own actions, our thoughts, and by the accumulation of our past deeds, or *karma*. He also emphasized that yoga does not reject Western medicine as an aid to help those who have fallen sick. "Yogic teachings and Western medicine can complement each other" he said, "and a person can derive benefits from both." Finally, Gurudev talked about the quality of life as being more important than the length of life. "It's not how long you live that's important," he stated. "Even if you live for only five years, be happy!. . . Some people think swamis just sit and meditate all day. But if you come to see me, you may see me working on a tractor or plowing the land, flying a plane or riding a horse. I do everything. Life must be an enjoyment."

Gurudev's teachings became the inspiration for many yoga-based health programs. Health professionals who were also devotees launched many successful programs for heart patients, cancer patients, lupus patients, AIDS patients, and others. Using the general practices of Integral Yoga, and aided tremendously by Gurudev's frequent direct guidance, they had amazing results. Perhaps even more amazingly, in this age of cunningly marketed fad diets and cures for just about everything, Gurudev's prescription remained simple and uniform. Enormous success was experienced in healing a wide variety of different disease conditions by following essentially the same basic practices that had been so freely shared all these years in regular yoga classes and retreats. *Asanas, pranayama,* deep relaxation, meditation, clean diet, proper mental attitudes — in short, Integral Yoga — this was the "magic cure-all."

"At the Baylor Medical College I conducted a year-long research program, under the guidance of Swami Satchidananda, using a complete vegetarian diet and yogic practices — Hatha Yoga, breathing practices, meditation — all in an environment that encouraged patients to feel less like victims and more capable of improving their own health. They were also asked to stop using cigarettes, alcohol and coffee. The program was very successful. At the end of the year, ten of the twelve patients who had taken part in the program were completely free from heart pain (most after years of constant or recurring pain). The other two patients had their pain greatly reduced."

Dean Ornish, M.D., Texas

"One cancer patient in our program had a swollen lymph gland in his neck the size of a golfball. He faithfully followed the yogic program, and when it ended, that diseased gland was the size of a pea. . .Another patient had leukemia. After the program, she called excitedly to say that her doctors were amazed. For the first time in years, her white blood count was normal."

Mitra Lerner, California

"He was fifty-five years old and had always had asthma. His wife, a yoga student herself, persuaded him to try yoga at the IYI. At first, he was really doing it just to please her; he didn't believe anything could help him after all these years. After a while, he even started to enjoy it; and he regularly practiced all the *pranayama.* After two months, he was feeling wonderful; and his doctor — who had been treating him for many years — just couldn't believe it. The asthmatic symptoms were gone."

P.M., Massachusetts

"This man looked at me with fear in his eyes. He had just been diagnosed as having ARC (AIDS-Related Complex). He wanted to know if a yogic program could help him. 'It depends on how seriously you take it,' I said, 'how dedicated you'll be to getting cured.' He was ready for anything. So I put him on a very strict program of exactly what Gurudev has taught all of us about good health: pure diet, *asanas*, *pranayama*, deep relaxation, meditation, proper mental attitude, and so on. In this case, I also recommended strict celibacy to strengthen the immune system. (Again, something Gurudev had told me.)

"He faithfully practiced this prescription. Several months later, he called to tell me that his latest visit to the doctor had shown that there was no longer a trace of the disease in his system."

Swami Nischalananda Ma,
California

"A friend asked me to talk with her father about yogic ways of dealing with his heart problem. He was about to have heart surgery, and she was hoping that yoga could help prevent it. But he wasn't interested. The surgeons performed quadruple bypass surgery, and he felt fine — for a while. In a year the pain returned, but the physicians couldn't operate again. His situation got worse and worse. Finally he came to see me. I had him practice gentle *pranayama*, a few select *asanas*, deep relaxation, and meditation. He was Jewish and the word *Shalom* had special meaning for him; he started using it for Japa Yoga. When he first started the yoga program, he couldn't walk even a block without pain. In three months, he was walking five miles each day and happily playing golf. Now, four years later, he is doing great and is still following his yoga practices. He even has his country club preparing special vegetarian meals for him! This is only one of many, many success stories I've witnessed, when people have put Gurudev's teachings to use for their health."

N.S., therapist, Connecticut

"My sister Grace was very seriously ill. Her liver was failing, due to the fact that she had had several major operations, the last of which was an intestinal bypass. She was literally dying before our eyes. The doctors felt that the only hope was another operation to re-establish intestinal continuity, but they could not promise she would survive the operation. And they were afraid she would lose her liver. At one of Gurudev's lectures, I gave him a letter explaining the situation. I asked that he pray for my sister and help us all to accept God's will. From that day on, Grace began to recover.

"The doctors could not believe she was getting better. Her hair was growing back, her strength and endurance were increasing and, most of all, her state of mind was improving. The doctors ignored all these signs and scheduled her for an operation. A liver biopsy was performed, which showed an improvement. The surgeons refused to operate because of this improvement, but all the other doctors were convinced that she would die. A six-hour argument between the internal specialist and the surgeons followed, resulting in a compromise of a month's delay. At the end of that time, if Grace's blood test showed no improvement, the surgeons would consent to the operation. Her health improved every day, and now she is living a normal life. The doctors are still confused about her recovery. They keep saying it's impossible; yet, it happened. When I told Gurudev about their confusion, his answer was, 'The doctors do not understand that prayer is more powerful than medicine.'"

G.D., California

John McKenzie worked at Blythedale Hospital. He invited Gurudev to come there and speak to one hundred sick and disabled children. John introduced him by saying simply, "I want you all to meet the best person I know."

The children were excited. Their inquisitive faces looked up at Gurudev. There were boys and girls of different races, different backgrounds. Some were very young, and some were a little older. But all of them shared a common problem. At least three-quarters of them were in braces or wheelchairs or on stretchers.

The children — divided into different groups representing different countries — were gathered on the lawn. They were dressed in the costumes of Holland, the Ivory Coast, India. They were about to take part in an "Olympic" games tournament and to learn the songs and customs of these countries. It was a special time for them, a time to transcend some of their limitations and experience some of the joys of normal childhood.

Gurudev stood in the warm sunlight, surrounded by this group of children who had never seen him before. He began softly.

"My sweet angels — yes, you look like angels to me — thank you for inviting me. I am so happy to be here to spend a few minutes with you and share in the joy of this festival." He stopped for a moment and gazed at them all. Then he took some flowers from a vase at his side. "I would like to ask you some questions. Will that be all right?"

"Yes," came the reply. The children were eager to participate.

Gurudev held up the flowers. "What are these?"

"Flowers," cried a dozen voices.

"Could you say that these are *my* flowers?"

"Yes," the children agreed.

"Fine. These are *my* flowers. But could you say that I *am* these flowers? Are these flowers me?"

"No, no." they replied, some of them giggling.

"Fine." Then Gurudev held up his hand. "This is my hand, is it not? This is *my* hand, but is it me?"

The children understood. "No!" they answered enthusiastically.

"This is my body," Gurudev continued, "but is this body me?"

"No!" shouted the children, now totally caught up in the game.

"But if this is not me, who am I?" This time the children were quiet. Some looked to their counselors for the answer. Gurudev smiled. "I am the soul. I *have* a body, but this body is not me. We live in the body, just like we live in a house. Sometimes our house needs repairs. But if my house is leaking, would you say that *I* am leaking?"

"No!" More giggles.

"Good. Then you must remember this. You have come here to get your body repaired. After some time, you'll go home with your body fixed. But you are not that body. You are a soul. You are always perfect and whole. You are all God's children. Do you understand?"

"Yes!" they replied. They did understand.

"Now I want to ask you something else." Gurudev pointed toward some balloons which would soon be released to begin the tournament. "In that green balloon, is there green air? Or in that red one, is there red air?"

"No," all the children answered.

"What color is air?"

"White!" shouted a little girl. Everyone laughed.

"Air has no color," Gurudev gently corrected. "Your souls have no color. No matter what our outer colors are, we are all children of the same God in heaven." He clasped his hands and glanced toward the sky, where the balloons waiting to be released would soon be flying.

There is one Cosmic Essence, all-pervading, all-knowing, all-powerful. This nameless, formless essence can be approached by any name, any form, any symbol that suits the individual. That is why we have all the religions. But we should never forget our essential unity.

(right) Saint Ramalingam

(below) Satya Jnana Sabhai - the Temple of Light, Vadalur.

(top) One light illuminates all the candles. All Faiths Day ceremony, 1977.
(below) All Faiths Symposium. Left to right: Murshida Taj Inayat, Rabbi Joseph Gelberman, Sri Gurudev, Brother David Steindl-Rast, O.S.B.; the Venerable Gesshin Prabhasa Dharma, Father Robert Beh.

347

Throughout his life, Gurudev had been inspired by the teachings of Saint Ramalingam. Born in 1823, Ramalinga Swamigal propagated the concept of using Light as a symbol of worship. He referred to the supreme omnipresent Being as *Arutperum Jyothi* — literally, "the light that bestows infinite grace." He wanted to travel beyond the evils of caste, creed, and clan. He aimed at the establishment of a universal religion; he taught others to understand the brotherhood of all humanity. In 1869, in the small village of Vadalur, he opened the first temple of light worship.

Unfortunately, most people came to see Ramalinga Swamigal for the wrong reasons. Rumors of his *siddhis* were rampant. "He can turn lead into gold," they said. "He can give life to the dead. He can cure disease and control the elements." Saint Ramalinga was a great *siddha*, but he knew that these powers had no real importance. For years, he had preached to the people, exhorting them to lead good lives, to practice meditation, to pray and to trust God. No matter what he said, they were still greedy for the *siddhis*. Most of them never even attempted to follow his teachings.

Tired of the hundreds of people who came because of desire for *siddhis* rather than thirst for Truth, Saint Ramalingam left for Mettukkuppam, a village south of Vadalur. A few sincere devotees went with him. There, in 1874, he entered a room and instructed his devotees to lock the door behind him and keep it locked. There was only one door and one very small window to the room.

Soon, the government authorities learned of this and went to investigate. "You can't keep someone locked in a room!" they said. "This door must be opened." The disciples refused to disobey their guru's orders. Finally, the officials opened the door themselves. There was no one inside. Ramalinga Swamigal had simply disappeared. He was never seen again.

The true devotees carried on his teachings. Over the years more and more people began to sincerely practice what Saint Ramalingam had preached. His beautiful, universal teachings and the Light Shrine at Vadalur were great inspirations to Gurudev as he planned to make public a wonderful vision he had pondered for many years.

Gurudev's work in behalf of ecumenism continued to grow. In 1977, he began to speak more often about his dream of an ecumenical temple, a place where people of all backgrounds and beliefs could silently worship together under one roof. While each worshiper prayed in his or her own way, the essential unity of all faiths could be experienced. For many years this had been Gurudev's vision. Now it was time for it to manifest, and plans began for the LOTUS (Light Of Truth Universal Shrine). The building would be in the shape of a lotus flower; because the lotus — which lives in the water but is not affected by it — is a symbol for the Spirit that pervades all of the physical world while remaining untainted. Inside, at the center of the shrine, there would be a light. Around that light would be individual shrines for all the different religions. The light from the center would go up to the ceiling and divide into rays that would come down to shine on each of the altars. If one looked upward from the central light, one would see that all the religions were illuminated by the same universal Light. If one looked from the individual altars back to the center, one could see that all religions ultimately lead to the same source. In the LOTUS, Gurudev said, people could come to pray at the altar of their own faiths, and, at the same time, be reminded of the underlying unity in the diversity of religions and philosophies. The experience of this spiritual unity, he taught, leads to true global fellowship, to love and understanding. That understanding is the fundamental remedy to all of humanity's divisiveness, greed and hatred. On the basis of drawings made by Gurudev, artists and architects began to sketch their ideas for the design to embody this great purpose.

On July 31 of that same year, the day after Guru Poornima, a deeply moving ceremony gave a living example of that unity in diversity. On that day, Gurudev brought leaders of five major religions together around one altar at Yogaville East to take part in an ecumenical service to the Divine in the form of light.

This landmark event, called All Faiths' Day, was a further step in Gurudev's lifelong effort to offer people the opportunity to experience their true oneness. As far back as 1952, he had been bringing people of various faiths together to worship and to help heal the religious disagreements that separated them.

The ceremony on All Faiths' Day was held outside in the ashram's large enclosed garden. The sun shone brightly on the proceedings as the acclaimed filmmaker John Goodell recorded the events. Five hundred people of all ages, backgrounds and religions watched and participated. They all joined in singing the Yogaville anthem: "Let us walk together. Let us talk together. Let us live together as one. . ."

The celebrants for the universal worship service were Sri Gurudev, Brother David, Rabbi Gelberman; the Venerable Gesshin Prabhasa Dharma, founder/president of the International Zen Institute of America; Murshida Taj Inayat, a leader of the Sufi Order and spiritual partner of Pir Vilayat Inayat Khan; and Father Robert Beh, C.S.C.,

Catholic chaplain of the Washington State Penitentiary. Each one used the rituals of his or her own tradition to worship the central light.

Two of the day's guests later wrote: "As we sat watching the pageant of All Faiths' Day — the incredibly beautiful ceremony, the flowers, the candles, the hundreds of loving faces, the chanting, the unity of purpose — we realized vividly how powerful this day was, and how important it was to the destiny of the world.

"We have been moved before in our lives. But the depth of our emotion that day distinctly revealed to us that if mankind were to survive, this would have to be the way — in a display of love and brotherhood and sisterhood that overcame all barriers, dissolved all differences, and demonstrated the great, overwhelming truth that we are all one. And in that oneness, we are one with God.

"Sitting next to us was a Catholic monk from a nearby monastery. He wept openly — as did we — during the service. When Gurudev and the others in the circle of Hindu, Jewish, Buddhist, Catholic and Sufi leaders embraced, we turned and embraced the monk. And we felt God's presence as never before."

After you have decided which path is right for you, stick to that path, but do not say to others that this is the only one. Recognize all of the paths and respect them. In the spiritual life, all paths lead to the same place.

In September of 1980, Gurudev flew to Switzerland for the annual meeting of the European Union of National Yoga Federations. This was the third year that he had been invited as a special guest speaker, and a tradition had begun. From then on, the members always asked him to attend and eagerly awaited his annual arrival. They asked Gurudev to serve as a Patron of the organization, and he had graciously accepted. The European Union of National Yoga Federations had come together through the guidance and inspiration of Mr. Gerard Blitz. Years before, he had founded the Club Mediterranean, but he later retired from Club Med to devote his life to teaching yoga and training yoga teachers in Europe. He had a deep affection and respect for Gurudev and acted as the most gracious of hosts each time Gurudev traveled to Switzerland.

Zinal, high in the Swiss Alps, was the lovely setting for these programs. In the clear, quiet mornings, one could see the cows grazing in the mountain fields and hear their bells ringing in the distance. The snow on the mountain peaks glistened in the sun. Forty teachers from all over Europe had come to spend a week with Gurudev. They ranged in age from twenty to seventy, and they had been trained in different schools of yoga.

Gurudev taught the Hatha Yoga class twice during the week. "*Asanas* should be easy but not lazy," he told the group. He guided them in the poses, watching with a master's eye. Precisely, he adjusted their posture. Now and then, he gave a short *satsang* on the tremendous value of the bow pose for proper insulin production, why a good diet is essential for flexibility, or some other guideline for health through yoga. He demonstrated the headstand, showing how to come out of it with perfect control, then showing how to come down if you lose your balance. He rolled out of the pose with the ease of a child.

After each class, Gurudev answered the group's questions and often illustrated his teachings with delightful drawings on a blackboard. For anyone else, it would have been quite a challenge to teach in a way that would appeal to this particular group of people — people who spoke a variety of languages and represented a variety of approaches to yoga practice. Gurudev, with his universal outlook, was more than equal to that challenge.

Some European schools of yoga do not consider vegetarian diet to be very important, and when Gurudev first started speaking in Zinal, the beautifully prepared meals had comprised mostly meat dishes with just a few items for vegetarians. At first Gurudev spoke gently about the benefits of a vegetarian diet. He gave an impressive array of reasons for vegetarianism. "I want you to understand and to be totally convinced that a vegetarian diet is the best diet for a yogi! No one should be disqualified from practicing yoga because of his or her diet; but, as teachers of yoga, you should know what is right." The next year there were a few more vegetarian dishes. The following year, there were more vegetarian than meat dishes. Eventually, the fare became almost totally vegetarian.

Each afternoon, Gurudev gave *satsang*. His subjects ranged from family life to building a house to realizing the Self. He showed how the essential teachings of yoga are at the heart of all religions. Although they express it differently, all affirm the need for purity, ethical perfection, self-control and a dedicated life so that one can experience God.

At their request, Gurudev led the group in meditation and answered many questions about meditation and *mantrams*. "Every religion has its sacred language and *mantrams*. The Christians used Gregorian chants to create the Divine vibration through sound." When he said this, many faces beamed with joy as they recognized the depth and meaning in the traditions of their childhood.

Gurudev gave five to seven hours of *satsang* each day along with informal teaching and personal counseling. Under his loving care, the participants were visibly transformed. When the week drew to an end, many of them said good-bye with tears in their eyes, and many were already planning to visit the ashram in America.

The husband of one of the participants came to pick her up. When she proudly introduced her husband to Gurudev, the gentleman said, "I'm really glad that my wife has been in good hands."

"Why do you say that?" Gurudev asked. "How do you know she's been in good hands?"

"I can tell just by looking at her. Her face is all shining!"

"There is a question that occasionally arises about the LOTUS: Is its sphere of influence limited to those fortunate people who will be able to travel to America to visit the Shrine? Can it have an effect on others who are far away? We recently received a letter that illustrates how the subtle healing power of the LOTUS is already being felt around the world.

"In Paris, France, Michele teaches catechism (religious instruction) to seven- and eight-year-old children. She is a joyful, radiant example of her Catholic faith. She also teaches her students some Hatha Yoga, meditation, and the yogic teachings which are so universal that they enhance the students' understanding of Catholicism. Her parish priest recently sent Michele an eight-year-old Vietnamese boy for religious instruction. This boy's father had been killed in the political strife in Vietnam, and the family fled to France. His mother was unable to raise her five children. He had been placed in a Catholic foster home. For the first time in his life, he felt secure and safe in this loving environment. He wanted to fully become a part of his new family and asked if he could become a Catholic.

"The family wisely realized that this might create another trauma for the child by separating him further from his mother and family, all of whom loved him very much and were Buddhists. The parish priest decided that Michele could help to bridge the gap.

"When Michele met this boy for the first time, she welcomed him and showed him a drawing of the proposed design for the LOTUS. 'You see,' she explained, 'there is one central light that lights the altars of all the different religions. Just like that, there is one God who teaches us how to live through the Catholic faith and the Buddhist faith, and all the other religions too. You are free to choose to follow God's teachings through Catholicism if you wish, but that doesn't mean you have to reject Buddhism. They both come from the same God.'

"The little boy could understand a picture and a symbol better than a presentation of rational arguments. This explanation seemed to please him and free him from the worry of feeling guilty or separated from his mother. It allowed him to feel fully loved and accepted exactly as he is in his new home."

LOTUS News

These days we hear a lot about religious rivalry and competition, so I wanted a place where we could feel the oneness — even though our approaches are many. Whenever we have an ecumenical worship service, the various clergy say afterward that they experienced the oneness. When I met with His Holiness Pope Paul VI for the second time, he told me how much he appreciated these happenings; and in a private interview, he spent almost thirty minutes asking me about them.

Detailed plans for the LOTUS were being prepared. Drawings and models had come in from around the country. Two devotees in particular — architects Viswanath Watson, of California, and Steve Au, of Hawaii — had lent their skills to the project and made the earliest architectural drawings. Eventually, Jagadish McCabe, architect and devotee from Florida, became the official LOTUS architect.

On one occasion, when Gurudev was talking about the LOTUS project at the Universalist Church in New York, someone in the audience asked him if the temple would be like a three-dimensional *yantra* that would radiate divine energy through its very structure. It was an unusual question, and Gurudev appeared to ponder it.

"Hmm. That's a beautiful question. I'm glad that somebody thought of it. Normally I don't want to elaborate on that too much, because these are very sacred things. There are a lot of hidden things. The minute you open them and talk about them, they become cheap.

(top) High in the Swiss Alps: The European Union of National Yoga Federations. (below) A warm exchange with Mr. Gerard Blitz, the inspiration and director for the European Union of National Yoga Federations.
(opposite) The children of Yogaville with Gurudev — the perfect Guide (top photo), the perfect Santa, the perfect playmate.

(top) Carole Karuna King (right of Gurudev), her two children, and some of the California devotees.
(below) A home for the LOTUS? The Santa Barbara Ashram.

But having received this question, I should say at least a little bit about it.

"As many of you already know, certain geometrical figures have the capacity to act as receptive objects to certain holy vibrations. Our *yantra*, for example. It has a tremendous capacity to receive the divine vibrations. According to the Hindu tradition, *yantras* and *mantras* have this power. Other faiths have this too. Our Jewish friends put something on the threshold, is it not so? Every house will have something inscribed to protect the house. Every letter emits its own vibration — whether you know it or not. A Star of David would emit certain holy vibrations. A cross would emit certain holy vibrations. You don't even have to be a believer for it to have a positive effect. Whether you believe it or not, if you put your finger in the fire, it will burn. So the holy objects have been given; those who have experienced them, who know what they are, have given them to us to use.

"So, yes, the LOTUS is like the *yantra*. The three-dimensional form, in the Hindu tradition is called a *mehru*. It's a structural form that attracts positive vibrations — like a lightning rod attracts lightning, for example. And that is the reason why most of the holy places have a pointed tower or spire. The Hindu temples also have that. They even have golden pinnacles to receive certain forces. And many of you might already know the effect of pyramids. So this structure also is like one of those. It has tremendous power. You don't even need to do anything special; if you simply go inside, you will feel the divine vibrations. It's going to be a beautiful healing place. It's designed that way. But I really don't want to say too much and make big promises. Let it happen. When there is something beautiful, it will reveal itself in its own time. When the flower opens there will be fragrance, and the bees will come."

At the same *satsang*, Gurudev addressed an issue that had been on many minds:

"The question may be asked: When there seem to be a lot of other needs, why should we spend our energy building the LOTUS? Here I would like to answer why. In a way, I think that this project and any similar project that will help bring people together to recognize the same Self in others, is the most important thing — more important than feeding the hungry, clothing the naked, providing shelter. You might wonder: How can he say that?

"What is the reason why there are millions of people starving? Is it because there is not enough food? Certainly not. The world has a population of about four and a half billion. We grow enough food to feed more than twelve billion. The world statistics clearly prove that there is plenty of food. Then why should there be hunger? It's because of the lack of concern about other people — the lack of love, of caring and sharing. It is the lack of these things that creates poverty and all the wars and calamities.

"Anything that you do to realize the spiritual oneness will help solve all the other problems. Certainly, if we are aware of our spiritual oneness, we will not be fighting with one another, starving one another, stealing from one another. The very purpose of religion is to bring that feeling of oneness, not to deny people. Universal love is religion. If that were instilled in our hearts, we certainly would not give room for these problems.

"Please don't misunderstand me. I am *not* saying that we should not give direct and immediate help to the hungry, the poor, the sick. On the contrary — we shouldn't even wait to be asked; we should look for ways to provide them with that help. What I am saying is that we should not *stop* there. If we stop with that, it is only temporary help.

"The Hindus describe four types of charity. Charity in Sanskrit is *dhanam*. The four *dhanams* or charities are *annam* or food, *swarnam* or money, *vidya* or education, and *jnanam* or wisdom. *Annadhanam* means offering food. When you give food to somebody, it lasts for a few hours. Afterward he or she has to find somebody to give more food. If you give money, *swarnadhanam*, maybe that person will be able to buy food for a week or a month. Still, it's only temporary. If you give somebody education, *vidyadhanam*, certainly that person will be able to earn enough money, not only for himself but for his family as well. But, again, that will not guarantee his peace. The educated one will be able to get money, but that won't make him or her a person of wisdom. There will still be trouble. Many people fight, not because they don't have enough food, but because of greed, hatred, jealousy. So even education is not enough.

"But if you give wisdom, *jnanadhanam*, if you help someone realize his or her Self and to see the same Self in everybody, you have really given help in the right way. Once that realization happens, food will come, money will come, health will come, peace will come, everything will come. 'Seek ye first the kingdom of God; everything else will be added unto you.'"

By this time, there was a second Yogaville West; this time it was on a beautiful piece of property in Santa Barbara, California. Many people thought this was the perfect spot for the LOTUS to be built, and preliminary plans were made. A few neighbors raised objections, and there were many discussions among ashramites and people in the surrounding area. One man was vehemently opposed. He lived on the hill opposite the proposed LOTUS site, and he said that he didn't want to see a "cigar-shaped building" in front of his house.

A meeting of the county environmental review board was called to discuss the matter. Gurudev listened patiently to the man's arguments. Finally Gurudev spoke, "If he is unhappy about it, we can plant some trees so that the shrine will be hidden from his view. We'll be glad to do whatever we can to accommodate him, but he can't stop us from building on our own property."

After a long discussion, the review board gave its approval for the LOTUS to be built at the Santa Barbara ashram.

"Thank you for your approval," Gurudev said, "but we have decided not to build it here."

The board members were astonished. "What? Why not? Why did you spend this time trying to get our approval?"

"I simply wanted to see how far it would go and what would happen. This shrine is not for me; it's not just for one group. It is for everybody. If even one person objects to its being here, that negative element will have a certain undesirable effect. So it seems Santa Barbara is not yet ready for something like this." That was the end of LOTUS construction in Santa Barbara, but the search for a LOTUS site continued.

Two magnificent gifts were presented to Gurudev in 1978. The first was from renowned singer and songwriter Carole (Karuna) King, a longtime devotee. For years she had wanted to donate her beautiful 300-acre estate on Music Mountain in western Connecticut to Gurudev. For all that time, Gurudev had gently declined her offer. For reasons beyond everyone's comprehension, he felt it was best to wait. He knew that there would be a certain amount of talk and criticism in the popular press, no matter what the circumstances of the gift. Some people would see it as a guru taking advantage of a devotee and getting rich. He wanted to be sure that if the land was given, Karuna would be fully prepared for this kind of attention from the press and that, regardless of what he should decide to do with the land — even if he sold it — she would be happy.

Finally, Karuna convinced him that she wanted to give him the land, no matter what. In the fall of 1978, the land was signed over. During the Thanksgiving holiday, Gurudev led a high-spirited group of Karma Yogis, who slept on the floor, cleaned all the buildings, and crowded into the living room of the main house for evening *satsang*.

For a while there was considerable speculation about what use would be made of the property. It was halfway between New York and the ashram, and some people thought it would be useful as a retreat site. None of the ideas bore fruit. Later Gurudev sold the property, and — true to his prediction — criticism appeared in certain magazines and newspapers. But before long, the true value of the gift became apparent.

In the fall of 1978, Gurudev received another gift; this too was a piece of land. The one hundred acres of land were mostly wooded and near the Connecticut ashram, with a beautiful, unspoiled river flowing over a waterfall on the property. It belonged to Tyagaraja Young, whose home in Dayville, Connecticut had been a kind of second home to the ashramites. This land was offered as a site for the LOTUS, and it was a perfect spot. It was near the ashram, yet not too close. It was out of the way, and yet accessible. It was undeveloped and unspoiled, and had great potential. The building of the LOTUS could now begin.

On the occasion when Tyagaraja signed over the land, Gurudev said, "One of my biggest dreams is going to be fulfilled. As you all know, we've been looking all over the country for some nice land on which to build the LOTUS. As the scriptures say, we search for God all over, while we have Him right in our hearts. Now we find that the very place is right next door.

"The Sanskrit word for dedication is *tyaga* and *raja* is king. We have a king of dedication here. He is offering almost his entire property. There's a perennial river running right in the middle. This is all proof that God approves, guides us, and fulfills our sincere wishes."

That winter, Gurudev was in Santa Barbara, California, in his West Coast home called La Paz. There he gave *satsang* and received many visitors. As always, many of his visitors were musicians. Over the years, many renowned musicians had been attracted to Gurudev's teachings and had become devotees: Alice Coltrane, Carole King, Laura Nyro, Felix Cavaliere, and others. Often, the evenings at La Paz were musical. On one such night Gurudev welcomed the famous flutist, Paul Horn, and another gifted musician, Bob Kindler. They played for Gurudev, and the quality of their musical skills was matched only by the depth of love in their offering. Later, Paul wrote Gurudev, "I shall treasure the memory of that evening for the rest of my life. Since you played on my flute, it has been playing better than ever! People have been commenting on the sudden increase in my musical ability, and I attribute it to you."

360

(right) Tyagaraja Young comes to the ashram to donate a beautiful piece of land. Gurudev honors the generous devotee by placing a beautiful shawl around him. (below) A place in Connecticut for LOTUS. The property donated by Tyagaraja is officially signed over.

Clearing the land for the LOTUS, Connecticut.

362

"It was Christmas, and I had gone out to get ornaments and gifts to decorate the tree beautifully for Gurudev. We worked and worked, and when everything was finished I clasped my hands and said, 'It looks really magical. I think all this will make Gurudev happy.'

"We hadn't known he was there and were startled when we heard him laugh and say, 'Nothing *makes* me happy, ma'am. I *am* happy.'"

Schools should be places where the children develop their own identities and good qualities. Each one has something special, something unique to give the world. So we should look into that natural tendency that each child has and then develop it. That is education.

By the summer of 1977 the parents in the community had begun looking seriously into the possibility of having a school on the ashram grounds. Many of the ashram children would be of school age in September, and the parents wanted a school where their children would be taught spiritual values at they same time they were getting a good academic education.

Sandra Snover, who later became Swami Sarvaananda Ma, was a school principal and a Ph.D. candidate in education. She happened to move to the ashram just at this time. With her professional background and excellent capabilities, she went through all the necessary legal preparations and found a facility. Satya and Sadasiva Greenstone — both excellent, experienced instructors — joined her to form the staff and teach in the primary school. Karuna Pirotta, another fine teacher, would work with the preschool children. There was much to be done to get a school going by the fall, but, almost miraculously, the school was operating by October of that year.

The Light of Yoga School, which was later renamed the Yogaville Vidyalayam, was run with special guidance from Gurudev himself. He often stopped by to spend time with the children and answer their questions, questions about everything from Raja Yoga to getting along with siblings and parents. He played with the little ones, listened seriously to their problems, showered them with hugs, kisses and love. They loved him dearly, and they learned from him beautifully.

The children also loved their teachers and their school. In their daily routine, they followed the principles and practices of yoga, including meditation and Hatha Yoga. Working with their teachers, they prepared their own nutritious vegetarian lunch each day. Often the children arrived at school before the teachers, and often they didn't want to go home after school. Occasionally a child would show up at the school building on Sunday and be terribly disappointed to find that it was not a school day.

"Before my involvement with yoga, I was training to teach elementary school. As an idealistic student, I had definite opinions about how a teacher should be. I was deeply committed to the idea that the student should always come first in the classroom, and that teaching was a full time occupation, not something that ended when the bell rang.

"My first experiences in a public school classroom were very disappointing. I saw myself manifesting the same qualities I had criticized in others. The main factor was that my personal untogetherness was affecting the children's education; that seemed very unfair to me. At first I tried to blame 'the system' but it soon became very clear that I was the problem. My lack of control over my own behavior and emotions led me to take it out on the children. They were innocent victims of my own unpredictable moods.

"Seeing that I really was just adding fuel to an already existing fire, I decided to get my personal life more settled before pursuing the teaching career. My desire for peace of mind led me eventually to Sri Gurudev and the teachings of Integral Yoga.

"After six years of living and studying in the Integral Yoga Institutes, Sri Gurudev put me back in the classroom — at the Light of Yoga School. He allowed me to practice teaching in order to learn more about myself and thus learn to teach.

"Gurudev himself is such a perfect example of the totally selfless teacher. He never hesitates to correct his students or to point out their faults, and is never shaken by their response — be it praise or blame. He is only concerned with the growth of the student, not with his own popularity.

"Working with the children is like constantly being in front of a mirror. They are like instant barometers reflecting the state of my own mind, and in a roomful of children the reflection is magnified that many times. Through the guidance of Gurudev's teachings I am coming to see that the atmosphere of the classroom is clearly a reflection of my own state of mind. So, if things become disorderly or chaotic I have nothing to blame but my own lack of concentration.

"It is a great blessing and joy to be a part of the Yogaville Vidyalayam. Truly this is a unique opportunity for both teachers and students to grow and learn together in an environment of loving acceptance, where the common goal is to know the Truth."

Satya Greenstone

"There have been times when I was worried about where the money would come from to provide facilities for the Vidyalayam. But God has truly taken care of everything; financial means were always provided, often by anonymous donations. When I see the results in the shining faces of the children, I know we are moving in the right direction. May we all enjoy the light we see shining forth through the Vidyalayam's angels."

Swami Sarvaananda Ma, Ph.D.

The children often expressed their appreciation of Gurudev and the school he had given them:

"Dear Gurudev, I like this school because it's fun. I learned to be stronger, how to overcome my fear of the ponies, and to cook tofu and like tofu. I learned new words I didn't even know, how to teach Hatha Yoga, and how to find someone to play with instead of just sitting alone. I learned new kinds of math. I learned to concentrate a little better and sit still in circle."

Dayalan, age 6

"Dear Gurudev, Thank you for the school. The school has helped me learn how to give and to share. The children have helped me feel comfortable here. When I first came here I always cried because I wanted to be with my mom. And now the school has helped me grow up. In fact just a month ago I saw that someone in the school had the same problem so I helped them get over it and they did. The school has helped me concentrate and know that I can work better too.

"So the school has done a lot for me and I'm glad I got to go to this school. I know there's not one more like it. The school has helped me learn how to play with all. I can love everybody. I love the children, the teachers and the school."

Radha, age 9

"Dear Gurudev, I think this school is special because it didn't only teach me schoolwork. It taught me to be one of the family in a school. And in my other schools I would be a solitary person at my private desk. In this school I feel one with all ages and types of children. But still there is the other level. The Hatha Yoga and meditation improved me in sports and schoolwork fifty percent. And in my other schools I never smiled, but now I'm always smiling."

Rivers, age 11

"Beloved Gurudev, thank you for bringing me here. Thank you for sacrificing your life for your disciples. Thank you for coming back and giving *satsang*. Thank you for giving me good as well as bad to teach me my lessons. Without you I would not have learned many lessons that I have learned. I love you."

Gopal K., age 11

The children also beautifully expressed Gurudev's teachings in their own words:

"People can't live without love. It's like a car trying to run without gas. Love equals devotion. You can't really love someone without being devoted to him or her. Love isn't just kissing and saying, 'Oh, honey, I love you so much.' It's much more. It's devotion and sacrifice."

Bala, age 11

"To really love Gurudev means you should like everything. I think it isn't easy to like everything. I think I should love everything because then I would feel great."

Gopal M., age 5

"The first thing a good parent should do is to be good so their children will copy them. Parents should never fight because it teaches the children fighting and it makes them feel bad. If the parents don't teach the children the right things no one will and the children won't be happy."

Ambha, age 5

"Prayer means talking to That you believe in without a doubt. You can pray for help or for thanks, but if you don't pray sincerely God may not respond.
"Service means doing something for others. If service to others makes you happy, your joy will never end."

Uma, age 8

"*Brahmacharya* is continence or storing energy for the time you need it. You cannot do things with your body when you are like a bowl of jelly. You have to be energetic, powerful, strong and willing! Would you like to be like that? Or do you want to be like a bowl of jelly?

"Conserve your energy! Storing your energy is what you think it is. It is not lying in bed and watching TV. You may think that is conserving energy because you are not doing anything but this is not the truth. This is draining your energy! To conserve you have to be active and get the energy flowing, then you can share it."

Dayalan, age 9

"Children may think that they cannot help world peace because they are just children. But really we can help. If all children were able to be friends and love their enemies, then most of the world's population would be peaceful. If each child becomes peaceful themselves then they can help other people be friends with each other.

"Peace and joy is our nature and it is our goal in life to always feel happy. It is our nature to be peaceful and joyful, not to be hateful. If each person from now on wouldn't hate or hurt anything forever then there would be world peace forever."

Padma, age 11

We are not building the LOTUS. We are simply acting as instruments. There is a great unseen Force, that cosmic Light, that wants to express itself through this construction; and it seems to be directing every aspect of this project.

In the spring of 1979, the work of clearing the land for the temple site was begun in Connecticut. At every opportunity, teams of ashramites went to the nearby spot for Karma Yoga. But early that summer it became apparent that a radical change was in the offing.

It began during a *satsang* at the ashram shortly after Gurudev had returned from a trip. He had heard about the difficulties that the ashram had experienced the previous winter, about the cold New England weather, the high cost of heating the ashram. He was told that it cost five to six thousand dollars a month during the winter and that, with inflation and the energy crisis, the expenses would only increase. With more and more people coming to live at the ashram, food bills were also rising. The large organic garden gave a rich harvest, but the growing season was so short. In addition, the fifty-eight acres was not nearly enough to accommodate all the families that wanted to live at the ashram and enroll their children in the school.

A new ashram is found! Satchidananda Ashram — Yogaville, Virginia.

368

Gurudev supervised and participated in all construction. Building a home at Yogaville, Virginia

(top) An expert helps ashramites rescue a piece of heavy equipment.
(bottom) A simple, dynamic ceremony for the LOTUS Lake groundbreaking.

It was time to seriously think about these things. Once the temple was built, that would be it. Then the ashram would stay where it was, no matter what conditions developed.

What Gurudev had in mind was a complete change: a search for new land, somewhere in a more temperate climate; land that would provide room to grow, land that was large enough so that the LOTUS could be located there too. It should also be warm enough to offer a longer growing season and lower food costs.

Gurudev made it clear that he was not telling anyone they would have to move or the ashram would have to relocate. All of these were only ideas and suggestions he was making for their consideration. He merely wanted everyone to think well about the future before laying the foundation for the LOTUS.

Everyone knew that their guru wasn't making these suggestions for himself. The ashram was for them and for others who would come, and Gurudev was thinking of their benefit.

Although the idea of uprooting and transplanting an entire community caused a stir of emotions, everyone knew it made sense from the most practical point of view. There was a great family spirit about these new plans. That, coupled with the clarity and wisdom of Gurudev's insights, led the entire group to courageously embark on this adventure.

In a meeting with Gurudev, the ashram family decided to look for a new ashram site during the winter. If they couldn't find something by spring, then that would be that. They would continue building in Connecticut.

> Yes, work seems to be our worship, our medita-tion, our *japa*. It looks like even our food is work nowadays. Well, it's not easy to build something this great. When you want to build a whole village you have to really work hard. But there's another way to look at it. To me, there is no overwork as such, because I enjoy it. That's my play. In a way, you could say that I don't work at all, because I feel it is play. I can play twenty-four hours a day. If your work is play, you will never get tired. If you make everything a playtime, you don't need to work at all!

Suddenly all the efforts to find a new home for Yogaville and the

LOTUS bore fruit. That winter, just as the new decade was coming in, the land was found. This new property consisted of 650 acres along the James River in Buckingham County in the heart of Virginia. A gorgeous site, it overlooked the broad James to the majestic foothills of the Blue Ridge Mountains, one of the oldest mountain ranges in the world. It was the sale of the Music Mountain property — which Carole King had given so lovingly, with no strings attached — that made possible the purchase of this beautiful acreage.

The new property satisfied every requirement. The winding river was unpolluted. The land was good for growing crops, and there was a perfect site for the LOTUS. The air was clear and serene; the atmosphere itself was meditative.

The one difficulty was that it would mean starting all over again, almost from scratch. There was only one building on the property, a large home which could house perhaps twenty people, but nothing else. The nearest city of any size, Charlottesville, was fifty minutes away. The land itself was beautiful and secluded. Everywhere one looked there were trees, fields, the river and sky, and nothing else. It would take a lot of work to create the new home of Yogaville, and the future site of the LOTUS. But the potential was there.

At first, just a few people came to Virginia from Connecticut to begin the work. The transition would take time; in fact, it would take years. There would be no sudden abandonment of what had been built up in Pomfret Center. The ashram in Connecticut would be kept and maintained as a retreat center for quite a few years before being sold. But the energy was definitely focused on Virginia.

Soon families from Connecticut began to move south to live on the new property or to live in nearby cities and towns. A branch of the school, the Yogaville Vidyalayam, followed quickly. A true yogi, Tyagaraja Young was not attached to having the LOTUS built on the land he had donated; soon he was one of the Virginia ashram residents. Things began to take root. There was a real pioneer spirit in this undertaking. Everyone felt that this sudden change, this transplantation to Virginia, was both a culmination of the years preceding, and a new beginning.

Buckingham County, Virginia was covered with rich, green foliage and flowers in full bloom. This beauty, the fresh air, and the soft calls of birds surrounded people from all over the country who had come to Yogaville, Virginia for the LOTUS Lake groundbreaking, on the 30th of April 1980. For most it was the first time they had seen the acres of forests, hills and fields which would eventually be the main headquarters for the Integral Yoga Institutes and a community of homes and cottage industries. The air was vibrant, fresh, undisturbed. The visitors who stayed in tents were lulled to sleep by the sounds of whippoorwills and other night birds.

The valley near the James River seemed to have designed itself just for the Shrine which would be built there. A large circle of trees and hills surrounded the area where the lotus-shaped building would sit, in the midst of a man-made lake. It was stirring and sweet to see the huge bulldozer waiting for the worship ceremony to begin. The big piece of machinery had been surrounded by ropes of dogwood blossoms and greenery and stood in front of a simple altar.

There was a gentle drizzle of rain as Gurudev arrived at the site to begin this auspicious event. Sri Kanagaratnam, visiting from Sri Lanka, chanted softly as Gurudev began the *puja*. The simple, beautiful ceremony ended dynamically as Gurudev stood holding the coconut that had been used in the service. Coconuts represent the hard egoistic shell. Gurudev raised it high above his head and shouted, *"Jai Sri Satguru Maharaj Ki!"* (Victory to the Divine!) as he forcefully dashed the coconut against the bucket of the bulldozer. That particular egoistic shell smashed into hundreds of pieces — a propitious sign.

Next, Gurudev climbed up onto the driver's seat and started the bulldozer. Powerfully, it moved through the dogwood ropes and began to dig up the rich, red earth. Gurudev spent almost thirty minutes beginning this digging for the LOTUS Lake. Auspiciousness does not necessarily mean somberness, and Gurudev played with everyone as he worked the bulldozer. A number of people followed along behind the machine, and Gurudev would turn it and gently chase them. At one point, he dumped a huge pile of earth from the bucket. The very last thing to come out was a bunch of flowers which landed right side up on top of the pile, as if by conscious design.

Sitting atop the bulldozer, the master paused briefly to address everyone present. "I am sure that by the Grace of God and the good wishes of all of you, this great project of the LOTUS will be achieved very soon so the world may know that we are all one in Spirit."

This glorious day was also the first full moon day of the Tamil year, *Chitra Poornami*. At dark, the crowning ceremony took place. Everyone gathered at the overlook — a beautiful point behind the only house on the property — which gave a marvelous view of the James River and the Blue Ridge Mountains.

Gurudev and two assistants gave a fantastic fireworks display. The show started with rockets that exploded into lights far above the river. Gurudev and his helpers got more and more inventive as they continued experimenting with combinations of sparklers, streamers and rockets. The audience was delighted by this fantastic display of lights and colors.

One beautiful memory from that night seemed to represent the majesty and import of the events of the day: Gurudev stood with a glowing sparkler raised high above his head. It was very dark, and the only light came from his sparkler and from the circle of children who stood around him, their delighted faces also lit by the sparklers they held. There they stood, Gurudev and the children, laughing together, all aglow, oblivious to the night's darkness.

> **I really believe that the necessary funds will come in, even as money has been coming all along. Yes, financial support has steadily come for the LOTUS even though we have never had a big formal fund-raising campaign. Every penny that comes for LOTUS should come with a convinced heart behind it. Don't ever think that you need to beg for money. It will come by itself. Those who are blessed will have the privilege of sharing in building this Shrine.**

A project like the LOTUS certainly needed money. Yet, Gurudev resisted the many good suggestions for launching a large-scale fund-raising campaign. He reminded the devotees of Sri Swami Chidbhavanandaji, who had turned down the money to build a school hall at the Ramakrishna Thapovanam because the potential donor had a selfish purpose for his "gift." Whatever money came should come from people who fully believed in the LOTUS and were giving happily.

"It is really that heartfelt belief that gets things done. I feel that our Pomfret Center, Connecticut, Yogaville was purchased thanks to one little boy named Prabhu. He collected all his pennies, put them in a jar and brought them to me, saying it was to buy a place for Yogaville. I didn't even spend that money; it's in a special display case. That kind of loving vibration will build the LOTUS."

The devotees began to think of ways to bring in financial support for the LOTUS without putting pressure on anyone. LOTUS fund-raising dinners were given at Integral Yoga Institutes across the country. Auctions were held. Children baked cookies and sold them for the

LOTUS. Just as architects and engineers volunteered their skills for the planning and construction of the Shrine, so other devotees offered their time and energy and skills.

A highlight of this effort came when Mrs. Rukmini Rasiah came to the United States with her son and daughter, Jeyarajan and Padmarani. A longtime devotee of Gurudev, Mrs. Rasiah served as the secretary of the Fine Arts Society in Kandy, for which Sri Gurudev was the founder and president. Jeyarajan and Padmarani were highly gifted performers of Bharata Natyam, the sacred classical dance of South India. In order to help raise money for the LOTUS, they traveled across the United States for almost five months, living out of trunks and following a very tight schedule. In performances of their sacred art, they captivated thousands of people who saw them perform in major cities of the United States and Canada. All the proceeds from these devotional concerts were joyfully offered to the Light Of Truth Universal Shrine. Through these programs, which were accompanied by LOTUS slide presentations, more and more people were finding out about this beautiful shrine for all faiths.

A person who has attained enlightenment will always be peaceful, will love everybody equally and will never get disturbed over anything. That person will never do things for his or her own sake. The entire life will be a sacrifice. An enlightened person won't be anxious to attain something; because he or she has already attained what is to be attained. The enlightened person is like a lit candle. It has light, but it doesn't run around saying, "Come on! Enjoy my light! I have light!" It *is* light, and wherever it goes it gives light.

The building of the LOTUS was now under way. Craftspeople and planners from around the world were working on various aspects of the shrine. Gurudev's great vision was going to manifest, but that didn't mean he would sit back in an easy chair and watch it all happen. He directed all planning and construction for the LOTUS, frequently operating the heavy equipment himself. He was always thinking of the LOTUS, finding new ways that it could be improved. He had frequent conferences with Mr. Lewis Thompson, Construction Superintendent for the general contractor, Andrews, Large and Whidden. At first the Swami from South India and the gentleman from the southern United States may have had some difficulty understanding each others' accents, but the real communication happened anyway. A deep mutual respect developed between them.

As the LOTUS construction continued and people began to see the blueprints, sketches, and models, they were awed by the design that was unfolding. Bedecked in delicate pink Italian mosaic tile, the LOTUS would sit resplendently on the banks of a fifteen-acre lake. Shaped like a lotus blossom, the Shrine would measure 108 feet in diameter to the outer petals. The domed interior would be twenty-seven feet in height with the crowning cupola and spire rising like a cosmic antenna for another fourteen feet into the sky. The LOTUS would appear to be floating on the water in the center of the 120-foot reflecting pond which would encircle it.

Approaching the Shrine from the reception buildings, the visitor would walk through the grand archway — with symbols of the world's religions overhead — and proceed alongside a long reflecting pool. Leaving all worldly thoughts behind, one would enter the healing, spiritual atmosphere of the main shrine in silence. Even from the archway one would be able to see the central column of light rising like a beacon in the center of the lotus. Within the main shrine could be seen the light, rising to the apex of the dome and descending in separate rays to illuminate the altars for each of the world's major faiths — Hinduism, Judaism, Shinto, Taoism, Buddhism, Christianity, Islam, Sikhism, Native American religions, and African religions — which would be housed in the alcoves formed by the Shrine's lotus petals. There would even be symbols respresenting all other known religions and all faiths as yet unknown, so that the LOTUS would be truly universal.

On the lower level, would be the All Faiths Hall, with displays of holy objects representative of the world's religious traditions. Statuary, carved granite, metal and wood work, and holy objects would come from around the world to be incorporated into the LOTUS.

In every place where Gurudev was invited to speak, people's imaginations were fired and their hearts were touched by the vision and ideals of the LOTUS. In their own ways, they tried to integrate these concepts into their lives. Clergy from all denominations and paths were inspired. Many began to incorporate Gurudev's ideas for ecumenical services into their own programs. Gurudev was very happy about this. He didn't want these aspirations or even the LOTUS to belong to one person or one organization. He wanted ecumenical understanding and ecumenical houses of worship to spread everywhere.

> **Just because you are going to be called ordained ministers does not mean that you automatically become ministers. You can be ordained, but the only way you can be a minister is to live like one.**

Some of Gurudev's householder devotees had long wished for a way to publicly commit themselves to a life of service. *Sannyasins*, of course, didn't have personal families; so this path was not possible for householders. Yet many devotees, although they were not monks, were deeply dedicated to service. Jaganath Carrera, of the New Brunswick, New Jersey, IYI, began to speak with Gurudev about forming a non-monastic ministry. Many months of planning gave birth to the Holy Order of the Ministry of Integral Yoga.

On Guru Poornima, 1980, Gurudev ordained eighteen devotees into the Ministry. Although the title "Reverend" now preceded their names, Gurudev made it clear that respect was to be earned, not automatically conferred with that title. The ministers, just like the *sannyasins,* should strive to lead exemplary yogic lives.

> **This is the only LOTUS in this country, but I don't want to keep it that way. When everyone sees the beauty of this, they will all want a LOTUS where people from all the churches can go and meet.**

Gurudev's travels hadn't stopped, or even slowed down. More than ever, he was being asked to speak at churches, colleges, organizations, and a variety of programs around the world. At least every two years, he returned to India, each time with a group of American devotees.

He also visited Hong Kong regularly. When any of the Harilela children got married, the devoted family always asked Gurudev to attend and give his blessings. They also invited him to bless their new businesses.

On one occasion, when they opened a Holiday Inn, the Harilelas asked Gurudev to come for the ribbon-cutting ceremony. He would be joined by the Reverend Billy Graham, who had been invited by the Chairman of the Board of Holiday Inns International.

Early in the morning, before the ceremony, there was a soft knock on Gurudev's door. "Swamiji, Ammi is not well. Please come." Ammi was the Harilela's beloved mother. After each morning's worship, they went to see her and get her blessings before going on with the business of the day. Now, on this very big day, she was suddenly in a coma.

Gurudev hastened to join the family members surrounding Ammi's bed. He led them in a prayer and then checked her weakening pulse. She opened her eyes and looked around at Gurudev and all her beloved children. Then she closed her eyes and passed away.

The gala hotel opening was only a few hours away. At first, the family didn't know what to do. Their revered mother, who had been expected to bless the ceremony, had passed on. Some family members thought of postponing the event. But others pointed out, "There are almost 1,500 people here. They've come from all around the world. We should not disappoint them." They decided that the event should go on as scheduled.

Still, it would be hard for them to participate in a celebration at this time. They decided not to attend the opening themselves. Instead, they asked Gurudev to take Sri Aaron Harilela, the ten-year-old son of Sri Hari Harilela, to the festivities. Gurudev and Aaron would serve as the family's representatives.

It was a little unusual. As Gurudev said later, "Can you imagine a Swami opening a hotel?" But, of course, he was happy to serve them in any way. He represented the Harilelas at all the day's functions. After the opening was successfully completed, Gurudev invited Reverend Graham to visit the Harilela home with him and say a prayer for Ammi. The famous minister was glad to join him in offering comfort to the family.

The next day, the cremation took place. The Harilelas were grateful to have Gurudev with them during this time. He managed to be there in times of joy and times of sorrow.

Everywhere he went, Gurudev's inspiration caused more interest in ecumenical understanding. Integral Yoga Institutes, Teaching Centers, and Meditation Groups continued to be organized in the United States and other countries.

378

(top) Captivating hearts with the art of Bharata Natyam — Jeyarajan and Padmarani.
(below) Some householder devotees formally commit themselves to lives of service. The first
ordination of Integral Yoga Ministers.

379

Visit to Rishikesh: (top) Satsang at Sivananda Ashram — left to right Sri Swami Madhavanandaji, Sri Swami Premanandaji, Sri Gurudev, Sri Swami Sankaranandaji.

(below) With American devotees on pilgrimage to Trincomalee.

Bathing in the Holy Ganges.

381

(top) Mr. and Mrs. Hari Harilela (left) were delighted to have Sri Gurudev bless their newly wed daughter Maya and her husband Ramesh.

(below) Hong Kong Holiday Inn ribbon-cutting ceremony: As the Harilela's official representative Sri Gurudev joins Mr. Rudiger Koppen, Holiday Inns International Vice President; the Reverend Dr. Billy Graham, the evangelist; Mr. Kemmons Wilson, Chairman of the board of Holiday Inns International.

382

(top) *The Holy Yantra is imprinted on the cover of the gembox, to become the floor of the meditation cave — the very center of the LOTUS foundation.*

(bottom) *Sri N. Mahalingam (left) and Sri Arumugam are seen discussing with Gurudev the shape of the* vimanam, *cupola, while the local temple architect observes.*

383

(above) Even the scaffolding was a work of art!
(below) LOTUS from the air, two months before it was finished.

(left) The placement of the central light. Another aspect of the LOTUS receives careful inspection. (below) A grand view with the reflecting pond that leads to the Shrine.

(top) In Leningrad, the Projects for Planetary Peace delegates meet with Russian Orthodox monks and many Soviet citizens who ardently hope for world peace.

(below) "It is the heart that brings us together." — Gurudev's sermon to the congregation in the Moscow Baptist Church, on the Ascension Day celebration. Dr. Orlov (standing beside Gurudev) interprets this message of love and peace.

386

The hearts meet. A warm exchange between Gurudev and Russian Orthodox Archpriest Adrian Dolzhikov.

"I give all my blessings and benedictions to your work." — H.H. Pope John Paul II to
Sri Gurudev.

One pioneering devotee, Krishna Yogi, came forward to start a Sat-chidananda Ashram-Yogaville in the beautiful remote countryside of Buchan, Australia. Australian devotees were soon talking about the possibility of an Australian LOTUS.

July of 1982 literally got off to a bang as the sound of fireworks echoed through Buckingham, Virginia, to announce the beginning of the foundation-laying ceremony for the Light Of Truth Universal Shrine. On the 1st of July, hundreds of people gathered in a quiet field to celebrate the start of the LOTUS building. Above the field, the sun was shining brightly; but its radiance seemed dim compared to the light radiating from the hearts of all present. It was a glorious and moving occasion. The physical reality of the LOTUS was being launched with this ceremony to lay the foundation for the Shrine.

The LOTUS site had been cleared in preparation for the construction that was about to begin. A temporary stage and altar had been erected on the site for this first ecumenical service at the Light Of Truth Universal Shrine.

Sri Gurudev was joined by his distinguished guest, Sri N. Mahalingam of the Ramalingam Mission in Madras, in representing Hinduism for the service. Other special guests were: Brother David, representing Catholicism; Mr. Satyendra S. Huja, Sikhism; Methodist minister John Ashley, representing Protestant denominations; Salima Erskine, Sufism; the Reverend Siva Ford, African religions; Jeevakan Abbate, Native American religions; and the Reverend Prahaladan Mandelkorn, Judaism.

At exactly 12:00 noon, Gurudev placed the first gem into fresh concrete for the centerpiece, or "gembox," which would be at the exact center of the Shrine's foundation. Representatives from the various religions, countries, and parts of the United States came forward to place the gems into the concrete. People from many nations had sent precious and semi-precious stones and metals for the gembox. There was even a rock from the moon. Holy waters, soil and stones from sacred places all over the world were also put in. All these auspicious and sacred substances were joined to form the permanent heart of the LOTUS' foundation. When the final bit of concrete was poured, it was smoothed over and a large metal framework of the sacred *yantra* was placed on the very top. In the wet concrete at the center, or *bindhu*, of this *yantra* Gurudev placed a large crystal.

Later when the concrete was hardening, the metal *yantra* was removed, leaving the imprint with the crystal in the middle as the covering for the gembox. All of this, combined with the holy and loving vibrations of the ceremony and those present — including those who were there in spirit — fully charged this central point of the Shrine so that it could begin to unfold like a magnificent blossom which springs from a well-planted and cultivated seed.

Even when I sleep now I dream of the LOTUS and Yogaville.

As the LOTUS grew, the Virginia ashram grew. It was very clear now that this was the hub of activity for the devotees. Gurudev's disciples were serving all around the United States and in other parts of the world, and that service would continue and increase. But many families and individuals began planning their move to the Virginia community.

The Yogaville Vidyalayam, which had started with a little preschool and primary school, soon added a secondary school. The numbers of students quickly expanded. Plans were soon underway for a high school and a university.

The international IYI coordination offices were now in Virginia — in addition to the audio/video department, publications department, credit union, large organic garden, natural foods store (in Charlottesville), cabinet shop, garage, gas station, and cottage industries. Some of the householders who moved to Yogaville started their own businesses. Many also moved to the nearby cities of Charlottesville and Richmond. There strong *sanghas*, closely connected to the ashram developed.

Living and working together as one beautiful family with total love. That is God.

It had been sixteen years since Gurudev's second meeting with His Holiness Pope Paul VI. The Vatican continued to be informed of Sri Gurudev's interfaith activities, and on the 30th of May, 1984, while Gurudev was visiting Rome, an opportunity was extended to him to have an audience with His Holiness Pope John Paul II. Gurudev presented to the Holy Father an album that gave an overview of his ecumenical activities and the LOTUS.

When His Holiness asked Gurudev about his other work, Gurudev answered, "My main work has been focused on bringing the religions together. Mainly I'm working in the ecumenical field."

The Holy Father responded, "That is very good. I am so glad to hear about this, and I give all of my blessings and benedictions to this work."

Gurudev presented a LOTUS pin to the Holy Father, who had been named an Honorary Patron of the LOTUS; and His Holiness presented Sri Gurudev with the Apostolic Medallion.

As Gurudev left St. Peter's Square, there were still crowds of people gathered who had come to hear the Pope speak. As Gurudev passed through the Square hundreds of thousands cheered and saluted him. Some handed him flowers, others shook his hand, and still others asked for his blessing.

> **There are so many people — adults and children — who have little or no food, who are destitute. To the best of your ability, find out which of your neighbors is in need. If your capacity allows you to give to the whole world, that's wonderful, but at least start in your own backyard. Do whatever you can to help others. . .Every time we have a celebration, we should think of the underprivileged (whether they are celebrating the same holiday or not) and give something to them.**

The surrounding community had been gracious and friendly to Yogaville from the start. Still, it was natural for some residents of rural Buckingham to be wary of so large a group moving into their midst. As always, the ashramites were open and friendly without being interested in preaching to or "converting" their neighbors. They were, however, interested in being of service to their neighbors; and ways to be useful began to make themselves clear. The ashramites learned that Buckingham was one of the poorest counties in Virginia.

"At Christmas of that first year in Virginia, we contacted the Social Services Agency of Buckingham County to see what we could do to help. They were very pleased to hear from Yogaville and asked if we could help deliver firewood to the elderly or infirm. We were happy to do it. We also collected used toys in good condition from among

391

ourselves, wrapped and labeled them for Social Service to give out. The Agency was so grateful for the little we did that it was quite touching. When I told Sri Gurudev about the project, he responded by saying, 'Why not have one of our people dress as Santa Claus and give out the presents ourselves?'

"When it came time to ask for donations and toys again, the response was great. Over and over, ashramites were saying, 'Don't give to us. Give to those more needy.' The ashram children — without any prompting from the adults — began to choose things from their own toy boxes to give to the poorer children.

"The next year, Social Services gave us a list of ten families, with the names and ages of all members, as well as directions to their homes. Gurudev was right, for it was with the greatest joy that we wrapped each toy and designated it for a particular child. Before ever meeting these people, we felt a great connection. We tried hard to be sure that each child in a family had presents of equal 'splendor' to avoid bringing grief instead of happiness. We bought large quantities of apples, oranges, canned goods, cheese, yams, potatoes. All the money, toys and food were donated by ashram family members. Gurudev recommended that each family imagine that they had one more child. Whatever amount was spent on each of the family's own children should be put aside to provide for a less fortunate child. Donations kept coming in, and it was soon clear that Santa and his elves would be making more than one trip. We spoke with some of our neighbors and got names of more needy families and elderly people. Three times before Christmas, the Santa Express left the ashram. Each time there was a different person acting as Santa with a different team of elves. They spent many hours on the country backroads and came home tired but thrilled at the reception they'd been given. They also felt chastened by what they'd seen of the living conditions of the recipients. For every family we knew about, there were five more we didn't. We quickly learned to have extra baskets of food and bags of toys for the unknown needy.

"Everywhere, we were received with such great love and gratitude that truly we received the greater blessings."

Reverend Lakshmi Levy

Soon Lakshmi Barsel joined Reverend Lakshmi Levy to head a year-round ashram program — formed in conjunction with the local social service agency — which would help provide emergency food relief. The two women from Yogaville found that the agency was staffed by many inspiring and dedicated "yogis" who had never before heard of that term. Through donations and yard sales, money was raised to purchase food, much of it provided wholesale by the ashram's natural foods store in Charlottesville. A program to provide "baby baskets" of needed food and supplies to indigent expectant mothers was also launched.

Gurudev was pleased with these programs, but he reminded the ashramites that it still wasn't enough. The best service to the poor, he explained, would be to start businesses which could employ local out-of-work people and transform at least some of those poor people into "rich" people. A new Yogaville Community Association, comprising householders in the surrounding communities, began actively pooling their energies and talents to help start such cottage industries at Yogaville, so that the dream of a complete yoga village could be realized.

When Virginia experienced its worst flood in one hundred years Yogaville was left relatively untouched by the high waters, but the nearby town of Scottsville was not so fortunate. The whole main street was completely flooded up to the second floor of all the buildings. Ashramites turned out in large numbers to help clean up. They worked day and night for several days, alongside other volunteers and towns-people, carrying out the debris and shoveling the thousands of gallons of mud. Gurudev was very proud of these efforts: "If our neighbors love us, then surely God loves us. 'Communion' comes after 'community.' Who are we serving in our neighbors? We are serving God Himself."

If a world war comes, there will be no winner or loser. But that terrible outcome can be averted. It is still in our hands.

For years, Gurudev had talked about the need for open, honest, trusting and friendly communications between the people of the United States and the people of the U.S.S.R. Now, in May, 1985, he was going on a peace mission to Russia. Projects for Planetary Peace had specially invited Gurudev to join Barbara Marx Hubbard, founder of Committee for the Future; Patricia Sun, spiritual teacher and healer; actors Mike Farrell, Dennis Weaver and Shelly Fabares; Swami Sara-swati Devyashram, spiritual head of the Rajarajeshwari Ashram; and other professional people and clergy on a journey meant as a big step toward peaceful communication between the two world powers.

Addressing his fellow travelers at the beginning of the trip, Gurudev said, "We are already united in spirit; we do not have to bring that unity anew. It is only a matter of recognizing that unity; and if that is possible, then world peace is achieved. But where to begin to experience that Spirit? It begins at home. Unless we raise ourselves to that spiritual level, unless we identify ourselves to be the Spirit — using these vehicles of body and mind — it is impossible for us to see the same Spirit in everybody and everything. . .It is not only charity that begins at home. Hope begins at home. Love begins at home. And, likewise, hatred begins at home. Whatever we are, we project; so let it begin in our hearts. . .May the Supreme Awareness give us this blessing to guide us to continue to remember this spiritual oneness. Let us go with that spiritual feeling, that love, with that peace in mind. As we walk, let others experience that supreme peace from us and through us. Let us know that our words have limitations. It is not the words that are going to conquer the world or bring unity; it is the heart. Let it come from the heart."

Wherever they traveled, the group — led by Dr. Ron Mann and Rama Jyothi Vernon — met with Soviet citizens. All were deeply moved by the sincere wish for peace they saw in these people. In spite of differences in language and ideology, there was a common bond among the hearts.

In Leningrad, American clergy and Russian clergy met as a group. Gurudev talked about adversities as blessings in disguise, and Russian Orthodox Archpriest Adrian Dolzhikov asked Gurudev to clarify this point in reference to World War II. "Do you mean to say, Swami, that even the last world war was a blessing?"

Gurudev answered, "I am not saying that we want war or that war in itself is a blessing. We all know that isn't true. But you were telling us that since the war more people have come to the church than before the war. So in that way, isn't it a blessing?"

The Archpriest nodded his head in understanding, but the translator was upset. She had even been reluctant to translate this statement. "How can you say it is a blessing?" she demanded. "We don't believe in blessings like this or in God." She was what the Soviets call a non-believer.

Gurudev asked her, "What is it that you, as a non-believer, don't believe in?" She couldn't find an answer. "Okay," Gurudev went on, "I will answer. You may not believe in the labels, rituals and churches; but don't you believe people should love each other, be friendly, care and share? Don't you believe in comradeship?"

"Yes," she replied.

"Well, that is the basic principle in any religion. You don't believe in the superficial things that divide people, but you believe in the essential principles."

The translator agreed, "Yes, I believe in that."

The priest looked at Gurudev in amazement. "We never could have answered this way to the non-believers!"

At the end of this session, the clergy all held hands, and Archpriest Adrian said: "For those who think of us, we shall think of them with love always. Please take our message to your families and to your friends: Let the skies be always blue and peaceful. Let war never come to our earth. Let our lives be always happy. Let us spend efforts and money for traveling and not for arms. We are all on the same planet; we have the same sky and we share the same home. If it is the same home which we inhabit, then we must stay friends, and we have to cooperate. The time for love and understanding has come."

The group was invited to attend a special Ascension Day service at the Moscow Baptist Church — the church that had sponsored the Reverend Billy Graham's tour of the Soviet Union — and the other group members asked Gurudev to speak on their behalf.

"Beloved and blessed friends," he began, "it is a great pleasure and privilege — not only for me but the entire group — to join you on the blessed day of the Ascension. The very day of the Ascension gives us a great message. It shows us that we all have to transcend our human limitations.

"We all look to Heaven and say 'our Heavenly Father.' We always address the Father as singular, not plural. It means there is only one Father. If there is a Father, then there must be a Mother. The Mother is the whole earth. That is why we call her 'Mother Earth.' It means we are all children of the same parents. No matter what our colors are, our nationalities are, our languages are — we are all one in heart.

"That is the reason Lord Jesus said, 'Blessed are those who are pure in heart; they shall see God.' So the one and only requirement to experience God is to have a pure heart, because it is the heart that brings us together.

"When I met your pastor and Dr. Orlov, I hugged them. That means our hearts met. Our heads didn't meet. If our heads meet, there will be a big noise. When two individuals get married they call each other 'sweetheart.' They never call each other 'sweethead.' It is impossible to be sweet in the head; it's always possible to be sweet in the heart. That is what we need — love and friendship. We must treat everybody as our brothers and sisters.

"This is a small beginning, and I am positive it will expand more and more. In the name of the entire globe, and particularly America, we offer our love and friendship to you all."

When Gurudev ended his talk, most members of the congregation were crying freely. There was no difference between the tears of the Russians and the Americans; citizens of both countries shared a common emotion. In spite of differences in ideology, government and language, everyone in that church felt the unity that lives in the hearts, not the heads.

Soon afterward, Gurudev returned to America. It had been a long and tiring journey through the Soviet Union, but as soon as he got back to Virginia he went to check the progress of construction on the LOTUS. It was right on schedule for the gala dedication in July, 1986. The LOTUS would be Sri Swami Satchidananda's great gift to humanity, to the entire world — a symbol of peace, love, and unity among all beings.

There is a joy in being together, in living together, and in thinking together. We have faced, we are facing, the terrible consequences of having lived apart, of having talked in terms of differences, and of having divided person from person in all possible ways. By such division, what have we gained? We are facing a great crisis. We have been sent into this world to live together, to enjoy the world, to make use of the capabilities bestowed upon us by nature for the benefit of humanity. But because of these divisions, we are making use of this very nature for our own destruction. The whole world has understood the danger of it. That is why we are together here. Everyone knows there is no other way to find peace and harmony except by rising above all these man-made differences, and realizing the oneness of the spirit. This is the need of the hour.

How are we to do this? How are people going to learn to love the whole world as their family? Not by law. Even that fails — whether it is a communist country or a democratic country, a socialist country or a capitalist country. Whichever way you call it, law is not going to make people change. Only spiritual knowledge will bring a change. Only when people realize their own spirit, and then see that same spirit in others, in everything — only then can they have that unlimited, unconditional love.

That is the very reason behind a shrine like the LOTUS. Of course, there are many shrines already. But there again, they are divided. Even religion divides us — not religion itself, but the so-called followers of religion, those who have never understood their own religion well. If they had understood their own religion, they could never deny another person. Neither Jesus nor Moses nor Mohammed nor Buddha nor Lao Tzu said to deny someone else. But the followers inject their egos into the religions. They say, 'My religion is superior to yours. Mine is the only way.' It is that which creates more problems than anything else. That's why the LOTUS does not belong to any one religion, to any one organization. It will be open to everyone. It is for everybody. That is why I'm convinced that this kind of shrine and the meaning behind it will bring peace to the whole world.

We can do it. If we cannot do it in America, we are not going to do it anywhere. Probably that's the reason why, though I had this dream for years, it started sprouting in America. And whatever happens in America happens automatically in other places. There will be many more such things. People will come together all over the globe. So we are really celebrating the dawn of such an era. This is only a beginning. OM Shanthi. Thank you.

Epilogue

In recounting the life of a person like Sri Swami Satchidananda, the most important things cannot be expressed. The endless activities, the untiring service, the myriad relationships, can only be listed. How can one tell the story of a great soul, who has touched and transformed the lives of countless others, in subtle, even invisible ways? As for the essence of the person, it can only be hinted at, alluded to. It is not something personal, and he himself does not speak of it as such. Instead, he speaks of that Essence which he sees in everyone. As for the meaning of his own particular life, perhaps the best summing up can be made by his own words:

"I have wondered why all this is happening around me in my name. I am not a scholar, I am not an M.A. or a Ph.D. I don't quote many books because I don't read that much. All I know is that I have surrendered myself to God's service — my God being the Cosmic Love, Cosmic Consciousness, Cosmic Peace.

"I never had the idea of setting up any centers or building any temples. Things are simply happening, and I am doing my part.

"I want to do it well. I want to be a good instrument, to serve you as well as I can. But if everything closed up tomorrow, that would be all right too. I really mean it. It would be God's will. That is why I'm always at ease and never anxious.

"If anything good comes, know that it comes from God. Be grateful to Him or Her or whatever name you want to use. Free yourself from selfishness. Become a good instrument in God's hands and leave the entire burden on God's shoulders. Your peace will be assured.

"May God bless you all. OM *Shanthi, Shanthi, Shanthi.*"

Chronology

22 December 1914	Sri Swami Satchidananda born as C.K. Rama-swamy Gounder in Chettipalayam, South India.
1921	Gives talk at the Sad Vidhya Sanmarga Sangam in Perur, South India.
1934	Appointed Manager of the Perur Temple. Joins Sri G. D. Naidu's National Electric Works as head of the welding division.
1945	Goes to Palani. Studies with Sri Sadhu Swami-gal, Sri Swami Badagara Sivananda, Sri Swami Ranga Nath and other great *siddhas*.
1946	Appointed manager of the Avinaasi Temple, South India.
	Enters the Ramakrishna Mission at Tirupurrai-turai under the direction of Sri Swami Chidbha-vanandaji Maharaj.
	Receives *brahmacharya diksha* and is named Sambasiva Chaitanya.
	Serves with Sri Bikshu Swamigal at Nature Cure Camp of Saraswati Sangam, Madras.
1947-48	Goes to Kalahasti to study with Sri Swami Rajeshwarananda.
	Goes to Tiruvannamalai to study with Sri Ramana Maharshi.
	Visits Pondicherry and has *darshan* of Sri Auro-bindo.
1949 May	Goes to Rishikesh to finally meet his Gurudev, H. H. Sri Swami Sivanandaji Maharaj.
	Makes 28-day Badrinath pilgrimage.
10 July	Receives *sannyas diksha* from Sri Swami Sivanan-daji and is named Swami Satchidananda.
September	Has enlightenment experience at Vasishta Guha.
1951 8 February	Requested by Sri Swami Sivanandaji to under-take All-India Tour.

1952

17 February	Gives lectures and organizes branches of the Divine Life Society in many parts of India.
December	Title of "Yogiraj" is bestowed upon Swami Satchidananda by Sri Swami Sivanandaji.

1953

1 February	Arrives in Trincomalee, Ceylon, where Sri Swami Sivanandaji has sent him to open a branch of the Divine Life Society.
July	Organizes the first "All Prophets Day" and embarks on an ecumenical mission.
7 November	Dedicates the Sivananda Ashram in Trincomalee. Inaugurates branches of the Divine Life Society in Colombo and Jaffna.

1955

29 October	Satchidananda Thapovanam is dedicated in Kandy and becomes the center for Gurudev's service throughout Ceylon. Appointed by municipality of Kandy to receive the President of India, Sri Rajendra Prasad during his official visit to Kandy.

1958

2 June	Begins Mount Kailash 138-day pilgrimage, climbing to 19,000 feet.

1959

1 March	Begins lecture tour throughout Hong Kong, Japan, Manila, Singapore and Kuala Lumpur, Malaysia.

1961

28 August	Returns to Ceylon.

1963

17 July	Returns to Rishikesh on the occasion of the Mahasamadhi of H.H. Sri Swami Sivanandaji Maharaj.
29 October	Returns to Ceylon.

1966

30 March	Leaves for the West on the invitation of Conrad Rooks.
April, May, June	Travels to Europe at the request of Conrad Rooks, stopping off at Cairo and Jerusalem on the way.

	Has audience with His Holiness Pope Paul VI.
31 July	Arrives in New York City as guest of artist Peter Max.
21 August	Devotees arrange for Gurudev to stay in Oliver Cromwell Hotel. Public classes start.
17 September	Performs first American *mantra* initiations.
7 October	Founding of the first Integral Yoga Institute (IYI) at 500 West End Avenue.
1 December	Speaks at Community Church in New York; introduced by Allen Ginsberg.
2 December	Interviewed by David Susskind.

1967

4 January	Travels to Chicago, Los Angeles, San Francisco, Honolulu, Tokyo, Hong Kong, Manila, Singapore and Malaysia.
25 February	Arrives in Ceylon.
1–4 May	Visits Prime Minister Indira Gandhi, Lama Govinda and His Holiness the Dalai Lama.
23 May	Returns to New York City.
10 June	Receives Martin Buber Award for Outstanding Service to Humanity.
1 August	Begins yoga ashram at Port Jervis.
16 November	First annual "Swami and the Rabbi" dialogue with Rabbi Joseph Gelberman.
30 November	Travels to Belgium and Europe. Participates as chief guest speaker at the First International Yoga Convention, Brussels.

1968

16 January	Interviewed by *LIFE* magazine.
31 January	Gives programs in Hawaii.
16 February	Begins Friday evening talks at the Unitarian Universalist Church in New York City.
22 February	Puerto Rican programs.
June	IYI begins weekend retreats at Ananda Ashram in Monroe, N.Y.
July	Center for Spiritual Studies incorporated with Brother David Steindl-Rast, O.S.B., Rabbi Joseph Gelberman and Eido Tai Shimano Roshi.
25 July	Receives resident visa as "Minister of Divine Words."
1 August	First group of students moves into the IYI at 500 West End Avenue.
	Gurudev leaves with a group of 25 American disciples on a five-month World Tour of Hawaii,

Japan, Hong Kong, Thailand, Malaysia, Ceylon, India and Europe.

1969

25 January	Returns to New York.
31 January	Gives lecture at Carnegie Hall.
22 May	Second annual "Swami and the Rabbi" dialogue.
9–15 July	Programs in Hawaii.
15–27 July	Programs in Los Angeles.
27 July	Speaks at the Esalen Institute.
12–13 August	Princeton University Ecumenical Program.
15 August	Opens the Woodstock Music and Peace Festival.
19 August	Interviewed by Mike Douglas.
31 August– 2 September	Attends the Val Morin True World Order conference.
8 September	Gala Sivananda Jayanthi Celebration in New York City.
25 September– 7 November	Programs and talks in Denmark, Sweden, Belgium, France, Italy, England and Switzerland.
9 November	Auroville Symposium at New York University.
15–16 November	International Congress of Religions in New York.
24 November	Records album of chants and *satsangs* for Columbia Records.

1970

12 January	Talk at UCLA and on NBC news.
20–22 January	Lectures in Dallas, Texas.
5–6 February	Participates in conference at Cornell University.
21 February	Nassau Yoga Conference.
19–20 March	Gives programs in Los Angeles.
21–22 March	Whole Earth Day.
8 April	Columbia University talk.
9 April	Stoney Brook College talk.
19 April	Washington Square Church talk.
22 April	Earth Day – speaks at Union Square Environmental Action Day program with Mayor John Lindsay.
23 April	Fordham University talk.
28 April	Montclair University talk.
30 April	Speaks at St. Mary Reparatrix Council, New York.
21 May	Talk for Horizon Center drug rehabilitation program.
4 June	Third annual "Swami and the Rabbi" dialogue.

5–11 June	Gives programs in Los Angeles, San Francisco and Detroit.
11–12 July	Speaks at Kentucky's "Inter-community H.O.P.E. for the 70s" and Gethsemane Trappist Monastery.
8–16 August	Canadian programs. Val Morin Music Festival.
28 August– 6 September	First Yoga Ecumenical Retreat at Annhurst College.
15–23 September	California and Colorado programs.
24 September	Congress of Religions, New York.
10 October	Meets with Secretary General U Thant at United Nations.
15 October	Dedication of Integral Yoga Institute at 227 West 13th Street, New York.
16 October	Begins six-month tour of London, Brussels, Amsterdam, Paris, Munich, Geneva, Lausanne, Nice, Milan, Bergamo, Florence, Assisi, Rome (audience with His Holiness Pope Paul VI), Bombay, Coimbatore, South India, New Delhi (World Scientific Yoga Conference), Malaysia, Singapore, Hong Kong, Japan, Philippines, Australia, New Zealand, Fiji and Hawaii.

1971

3 April	Returns to United States. Programs in Los Angeles, San Francisco, Dallas and Detroit.
26 April	Miami University lecture.
30 April	Hunter College lecture.
June	Tulane University lecture.
23 June– 2 July	Second annual Yoga Ecumenical Retreat at Annhurst College.
July	*Satsang* at Horizon Drug Rehabilitation Center. Programs at second Yoga Ecumenical Seminar (YES) program, Saugerties, N.Y.
August	Programs in Washington, D.C. Talk at Lorton Prison. Speaks at benefit concert in Chicago – with Peter Max, Felix Cavaliere and Alice Coltrane. California programs.

1972

1–5 February	Programs in Boulder, Colorado, Kansas, and Missouri.
19 February	Dedicates Ananda Moya Ma Ashram in Oklahoma City.

20 February	Dallas lecture.
26 February	Boston lecture.
4–5 March	Programs in Toronto.
12 March	Speaks at Gethsemane Trappist Monastery, Kentucky.
21 March	Participates in Earth Day at the United Nations.
22 March	Talk at New York University.
26 March	Talk at Danbury Prison. Opens the Natural Foods Store at the New York IYI.
13–14 April	Programs in Chapel Hill, North Carolina.
15 April	Lorton Prison *satsang*. Yogaville West is founded.
23 April	Speaks at Whole Earth Day Festival, California.
6–8 May	Montreal programs.
11 May	Annual "Swami and the Rabbi"
14 May– 27 June	Travels to London, Belgium (Mons Yoga Festival), Paris, Geneva, Germany, Italy, Greece and Israel (Tel Aviv Integral Yoga Retreat).
5–6 August	Speaks at annual Yoga Ecumenical Seminar (YES).
27 August– 1 September	Mt. Saviour Monastery "Word Out of Silence" Symposium.
October	Participates in Center for Spiritual Studies program at Fordham University. Talks and gives classes at the annual meeting of the American Academy of Psychotherapists in New York City.
November	Speaks at Adelphi College Drug Prevention Training Program.
1–19 December	18 day trip around the world.
1973	
18 January– 15 March	Talks in Portland, Seattle, San Francisco, San Diego and other parts of California.
17 February	Initiates first group of American disciples into *presannyas* at Yogaville West.
15–25 March	Dallas and Missouri programs.
25–27 March	Gives all-day program at the Notre Dame University Conference, "Doing Prayer."
30 March	Gives talk at Palmer Chiropractic College in Iowa.

4 April	Tapes "Yoga for the City," Channel 13 New York. Talks at Fordham University.
6–7 April	Montreal programs.
11–12 April	Oklahoma programs.
14 April	Official opening of Yogaville East in Pomfret Center, Connecticut.
25 May	Hunter College program.
31 May	Annual "Swami and the Rabbi" talk.
15–25 June	Conducts 10-day Integral Yoga Retreat at Monticello, N.Y. with Sant Keshavadas, Swami Nirmalananda, Rabbi Gelberman, Shlomo Carlebach, Ram Dass and Brother David.
30 July	Talks at the Morris County prison in New Jersey.
20–22 September	Talks at Soledad Prison and Tracey Prison. Attends Meeting of the Ways Ecumenical Conference.
4 October	Talks at Chiropractic Conference, Salisbury, Ct.
9–11 November	Canadian programs.
15 November	Union College talk, Schenectady, N.Y.
13–31 December	Travels in Hong Kong, Manila and the Far East.

1974	
1–4 January	San Francisco and Los Angeles programs.
5–8 January	Los Alamos, New Mexico programs.
17–31 January	Programs in Spain.
19–27 February	Dallas, Austin, San Antonio, Denver, Los Angeles, San Diego, San Francisco programs.
6–30 March	Travels to New Zealand as the chief speaker at the International Yoga Teachers Association Conference.
26 April	University of Connecticut talk.
2–8 June	Denver, Boulder, Dallas, Detroit programs.
18 July	Annual "Swami and the Rabbi" talk.
19 July	Talk at Morris County Prison, N.J.
20 July	Montreal programs.
31 July– 9 August	Oregon, Seattle, Spokane (Expo'74 Health Symposium), San Francisco, San Jose, Santa Cruz and Los Angeles programs.
10–13 August	Chicago programs.
24–25 August	Virginia Beach programs.
1 September– 2 December	Three-month trip to India, Sri Lanka and Hong Kong.

21 November	The Satchidananda Clinic is inaugurated at Gurudev's birthplace in Chettipalayam, South India.
23 November	The first Integral Yoga Institute in India is formed in Coimbatore, with Sri Sengottuvelan as its secretary.
22 December	60th Jayanthi (birthday) celebrated at the Beverly Wilshire Theater.

1975

22–27 January	San Francisco, Olympia, Seattle programs.
31 January– 11 February	Hawaii programs.
20–22 February	Dallas programs.
8 March	Presented the key to the city of Orlando, Florida by the Mayor.
21 March	Dedicates the opening of Integral Health Services and of Anna Poorna Natural Foods Store, both in Putnam, Ct.
25 March– 1 April	Attends the International Yoga Conference in Nassau.
30 April	European programs.
31 May–1 June	State of Brotherhood Ecumenical Symposium in Oregon.
13–22 June	Conducts the Annhurst III Integral Yoga Retreat; Brother David, Zen Master Seung Sahn, Rabbi Gendler, Andre Van Lysebeth, and Sri N. Mahalingam of India attend; Children's Ten-Day Retreat held at the Ashram.
23 July	Guru Poornima; Initiates first group of American disciples into the Holy Order of Sannyas.
1–27 August	The first month-long intensive Teacher Training Program is held at the Ashram.
22–23 August	Speaks at the annual World Vegetarian Congress in Orono, Maine.
27–28 September	Montreal and Ottawa programs.
1–11 October	Venezuela, South America programs.
23–24 October	Takes part in Spiritual Summit Conference, New York, honoring the United Nation's 30th Anniversary.
25–27 October	Speaks at the Roundtable of the Light Conference in Miami.
20–30 November	Dallas, Houston, Austin, San Antonio programs. Dallas Integral Yoga Retreat.

10 December	Two-month trip to India and Sri Lanka with thirty-four disciples.
1976	
4 February	Takes part in re-dedication ceremony of the Perur Temple, South India.
15 February	Returns from India.
20 February	Receives U.S. citizenship.
13-14 March	Addresses the Symposium on the Healing Arts in Vancouver.
14 March	San Francisco lectures.
21 May	Lecture at Pratt & Whitney Aircraft Club, Hartford, Ct.
29 May	Takes part in dedication of Yogi Amrit Desai's Ashram in Pennsylvania.
17-19 June	Participates in the inauguration of the Himalayan Institute's International Congress on yoga and meditation, Chicago.
21 June	WNEW-TV, Channel 5, "Midday Live" program with Ram Dass.
30 July	Public celebration – at the Cathedral of St. John the Divine, N.Y. – of Gurudev's ten years of service in America.
25 September	"Living Yoga" filmed.
26 September	Speaker at the farewell dinner for former Indian Ambassador T.N. Kaul.
2 October	Awarded Honorary Fellowship of Concordia University, Canada.
3 October	Lecture at Rutgers University.
19 October	Fifth World Tour, including Scotland, England, Belgium, Rome, India, Sri Lanka, and Hong Kong.
1977	
25 March	Guest Speaker for symposium at the Himalayan Institute, Chicago.
1 April	Addresses the Conference of the American Medical Students Association, Chicago.
7 April	Lecture at Barnard College.
11 April	Lecture at Johns Hopkins University Medical School.
16 April	European Tour–including England, Belgium, Germany. Guest speaker at Dartington Hall Conference and the Festival of Mind, Body and Spirit in England.

19 May	Lecture at the National Institutes of Health, Washington, D.C.
10 June	Speaks at the Conference of East-West Monastics in Massachusetts.
16 June	Guest speaker at the Himalayan Institute's Annual International Congress, Chicago.
	Attends dedication of Hindu Temple of New York.
14 July	Conducts All-Faiths Day celebration in Ct.
	Documentary of Yoga Ecumenical Service made by Oscar nominee John Goodell.
30 August	European Tour, including Switzerland, Italy, Greece, and Spain.
	Guest speaker at the annual conference of the European Union of National Yoga Federations, Switzerland. Named as a patron of the EUNYF.
1 October	Lecture at Rutgers University.
3 October	Annual "Swami and the Rabbi" dialogue. "Midday Live" TV show.
6 October	Lecture at Baylor College of Medicine, Texas.
13 November	Tour of India with twenty American students.

1978

13 January	Lecture at Portland Chiropractic College.
15 January	Lecture at University of Washington.
28 January	Lecture at "Awakening Conference" in Los Angeles, with Buckminster Fuller.
30 March	Tour of Spain.
	Attends National Congress of Yoga.
22 April	Guest speaker for symposium at the Himalayan Institute, Chicago.
27 April	Lecture at Haverford College.
28 April	Lecture at Fairleigh Dickinson University.
2 May	Lecture at the University of Connecticut.
5 May	Lecture at the University of Rhode Island.
6 May	Guest speaker at the International Institute of Integral Health Science Conference, Montreal.
17 May	Lecture at Baylor College of Medicine, Houston.
26 May	Guest speaker at the International Religious Convocation for Human Survival held at the United Nations.
	Integral Health Services, N.Y., opens.
27 May	Guest speaker at Seven Hills Healing Arts Festival, Florida.
15 June	Guest speaker at Himalayan Institute's Annual International Conference, Chicago.

22 August	Guest speaker at Thanksgiving Square, Dallas.
26 August	Guest speaker at the Holistic Health Conference, San Diego.
7 September	Annual "Swami and the Rabbi" dialogue in New York.
23 September	Guest speaker at the Western Congress on Meditation, Los Angeles.
8 October	Guest speaker at the Meeting of the Ways Conference, Rutgers University.
17 October	Pillsbury Company representatives visit to discuss nutrition with Gurudev.
12 November	Ravi Shankar benefit concert for LOTUS in California.

1979

20 January	Guest speaker at the International Cooperation Council Conference, Los Angeles.
24 January	Tour of New Zealand, Fiji, Hawaii.
13 February	California programs.
30 March	Lecture at University of Detroit symposium.
6 April	Guest speaker at the Roundtable of Light Conference, Miami.
9 April	Tour of England, Belgium, Holland, France, Greece, and Italy.
19 May	Attends Dedication of Hindu Temple of Pittsburgh.
26 May	Named as Honorary Advisor to the Connecticut Hindu Temple Society.
31 May	Tour of Scotland.
14 June	Guest Speaker at the Himalayan Institute's Annual International Congress, Chicago.
31 July– 29 August	Tour of India with medical doctors.
1 September	European tour, including Switzerland and England.
	Guest speaker at the Annual Conference of the European Union of National Yoga Federations, Switzerland.
19 September	Tour of Australia and New Zealand.
	Guest speaker at International Yoga Teachers Association Conference.
	Named as Honorary Advisor to I.Y.T.A., Australia.
28 September	Satchidananda Ashram, Yogaville, Virginia is acquired.

19 October	Meets with His Holiness the Dalai Lama and Werner Erhard in Boston.
1 November	Annual "Swami and the Rabbi" dialogue, New York.
	Lecture at the University of Washington.
15 November	Lecture at the Naturopathic College, Seattle.

1980

11 March	Lecture at California State University.
20 March	Tour of Hong Kong and Japan.
	Guest speaker at the first World Zen Yoga Convention.
	Guest speaker at the International Yoga Teachers Association Conference, Japan.
29 April	LOTUS groundbreaking.
23 May	Lecture at Concordia University, Montreal.
12 June	Guest speaker at the Himalayan Institute's Annual International Congress, Chicago.
23 July	Guest speaker at the 7th International Human Unity Conference, Chicago.
28 July	First Integral Yoga Ministers receive ordination.
11 August	Lecture at Goddard College, Vermont.
14 August	Guest speaker at the North American Vegetarian Congress, N.J.
29 August	Tour of Switzerland and England.
	Guest speaker at the annual conference of European Union of National Yoga Federations, Switzerland.
18 October	Guest speaker at Human Survival Conference, N.Y.
20 October	Lecture at Rutgers University, N.J.
21 October	Lecture at Ramapo College, N.J.
30 October	Lecture at Virginia Commonwealth University.
18 December	Annual "Swami and the Rabbi" dialogue, New York.

1981

20 January	Tour of Australia.
30 January	Dedication of Ontos Yogaville, Australia.
11 March	Lecture at California State University.
28 March	Lecture at George Washington University.
5 May	LOTUS Lake dedication.
5 June	Lecture at the University of Toronto, Canada.
6 June	Guest speaker at ecumenical conference, Montreal.

10 June	Guest speaker at the Himalayan Institute's Annual International Congress, New York.
12 June	Tour of France and Belgium.
	Guest speaker at Paris Yoga Congress.
30 June	Gives talk at the offices of the *New York Times*.
30 July	15th Anniversary of Service in the United States celebrated at Satchidananda Ashram – Yogaville, Virginia.
24 August	Guest speaker at the Omega Institute, Vermont.
4 September	Annual conference of the European Union of National Yoga Federations, Switzerland.
20 September	Tour of India, Malaysia, Singapore, Sri Lanka and England.
1 December	Named as Honorary Fellow of World Thanksgiving by World Thanks-giving Council, Texas.
10 December	Annual "Swami and the Rabbi" dialogue, New York.

1982

10 February	Guest speaker at the Unity in Diversity Symposium, Seattle.
23 February	Address to Cancer Victors Association, California.
28 March	Guest speaker at the Meeting of the Ways Conference, Stanford University.
29 March	Appointed as Advisor of the Hartley Film Foundation, Ct.
23 April	Appointed as Honorary Council of Patron Members of the Universal Temple, France.
8 May	Speaks at the School of Spiritual Healing, North Carolina.
8 June	Speaks at the Reverence for Life Conference, New York.
17 June	Guest speaker at the Himalayan Institute's Annual International Congress, New York.
20 June	Guest speaker at the Faith for Security Conference, New York.
	Speaks at the International Religious Convocation at the Cathedral of St. John the Divine.
1 July	LOTUS foundation pouring ceremony.
4 September	Tour of Switzerland and France.
	Guest speaker at the annual conference of the European Union of National Yoga Federations, Switzerland.
13 September	Presented with the key to the village of Varredes, France.

1 October	Named as Patron of the United States Center of the Bharatiya Vidya Bhavan.
3 October	Speaker during panel discussion with Professor John Kenneth Galbraith at Columbia University, New York.
24 October	Tour of Australia and New Zealand.

1983

6 January	Tour of Hong Kong, Sri Lanka, India and Malaysia.
25 January	Attends Silver Jubilee of Bharatiya Vidya Bhavan, Madras. Governor of Tamil Nadu awards Gurudev honorary title "Perarul Perumunuvar" (Grace-filled Great Sage).
29 January	Official presentation, in South India, of Tamil version of *To Know Your Self*.
24 February	Guest speaker at Unity in Diversity Conference, Seattle.
15 April	Meeting with Senator Claiborne Pell at the Capitol, Washington, D.C.
21 April	Lecture at Oblate School of Theology, San Antonio, Tx.
22 April	Mexico programs.
30 April	Guest speaker at the World Conference of Religions for Peace, Montreal.
22 May	Yoga Ecumenical Service performed at the Cathedral of St. John the Divine, New York – Gives Pentacost sermon.
26 May	Speaks at the Bharatiya Vidya Bhavan, New York.
17 June	Participates in Himalayan Institute's Annual International Congress, Pennsylvania.
1 July	Guest speaker at the First Southeastern Vishwa Hindu Parishad Conference, Florida.
10 August	Tour of India, Malaysia, Belgium, Switzerland, England and Scotland.
20 August	Guest speaker at the Divine Life Society Silver Jubilee, Kuala Lumpur.
4 September	Annual Conference of European Union of National Yoga Federations, Switzerland.
16 September	Lecture at the British Wheel of Yoga.
18 September	Lecture at the Theosophical Society, Glasgow, Scotland.
19 September	Lecture at the Bharatiya Vidya Bhavan, London.

30 September	Attends the opening of India Week in San Francisco.
4 October	Meets with Mayor Diane Feinstein of San Francisco and with India Week dignitaries.
5 October	Lecture at the University of California, San Diego.
9 October	Attends the inauguration of the Bharatiya Vidya Bhavan's Boston Center.
	Attends reception at the Harvard School of Divinity.
12 October	Receives honorary award from the Mayor of Baltimore as Patron of the Bhavan.
13 October	Joins reception at the Indian Embassy with Bhavan members, Washington, D.C.
11 November	Attends groundbreaking for the Hindu Temple of San Francisco.
12 November	Guest speaker at the Unity in Yoga Conference, Oregon.
10 December	Special guest at the Earth Mass, National Shrine of the Immaculate Conception, Washington, D.C.

1984

25 January	Tour of India.
25 March	Lecture at Bharatiya Vidya Bhavan, Bombay.
30 April	Yoga retreat at Rio Caliente, Mexico.
8 May	Lecture at Southwest Research Foundation, Texas.
22 May	Guest speaker at 10th Anniversary Conference of the Italian Yoga Foundation.
30 May	Audience with His Holiness Pope John Paul II.
10 June	Second annual Ecumenical Service at the Cathedral of St. John the Divine, New York.
	Receives Honorary Doctor of Divine Wisdom degree from the New Seminary, New York.
14 June	Guest speaker at the 9th International Congress of the Himalayan Institute, Pennsylvania.
6 July	Guest speaker at the 10th Vishwa Hindu Parishad Conference, New York.
4 August	Guest speaker at the World Vegetarian Congress. Nominated as "Honorary Fellow of the World Vegetarian Congress."
1 September	Guest speaker at the annual conference of the European Union of National Yoga Federations, Switzerland.
7 October	Guest speaker at the Spiritual Summit VI.
30 October	Tour of India.

11 November	Lecture at Bharatiya Vidya Bhavan, Madras.

1985
12 February	Tour of Australia, Hong Kong, Taiwan, Japan and India.
16 April	Public lecture at Shell Auditorium, Brussels.
18 April	Addresses Light of the Orient Festival as guest of the mayor of Lille, France.
19 April	Guest speaker at Serenity and Efficiency Seminar, Paris.
21 April	Yoga Ecumenical Conference, France.
24 April	Guest speaker at the Italian Yoga Federation Conference.
13 May	Visits Finland and the U.S.S.R. as guest of Projects for Planetary Peace.
23 May	Gives Sermon at the Moscow Baptist Church.
26 May	Ecumenical Service at the Cathedral of St. John the Divine, New York.
26 May	Guest speaker at the Tamil Nadu Foundation Conference.
13 June	Attends inauguration of the Festival of India with American Vice President George Bush and Indian Prime Minister Rajiv Gandhi.
15 June	Guest speaker at the 10th International Congress of the Himalayan Institute, Pennsylvania.
21 June	Seminar at the Joy Lake Mountain Retreat – Appointed to the Joy Lake Mountain Retreat Advisory Board.
14 August	Guest speaker at the Dag Hammarskjold Auditorium at the United Nations, sponsored by the Bharatiya Vidya Bhavan.
21 August	Tour of Hong Kong, Singapore and Switzerland.
27 August	Officiates at the opening of the Holiday Inn – Parkview, Singapore.
1 September	Guest speaker at the 11th annual conference of the European Union of National Yoga Federations, Switzerland.
15 September	Appointed advisor to the Center for Soviet-American Dialogue.
28 September	Officiates at the Foundation Ceremony for the Hindu Society of Virginia.
3 October	Guest speaker at the Interfaith Program of the Brotherhood Synagogue.
4 October	Speaker at the International Press Conference, United Nations.

	Annual "Swami and the Rabbi" dialogue, New York.
28 October	Participates in the Interreligious Dialogue with Francis Cardinal Arinze at Thanksgiving Square, Dallas.

1986

January–February	Programs in Hong Kong, Australia and Hawaii.
15 April	Guest of honor at British Wheel of Yoga Congress.
5 May	Meets with Bernard Cardinal Law, Boston.
12 May	Named as member of International Advisory Council for World Peace Project.
19 July	World Faiths Symposium, Charlottesville, Va.
20 July	Grand Dedication of the Light Of Truth Universal Shrine (LOTUS), Buckingham, Va.

This Chronology *only gives highlights from Sri Gurudev's schedule up to the LOTUS Dedication. He has given many more talks, programs and other kinds of public service than could possibly be listed here.*

Appendix

Glossary of Sanskrit
and Tamil Terms

A

abishekam: during worship, pouring milk or water over an image of the Lord
ahimsa: non-injury
asana: pose, seat (Hatha Yoga)
ashram: a spiritual community where seekers practice and study under the
  guidance of a spiritual master
Ashtanga Yoga: the Yoga of eight limbs; another name for Raja Yoga
ayurveda: (lit. scripture of life) one of the Indian systems of medicine

B

bhakti: one who follows the path of Bhakti Yoga; a devotee of God
Bhakti Yoga: the path of love and devotion to God, to an incarnation of the
  Divine or to a spiritual teacher
bhajan: song or prayer in praise of the Lord
Bharata Natyam: a classical devotional Indian dance form
brahmachari: one who practices sense control; a celibate
brahmacharyam: continence, sense control, celibacy
Brahman: the unmanifest Supreme Consciousness or God
Brahmin: a member of the priestly caste, the highest caste in Hindu society

C, D

choultry: housing provided by temple authorities near places of pilgrimage
  in India
darshan: vision or experience of a divine form or being
deva: celestial being; controller of an aspect of nature
dhal: lentils
diksha: initiation; consecration

G, H

ghee: clarified butter
guru: (lit. remover of darkness) spiritual guide, teacher
Hatha Yoga: the physical aspect of yoga practice — including postures (*asanas*),
  breathing techniques (*pranayama*), seals (*mudras*), locks (*bandhas*), and
  cleansing practices (*kriyas*)

I, J

idli: steamed cake made of ground rice and *dhal*
japa: mantra repetition
Japa Yoga: science of *mantra* repetition
jayanthi: birthday
Jnana Yoga: the path of self-inquiry
Jnana Yogi: one who follows the path of Jnana Yoga

K

karma: the law of action and reaction
Karma Yoga: performing actions as selfless service without seeking reward
kundalini: (lit. coiled energy) the energy stored at the base of the spine. Upon awakening, it rises through the spinal column, passing through seven centers *(chakras)*

L, M

lingam: a symbol of Lord Siva
mahasamadhi: (lit. great *samadhi*) the final *samadhi* in which the consciousness of a saint separates from the body and the physical plane
mala: beads used for counting the number of *mantra* repetitions
mantra diksha: initiation in which the disciple receives a *mantram* from his or her guru
mantram: a sound formula for meditation
mudra: sign, seal or symbol

N

Namaskar: a form of greeting
Nataraja: Lord Siva in the form of the Cosmic Dancer

P

prana: the vital energy
pranayama: the practice of controlling the vital energy, usually through control of the breath
prasadam: consecrated offering
puja: worship service

R, S

Raja Yoga: the "Royal Yoga"; path of concentration and meditation, based on ethical perfection and control of the mind
sadhana: spiritual practice
sadhu: a spiritual person, often a wandering mendicant
samadhi: contemplation, superconscious state, absorption
sannyas: renunciation

sannyas diksha: initiation into *sannyas* (monkhood)

sannyasi: a renunciate; member of the Holy Order of Sannyas, having taken formal initiation from another *sannyasi*

satsang: spiritual company; a spiritual gathering

siddha: an accomplished one, often with supernatural psychic powers

siddhi: accomplishment; psychic power

swami: (lit. master of one's own self) renunciate; member of the Holy Order of Sannyas

T, U

Tantra Yoga: a practice involving *mantram* and *yantram* to experience the union of Siva and Shakti – the masculine and feminine (positive and negative) forces – within the individual

upma: a South Indian dish containing creamed wheat, onions, cashews, and various other ingredients

V, Y

Vedanta: final experience of the study of the Vedas

yantram: a sacred geometrical figure representing a particular aspect of the Divine

Index of People and Places

Photographs

431

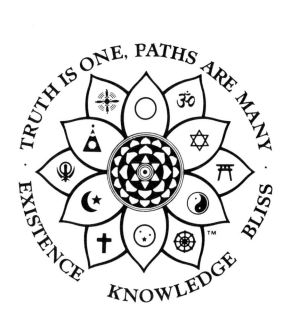

"Truth is One, Paths are Many": the All Faiths Logo designed
by Sri Swami Satchidananda. The symbols appearing in the lotus petals
represent: (clockwise, starting from one o'clock) Hinduism, Judaism,
Shinto, Taoism, Buddhism, All Other Known Religions, Christianity,
Islam, Sikhism, African Religions, Native American Religions, Those
Religions Not Yet Known.